Bundesleiter Fritz Julius Kuhn (1896–1951), the American Führer, 1938. (National Archives.)

THE NAZI MOVEMENT
IN THE UNITED STATES
1924-1941

SANDER A. DIAMOND

CORNELL UNIVERSITY PRESS | ITHACA AND LONDON

First published 1974 by Cornell University Press.
Published in the United Kingdom by Cornell University Press Ltd., 2-4 Brook Street, London W1Y 1AA.

International Standard Book Number 0-8014-0788-5
Library of Congress Catalog Card Number 73-16654

Printed in the United States of America by Vail-Ballou Press, Inc.

To SUSAN,
MEREDITH,
and MATTHEW

Preface

In the late 1930's, Adolf Hitler commanded the veneration of millions of people in Germany and, after the *Anschluss*, in his native Austria. By the autumn of 1938, the road to Eastern Europe was open for a German push. Statesmen, diplomats, and journalists courted the German Führer; tourists visited the new Germany in record numbers. In 1938, Hitler's Germany was on display. The chancellery in Berlin and the Führer's residence at Obersalzberg symbolized the style of the Third Reich; both were seen as befitting the man in whom many perceived the new Luther. Furthermore, Germans and foreign observers viewed the new public buildings as the Third Reich in microcosm; the granite and the marble represented permanence. Hitler's architectural megalomania mirrored his larger designs for remaking the world. The domed Great Hall planned for Berlin and the Great Stadium scheduled for Nuremberg were supposed to surpass other great buildings in history.

The Führer had imitators and supporters on the Continent and in the New World, including the United States. Hitler's followers in America, the Bundists—members of several pro-Nazi organizations that carried on what was known as the Bund movement—argued that National Socialism was the solution to America's manifold problems. Someday in the distant future (on *Der Tag*—"The Day"), the Bundists asserted, the followers of Adolf Hitler would cleanse America, free it from the grip of the Jews, the Communists, and other alleged "parasites," as Hitler had cleansed Germany. Echoing Hitlerian invective, they denounced the Jews as America's misfortune.

Most of the men and women who participated in the Bund

movement were not native-born Americans; they were Germans who had emigrated to the United States in the 1920's. Many were members of Hitler's infant Nazi Party; others had participated in the Freikorps and other right-wing paramilitary groups before they left Germany for America. In sum, many Bundists were predisposed to the Hitlerian viewpoint before they left their native land. Within weeks of Hitler's advent to power, they emerged as outspoken supporters of the new regime. Adhering to Nazi cosmology, the Bundists maintained that the magnetism of blood was stronger than that of place of birth. In consequence, they believed that their "racial brothers," the millions of German-Americans (Americans descended from Germans) in cities from coast to coast, would drop their hyphens, recognize their racially dictated responsibilities, and join the Bund or one of the numerous Bund-related groups. They did not. Shortly before the Munich crisis, the Bund's German-born leader, Fritz Julius Kuhn, dismissed his racial brothers as Americans contaminated by Americanization. Increasingly, the Bundists and their sympathizers remained in their haunts in New York City's "Germantown"—the Yorkville section in Manhattan's East Eighties—and in Yorkvilles in Chicago, Milwaukee, and elsewhere. They also sealed themselves off from American society in their camps: Siegfried, on Long Island; Nordland, in New Jersey; and Hindenburg, in Wisconsin. From these enclaves they lashed out at the President, the German-American community, the Jews, the Blacks—at anyone who did not share their view of America's and Germany's destiny.

By 1938, Americans' willingness to tolerate Hitler's followers had markedly diminished. Local, state, and Federal investigators of the Bund's internal affairs labeled it un-American, its youth camps immoral, and its membership's allegiance to Nazism incompatible with American citizenship. Investigations also revealed that a large majority of the Bundists were not Americans of German extraction but recently naturalized Americans recruited from the ranks of the nearly 430,000 Germans who had entered this country between 1919 and 1932. Sensing that their activities might be considered treasonous, several hundred Bundists packed their belongings and

returned to Germany. They found there what they had tried to create in America, a complete National Socialist experience. Almost
all of them were returning to Germany for the first time since they
had emigrated to America in the preceding decade. The majority
of the Bundists chose to remain in the United States. Their worst
fears were borne out; they found themselves abandoned by their
ideological mentors in a hostile environment, exiled from the Germany that Hitler had moved to the center of the world stage.

The sources revealing the history of the Bund are voluminous. I
have tried to extract from the mountains of documents left behind
by the Bund and its members the material for a significant story.
The inevitable problem of translation created some difficulty.
Many of the documents left behind by the Bundists are in ungrammatical German and are filled with Nazi jargon. Errors in translation and in interpretation are wholly my responsibility.

I am particularly indebted to George H. Stein for his advice, en-
couragement, patience, and interest in this project; to Alfred B.
Rollins, Jr., who introduced me to the world of scholarship and
who, together with Professor Stein, taught me the value of teaching; to James McPherson, my friend and neighbor, for reading the
manuscript and suggesting many changes in style; to friends, li-
brarians, and professional colleagues for their criticism and many
kindnesses; and to Ann Westbrook, my friend and assistant.

To the Office of the Attorney General I am grateful for giving
me access to documents at the Washington National Records Center, Suitland, Maryland; and to Kurt J. Bachrach-Baker and Jerome
Bakst for making available the German-American Bund collection
of the Anti-Defamation League of B'nai B'rith, New York. Hans
Thomsen, chargé d'affaires at the German Embassy in Washington
before the outbreak of World War II, and Heinz Kloss, formerly of
the German Foreign Institute in Stuttgart, have generously provided information and answered questions. I also appreciate the
assistance of the Wiener Library, Institute of Contemporary
History, London; the Federal Records Center, New York; the
Franklin D. Roosevelt Library, Hyde Park, New York; the Na-

tional Archives and the Washington National Records Center; the New York Public Library; and the library of the State University of New York at Binghamton.

For permission to quote from documents available in their collections I am grateful to the following: the Anti-Defamation League of B'nai B'rith, from "Outline of Evidence against the German-American Bund," publications of the German-American Bund, Bund commands, and William B. Herlands, "Report of the [New York] City Emergency Tax Investigation of the German American Bund and Related Groups and Concerns"; the Hoover Institution on War, Revolution and Peace, Stanford, California, from the *NSDAP Hauptarchiv* Collection; Heinz Kloss, from his manuscript "Die 'Amerikaarbeit' des DAI im Dritten Reich"; and the Archives, YIVO Institute for Jewish Research, New York, from the Noah Greenberg Collection of Anti-Semitic Materials Distributed in the New York Metropolitian Area, 1933–1945, papers of the Reich Ministry of Interior, and financial reports of the German Foreign Institute.

For permission to reprint portions of two of my articles that were published in journals I thank the editors: "The Years of Waiting: National Socialism in the United States, 1922–1933," *American Jewish Historical Quarterly*, 59 (1970); and "The *Kristallnacht* and the Reaction in America," *YIVO Annual of Jewish Social Science*, 14 (1969).

Financial assistance from Keuka College and the College Center of the Finger Lakes is gratefully acknowledged.

My work was made more enjoyable by the patience and concern of my wife, Susan Lee Diamond. She shared with me the excitement of research and writing.

SANDER A. DIAMOND

Keuka Park, New York

Contents

Illustrations

Tables

Abbreviations

ADL	Anti-Defamation League of B'nai B'rith, New York.
AO der NSDAP	Auslandsorganisation der NSDAP (Foreign Organization of the National Socialist German Workers' Party).
APA	Aussenpolitisches Amt der NSDAP (Foreign Affairs Office of the National Socialist German Workers' Party).
BANS	Bund Amerikanischer Nationalsozialisten (American National Socialist Bund).
BdA	Bund der Auslandsdeutschen (Organization of Foreign Germans).
DAI	Deutsches Ausland-Institut (German Foreign Institute).
DAWA	Deutschamerikanischer Wirtschaftsausschuss (German-American Business League).
DGFP	*Documents on German Foreign Policy, 1918–1945.* Series C (5 vols.; 1933–1937) and D (13 vols.; 1937–1941). Washington, D.C., 1949——.
DKV	Deutscher Konsum Verband (German Consumers' Cooperative).
"Evidence"	Justice Department. "Outline of Evidence against the German-American Bund." 1942. Anti-Defamation League of B'nai B'rith, New York.
FDRL	Franklin Delano Roosevelt Library, Hyde Park, New York.
FONG	Bund der Freunde des Neuen Deutschland (Friends of the New Germany).
FRC	Federal Records Center, New York.
Hearings	U.S. House of Representatives, Special Committee to Investigate Un-American Activities and Propaganda in the United States. *Hearings.* 75 Cong., 2 Sess.; 76 Cong., 1 and 2 Sess. 16 vols. and

	appendix. Parts II, III, IV. Washington, D.C., 1939–1941.
NP	U.S. House of Representatives. *Investigation of Nazi Propaganda and Investigation of Certain Other Propaganda Activities: Public Hearings before the Special Committee on Un-American Activities.* 73 Cong., 2 Sess. 2 vols. Washington, D.C., 1934–1935.
NSDAP	Nationalsozialistische Deutsche Arbeiterpartei (National Socialist German Workers' Party, or Nazi Party).
OD	Ordnungs-Dienst (Uniformed Service).
PRDR	*Papers Relating to the Diplomatic Relations of the United States, 1933–1941.* Washington, D.C., 1949——.
RG 59	Department of State. *Special Interrogation Mission: Reports on Interrogation of German Prisoners-of-War, Made by Members of the Department of State Special Interrogation Mission (September, 1945 to September, 1946), Headed by DeWitt C. Poole.* General Records of the State Department. Record Group 59. Microcopy 679. National Archives, Washington, D.C.
RG 131	Office of Alien Property, APA World War II Seized Enemy Records. Record Group 131. Washington National Records Center, Suitland, Maryland.
SA	Sturmabteilung (Storm Troopers of the National Socialist German Workers' Party; also known as Brown Shirts).
SS	Schutzstaffel (Protection Squad), originally the elite corps of the Nazi Party.
T-81	*Records of the National Socialist German Labor Party.* Microcopy T-81. National Archives, Washington, D.C.
T-120	*Records of the German Foreign Ministry Received by the Department of State.* Microcopy T-120. National Archives, Washington, D.C.
T-611	*World War II Collection of Seized Enemy Records: Captured German Documents Filmed at Berlin.* Microcopy T-611. National Archives, Washington, D.C.

UA	U.S. House of Representatives. *Investigation of Un-American Propaganda Activities in the United States.* 76 Cong., 1 Sess. Report no. 2. Washington, D.C., 1939.
UGS	United German Societies of Greater New York.
VDA	Verein für das Deutschtum im Ausland (League of Germans Abroad). After Hitler came to power, "Verein" was changed to "Volksbund"; the same initials were retained.
VoMi	Volksdeutsche Mittelstelle (Ethnic German Office).
VR	Volksdeutscher Rat (Ethnic German Council).

THE NAZI MOVEMENT
IN THE UNITED STATES
1924–1941

Introduction

For many Americans who followed national events in the late 1930's, the name Fritz Julius Kuhn conjures up memories of what William Leuchtenburg has called the "fascist challenge." [1] Although Kuhn, Hitler's imitator in America, never attracted more than twenty-five thousand followers to the Amerikadeutscher Volksbund and related organizations (or, simply, the Bund), his bellicose statements and elaborate fanfare engaged the public's imagination at the time Hitler was becoming the central figure in the world events. Many Americans believed that the Bundists intended to establish a Nazi dictatorship in the United States. In retrospect, this assertion seems ludicrous; in the context of the late 1930's, however—when a permanently fascist Europe seemed possible—the belief that a Trojan horse was being readied by Hitler's supposed agents was not considered farfetched. [2]

[1] William E. Leuchtenburg, *Franklin D. Roosevelt and the New Deal, 1932–1940*, New American Nation Series (New York, 1963), ch. xii.

[2] The term "Bund" is used to designate several organizations that carried on the Nazi movement in the United States between 1924 and 1941 in four distinct though interrelated organizational stages: (1) Nationalsozialistische Vereinigung Teutonia (Teutonia Association), 1924–1932; (2) Gauleitung-USA (or Gau-USA), a unit of the German Nazi Party, 1931–1933; (3) Bund der Freunde des Neuen Deutschland (Friends of the New Germany), 1933–1936, and a subdivision, Freunde von Deutschland (Friends of Germany), 1933–1934; (4) Amerikadeutscher Volksbund (American German Bund or German-American Bund), 1936–1941, and related groups and organizations. The findings of several congressional investigations (by the McCormack-Dickstein Committee and, later, the Dies committee) constitute the first informal history. The volumes, published between 1935 and 1941, remain standard reference works on the intrastructure of the Bund. More recent studies that touch on the Bund and on Nazi propaganda activities in general in the American hemi-

To be sure, the activities of German nationals and a handful of Americans of German extraction in the Bund movement never posed a serious threat to America's security. But many irate congressmen and senators, presidential advisers, anti-Nazis and anti-fascists, patriotic leagues, Jewish organizations, and leaders of organized labor asserted that Hitler's Germany was supporting a gigantic conspiracy bent on destroying the American system of government. They labeled Bundists "un-American."

Historically, the definitions of "Americanism" and "un-Americanism" have been inextricably related to the involvement of the United States with real or imagined foes. Any individual, ethnic group, or organization subscribing to a foreign ideology or demonstrating sympathy for another nation or foreign ideology was assumed to be a present or potential enemy. Refusal to conform to the dominant culture was often regarded as un-American. Throughout the interwar period, many Americans believed that Bolshevism and fascism, and later Communism and National Socialism, were un-American ideologies. In the 1920's, some contended that Italian-Americans gave supranational allegiance to Mussolini's Italy; others argued that the Left was in sympathy with Soviet Russia. By the middle of the decade and into the 1930's, most Americans were too greatly preoccupied with the economic dislocations of the period to be concerned about either the "Reds" or the Black Shirts. It was not until the end of the 1930's that the alleged Communist threat again emerged as a major national issue. National Socialism, however, commanded public attention throughout the New Deal era, especially in the Northeast, which was

sphere include Alton Frye, *Nazi Germany and the American Hemisphere, 1933–1941* (New Haven, 1967); Hans-Adolf Jacobsen, *Nationalsozialistische Aussenpolitik, 1933–1938* (Frankfort on the Main, 1968), pp. 528–549; Klaus Kipphan, *Deutsche Propaganda in den Vereinigten Staaten, 1933–1941* (Heidelberg, 1971); Arthur Smith, Jr., *The Deutschtum of Nazi Germany and the United States*, International Scholars Forum, No. 15 (The Hague, 1965); Geoffrey S. Smith, *To Save a Nation: American Countersubversives, the New Deal, and the Coming of World War II* (New York, 1973), pp. 87–100; and Leland V. Bell, *In Hitler's Shadow: The Anatomy of American Nazism* (New York, 1973). A general discussion of the antifascist and anti-Nazi vocabulary ("Trojan horse," "Fifth Column") is in Louis De Jong, *The German Fifth Column in the Second World War*, trans. C. M. Geyl (Chicago, 1956).

attuned to European affairs and had a large Jewish population.[3]

Articles published in popular magazines during this period betray a fascination with Nazism and its leader, Adolf Hitler. Although most writers dismissed Hitler's racial-political theories as nonsense and were not sure whether he was a slick politician or a madman, they conveyed the impression that America had something to fear from Hitlerism. Many writers were more interested in the barbaric elements of Nazism—in its use of concentration camps, murder, and brutality—than in its political ramifications. Consequently, by the middle of the decade segments of the American public believed that the Nazis were gangsters and sadists. Their negative feelings were transferred to the Bundists, Hitler's followers in this country. The Bundists aroused great public excitement during the New Deal era. Their activities also contributed to the "atmosphere of mutual tension and hostility" between Franklin D. Roosevelt's America and Adolf Hitler's Germany.[4]

Diplomatic relations between Nazi Germany and the United States have been the object of much scholarly attention in recent years.[5] The salient question emerging from research has been formulated by Ernest R. May: "How could the German government have been so blind, so stupid, or so clumsy as once again to arouse

[3] "Un-Americanism Defined," UA, p. 10. On the activities of the Italian fascists (Count Ignazio Thaon di Revel and the Fascist League of North America, or FLNA), see John P. Diggins, Mussolini and Fascism: The View from America (Princeton, N.J., 1972), and "The Italo-American Anti-Fascist Opposition," Journal of Modern History, 54 (Dec. 1967), 579–598; and Frank Hanighan, "Foreign Political Movements in the United States," Foreign Affairs, 16 (Oct. 1937), 1–20.

[4] Saul Friedländer, Prelude to Downfall: Hitler and the United States, 1939–1941, trans. Aline B. Werth and Alexander Werth (New York, 1967), p. 3.

[5] James V. Compton, The Swastika and the Eagle: Hitler, the United States, and the Origins of World War II (Boston, 1967); Gerhart Hass, Von München bis Pearl Harbor: Zur Geschichte der deutschamerikanischen Beziehungen, 1938–1941 (Berlin, 1965); Arnold Offner, American Appeasement: United States Foreign Policy and Germany, 1933–1938 (Cambridge, Mass., 1969); Robert Dallek, Democrat and Diplomat: The Life of William E. Dodd (New York, 1968); Hans-Jürgen Schröder, Deutschland und die Vereinigten Staaten, 1933–1939 (Wiesbaden, 1970); Gerhard Weinberg, The Foreign Policy of Hitler's Germany: Diplomatic Revolution in Europe, 1933–36 (Chicago, 1970), ch. vi; Friedländer; Frye; Jacobsen; and Kipphan.

a hostile coalition that included the United States?"[6] To answer this question, historians generally find it necessary to examine the reasons for the tension that existed between the two nations throughout the 1930's.

That tension, characterized by distrust and mutual recriminations, heightened as war became imminent in Europe. After the anti-Jewish pogroms in November 1938, on the *Kristallnacht* ("Night of Broken Glass"), diplomatic relations were no longer conducted on the ambassadorial level. Much of the diplomatic anxiety of the era can be attributed to the ideas and commitments of the German Führer. Rarely has the modern world witnessed a leader consumed by such infectious and obsessive hatred—hatred that nearly shattered the existing world order. A German victory over the Allies would have brought about a total reorganization of the Western world. The terror and horror unleashed by the Third Reich were so overwhelming and unpredictable that, in retrospect, they take on a surrealistic effect. But Nazism was not an uncontrollable dream, and the artifacts of Hitler's ill-fated New Order attest to its reality.

The totality of the National Socialist experience has not been thoroughly explained. Scholars have employed a variety of analogues. In an effort to explicate the roots of Nazism, some have emphasized that it was a last-ditch effort by the capitalists working in conjunction with the military and supported by the middle class to preserve the capitalist order; others have viewed National Socialism as the fulfillment of Germany's destiny and have placed stress on Germany's grotesque pursuit of power in World War I. As evidence, they cite Germany's prewar egotism and overbearing self-confidence, which were transformed into a fantastic expansionism once the war began. In essence, the Great War of 1914 was a dress rehearsal for Germany's madness under the National Socialists. Some scholars have depicted Nazism as a revolution of nihilism, and others have employed multifactor analysis, stressing that, after the defeat in 1918, the Germans experienced a series of internal dislocations which culminated in the advent to power of Hitler.

[6] "Nazi Germany and the United States: A Review Essay," *Journal of Modern History*, 41 (June 1969), 207.

To be sure, the list of explanations for the emergence of Nazism is by no means complete, and the scholarly preoccupation with its origins continues. Only recently have scholars started to probe the psyches of Hitler and other members of the Nazi elite. Even this approach has defects.[7]

It is clear, however, that though Hitler was obsessed with attaining his own goals, the ideas that made up his *Weltanschauung* (world view) were not exclusively his. They were not formulated in a vacuum. National Socialism was the product of differing conceptions of the perceived social and economic needs of the German people in an era of unprecedented social and economic dislocation. Unlike many of his adversaries, Hitler preyed on fear and exploited it in a selfish and opportunistic way. But millions of Germans found in National Socialism a solution to the Depression, a strong anti-Communist stance, promise of social reforms, and a reversal of the course allegedly set by the leaders of the Weimar Republic. Then, too, many Germans viewed the Nazi successes at the polls as evidence of Nazism's "inevitability." [8] Although it would be wrong to maintain that militarism, biological nationalism, and irrationality did not contribute to the emergence of National Socialism, one must also stress the immediate determinants; and in 1933, few Germans knew how Nazism would end. Still unexplained, however, is why most levels of German society succumbed to a collective megalomania that culminated in the annihilation of millions of people.

While an inmate of Landsberg Prison, Hitler wrote *Mein Kampf.* Borrowing heavily from the Social Darwinists and neo-Hegelians, he glorified brute force and eternal struggle as the mainsprings of life. At the center of his constellation of ideas were the beliefs that

[7] An excellent review of recent literature on National Socialism by Geoffrey Barraclough is in the *New York Review of Books,* Oct. 19, Nov. 2, and Nov. 16, 1972. On the use and misuse of the psychohistorical approach, see Jacques Barzun, "History: The Muse and Her Doctors," *American Historical Review,* 77 (Feb. 1972), 36–64; see also Robert Coles, "Shrinking History–Part Two," *New York Review of Books,* March 8, 1973.

[8] An excellent study that helps to account for German voting behavior is William S. Allen, *The Nazi Seizure of Power: The Experience of a Single German Town, 1930–1935* (Chicago, 1965).

the Aryan race was superior to other races and that race alone propelled the historic process—that history was simply the record of the rise and fall of races and racial communities (*Völker*). According to Hitler, the inexorable laws of history and the demands of blood made Aryan hegemony over the world inevitable and, in addition, presented the Aryan race with the historic task of awakening the world to the threat posed by the Jewish race. He saw the Jews—the antithesis of the Aryans—as the incarnation of all the evil in the world and the progenitors of modernism or, more precisely, of everything he hated and feared: liberalism, Marxism, democracy, and the rootlessness of men in the industrial age. Although many of Hitler's biological-anthropological ideas had been promulgated by others before the appearance of *Mein Kampf*, Hitler made biological nationalism a political concept. Thus, the history of Germany between the wars can be seen as the transfer of biological nationalism from the cultural to the political sphere and the emergence of an exclusive and destructive ideology that eventually extended beyond the borders of the Reich.

After Hitler was appointed Chancellor in January 1933, he imposed his world view on the German nation. By 1938, few segments of German society remained unaffected by the Führer's pseudoscientific and geopolitical ideas. Hans-Adolf Jacobsen has demonstrated, in his monumental study of Nazi foreign policy, *Nationalsozialistische Aussenpolitik, 1933–1938*, that the German Führer had complete control over his country's foreign relations by 1938 and that his racial-political views became the base upon which Nazi foreign policy was constructed. Since the German nation represented the collective historical ambitions of the Aryan race, Hitler believed that it was Germany's destiny to counteract the satanic machinations of international Jewry. He wrote in *Mein Kampf* what would later constitute the quintessence of his world view:

As often in history, Germany is the great pivot in the mighty struggle. If our people and our state become the victim of these bloodthirsty and avaricious Jewish tyrants of nations, the whole earth will sink into the snares of this octopus; if Germany frees herself from this embrace, this greatest of dangers to nations may be regarded as broken for the whole world.[9]

Hitler believed that it was Germany's mission to unify millions of Germans (or racial comrades) living outside the Reich into a world-wide racial community. To attain that end, Nazi Party officialdom created numerous agencies. Jacobsen has traced, not only the growth and proliferation of these agencies, but also the history of Nazi Germany's intrusions in the internal affairs of states with large German populations in Central and Eastern Europe, in Africa, and in the American hemisphere.[10]

Clearly, however, many Nazi policies and decisions were tempered by German experiences in the past. A new regime inherits, upon assuming power, the machinery of government, the bureaucracy, and the legacy of past decisions. Hitler's administration acquired an intact and extremely traditional foreign service that included many men who had spent their youth and received their training in the late imperial period. Traditionalism was an extremely difficult problem to the impatient Nazis, who wanted to accelerate the pace of implementing foreign policy. In spite of Hitler's failure immediately to weaken the influence of the traditionalists in the Wilhelmstrasse (Foreign Ministry) and the more conservative supporters of the new regime in the military, he pursued a foreign policy that was distinct from the policies of the State. It was only after Joachim von Ribbentrop's appointment as foreign minister on February 4, 1938, that the foreign policies of the State and the Party were finally fused, although it can be stated with some certainty that Ribbentrop's predecessor, Constantin von Neurath, was in accord with many of the wishes of the German Führer. Disagreements between Foreign Ministry personnel and the Party were confined to the question of the accelerated pace of foreign policy and annoyance over intrusions into what the ministry considered its domain. For almost five years Germany's foreign policy was characterized by a dichotomy between the racial-political activities of the Party and the more traditional methods of the

[9] Adolf Hitler, *Mein Kampf*, trans. Ralph Manheim, Sentry Edition (Boston, 1962), p. 623.
[10] Jacobsen, pp. 445–597.

Foreign Ministry. That division was especially apparent in Germany's relations with the United States between 1933 and late 1935.

A few weeks after Hitler assumed the chancellorship, American diplomats became aware that the new regime in Germany was pursuing a dual foreign policy. On the one hand, the Foreign Ministry continued to follow a policy laid down during the Weimar period. Controversies between Washington and Berlin were confined to economic problems—tariff regulations and the payment of old debts. On the other hand, foreign-policy planners in Nazi-created and recently Nazified agencies called for the unification of Germany's "racial comrades" in the United States. The Party's efforts to bring about the unification of the German-American community were at the root of much of the ill-feeling directed against the Nazi regime.[11]

According to the official Nazi viewpoint, the German element in America was uncontaminated by the pernicious influence of the "melting-pot philosophy," which was labeled a "Jewish invention." This contention received support from a number of ethnologists and racists in the Party's Foreign Organization (Die Auslandsorganisation der NSDAP, or AO), the German Foreign Institute (Deutsches Ausland-Institut, or DAI), and the League of Germans Abroad (Volksbund für das Deutschtum im Ausland, or VDA), and a host of other Nazified agencies. Several of these groups were active in what the Nazis called "American work." Many of their records were destroyed during the war, but those that survive give a clear indication of the extent and scope of Nazi activities in the United States; they also show how a racial-political view of America's past was transformed into an active policy.[12] The DAI, which was founded in 1917 and was not part of the traditional academic structure, was prominent in effecting this transformation. After the DAI's incorporation into the Nazi administrative organization, its

[11] An excellent summary of the manifold problems that confronted the two powers can be found in Weinberg's *The Foreign Policy of Hitler's Germany*. Offner's *American Appeasement* presents a much more elaborate history.

[12] The German Foreign Institute was reorganized after World War II and is now known as the Institut für Auslandsbeziehungen (Institute for Foreign Relations). It is located in Stuttgart.

studies of the world-wide German community were used to justify the Party's and later Germany's supranational adventures.

Although the conclusions the DAI derived from its studies of the German-American community often differed from those of the Party, Nazi race theorists and foreign-policy planners adjusted divergent views to meet the demands of ideology. In general, what emerged were hybrid concepts that usually adhered to the Party line. Party theorists maintained that an estimated six to seven million German-Americans still spoke German as their primary language in 1930 and that about a fourth of the American population was of German extraction. Some of the Party's personnel in the Auslandsorganisation concluded that the progeny of the millions of German settlers who had arrived in America in the eighteenth and nineteenth centuries could be unified into a viable political force. Thus decisions implemented what was assumed to be fact, and facts were remolded to the Hitlerian racial interpretation of history. The past was perverted to justify the present; but for the Nazis, truth was not attained by using an inductive-empirical method. Policies and decisions conformed to an a priori view of the world: a view dictated by a belief in the magnetism of blood and an alleged world-wide Jewish-Communist conspiracy.

Moreover, the Nazis had inherited from Germany's recent past an array of ideas concerning America and its people. The vague and amorphous structure of myths that contributed to German national awareness perpetuated two fictions: that the people of the United States were as much Germanic as Anglo-Saxon in origin, and that America was rapidly becoming a decadent and corrupt nation. The first was at the root of the Nazi concept of American *Deutschtum* (the word *Deutschtum* can be translated as "Germandom" or "Germanness" and in Nazi usage connotes the superiority of German racial bonds to state ties); the second was manipulated to accord with the view of world Jewry. America was a Jew-ridden plutocracy whose salvation would come from the still untainted German element.

Whether the entire Nazi hierarchy shared these beliefs is not important; what is important is that many of its members acted upon them during the first years of the Nazi regime. The ideas manifested themselves on the decision-making level in two distinct ways. First, throughout the 1930's, Hitler believed that the United States was incapable of sustaining itself in war. In retrospect this seems incomprehensible. After all, America had accelerated the pace of Germany's defeat after 1917. Though several knowledgeable Germans tried to caution Hitler and his immediate entourage about repeating the mistakes of the leaders of imperial Germany, he, like his predecessors, was dazzled by the myth of German invincibility. Second, in keeping with the Nazi world view, many highly placed Gemans—including Hitler's deputy Rudolf Hess and AO chief Ernst-Wilhelm Bohle—believed that the dictates of blood demanded that Berlin support its racial comrades in America. Thus, between 1933 and 1935, various Party agencies supported pro-Nazi groups collectively known as the Bund, which was founded and organized by German nationals living in the United States. When the Bund failed to develop into a viable force in American life and proved to be a troublesome burden, the Party severed most of its connections with it in 1935. More by accident than design, however, the organization created before Hitler came to power did not die in late 1935; with little German support, it lasted until December 1941.

During the history of the Bund, its long-range purpose was to unify the amorphous community known as German-America, producing a "united Germandom" (*Einigung des Deutschtums*) that could counteract the monopoly of power allegedly held by American Jewry. Its short-term goal was to combat the unfavorable image of the new Germany that Americans were obtaining from those who "rake the gutters for filth to fling at the Germans"—that is, the Jews.[13] The succession of men who led the Bund failed in their attempts to unify Geman-America into a political force. Their abortive efforts to rekindle the feeling of Germanness in America and to transplant racial anti-Semitism constitute the story of the failure of the Nazi movement in the United States—a failure caused in part by the diplomatic web in which Nazi Germany found itself entangled, in part by the internecine conflict that characterized the entire history of the Bund. Furthermore, Nazi over-

[13] *Deutscher Beobachter,* Dec. 1, 1934, p. 4.

tures to German-America were predicated on the assumption that blood was stronger than citizenship. The leading Bundists, who were native Germans, did not, and perhaps could not, understand how profoundly and irrevocably the melting-pot philosophy and the excesses directed by Americans against German-America during World War I had altered the lives of the people they were attempting to attract.

In general, recent studies of the Bund have emphasized the group's chronological development and its relationship with Germany. This book, which uses the chronological approach, also examines Germany's evolving views concerning Americans of German ancestry. It is not only a history of the Nazi movement in the United States—its origins, leaders, members, and ideology—but also a study of the ideas that prompted Germany to embark on its ill-fated adventure in the United States.

I

PENETRATING THE GERMAN - AMERICAN COMMUNITY

CHAPTER 1

From Cultural to
Racial "Deutschtum"

On March 22, 1938, just nine days after Austria was incorporated in the German Reich, Hugh Wilson, who had recently replaced William Dodd as ambassador to Germany, was received by Joseph Goebbels at the Ministry of Propaganda. After a cordial but brief welcome, Goebbels told Wilson that he was deeply distressed by the "slanderous attacks upon the person of the *Führer*" by members of the American press. He reminded Wilson that, far from being a "bandit" or a "robber," Hitler was a "man of the most unquestionable character and honesty of purpose," a man whom the German people considered "holy." Wilson did not deny that the American press had consistently and bitterly attacked Hitler. The widespread disdain for Hitler and the National Socialists, argued Wilson, could be understood by employing a Freudian analogy: "Americans of my age and generation had been accustomed to see the best intellectuals in our country go to Germany for education . . . ; thousands of houses, among them mine, had had German girls as governesses for their children, . . . tens of thousands of families had German relatives. Thus, the bonds between the two lands went so deep that we could not regard what happened in Germany with indifference." He could prove the closeness of the two nations, he said, simply by summoning a dozen of Goebbels' aides and asking them if they had relatives in America. Goebbels would find that each had a relative "or some branch of the family established in our country for almost 100 years." The war, continued Wilson, Hitler's rise to power, and the persecution of the Jews had weakened the bonds between America and Germany, and the "deep affection" Americans once felt for the Germans had inevitably turned to "hatred and not to indifference."[1]

Admittedly, Wilson's interpretation of the Nazi phenomenon was highly subjective. His type of reasoning was characteristic of his generation, which could not fully comprehend the rise of a thoroughgoing irrationalism in Germany. Many members of America's traditional elite—especially in the universities and the diplomatic corps—had come to respect Germany during their university years. German democracy, which had taken questionable form in the Weimar Republic, at one time represented a partial fulfillment of the newly assumed American world mission of spreading the concept and furthering the adoption of democracy. The rapidity with which the National Socialists consolidated their power, the emergence of a virulent strain of racism in German life and politics, and the resurrection of militarism caused scholars, diplomats, and other Americans to question their suppositions concerning the Germans. In spite of their dismay, many Americans held fast to the belief that Hitler and the National Socialists represented an aberration in German history; they were unexplainable scourges inflicted on the Germans. One result of their disillusionment was an attempt to separate the "good Germans" from the "bad Germans," the Nazis. Accordingly, the "bad Germans" were gangsters and perverts, recruited from the social debris of the underworld. The Nuremberg Trials later did much to dispel this belief, but it is clear that the "other Germany" explanation of Nazism had its roots in the pre–World War II era. The classification of the Germans into two distinct categories reflected a desire to minimize the extent to which Nazism was accepted in a country that had served as the intellectual and spiritual host for American scholars and scientists.

Many Americans, including, of course, American Jews and millions of Americans of German ancestry, were perplexed by the rise of Nazism. Part of the Bismarckian legacy to the United States was

[1] Memorandum of a conversation between Hugh Wilson and Joseph Goebbels, Berlin, March 22, 1938, enclosed in a letter from Sumner Welles to President Roosevelt, April 22, 1938, Hugh Wilson folder, President's Secretary's File, Germany, FDRL.

an admiration for German efficiency, thrift, cleanliness, thoroughness, productivity, and orderliness. These supposed "German virtues" have been incorporated into American folklore and, to be
sure, have been skillfully exploited by German public-relations
firms and businesses. But, as Hitlerism became synonymous with
organized brutality, American admiration for these "German qualities" gradually waned. With the onset of the war, German efficiency and thoroughness were equated with the repugnant characteristics of Hitler's New Order.[2]

Ambassador Wilson's contention that a "Freudian relationship"
existed between the two peoples is a reflection of one of the then
popular explanations of Hitlerism. Doubtless Americans have a
stereotyped image of the Germans, just as they do of other national
groups. Unfortunately, people tend to see each other, not as individuals, but as members of collective entities. The organic theory
of the national state, the concept of the state as a living thing, is
but one manifestation of this historical tendency, and derives from
the cultural and political climate of the last century. Whether
based on myth or fact, the popular presentation of foreign national
or ethnic groups is often translated into policy. Realistic reapprais-
als often come too late, especially when a nation's foreign policy
has been constructed on the basis of a mythical image of another
nation and its people. To some extent, the history of the present
century has been the history of misrepresentations of other peoples
and how they might react in a particular situation. An outstanding
example is Adolf Hitler's distorted image of the world, especially
of the New World.

[2] The image of the German craftsman hand-tooling each product is part of
the traditional American image of the Germans. Commenting on the Bismarckian legacy, the editor of the *New York Evening Journal* (Feb. 28, 1902)
wrote, "German thought has set before the world an invaluable example of
thoroughness; the Germans are original, imaginative and they have excelled in
war, in all of the arts, in commerce—in every form of human effort"
(T-81/617/5411641). Discussing Holger Herwig's discovery, in 1971, of German documents alleging that the Kaiser had plans to invade the United States,
Russell Baker of the *New York Times* wrote: "The Government would be run
by people with Germanic names, like Kissinger, Ehrlichman, Haldeman, Zie-
gler, Klein, Kleindienst, and Schultz. Our streets would be filled with Volks-
wagens instead of Hupmobiles" ("If the Kaiser Had Won," April 29, 1971).

In the history of both the United States and Germany, January 30, 1933, is a crucial date. In Germany, Hitler was appointed Reich Chancellor of a deeply divided nation. At the time of his appointment, the Republic was a moribund reminder of political failure. On that day in January, Germany's fate was placed in the hands of a man who was an untested political leader, at least on the national level. There were no clairvoyants, in 1933, who could see that Hitler was to become the central figure in human events, that his years in power would transform the world, or that the eventual demise of the Third Reich would remove Europe from its central position in world affairs. Most westerners were too much concerned with the dislocations engendered by the Depression to be greatly interested in Germany's internal affairs. There were, however, two groups that viewed events in Germany circumspectly: world Jewry and the overseas German community. In the United States, especially, the large and influential Jewish population and the even greater number of Americans of German extraction were wary.

From the beginning of the Nazi regime, the leaders of the American Jewish community exhibited great concern for their coreligionists in Germany. But during the first years of the Third Reich, American Jewry's vigilance did not result in the coalescence of Jewish groups into a genuine anti-Nazi front. Several important Jewish leaders counseled against any action which might antagonize the Nazis; caution became the watchword. Later, as Hitler's intentions became clear and his obsessive racial anti-Semitism could no longer be rationalized as revolutionary fervor, the leaders of American Jewry found that there was little they could do to alter the course of German history. Instead, they turned their attention to the most conspicuous representatives of Nazism at home, the Bundists—the members of the Nazi movement on American soil.[3]

By the middle of the decade Jews and millions of other Ameri-

[3] On American Jewry's reaction to National Socialism in 1933–1934, see Moshe Gottlieb, "The First of April Boycott and the Reaction of the American Jewish Community," *American Jewish Historical Quarterly*, 57 (1968), 516–556; and Offner, *American Appeasement*, pp. 59–65.

cans were convinced that Hitler had an undetermined but alarmingly large number of followers in the United States. That conviction was supported by the exposure given to the Bund by the news media. Popular writers capitalized on the sensationalism inherent in the Bund's extremist activities, and the reading public responded with insatiable interest, devouring books and articles at a great rate. The Bundists' raucous anti-Semitism, riotous meetings in beer halls in New York's Yorkville, St. Louis, and Chicago, and street fights with Jewish war veterans became front-page stories. Even a cursory examination of several widely circulated journals published in the late 1930's suggests that the Bundists were catapulted into the national limelight at the very moment when the fascist or fascoid regimes and Nazi Germany were threatening the already weakened international structure. The Bund's inner machinations made for interesting reading—intrigue is inherent in oath-bound organizations owing allegiance to a foreign power—but few writers attempted to assess the movement's broader connotations.

Among the salient features of denunciations of the alleged fascist menace was the consistent characterization of Nazis and other fascists as gangster types, thugs recruited from the gutters and flophouses of the world to serve as Hitler's willing henchmen; in America, the Bundists were portrayed as beer-drinking bullies, scum from the lowest level of society. Moreover, they were depicted as illiterate and irrational men who were predisposed to violence; it was not unusual for writers to use the terms "thug," "social misfit," and "Nazi" interchangeably. This caricature can be traced to the early days of Nazism. Even Hitler was concerned with the popular image of the Party after his advent to power. The purge of Ernst Roehm in June 1934 can, in part, be explained by Hitler's desire to make National Socialism appear more respectable to the middle class and the old elite of German society.

Surprisingly, the allegation that the Bundists were part of Hitler's advance guard in the United States was never applied to the German-American community, perhaps because it shared the dominant popular view of the Bundists. Furthermore, though many American-born and naturalized German-Americans may have been proud of the re-emergence of Germany as a great power, they wisely eschewed German and Bundist efforts to propagandize them, especially in the wake of several state and Federal investigations of German activities in the 1930's. So strong was the belief, in some quarters, that the Bundists were bent on destroying the Republic that pressure was brought to bear on Congress to investigate the group's supposed un-American activities within a year after Hitler was appointed Chancellor. The first investigation was led by Congressmen John McCormack of Massachusetts and Samuel Dickstein of New York, later probes by Martin Dies of Texas, who chaired the House Committee to Investigate Un-American Activities. Unlike their compatriots in the period 1914 to 1918, however, few Americans in the 1930's argued that their German-American neighbors were hyphenates with divided allegiance.

The German-American community did figure in Nazi Germany's plans regarding the United States. Like the Jewish community, it experienced a feeling of heightened ethnic identity during the Hitler years as it became conscious of a new pivotal importance in the eyes of some Nazi ideologues. The National Socialist *Weltanschauung* maintained that all those of German blood, irrespective of nationality, owed primary allegiance to the ancestral homeland. Blood was stronger than citizenship or place of birth, and the magnetism of *völkisch* (racial) bonds transcended time and space. Accordingly, Germans in the Volga, in the Argentine, and in the United States were members of racial communities and were labeled "racial comrades"; it was their duty to assert their Germanness, or *Deutschtum* (the word connotes the totality of the experience of being an ethnic German). In short, it was the historical and biological duty of all Germans to unite around the concept of race. After the Nazi consolidation of power, *völkisch*-national theories were politicized and Germany propagated a supranational ideology. America, which allegedly had more "German blood" than any other nation, became a prime target for Nazi propaganda. If Americans of German ancestry could unite, some Party officials in Germany believed, they could exert considerable influence in Washington. Many high-ranking members of the NSDAP fervently believed in the political potential of German-America, especially since their theorists indicated that millions of Americans could claim two or more German grandparents.

The tendency of some Germans to view German-America as a cultural and ethnic monolith predated the rise of Nazism. For several generations, German schoolchildren had been taught, correctly, that millions of their countrymen had left their homeland for America for religious, social, and economic reasons. Schoolbooks in the Wilhelminian period praised the exploits of the legendary Baron Friedrich von Steuben in the cause of American independence, told of the death of thousands of Germans in the Civil War, extolled Carl Schurz's attempt to cleanse America of corruption, and claimed the existence of "German states" in the Union. Naturally, many Germans grew up believing that America was as much German as Anglo-Saxon. This view was reinforced at the turn of the century by the large number of American academicians —the so-called Teutonists—who were attracted to the German universities and by the quality of German scholarship. By the time German troops marched through Belgium in the summer of 1914, the fact that millions of Germans lived in the United States had evolved into the myth that they could exert influence on American domestic and foreign policy. Belief in the myth was so strong in some quarters, especially in the Kaiser's circle, that it seemed inconceivable that America would ever come to the aid of Germany's enemies. And there seemed to be good reason for this feeling. The two-million-member pro-German National German-American Alliance implied that it could exert pressure on Washington at the crucial moment. Yet three years later America and Germany were at war, and German-Americans were being subjected to social and political harassment. The many Germans who found this situation incredible revealed, not only their belief in the myth, but also their ignorance of American political behavior.[4]

[4] On German immigration to the United States, see Appendix I, below, and "Immigrants, by Country: 1820–1957," in *The Statistical History of the United States from Colonial Times to the Present* (Stamford, Conn., 1965), Series C 88–114, pp. 56–57. Among the numerous works which furthered the myth of a Germanic America are: Frederick Kapp, *Geschichte der deutschen Einwanderung in Amerika* (Stuttgart, 1868); Albert Faust, *Das Deutschtum in den Vereinigten Staaten* (Leipzig, 1912; Hildesheim, 1970), trans., *The Ger-*

But a myth with a basis in fact is hard to dispel. The rapidity with which Germany and the United States resumed normal relations after the war led some Germans to believe that America had been tricked into entering the conflict by the British: if British propaganda had not been so direct and well planned, German-America could have asserted itself to keep the nation out of the conflict. This argument received additional support when some Americans, especially members of the academic community, began to question the severity of the Versailles Treaty and, more important, publicly asserted that America's entrance into the war had been the result of British intrigue. By 1919, large segments of the defeated and disillusioned German population believed that although America had facilitated the Allied victory, the real enemies were still Britain and France.[5] This view, propagated by many academicians in Germany's universities and ethnological institutions, was linked to the myth that America was largely a Germanic nation. One such institution was the Deutsches Ausland-Institut, or DAI (German Foreign Institute), in Stuttgart.

Having created the DAI in January 1917 because of the exigencies of the World War, the German government hoped that it would further national business interests overseas and re-establish the many contacts that had been severed during the war. This element of the Institute's work was reflected in the large number of business leaders on the advisory board. With victory in sight,

man Element in the United States (Boston, 1909); and Georg von Bosse, Das Heutige Deutschtum in den Vereinigten Staaten (Stuttgart, 1904). On the German-American National Alliance, see Clifton Child, The German-Americans in Politics, 1914–1917 (Madison, Wis., 1939).

[5] The history of the revisionist movement in America has been studied in considerable detail. Of special note are Selig Adler, "The War-Guilt Question and American Disillusionment, 1918–1928," Journal of Modern History, 23 (March 1951), 1–28; and Warren Cohen, The American Revisionists: The Lessons of Intervention in World War I (Chicago, 1967). German-American diplomatic relations in the 1920's have not been thoroughly examined. Sections of Selig Adler's The Isolationist Impulse: Its Twentieth Century Reaction (New York, 1957) outline the broad contours. More recently, the topic has been examined by Earl Beck, Germany Rediscovers America (Tallahassee, Fla., 1968), and Peter Berg, "Deutschland und Amerika, 1918–1929," Historische Studien, 385 (1963), 7–162.

many of these businessmen foresaw a bright future for the DAI in the postwar period and lent their financial support to the Institute. They believed that it could easily be converted from a wartime appendage of the propaganda machine into an instrument to market German goods. But as the war dragged on, many of the heavy contributors channeled their funds directly into the war effort, and the infant DAI was one of the first casualties. When defeat came in November 1918, there seemed no further reason for German businessmen or the government to underwrite the DAI.[6]

Not everyone agreed with this reasoning. Believing that Germany's international image was so tarnished that it was now more important than ever to present the nation in a favorable light, the DAI's director, Fritz Wertheimer, petitioned Germany's new leaders and the business community for renewed support. He was at first unable to convince the leaders of the unstable Weimar Republic that money should be diverted from more pressing needs to support a wartime undertaking. He did, however, elicit much financial support from such firms as Krupp, I. G. Farben, and the Hamburg-American Shipping Line, all of which had had extensive overseas business connections. Thus, four months after Germany's new leaders reluctantly accepted the Versailles Treaty, the DAI started to renew its contacts with business leaders throughout the world.[7]

[6] On the founding of the DAI, see "Schirmherr: Seine Majestät König Wilhelm II," n.d., T-81/603/5392769; and "Das DAI im Jahre 1925," in "Rundfunk-Vorträge des DAI," 2, no. 25, T-81/453/5205954–57. Among the notables who lent their names in support of the DAI were Matthias Erzberger, the directors of Germany's "D" Banks, Grand Admiral von Koester, and Constantin von Neurath (T-81/603/5392617). On contributions from Krupp, Siemens, and Rothschild, see "1918 Bericht," T-81/603/5392618.

[7] "Protokoll über die dritte Verwaltungsrats-Sitzung, 31. Mai 1919 im Sitzungssaal des DAI," T-81/603/5392760–4. Much of the money contributed to the Institute was used for operational expenses and to maintain a museum which housed a collection of materials relating to the history of overseas Germandom (T-81/453/5206272–80). An organizational chart indicating sources of income in the pre-Hitler period is in T-81/603/5392763. After 1933, the Ministry of Interior underwrote the DAI's daily operations. On financing in the Hitler period, see "Haushaltplan," T-81/425/5123440, 5172281, 5172199–225; and "Reichsministerium des Innern, Abteilung III: Forschungsstelle für Auslandsdeutschtum und Auslandskunde, 1927–1934," file NFI 18, pp. 230–261, Archives, YIVO Institute for Jewish Research, New York.

Inextricably linked to the DAI's economic endeavors was the desire to re-establish contacts with the Germans who had left the Reich in the years immediately preceding the war. Wertheimer reasoned that these people were an excellent potential market for German products and, more important, that they could help to create an atmosphere in their adopted homelands amicable to the newly formed Weimar Republic. He also believed that they should be informed of events in Germany and that some effort should be made to keep their feelings for Germany alive. Accordingly, in October 1919, the DAI sent copies of several of its publications to a select group of Germans in the United States and elsewhere.

The DAI's revival was only a meager beginning; the organization could not function without a continuous flow of money, preferably supplied by the government.[8] In late 1922 the DAI had an unexpected windfall when the Reichstag approved funds for it, amid much opposition from members of the Social Democratic Party, who maintained that the Institute was simply a mouthpiece for big business.[9]

Now that the Institute enjoyed both private and public support, Wertheimer attempted to reform the structure and methods of the organization. His first step was to create the Press Correspondence Section to collect foreign newspaper articles dealing with Germany and the overseas German community. Then he established a massive card index containing the names and last known addresses of

[8] In the middle of the decade, Wertheimer wrote, "It was during those troubled years, 1918–1920, that the Institute received a new purpose. It was our hope that the DAI could re-establish economic and cultural ties with the German overseas community and provide some help for those Germans cut-off from the homeland because of the Peace Settlement" ("Das DAI im Jahre 1925," T-81/453/5205954–7). See also Fritz Wertheimer, Das Deutsche Ausland-Institut (1929), T-81/453/5206270. Wertheimer outlined his ideas and views in numerous memoranda. A former colleague, Heinz Kloss, commented that Wertheimer was "certainly deeply committed to the cause of the German language and Volk" (Heinz Kloss to the author, March 2, 1972).

[9] The Social Democrats were opposed to underwriting the DAI; their spokesmen argued that the DAI's overseas activities would give rise to the suspicion that Germany was reviving the Kulturpolitik ("cultural politics") of the prewar period. The bill was passed, and the government also provided funds for the construction of a permanent headquarters (Der Auslanddeutsche, 4 [1921], T-81/426/5174266; 625/5421096–97).

Germans who had emigrated during the latter half of the nineteenth century. Finally, arrangements were made for Germans living abroad to send reports on the current status of their German communities. By the end of the decade, the press section was receiving more than 140 German-language newspapers a year and had a card index containing the names and addresses of an estimated 28,000 German organizations abroad. All this material, together with a 40,000-volume library dealing primarily with German immigration and the history of the overseas German community, was housed in the newly constructed, government-subsidized headquarters, the House of Germanism (Haus des Deutschtums) in Stuttgart.[10]

Wertheimer had long believed that merely to contact Germans living abroad was not enough. Somehow the clusters of Germans in the old Habsburg domains, in Russia, and in the New World had to be reminded of each other's existence; somehow their feeling for Germany had to be kept alive, their use of the German language encouraged, and their preference for German goods strengthened. If Germany did not establish contacts with these people, Wertheimer reasoned, the overseas German community would be lost to Germany forever. To influence them politically would be futile, since many, if not most, were loyal citizens of their adopted countries. He maintained that the DAI should approach them on a strictly cultural basis, reminding them that they had an obligation to prevent their assimilation into the dominant cultures of their new homes. If Germanism was treated as a cultural matter, Germany could not be accused of violating the sovereignty of other nations or of cultivating supranational feeling among her former subjects.

The industrious Wertheimer believed that the most expedient way to rekindle the feeling of *Deutschtum* was to create a worldwide *Verein* (association), which Germans at home and abroad

[10] The name selected for the DAI's headquarters disturbed not only the Social Democrats, but also irritated the French ("La Maison de la Germanie," *L'Avenir* [Paris], April 3, 1930, T-81/453/5206369–70). On the reorganization of the DAI, see T-81/453/5206347–62. See also Fritz Wertheimer, in *Kultur und Politik*, 6 (1932), 164–169.

would be invited to join, to sustain each member's feeling of Germanness. In 1919 or 1920, Wertheimer received approval for his scheme from the DAI's advisory board. Embossed invitations were sent to several hundred Germans living overseas and at home, describing the Institute's functions: to encourage loyalty to the German language and to enhance Germany's economic position. At first the response was disappointing, but as memories of the war faded and the young republic earned the confidence of other nations, many overseas Germans overcame their initial reluctance to re-establish ties with Germany. Wertheimer's task was simplified after he gained access to the lengthy membership lists of two important organizations in Central Europe and the New World, the Union of Germans Abroad (Verein für das Deutschtum im Ausland, VDA) and the Organization of Foreign Germans (Bund der Auslandsdeutschen, BdA). For a short period in the early 1920's, the VDA and the DAI operated as joint organizations, thus avoiding a duplication of effort. But after 1923, the two groups parted company, and each assumed its former autonomy. By the end of the decade, both the DAI and the VDA branches outside Germany had large memberships in Europe and North America.[11]

Whereas the VDA remained a cultural and nationally oriented institution, the DAI had broadened its base to include the academic study of *Deutschtum*. At the onset of the Depression, the DAI emerged as one of the most prestigious, broadly based, and

[11] Members of the BdA were encouraged to join the DAI overseas *Vereine*. For a short while the BdA and the DAI worked together, and the DAI assumed the title of the BdA's publication, *Der Auslanddeutsche*. After 1939, the DAI's publication was known as *Deutschtum im Ausland* ("Satzungen des Bundes der Auslandsdeutschen, Berlin," n.d., T-81/603/5392796; BdA program, 1920, T-81/351/5080804–6). On the DAI-VDA relationship, see "Abkommen zwischen dem VDA und DAI, Okt. 1920," T-81/423/5170023–6. In the Weimar years, Hans Luther, once Chancellor of the Republic, president of the Reichsbank, and ambassador to Washington (1933–1937), Gustav Stinnes, and Constantin von Neurath were associated with the VDA's advisory board. After the VDA's integration into the Third Reich, "Verein" in its title was changed to "Volksbund"; thus the organization retained the same initials. On the VDA in the 1930's, see Carl Bell, "VDA-Geschichte in Sichworten," T-81/502/5265236–60; cf. Otto Schäfer, *Sinn und Wesen des V.D.A.* (Berlin, 1933). See also Hans-Adolf Jacobsen, ed., *Hans Steinacher, Bundesleiter des VDA, 1933–1937* (Boppard, West Germany, 1970).

well-financed institutes in its field in Germany. There were other organizations duplicating some of the DAI's cultural and ethnic work—the Fichtebund, the VDA, the Goethe Institut, and the Munich-based German Academy—but the industrious Wertheimer had expanded the economic aspects of the Institute's work to include an intensive investigation of the history of the overseas German community. He gave the DAI a reputation as the institution in pre-Nazi Germany best qualified to study the phenomenon of *Deutschtum*. In fact, it was partially owing to the Institute's activities and studies that a feeling developed in the German academic community that ethnology was a respectable scholarly field.[12]

Broadly defined, ethnology is the study of the distinctive characteristics of the subdivisions mankind—their origins, speech, culture, and institutions. To Wertheimer and to most of his co-workers, the study of the ethnological background of the German people was synonymous with the study of *Deutschtum*. In postwar Germany, ethnology thrived, owing to some extent to the changes of boundaries and the transfers of populations that followed the signing of the several peace treaties. Professional ethnologists found employment in the universities, in the government, and in numerous academic institutions that flourished during Weimar. They were a heterogeneous group. Among any given number of ethnologists were former members of the Pan-German League, extreme right-wing nationalists, renowned scholars, pseudo intellectuals, and racists. Unfortunately for Wertheimer, who thought ethnology of secondary importance in the work of the DAI, a group of young men joined the DAI in the mid-1920's. These men were gradually equating *Deutschtum* with the mystical qualities of the German *Volk*—an equation that would result in the brutalization of German society. The equation of *Deutschtum* with racial characteris-

---

[12] On the creation of institutes outside the traditional academic structure, see Peter Gay's comments in *Weimar Culture* (New York, 1969), p. 30. Many prominent social scientists, ethnologists, geopoliticians, and anthropologists were affiliated with the DAI—for example, Max-Hildebert Boehm, Hermann Ullmann, Wilhelm Stapel, Hans Grimm, Werner Sombart, and Karl Haushofer. These men served in an advisory capacity. After the DAI was absorbed into the Nazi administrative structure, the relationship with the DAI that these men enjoyed in the 1920's continued into the next decade.

tics was not new to some segments of German society. What was new was the elevation of the study of *Deutschtum* to the academic level and its eventual evolution into a political ideology.[13]

Between 1923 and 1932, Hermann Rüdiger, Otto Lohr, Gustav Moshack, Wahrhold Drascher, and Heinz Kloss joined the Institute.[14] Throughout the decade each enhanced the organization's prestige by writing and editing a number of ethnological studies. Their unpublished and published writings reflect a change in the meaning of *Deutschtum;* the emphasis was more on *völkisch* solidarity than on culture and ethnicity. Wertheimer seems to have agreed with their views. He could not know that *Deutschtum* would become a political issue and that some of these men would facilitate the DAI's integration into the NSDAP's administrative structure. Nor could he have imagined that they would oust him from his position as general director, claiming that a Jew could not serve the New Germany.

During the Weimar years, the DAI's conception of *Deutschtum* was still cultural, and Wertheimer and his subordinates were concerned with the preservation of the German language and the traditional way of life of the overseas German communities. When Hitler came to power, the Institute's functions differed little from those outlined in Wertheimer's proposals of fourteen years earlier. Although it had a forty-thousand-volume library, enjoyed far-

---

[13] The so-called ethnic vocabulary often associated with the Nazis was developed in the previous decade. Z. A. B. Zeman's *Nazi Propaganda* (London, 1964) illustrates its evolution. Among the words and expressions are: *Grenzdeutsche* (ethnically homogeneous areas bordering on Germany's frontiers); *Inselddeutsche* (compact settlements of Germans in Central Europe and Russia); *Reichsdeutsche* (German nationals, usually living outside the Reich); *Auslandsdeutsche* (foreign Germans, i.e., as distinguished from *Reichsdeutsche*—German nationals who were German citizens); *Volksdeutsche* (ethnic Germans, i.e., persons of German stock but not of German nationality living outside Germany) (p. 64). Under the National Socialists, these ethnic classifications had distinct racial overtones. Some of the more important works dealing with *Deutschtum* in the 1920's are: Karl von Loesch, ed., *Volk unter Völkern* (Berlin, 1925); Loesch, ed., *Staat und Volkstum* (Berlin, 1926); Loesch and Max-Hildebert Boehm, eds., *Zehn Jahre Versailles: Die grenz- und volkspolitischen Folgen des Friedensschlusses* (Berlin, 1930); and Hermann Haach, *Das Deutschtum der Erde* (Gotha, 1930).

[14] More detailed accounts can be found in the DAI's personnel folders (1920–1942), T-81/349/5078211ff.

reaching contacts with the overseas German community, and was probably Germany's major depository of archives documenting the history of the overseas German community, the DAI was still, as its detractors claimed during the Reichstag debates, a publicity agent for Germany's captains of industry. It was, however, potentially a leading ethnological institution in a nation that would shortly make ethnology a national preoccupation.

Hitler's appointment as Chancellor marked the end of the study of Germanness as a private and seemingly harmless endeavor. After January 1933, the cultural Germanism of the Weimar years became the political and racial *Deutschtum* of the thirties. Shortly after Hitler assumed the chancellorship, Rudolf Hess told an audience, "You know as well as I do that the one great mistake of the former regime was in not keeping up ties of blood which connect the Germans in their home country with Germans abroad." *Deutschtum*, concluded Hitler's deputy, had to be used abroad politically; it was the "special duty of the National Socialist state to rectify this mistake." [15] Designated by Hitler as the overseer of the entire overseas German community, Hess hoped that all ethnological institutions would lend their aid in a national effort to correct the mistakes of Weimar's leaders. Moved by fear and opportunism, many of these institutes acquiesced in Hitler's appointment and immediately gave their support to the new regime. Some organizations, like the VDA and the Fichtebund, considered racial *Deutschtum* indistinguishable from the ethnology of the Weimar years and welcomed the national revival of Germanism under Hitler. Much to the surprise of the new regime, opposition to its goals came from the DAI, the one organization Hess believed likely to give its overwhelming support to Hitler.[16]

[15] Rudolf Hess, *Reden* (Berlin, 1938), p. 34.

[16] On the coordination of German institutions and agencies with the needs of the State and the Party see Karl Dietrich Bracher, Wolfgang Sauer, and Gerhard Schulz, *Die nationalsozialistische Machtergreifung* (Cologne and Opladen, 1962); Jacobsen, *Nationalsozialistische Aussenpolitik*, Sect. II, pp. 16–318; Donald Norton, "Karl Haushofer and the German Academy," *Central European History*, 1 (March 1968), 80–99; Nelson Edmondson, "The Fichte Society: A Chapter in Germany's Conservative Revolution," *Journal of Modern History*, 38 (1966), 161–180; and Kipphan, *Deutsche Propaganda*, pp. 21–55. On the DAI's staff and the Nazis, see "Nationalsozialismus und Auslanddeutschtum," DAI, Bericht-Archiv, 1933, T-81/443/5194422–5.

The Institute's chiefs were reluctant to endorse the new government for several reasons. First, most of the DAI's financial backing came from Germany's business leaders. Some of these men considered Hitler a dangerous radical and were hesitant to support him. Believing that Hitler's conception of *Deutschtum* and the NSDAP's desire to unite the overseas German community on the basis of race would do considerable damage to their world-wide business contacts, many of them simply refused to jump on the Nazi bandwagon. Furthermore, several important members of the DAI's advisory board were Germans of Jewish origin. In addition, segments of the population of Stuttgart (home of the DAI) were reputed to be opposed to National Socialism. During the spring of 1933, these factors led to the emergence of a genuine, though weak, anti-Nazi opposition. In late 1933, the new regime, intolerant of any opposition, decided to bring the city of Stuttgart and the prestigious Institute firmly inside the Nazi orbit.[17]

The first sign that the party intended to force Stuttgart into the Nazi mold came in the fall of 1933, when Karl Strölin was appointed Lord Mayor of Stuttgart.[18] At the same time, he was named honorary president of the DAI, a position and title that suited neither his personality nor his qualifications. Strölin believed that if the supranational appeal of National Socialism could be combined with the ethnological endeavors of the DAI, Stuttgart could easily become a central base for Nazi overseas adventures, thus becoming one of the key cities in the Third Reich.

Shortly after the start of the new year, Strölin got in touch with a group of the city's most prominent businessmen who contributed money to the DAI from time to time. He offered them a scheme to "publicize the city" as the center of Germany's world-wide business

[17] Wertheimer's file, clipping, "Wir pflanzen des Banner der deutscher Revolution in Stuttgart auf," *NS Kurier*, March 8, 1933, T-81/597/5384812.

[18] After World War II, Strölin told Allied interrogators that his position was honorary; by inference, he had no impact on the DAI's activities. His position was far from ornamental. He helped bring the Institute into the Nazi orbit and played a major role in the DAI's American work after 1934 (RG 59, "Strölin Interrogation," 551). See also Karl Strölin, *Verräter oder Patrioten* (Stuttgart, 1952) and Gerhard Ritter's comments on Strölin in *Carl Goerdeler und die deutsche Widerstandsbewegung* (Stuttgart, 1954), pp. 152, 390ff, 538.

interests and to make Stuttgart famous the world over—to make it what the Nazis later called the "City of the Foreign-born." The fragmentary evidence suggests that he quietly assured them that the only radical aspect of Hitler's program was his desire to see the rebirth of Germany. Reassured, they told Strölin they would support the new government and promised to facilitate the accommodation of the DAI to the needs of the Third Reich.[19]

Strölin felt that it was now time to bring the Institute under Nazi control. He appointed three staunch Nazis to the advisory board and dismissed Wertheimer, together with many key members of the DAI, most of whom found National Socialism personally repugnant or were of Jewish ancestry. Their positions were immediately filled by outsiders or by former colleagues who were waiting for Hitler's assumption of power to emerge publicly as Nazis.[20]

By the spring of 1934, the Institute was apparently conforming to the Nazi model, and Strölin wanted the Party to make it the nucleus around which Germany would build its policy to attract the overseas German community to Nazism. But his bid came too late; the DAI was only one of many Nazified agencies studying *Deutschtum* and maintaining diverse overseas contacts. More important, the Party had decided to use its own foreign apparatus, the Foreign Organization (Die Auslandsorganisation der NSDAP, or AO) and the Foreign Affairs Office (Das Aussenpolitische Amt der NSDAP, or APA) to achieve one of its cardinal goals—the unification of the world-wide German community into a bloc in favor of the new regime. Both these agencies wanted to avoid any competition from the DAI; the leaders of the AO and APA even hoped to absorb it, to take advantage of its rich archival depository and extensive world-wide contacts.

[19] RG 59, "Strölin Interrogation," 556.

[20] After the Nazification of the DAI, Hermann Rüdiger headed the press division, Wahrhold Drascher took charge of the overseas section which handled shortwave broadcasts, and Richard Csaki replaced Wertheimer as general director. Rüdiger replaced Csaki in July 1941. On Csaki, see T-81/331/5055041ff. Wertheimer left Germany in 1938 and settled in Porto Alegre, Brazil. He died in Germany on September 6, 1968 (Gertrud Kuhn, director of the library. Institut für Auslandsbeziehungen, to the author, March 17, 1972).

Throughout most of 1934 a virtual intraparty war was fought for the control of the DAI. Strölin took advantage of this conflict by attempting to publicize the Institute's work. In November 1934, he instructed Wertheimer's former colleague Hermann Rüdiger, now director of the press division, to meet with Friedrich Schmidt, one of the NSDAP's chief agents in Stuttgart and deputy *Gauleiter* of Württemberg.[21] On the twenty-first, Rüdiger told Schmidt that the DAI would place itself at the service of the Party. During the next few weeks, Rüdiger gave a series of talks to high-ranking members of the Nazi hierarchy. The underlying theme of each speech was the same: the DAI was more than willing to work for the Party but did not want to be absorbed by any agency.[22] On November 29, Rüdiger gave an address entitled "The Basic Racial-Political Questions in the German Overseas Community" to a gathering of Nazi "racial specialists" in Hamburg that included the AO's two experts on *Deutschtum,* Emil Ehrich and Karl Klingenfuss. He said that the DAI was the best qualified and most appropriate body in Germany to study *Deutschtum* in its new context, and furthermore, that its world-wide contacts, its network of overseas representatives, and its index of emigrants and German nationals residing abroad could facilitate the rapid unification of the entire overseas German community. During the next two weeks Rüdiger stressed the same ideas to representatives of various Party offices and Nazified organizations.[23] In sum, NSDAP members at the DAI took advantage of administrative uncertainty in the Party regarding the

[21] Memorandum by Hermann Rüdiger, Dec. 1934, T-81/346/5073584; Rüdiger, "Stuttgart und das Auslanddeutschtum," copy of an address, n.d., T-81/346/5073629. See also "Nationalsozialismus und Auslanddeutschtum," 1933, T-81/443/5194174ff. During the week of November 21, 1934, Rüdiger met with Friedrich Stieve of the Auswärtiges Amt (Foreign Ministry), Friedrich Carl Badendieck (VDA), and Georg Leibbrandt (APA). On the final coordination of the DAI, see Rüdiger, "Grundfrage der volkspolitischen Lage des Grenz- und Auslanddeutschtums," T-81/346/5073584; "DAI an Stadtrat Dr. Cuhorst, NSDAP, Kreisleitung Stuttgart, vom 9. Oktober 1934," T-81/404/5147304-5.

[22] "Rüdiger Bericht," Dec. 1934, T-81/346/5073584. During the war, Schmidt held the rank of SS *Standartenführer* and was attached to the notorious Ostministerium.

[23] T-81/316/5073629, 346/5073584. Emil Ehrich published a history of the Auslandsorganisation in the late 1930's, *Die Auslands Organisation der NSDAP,* Vol. II, Part I, of *Das Dritte Reich im Aufbau* (Berlin, 1939). Ehrich

place of the DAI in the new Germany by disseminating propaganda about the virtues of the organization through a series of lectures.[24]

By Christmas 1934, Rüdiger reported that the DAI had completely coordinated its work with other agencies that had overseas contacts: the Ministry of Propaganda, the AO, the VDA, the APA, and the German Student Union. The DAI was to make available to the State and the Party its numerous foreign connections. In keeping with its new status, the Institute had three principal duties: to serve as a center for "the collection, investigation, and documentation of the lives of Germans overseas"; to "study all questions relating to the mutual relations between the Reich, foreign nations, and the overseas German community"; and, most important, "to enlighten all overseas Germans about the new regime and the meaning of *Deutschtum*." [25] On the surface, the DAI's new goals were similar to those Wertheimer had envisioned for it following the war. The contrast between his plans and Strölin's was, however, as striking as the distance between the ethnology of the Weimar period and the racial politics of the Hitler years.

Although the Institute was firmly integrated into the Nazi administrative structure by December 1934, the Party decided to foster the illusion that it was a private agency, independent of the State and the Party. This decision was made because it was believed that most people of German extraction in foreign countries did not understand the meaning of National Socialism and might be more receptive to DAI overtures if it was a private institution. To ensure the credibility of the DAI's private status, the Party asked the chairman of the Hamburg-American Line to chair the advisory board and persuaded more than a hundred prominent

---

was an aide to Ernst-Wilhelm Bohle, who was appointed *Gauleiter* of the Auslandsorganisation in 1934. About Bohle, see Appendix III. Klingenfuss was chief of the cultural section in the Auslandsorganisation until 1936. From 1936 to 1944 he was attached to the German Embassy in Berne (RG 59, "Bohle Interrogation," 148).

[24] Gustav Moshack (Moshack is the correct spelling, although some authors have used Moshak), for example, gave an address to the NS Frauenschaft, "Die Frau im deutsch-amerikanischen Abwehrkampf," and Rüdiger gave an address, "Stimmungen und Strömungen im Deutschtum Amerikas" (T-81/346/5073585ff).

[25] "Neue Aufgaben des DAI," Oct. 23, 1934, T-81/346/5073602–3; DAI, Bericht-Archiv, II, 1934, T-81/346/5073590–2.

business leaders to permit their names to be used in DAI publications. Their support enabled the DAI to appear to be a privately endowed organization.[26]

After a year of uncertainty, the DAI's researchers settled down to the study of the world-wide *Deutschtum* in its new racial context. Their scholarly inclinations would lead them to the Volga Germans and to other clusters of Germans in Africa, in South America, in Central and Eastern Europe, and in the American hemisphere. One of the most fascinating aspects of the DAI's research was the study of American *Deutschtum* undertaken by its experts on America.[27] Investigations of the history of Americans of German ancestry completed during the Nazi years lent statistical support to those persons in Germany who believed that German immigrants in the United States had made great contributions to that nation's historical development. The Institute's "American work" coincided with the Party's desire to unify German-America into a political force that could exert pressure on Washington. Thus, as a result of its reorganizations in the early 1920's and its absorption by the Party, the DAI had evolved from a servant of the business community to a subordinate of the NSDAP. In its new capacity, the DAI was in a position to support and justify the aims of German foreign policy.

[26] "Wirtschafts-Abteilung der DAI," T-81/463/5216716–48. On the DAI's relationship with other Nazi agencies, see Kloss, "Die 'Amerikaarbeit' des DAI im Dritten Reich," p. 2.

[27] In a technical sense, the DAI did not have an American Department. Several departments—or rather subsections (*Referate*) which handled emigration and historical research—maintained extensive connections with American *Deutschtum*. In 1938, a Nordamerika Referat was created to coordinate the increased activity in the United States and was headed by Gustav Moshack. It was dissolved in 1940.

Germans Look at Their
American Cousins

The new status of the German Foreign Institute signified more than the incorporation of an institution concerned with *Deutschtum* into the structure of the Third Reich. As we have seen, the opening of its archives gave the Party one of the most comprehensive and centralized collections of materials dealing with the historical evolution of world-wide *Deutschtum* then in existence. After 1934, ideas exemplified in the materials collected by researchers in the preceding decade were absorbed into the Nazi *Weltanschauung*. One example of the merging of the DAI's studies with the NSDAP's racial activities was the investigation of Americans of German ancestry. What emerged was a picture of a racially intact German-America. This impression of German-America and Germany's subsequent attempt to accommodate it to the needs of German foreign policy challenged the American concept of a nation, gave rise to widespread anti-Nazi feeling in the United States, and contributed much of the tension between Washington and Berlin.

The idea of American *Deutschtum* that had evolved during the Weimar years had few of the political or racial overtones of the Nazi period. In 1921, the DAI, wishing to study and stimulate German interest in Germans abroad, started to collect information about the German element in the United States. Most of the research was carried on by men who were aware of the numerous links between America and Germany before 1917. Careful ethnological studies were made of the way eight million first- and second-generation Germans in America had maintained their

Deutschtum by establishing German schools, theaters, and churches. The researchers were fascinated by the widespread acceptance of Rankean empiricism in academic circles and by the adoption of the German model by many American universities in the last decades of the nineteenth century. They asked how it was possible for the National German-American Alliance, which boasted more than two million members in 1914, to exist in a nation that prided itself on its ability to amalgamate its minorities with the dominant Anglo-Saxon culture. They concluded that the melting pot had not functioned in the case of American *Deutschtum*, and by inference, was nothing more than a widely accepted myth created by those Americans who wanted to foster a concept of American nationality. Though they were impressed by the healthy state of *Deutschtum*, their optimism was tempered by the realization that German-America had collapsed as a political force under the impact of national hysteria and the outpouring of hate engendered by the war. From the outset of these investigations, the members of the DAI's research section hoped to make a realistic reappraisal of American *Deutschtum* in the light of what one author has called the "dissolution of the hyphen," that is, the desire of Americans of German extraction to become Americans only.[1]

The war left the German-American community split, disillusioned, and badly shaken by the "one-hundred per cent Americanism" of the previous few years. The once powerful National German-American Alliance had been disbanded by congressional action, and most of its members had withdrawn from public life.

---

[1] John Hawgood, *The Tragedy of German-America* (New York, 1940); H. C. Peterson and Gilbert Fite, *Opponents of War, 1917–1918* (Madison, Wis., 1957). In general "German-America(n)" is spelled with a hyphen, as is *Deutsch-Amerikaner*. Often, "German-Americans" was used interchangeably with *deutschen Stammes* ("of German stock") or *Abstammung* ("German descent"). After 1933, the Nazis and their German supporters in America preferred "American Germans" (*Amerikaner deutschen Blutes*); in fact, the name selected for the Bund movement in March 1936 was Amerikadeutscher Volksbund. It was argued that the hyphenated name implied that German-Americans had become Americans; the Bundists viewed themselves as Germans *in* America or American Germans. In a word, blood was stronger than citizenship or place of birth. A more detailed discussion can be found in Chapter 8, below.

The thousands of German organizations that had once honey-combed the major German centers—New York, St. Louis, Milwau-kee, Chicago, Cincinnati—were dissolved. German-language in-struction had almost vanished in the public schools, and academic Teutonism of any sort was minimal. But with the dissolution of the German Empire and the creation of the Weimar Republic, Ger-man-Americans and the threat of German hegemony were no longer real issues either in America or on the Continent.[2] In Amer-ica, the Red Scare, according to Robert Murray, "was the major vehicle on which the American nation rode from a victorious war into a bankrupt peace." [3] The German element was replaced as a topic of conversation by the Blacks and their "new ways," the re-vival of the Ku Klux Klan, the withdrawal into isolationism, and the Bolshevik menace. The mores and life styles of prewar America were gone, along with Wilsonian idealism.[4] These factors, as well as the stable relationship between the United States and republican Germany, facilitated the re-emergence of a small but vocal seg-ment of German-America.

In May 1919, the Steuben Society of America was founded for the express purpose of changing the image of Germany and Ger-mans that had developed during the World War. It hoped to con-vince Americans that Germany was not the nation of Huns in spiked helmets portrayed in the wartime press, but the home of a highly cultured and sophisticated people. The society's founders

[2] On German-America in the 1920's, see Richard O'Connor, *The German-Americans* (Boston, 1968), pp. 429ff. On the life and thought of the pro-German George Sylvester Viereck in the 1920's, see Niel M. Johnson, *George Sylvester Viereck: German-American Propagandist* (Urbana, Ill., 1972), and Phyllis Keller, "George Sylvester Viereck: The Psychology of a German-American Militant," *Journal of Interdisciplinary History*, 2 (1971), 59–108. On the de-cline of the German-language press in this period, see Carl Wittke, *The Ger-man-Language Press in America* (Lexington, Ky., 1940), pp. 238ff.

[3] Robert K. Murray, *The Red Scare: A Study in National Hysteria* (Minne-apolis, 1955), p. 17; Paul L. Murphy, "Sources and Nature of Intolerance in the 1920's," *Journal of American History*, 51 (June 1964), 60–76; Louis Ger-son, *The Hyphenate in Recent American Politics* (Lawrence, Kan., 1964).

[4] An excellent survey of the 1920's is John D. Hicks, *Republican Ascen-dancy, 1921–1933*, New American Nation Series (New York, 1960). On the changing picture of the 1920's, see Henry May, "Shifting Perspectives on the 1920's," *Mississippi Valley Historical Review*, 43 (Dec. 1955), 405–424.

also stressed the view that German-Americans, far from being "mongrels with a divided allegiance, . . . hyphenates, whose hyphen, like the kiss of Judas, is linked to treachery," were and always had been loyal Americans.[5] Another aim of the organization was to popularize the view that the war had been the result of a Russo-French conspiracy and that Germany had become involved, not to gain territory, but to maintain the balance of power on the Continent. The society's task was made easier by the growing desire of Americans for a return to normalcy and by the transfer of their hate from German-Americans to other minorities. The image changers were aided by a loose alliance with the liberal-academic community and by unintentional support from anti-Wilson Republicans, isolationists, and idealists who viewed Germany's transition from monarchy to republic as a triumph of American democracy. The first number of the society's magazine *Issues of To-Day* appeared in October 1920 and along with its more popular publication, *The Progressive,* helped to publicize its views about the origins of the war.[6]

During the next few years, the society also had a powerful ally in Senator Robert M. La Follette, who had opposed America's entrance into the war and who now regarded the harsh terms of the Treaty of Versailles as a tragic mistake. The society also found a spokesman in the American ambassador to Berlin, Alanson B. Houghton, who fostered the view that Weimar Germany was the first line of defense against the creeping menace of Bolshevism from the east. Upon his return to the United States in 1925, Houghton was replaced by Jacob Gould Schurman, who became such an ardent supporter of anti-Versailles forces in Germany that the State Department recalled him several years later.[7]

[5] Frederick Schrader, "The Genesis of the Steuben Society in America," *The Progressive* (Feb. 15, 1927), 205–208; Adler, *Isolationist Impulse,* pp. 85–86.

[6] The Steuben Society received most of the material it distributed directly from Germany. Many of the articles that appeared in *Issues of To-Day* and *The Progressive* first appeared in the journal *Die Kriegsschuldfrage,* which was published by the Zentralstelle für Erforschung der Kriegsschuldfrage in Berlin. On the role played by the Kriegsschuldreferat, a subsection in the Foreign Ministry, see Imanuel Geiss, "The Outbreak of the First World War and German War Aims," *Journal of Contemporary History,* 1 (July 1966), 75–78.

[7] Adler, *Isolationist Impulse,* pp. 164–165. Schurman, a one-time president of Cornell University, remained active after his return to America. During the

The most articulate support of the Steuben Society's cause, however, came not from the activities of politicians and statesmen but from the writings of scholars and publicists—the so-called revisionists—who argued that the blame for the war did not rest solely upon Berlin. Although not all the writers were pro-German, many were either isolationists or internationalists. To support their argument that Germany was not exclusively responsible for the conflict, they found ample documentation in the archival collections made public in the 1920's. Soon Harry Elmer Barnes, Sidney B. Fay, and several contributors to the *New Republic* became the leading spokesmen of the revisionist school in the United States. Their writings, as well as America's failure to ratify the Treaty of Versailles, led some Germans to conclude that there was widespread sympathy for Germany in America. By 1924, Germany was sending great quantities of material dealing with the war-guilt question to the United States to be distributed by the Steuben Society.[8]

Sensing the subtle changes in American public opinion, some Americans of German extraction slowly re-entered public life. German-American sport associations, church groups, and schools started to reappear in German-speaking centers. Their activities did not go unnoticed by the DAI researchers and members of a branch of its *Verein* in America. In the middle of the decade, the Institute undertook an ethnological study of American *Deutschtum* to determine what percentage of the population was of German stock (*Stamm*). More important, the DAI wanted to learn whether the German element was in any way ethnically or politically united. At this juncture, it must be emphasized, the Institute's seemingly great interest in American *Deutschtum* sprang from the economic motive of conducting what Americans have come to know as marketing research.

Basing their findings largely on the census reports published by Washington, on the writings of historians Albert Faust and Emil

Nazi years, he attempted to secure teaching positions for refugee intellectuals. Materials dealing with aspects of his ambassadorship and his activities in the 1930's are in the manuscript division of the Cornell University Libraries, Ithaca, New York.

[8] Adler, "The War-Guilt Question," pp. 1–28.

Mannhardt, and on the information sent from members of the *Verein* to the DAI, the Institute's researchers calculated that nearly 22 per cent of the total American population was of German stock; moreover, they concluded that as many as five to six million naturalized Germans and native-born German-Americans used German as their primary language, thus indicating that they were still unassimilated but that future generations were not beyond the reach of the melting pot. When this information was correlated with the statistics kept by German state governments, it was found that of the two million Germans who had emigrated to America between 1871 and 1914, nearly two-thirds were from southwestern Germany. Generally Catholic, these so-called *schwäbisch* Germans had left their homeland for a variety of social and economic reasons.

Following their inclination for ethnic arithmetic, the DAI's research staff next launched a full-scale investigation of German-America's historical development. With interests comparable to those of the German-American Historical Society, researchers combed the history of the United States for examples of famous Americans of German ancestry. Biographical sketches were written examining the lives of Germans prominent in the history of the United States: the Steinway brothers, August Gräbner, Julius Goebel, Carl Hexamer, William Nast, August Kautz, and Friedrich Hocke. Materials were collected documenting the histories of states with large German-speaking populations, and detailed studies were prepared of the Pennsylvania Dutch—or Pennsylvania Germans—and of other German religious sects unaffected by Americanization or industrialization. Some of this material appeared in the DAI's journal, *Der Auslanddeutsche*. Although most, if not all, of these studies were not published until after the DAI's incorporation into the Nazi administrative structure, some members of the Institute's house staff used these findings to support the contention that American *Deutschtum* had remained ethnically intact in a land that took pride in its ability to integrate most of its major ethnic groups.[9] Thus these articles reinforced the view that

[9] The study of ethnic roots was by no means a monopoly of the Germans. A cursory survey of the literature of the 1920's indicate that the Jews, the Irish, the Italians, and other ethnic groups in America had their ethnic spokesman. On the Germans, see Frederick Schrader, *The Germans in the Making of*

the United States was partly a Germanic nation. The data were not utilized for political purposes until after the Nazis came to power, but the DAI's researchers were unwittingly creating a rationale for future German encroachments in American affairs by providing statistical "proof" of the existence of a potentially powerful German-American community.[10]

During the Weimar years, the man most responsible for perpetuating this belief was Otto Lohr. Between 1927 and the Nazi victory in 1933, Lohr assembled an impressive biographical compendium of famous German-Americans. During the 1930's he published numerous brief biographies in the DAI's and other publications destined for consumption in Germany and overseas. In view of his rapid conversion from ethnological *Deutschtum* to Hitlerian racial ideology, his early works suggest that he did not subscribe to the view that *Deutschtum* was an exclusively cultural phenomenon; rather, he viewed the German *Volk* as the embodiment of a spiritual essence, as a unique product of history, possessing immutable qualities that transcended the immediate historical experience; Germans the world over enjoyed a special solidarity. In December 1931, for example, he published an article in *Der Sammler,* a Munich-based literary journal. The article dealt with a relatively unimportant German-American, Paul Schrick, an immigrant pastor of the seventeenth century. Using the biographical materials collected by his colleagues, he attributed to Schrick an exceedingly important role in the founding of New Amsterdam and erroneously asserted that the city had been more German than Dutch. In October of the same year, Lohr had published an excerpt from a long essay he was preparing, "The Bavarians in the History of the

---

America, Knights of Columbus Racial Contribution Series (New York, 1924); and J. Russell, *The Germanic Influence in the Making of Michigan* (Detroit, 1927). On the DAI's American studies, see E. Stricker, "Die Schwaben und ihre Beziehungen zum Ausland in Vergangenheit und Gegenwart," *Der Auslanddeutsche,* 6 (1923), 158–162. The DAI also circulated its views of the overseas German community in annual publications: *Picture Calendar* (1925——), *Bibliographie des Deutschtums im Ausland* (1937——), *Jahrbuch für auslanddeutsche Sippenkunde* (1936——), *Auslanddeutsche Volksforschung* (1937——), and after 1939, *Volksforschung.*

[10] The population of the United States was 115,832,000 in 1925. The DAI derived its statistics and materials concerning population patterns from the

United States." The appearance of the article coincided with the celebration of the founding of Germantown, Pennsylvania. Subtly manipulating his documentary evidence, Lohr led his readers to believe that Germantown was America's "German City" and that its population was an example of how Germanness could be preserved in an Anglo-Saxon area.[11]

Though Lohr was not a major scholar, his published writings were symptomatic of a problem of German society: the gradual erosion of German scholarship. When the DAI's studies are viewed as a whole, they indicate the emergence of a *völkisch* German language, replete with its own jargon. Together with other institutes of its type, the DAI was elevating the study of *Deutschtum* to the level of acceptable scholarship and, by inference, suggesting that German ethnocentrism was a topic worthy of scholarly endeavor. For a man like Otto Lohr the transition from cultural to racial *Deutschtum* would never pose an intellectual problem; for

---

U.S. government *Annual Report on Commerce and Immigration.* See T-81/337/5063073. On the use of these materials, see Max Miller, "Ursachen und Ziele der schwäbischen Auswanderung," in DAI, Staatsarchiv Stuttgart, 1919–1932, T-81/614/5406985ff. A DAI study undertaken in 1928 estimated that twenty-five million, or 22 per cent, of the American population was of German origin. As will be seen, these statistics became especially important in the next decade ("Übersicht über die vermutliche Stärke des Deutschtums in den einzelnen Ländern der Erde," May 1929, T-81/617/5411384). See also "Anzahl der Deutschen in der Welt ausserhalb Deutschlands," *Deutsches Volksblatt,* Spring 1928, T-81/346/5073524; and "Wanderungsbewegung im Rechnungsjahre, 1820–1928," DAI, Bericht-Archiv, T-81/337/5063061ff. Cf. Albert Faust, II, 24. On the use of these statistics in the Hitler years, see Heinz Kloss, *Statistisches Handbuch der Volksdeutschen in Übersee* (Stuttgart, 1943), and *Um die Einigung des Deutschamerikanertums: Die Geschichte einer unvollendeten Volksgruppe* (Berlin, 1937), p. 13. Compare Carl Wittke's use of these materials in "German Immigrants and Their Children," *Annals of the American Academy of Political and Social Science,* 223 (Sept. 1942).

[11] Although this study uses Otto Lohr as a case in point, the writings of Katharina Reimann are worth examining (see T-81/597/5383721). Among Lohr' writings are: "Pastor Paul Schrick," *Der Sammler,* T-81/617/5410999–5411009; "Bayern in der Geschichte Amerikas," T-81/617/5411010; "Die ersten Deutschen in der neuen Welt," *Deutschtum im Ausland,* 14 (Feb. 1932), 80–83. For Lohr's studies of famous (and not so famous) German-Americans, see T-81/602/5414628ff and 618/5413059ff. Several examples of Lohr's writings in the 1930's can be found in *Der Auslanddeutsche,* 19 (March 1936); 20 (June 1936); 21 (Sept. 1938).

others, the transition presented an intellectual rather than a political problem.

Nowhere in Lohr's writings does one find a call for the unification of the German-American community. In fact, his view of contemporary American *Deutschtum* was shared by his colleagues. Many of them believed that most German-Americans were rapidly severing their ancestral roots in order to conform to the dominant culture. Even though there were hundreds of large and influential German social and cultural associations in prewar America, and though numerous religious sects maintained ethnic separateness, the DAI researchers had little hope for the future of American *Deutschtum*. Their studies seemed to point to one conclusion: the World War had left a once powerful and united German-America politically fragmented; more important, the war had accelerated the process of assimilation. No matter how each researcher defined *Deutschtum*, they all agreed that prewar German-America was irrevocably gone.

This view was supported by reports sent to the Institute from members of its *Verein* and by German travelers in the United States that predicted a gloomy future for Americans of German ancestry. German-Americans, wrote a German exchange student in the summer of 1928, wanted to drop the hyphen forever and simply be Americans. He concluded that the prewar *Deutschtum* had collapsed as a political and cultural force.[12] This report reaffirmed the findings of an informal study completed in the previous year by Martha Schreiber, a German exchange teacher at the University of Wisconsin. Her discussion, entitled "The Future of North American *Deutschtum*," had been forwarded to Wertheimer by the Institute of Sociology in Berlin.[13]

Schreiber maintained that the wartime prohibition against the teaching of German had all but destroyed the cohesiveness Ameri-

[12] "Bericht über meine Studienreise nach Kanada und Amerika, 5. Mai bis 21. August 1928," DAI, Bericht-Archiv, T-81/436/5186140–158.

[13] Martha Schreiber, "Die Zukunft des nordamerikanischen Deutschtum, 1927," *ibid.*, folders 601–630, T-81/434/5184256–61. See also Anna Penck, "Möglichkeiten deutscher Einwanderer in Amerika," Nov. 1928, *ibid.*, 1188, T-81/440/5191046–61; and "Denkschrift betreffend Rückwanderer aus Amerika nach dem Krieg," 1930(?), *ibid.*, 1081, T-81/438/5189239–46.

can *Deutschtum* had once possessed. Furthermore, German-Americans were reluctant to reassert their Germanness either on the political or cultural levels in the post-war period. With few options open to them, they viewed the total adoption of the dominant Anglo-Saxon culture as the only way to gain the complete acceptance of their non-German neighbors. "But all of the difficulties," she added, "do not come from the American side alone; on the contrary, part of the problem rests with Germany." The Weimar Republic, she argued, had not done enough to make German-Americans want to reassert their Germanness. She offered several suggestions for rectifying this condition. First, German centers displaying the finest examples of German books, magazines, and pictorial art should be established in cities with large German-American concentrations. In addition, the German government should urge upon the members of large and influential German associations the duty of becoming members of the world-wide German community. In brief, what was needed was a revival of the *Kulturpolitik* of the Kaiser's Germany. She concluded, "If this does not happen, they [German-Americans] will ruin themselves by indulging in individualism and materialism. Hopefully, Germans abroad, especially in the United States, will set the example of unity and loyal cooperation with their Motherland." In view of Schreiber's somber appraisal of American *Deutschtum* and her proposals (some of which did not come under the Institute's jurisdiction), it is not surprising that Wertheimer placed her study in the file marked "Reprint Forbidden." [14]

Schreiber's belief that Germany must aim for the revival of *Kulturpolitik* or suffer the irrevocable loss of the overseas German community should not be construed as dramatically *völkisch*. It is doubtful that Schreiber or the recipients of these reports were of the same ilk as the sectarian race theorists of that era. For men such as Nathaniel Jünger, Werner Jansen, and, of course, Adolf Hitler, *völkisch* nationalism differed from the prewar cultural nationalism in that it regarded cultural differences as differences of blood. The reports arriving from America and elsewhere reflected,

[14] Schreiber.

however, a deep sense of frustration: the failure of Germany to establish a *Weltreich* (world empire) in the Great War also meant the demise of *Kulturpolitik* on a world-wide scale. For some, the gulf between the two eras was bridged by the ideas of the National Socialists, with their emphasis on uniqueness, national community, biological nationalism, and creativity determined by blood, all of which became features of the Nazi *Weltanschauung*.

The DAI had to revise its cultural-ethnological orientation to meet the needs of Nazi racial-politics after it was incorporated into the structure of the Third Reich. The Institute's conversion to racial *Deutschtum* was not as rapid as that of other such institutions. The DAI's failure to accept immediately the National Socialist viewpoint was not caused by any lack of zeal for the new regime. In fact, the men who facilitiated its take-over by the Nazis—Otto Lohr, Gustav Moshack, Herman Rüdiger—welcomed National Socialism as a boon to the study of *Deutschtum* and as a spur to German overseas adventures. But they were reluctant to accept some of the precepts of the Hitlerian world-view, especially those which did not agree with their findings. These men considered themselves academicians and scholars whose theories and opinions were based on scholarly research rather than conjecture and speculation. Although the DAI's predilection for scholarship never resulted in overt hostility to the Party, the relationship between the NDSAP's overseas agencies and the Institute was tense, particularly as that relationship affected *Deutschtum* in the United States.[15]

After the Nazification of Germany, studies that had been undertaken before 1934 were reinterpreted and rewritten to conform to Nazi cosmology. The DAI was a forerunner of the "think tank." Its function under the Third Reich was to study and investigate problems affecting the overseas German community in the light of the most recent developments in Germany's foreign needs, in short, to bridge the gap between the ideal and the reality of racial-politics abroad. Various agencies addressed questions to the Institute's researchers, for example: How could the unification of the German-

[15] On the DAI's activities in America, see Kipphan, *Deutsche Propaganda*, Part I, pp. 26ff; and Smith, *The Deutschtum of Nazi Germany and the United States*, ch. ii.

American community be best accomplished? What was the current state of racial awareness among the Volga Germans? What impact were radio broadcasts having on the pockets of Germans living in the former Habsburg lands? From time to time, the Institute's staff prepared reports that were at variance with the Party's preconceived image of the world. These reports were shelved or reworked. Thus, the Institute never decided anything; it implemented policy in only a limited sense. Rather, the reports and special studies were used to justify existing policy or to provide a rationale for a particular undertaking. This procedure, to be sure, brought some members of the DAI's staff into conflict with Party ideologues. The conflict was apparent when one of the DAI's specialists on American *Deutschtum*, Heinz Kloss, dismissed the writings of the Nazi propagandist Colin Ross as crude, naïve, unrealistic, and unscholarly.[16]

Kloss had little use for Ross, who had found favor with some members of the Nazi hierarchy. Kloss and his colleagues asserted that their findings had led them to a conclusion concerning the future of *Deutschtum* in the United States: the task must be entrusted to native German-American organizations operating on a cultural rather than a racial-political basis. The unification of the overseas German community in America and elsewhere could not be accomplished by approaching the task monolithically; any approach had to take into account the indigenous needs of each community. Only when the feeling of *Deutschtum* had been rekindled sufficiently could Germany hope to influence political attitudes or behavior. Thus, any effort to superimpose a party structure analogous to the NSDAP's on the German-American community was not only premature; it was also a product of sheer fantasy, especially in view of the disastrous effects of the Great War on American *Deutschtum*. After 1934, the Institute chose what its researchers considered the most realistic approach to American *Deutschtum*, that is, working for "minority group rights."

---

[16] The conflict between Colin Ross, a German propagandist whose works are examined in subsequent chapters, and the DAI's Heinz Kloss is discussed in a memorandum prepared by Kloss: "Buchbesprechung von Heinz Kloss über Colin Ross, 'Unser Amerika' vom 7. Sept. 1938," T-81/351/5080000ff.

It will be recalled that during the Weimar years, the Institute had completed detailed studies of American Germandom in its historical and contemporary settings. Those studies led the researchers to conclude that the United States was a pluralistic nation composed of numerous minority groups. Of course, there was nothing novel about their interpretation. Americans and knowledgeable Europeans had made similar interpretations for years. Like the American sociologist Henry Pratt Fairchild, DAI men asked whether the melting pot had ever worked and whether it could ever throughly assimilate all of its hyphenates. During this period, these queries remained cultural rather than political; although some DAI researchers tended to exaggerate the historical importance of American *Deutschtum,* no one seems to have phrased his conception of it as a racial-political question.

It is noteworthy that during the same period and into the next decade some American intellectuals and social theorists had begun to display the same skepticism about the melting-pot philosophy. The New Deal, with its emphasis on cultural pluralism and a heightened interest in the political role of minority groups, transformed this questioning into a political as well as a cultural phenomenon. Some New Dealers suggested that America was governed by coalitions of the major ethnic groups and that America's minorities could preserve their cultural traits within the framework of the dominant Anglo-Saxon culture. They did not maintain that all minorities were outside the melting-pot, but they argued that cultural and ethnic diversity was a desirable national goal. This argument did not imply, as the Nazi Party's race theorists and specialists on America later maintained, that representation in government should be based on the extent of a group's sense of ethnic (or racial) oneness or on its contribution to the historical development of the United States. According to the official Nazi viewpoint, German-Americans had made extraordinary contributions to the historical evolution of the United States and therefore deserved a proportionate share of political power.

Obviously, the German experts on America and some New Dealers reached similar conclusions concerning the melting pot by starting from entirely different premises. The New Deal questions about the then dominant theories concerning the melting pot had been asked by Randolph Bourne before America's entry into the World War. Bourne, who had opposed America's entry into the war and had gained a reputation as a literary radical, had outlined his views in the *New Republic*. He argued that America's desire to blend its minorities into a homogeneous whole was a serious mistake "because it did not really mean creating a new culture which would be an amalgam of the various immigrant cultures with the Anglo-Saxon civilization but actually meant a forcing of the immigrants into the Yankee mold." Instead of forced assimilation, which made memories of Europe more intense, America's goal should be a cosmopolitanism that permitted each culture expression. Only by attaining this goal could the United States become a truly "transnational" state made up of heterogeneous peoples.[17]

Two decades after his death in 1918, some New Dealers found such ideas appealing as antidotes to the white-Anglo-Saxon-Protestant Republicanism that was in the ascendancy in the 1920's. The New Deal conception of pluralism found expression in much of the literature and legislation, and in many of the federally sponsored art projects of the 1930's. In fact, emphasis on the individuality of America's minorities became part of the liberal credo during the Roosevelt years.[18]

To researchers at the DAI during the Hitler years, in contrast, cultural pluralism was synonymous with a racial interpretation of American history. The man largely responsible for this equation was Heinz Kloss. Born in Germany in 1904, Kloss joined the DAI's staff in May 1927 and was later appointed director of the Institute's library. Kloss was obviously an opportunist, but he was also

[17] Bourne, as quoted in David Shannon, ed., *Progressives and Postwar Disillusionment*, Vol. VI of *A Documentary History of American Life* (New York, 1967), pp. 179–191. On the development of Bourne's ideas, see Christopher Lasch, *The New Radicalism in America* (New York, 1967), pp. 65–103; and John Moreau, *Randolph Bourne: Legend and Reality* (Washington, D.C., 1966).

[18] See William Leuchtenburg's comments on the federal theater in *Franklin D. Roosevelt and the New Deal*, pp. 126–128. The Life in America series (1934–1938) is one example of the stress on ethnic differences. On the political ramifications of pluralism, see Carl Degler, "American Political Parties and the Rise of the City: An Interpretation," *Journal of American History*, 51 (June 1964), 41–59.

an extremely competent researcher and writer.[19] Between 1934 and 1942, he published many articles and wrote three detailed studies outlining his conception of "minority group rights" and of German-America's historical development.[20]

Kloss's writings illustrate the deterioration of German historical empiricism under the National Socialist regime—the misuse of historical methodology in an effort to fulfill the assumed needs of German overseas policy and to provide a rationale for what the Germans called "American work." His studies also show that the Nazi view of American *Deutschtum* was not a temporary aberration but that much of the groundwork had been laid during the Weimar years. Unquestionably, Kloss's most important work was *Das Volksgruppenrecht in den Vereinigten Staaten von Amerika*, a two-volume examination of minority-group legislation in the United States. In it he asserted that the United States had failed to develop a dominant American nationality composed of thoroughly assimilated ethnic and racial minorities. Attempts to do so had failed because the proponents of Anglo-Saxon culture had not realized that the attraction of ancestry was in some cases stronger than the desire to conform to the cultural norm. In areas in the United States where this was realized, special minority-group legislation had been passed. "A unified national America was an illusion," he argued; accordingly, the United States was a heterogeneous nation composed of sometimes friendly, sometimes antagonistic racial and ethnic minorities.[21]

To substantiate his argument, Kloss examined the legislation

[19] For biographical data about Kloss see Appendix III. About some of his trips to America, see Kloss, "Die 'Amerikaarbeit' des DAI," pp. 7, 14. On his background, see DAI personnel folders, T-81/389/5078210ff.

[20] Kloss's most important works include *Um die Einigung des Deutschamerikanertums;* his introduction to *Brüder vor den Toren des Reiches* (Berlin, 1937); *Das Volksgruppenrecht in den Vereinigten Staaten von Amerika* (2 vols.; Essen, 1940–1942; reissued 1963, *Das Nationalitätenrecht der Vereinigten Staaten von Amerika*); *Statistisches Handbuch der Volksdeutschen in Übersee; Pennsylvaniendeutscher Text—Poesie und Prosa* (Wiesbaden, 1936); "Volkstums- und Rassenfragen," *Denkschrift* (1942), T-81/423/5169629–5169832.

[21] Kloss to the Ministry of Propaganda and Enlightenment, Sect. VII (*Ausland*), Berlin, July 12, 1939, T-81/140/177342; 177322–51. On Kloss's use of materials collected by Otto Lohr in the previous decade, see *Volksgruppenrecht*, I: *Die Erstsiedlergruppen*, 29, 30, 93n, 137–138.

passed in states with large ethnic and racial minorities. He discovered that in almost every state where a transplanted minority had settled, its language was taught in public or private schools. In accordance with the evidence as he interpreted it, Kloss concluded that the desire to perpetuate ethnic and racial separateness was far greater than the desire to blend with the dominant Anglo-Saxon culture. Exclusiveness was not a monopoly of the recently arrived; it was characteristic of the American way. In the preface to *Volksgruppenrecht*, Kloss wrote, "It is with a feeling of admiration for American farsightedness and practical wisdom that this book has been written." Kloss welcomed the coming of the New Deal because of its stressing of minority and racial diversity. In his opinion, the history of the United States was a series of collisions between various minorities and the dominant culture. Now that the federal government was placing greater emphasis on racial and ethnic pluralism, Kloss implied, the submerged groups could reappear and claim a readjusted place in the historical and political development of the United States.

In 1937, several years before the appearance of *Volksgruppenrecht*, Germany's Volk und Reich Press published Kloss's *Um die Einigung des Deutschamerikanertums*, a comprehensive history of German-America's striving toward unity since colonial times. To the uncritical student of Nazi racial-political theory, this work might seem a substantial piece of scholarship; it has none of the crude propagandizing of a Colin Ross or an Alfred Rosenberg. In the April 1938 number of the *American Historical Review*, Carl Wittke reviewed the book and pointed out several misrepresentations. Wittke concluded that "the title of this book might lead one to expect some conclusions as to the intrinsic merits of many 'reclamation' projects tried on German-Americans or an opinion about Nazi techniques of the *Amerikadeutscher Volksbund*, organized in 1936, but here the author is discreetly silent." [22] Kloss was quite correct when he wrote that at one time the Germans represented one of the largest non-English-speaking minorities in the United States. He was also correct in stating that there had been a

[22] *American Historical Review*, 42 (April 1938), 644–666.

number of attempts to unify the German-American community in the nineteenth and early twentieth centuries. Only when his writings are viewed in the light of Nazi attempts to amalgamate American *Deutschtum* and German racial-political theory can his purpose be understood: Kloss and other specialists on America at the Institute and in the other Nazified agencies were attempting to illustrate the continuity of the *Volk* in North America and to demonstrate that Germany's recent attempts to unify the progeny of the original German settlers were not without precedent. In essence, Kloss was supplying the connective links between theory and politics.[23]

Kloss's racial-political interpretation of American history was not new, as he was well aware. In "Volkstums- und Rassenfragen," a lengthy treatise prepared in 1942, Kloss cited Madison Grant, John William Burgess, and Griffith Taylor as Americans who appreciated the fact that race was the key to history.[24] As in his previous studies, he ransacked the entire spectrum of American history to give credence to the contention that American *Deutschtum* had made a great contribution to the development of the United States. Unquestionably, Kloss's most important sources were his firsthand knowledge of the United States and the North American atlas project, which was started in the mid-1930's. The atlas was the Institute's most ambitious attempt to provide documentary proof of the Party's contention about American *Deutschtum*'s contributions to American history. From the beginning of the project, the DAI's archives were combed for studies of German-Americans undertaken during the previous decade, and contacts were made with aca-

---

[23] Cf. Otto Lohr, "Deutschsprachige Zeitschriften in den Vereinigten Staaten (von 1789–1935)," *Deutschtum im Ausland*, 22 (June 1939), 364–371; and "Stuttgarter in Nordamerika," *Der Auslanddeutsche*, 19 (March 1936), 175–179.

[24] In "Volkstums- und Rassenfragen," Kloss's comments on the "Negro question" (*Negerfrage*) are worth noting. Kloss did not condemn racism in American life. He saw it as an acceptable part of the Western tradition. Echoing the Nazi contention that the Civil War was the decisive turning point in American history, he wrote that "the victory of the North over the South . . . did not mean a victory for the Negro; rather it placed the entire race question at the feet of the government," which he believed was incapable of handling what he considered an insolvable question.

demicians in the United States. Under Kloss's careful guidance, materials were rewritten to conform to the exigencies of National Socialist scholarship. Obscure privates in America's wars became heroes; German troopers in the Civil War took on pivotal importance in the North's victory over the South; "ethnic maps" of New York, Chicago, St. Louis, and the so-called German states (Texas and Wisconsin) were prepared to indicate the "pockets of Germanism in North America." Although the atlas was never completed, excerpts were published in journals and magazines destined for consumption in Germany and abroad. For uninformed readers—many of whom had subscribed to the long-standing myth that America was as much German as Anglo-Saxon—this material led to one conclusion: America was built by German immigrants, the Hitlerian 'Viking types." [25]

The atlas was scheduled to be a multivolume work. If the war had not interrupted and changed the DAI's activities, it would have been a comprehensive Nazi history of German-America. According to the plans, one volume was to be devoted to the Pennsylvania Dutch, descendants of eighteenth-century settlers from Germany, now numbering about 400,000. Even before the advent to power of the National Socialists this group had been somewhat of a historical curiosity to the Germans. These North American cousins, who eschewed modern conveniences in favor of traditional modes of life, were a living link with Germany's past. In fact, during the Weimar years, researchers at the Institute had begun to compile a dictionary of their indigenous dialect and had completed several historical studies. Once the atlas project got under way, Kloss had his staff reinterpret the materials in the framework of Nazi race theory. They maintained that the Pennsylvania Dutch represented the very essence of *Deutschtum*, the Nazi ideal type: the simple peasant unaffected by modernity and cultural amalga-

[25] "Atlass des Amerikadeutschtums," Sept. 23, 1940, T-81/425/5172809ff. Excerpted portions of the atlas were published in numerous journals. See Otto Lohr, "Emil Mannhardts Studien für die deutsche Bevölkerung des Staates Illinois," and "Beziehungen zwischen deutschen und jüdischen Einwanderern aus dem Reichsgebiet in den USA, 1815–1914," *Der Deutsche in Nord-Amerika*, Dec. 1936, T-81/619/5414197. On planning for the atlas project, see T-81/614/5406497ff.

mation. More important, by actively resisting modernism and remaining insular, they had remained racially pure. They were unlike their cosmopolitan racial brothers who had settled in the
cities. Kloss was not disturbed about their avowed pacifism, an attitude which was anathema in the Nazi cosmology. Kloss was concerned only with the image they projected. He hoped that once the
atlas was published and distributed in America, their resistance to
modernism would serve as a model to all Americans of German extraction: an illustration that *Deutschtum* could be preserved in an
Anglo-Saxon framework.[26]

Not only the Pennsylvania Dutch, but also their spiritual brothers in Ohio, Missouri, and elsewhere received an honored place in
the history of American *Deutschtum*. Histories of their religious
communities in Salem, Canaan, and Bethlehem in Pennsylvania
and of the cities of Dresden, Spires, Hanover, and Berlin in Ohio
were prepared for the atlas; new importance was ascribed to such
towns as Hermann, whose founders had perpetuated the memory
of the ancient German conqueror Arminius (Teutonized as Hermann), and to the villages of Holstein and Hamburg in Missouri.
Each study repeated the same theme: these were "Viking-like"
Germans who had emigrated from the homeland but had successfully resisted total assimilation. Interestingly, when the Party's foreign-policy planners permitted the DAI to translate some of its theories into an active program, Kloss and his colleagues agreed that
approaching those religious sects would be unprofitable for Germany, since they were pacifists and wanted little or no involvement with the outside world.

The millions of Germans living in the cities and most areas of
the Midwest and Northeast were very different. Worldly rather
than ascetic, these groups became prime targets for German propaganda. In general, they were less readily distinguishable than the
religious sects. Sensitive to the native loyalties of German-Americans and aware of the limitations of crude anti-Semitic and
strident Pan-German propaganda, the DAI wisely eschewed politi-

[26] T-81/614/5404536ff. On the DAI's involvement with these groups, see
Smith, *The Deutschtum of Nazi Germany and the United States*, pp. 34,
37–40, 42, 144.

cal agitation in favor of a subtle approach that stressed the attractions of German culture. Recognizing the practical and financial obstacles to approaching individual German-Americans, the experts on America hoped to rekindle the feeling of *Deutschtum* by offering free film strips, foreign exchange programs, reduced rates for vacations in Germany, and a host of other cultural benefits. Since the DAI already had in its possession the names and addresses of most German-American organizations, the planners thought that the task of translating theory into reality would be relatively simple. In spite of their well-constructed theories, their widespread contacts with hundreds of German-American groups, and the large sums of money they spent on research and implementation, their plan failed.

Moreover, it clashed with the inelastic and intransigent demands of a handful of high-ranking Party members pursuing their own aims in the United States.[27] Although Kloss and his co-workers echoed Hitlerian invective, their works seem sophisticated and historically sound when compared with the writings of their counterparts in the Auslandsorganisation and other Nazified agencies. But it was precisely these party hacks, not the DAI's specialists on America, who were creating the Hitlerian image of the United States. To criticize their works was to condemn the ideas of the Führer himself.

Hitler's image of the United States had been studied in great detail.[28] After piecing together the diverse sources which helped Hitler to formulate his conception, James Compton has written, "there emerges a quite consistent picture of America as seen through the eyes of the Führer." [29] Hitler's private and public utterances and his writings are filled with scorn for the United States. A cursory examination of these diffuse sources might lead one to conclude that Hitler considered the American nation solely as a Jew-ridden

[27] "Pläne und Aktivitäten der freien Arbeitsstellen für das Deutschtum im Ausland," in Kipphan, *Deutsche Propaganda,* pp. 30ff.

[28] Frye, *Nazi Germany and the American Hemisphere,* ch. ii; Compton, *The Swastika and the Eagle,* ch. i; Gerhard Weinberg, "Hitler's Image of the United States," *American Historical Review,* 69 (July 1964), 1006–1021, and *Foreign Policy of Hitler's Germany,* ch. i.

[29] *The Swastika and the Eagle,* p. 3.

country of "millionaires, beauty queens, stupid records, and Hollywood." [30]

Much of Hitler's early knowledge of America came from the stories of the American West written by the German novelist Karl May (who had never visited the United States and knew little about it); from the personal accounts of his one-time favorite the Harvard-educated *bon vivant* Ernst ("Putzi") Hanfstaengl; and from Kurt Lüdecke, a disappointed Party hack who had spent several years in North America. Hitler modified his image of the United States to accord with his dream of Aryan supremacy. Behind his ravings about a Jew-infested communist-dominated American plutocracy there emerged the picture of a nation with a German backbone.

Hitler believed that America had once been a potential citadel for Aryan man. A turning point came during the Civil War, when the "beginnings of a great new social order based on the principle of slavery and inequality were destroyed." [31] The war had smashed the "embryo of a future truly great America that would not have been ruled by a corrupt caste of tradesmen, but by a real *Herren*-class" and had led to a victory for the "falsities of liberty and equality." [32] But all had not been lost during this epochal struggle. America's "political and mental resurrection" would come from its German element, which was largely uncontaminated by racial pollution. Even as late as February 1945, Hitler said that he was "deeply distressed at the thought of those millions of Germans, men of good faith, who emigrated to the United States and are the backbone of the country." Then, giving full vent to the bitterness engendered by imminent defeat and the rejection of his ideas by those "men of good faith," he went on to say:

[30] Ernst Hanfstaengl, *Unheard Witness* (London, 1953), p. 42. After the war, Hitler's interpreter, Paul Schmidt, told Allied interrogators that Hitler formed his picture of the world from "elementary school textbooks, his personal knowledge of the old Austro-Hungarian Empire, and the old ways of dealing with these peoples" (RG 59, "Schmidt Interrogation," Annex IV, p. 21).

[31] Hermann Rauschning, *The Voice of Destruction* (New York, 1940), pp. 68–69.

[32] *Ibid.*

For these men, mark you, are not merely good Germans, lost to their fatherland; rather, they have become enemies, more implacably hostile than others. . . . Transfer a German to Kiev, and he remains a perfect German. But transfer him to Miami and you make a degenerate out of him—in other words—an American.[33]

To the very end, Hitler believed that it was not racial amalgamation that had ruined Americans of German ancestry; it was their failure to resist the pernicious influences of American culture. It became one of the basic aims of Nazi activities in the United States somehow to extricate German-America from the sinister influences of those whom Hitler referred to as "the tradesmen"—namely, the Jews.

Thus, together with anti-Semitism, anti-Bolshevism, and theories of the inherent racial superiority of the Germans, Hitler's distorted image of the United States formed a part of his *Weltanschauung*. After Hitler gained control of Germany, he attempted to impose his ideas and theories on people who were gradually accepting National Socialism as a new form of religious exaltation.[34] Hitler told the Germans that they were superior to other peoples by virtue of their genetic and cultural heritage and that they were linked to their racial comrades outside Germany's borders by a community of blood. Germans living outside the Reich were "Viking-like Germans . . . who went out into the wide world as bearers of culture and belong to the great German racial family."[35] A German was a

---

[33] *The Testament of Adolf Hitler: The Hitler-Bormann Documents, February–April 1945,* ed. François Genoud (London, 1961), p. 46.

[34] Weinberg has concluded that Hitler's "basic hostility remained, but concern about America's racial strength had vanished" (*Foreign Policy of Hitler's Germany,* p. 22). This point is of cardinal importance. Subsequent chapters will show that Hitler's image of a racially pure German-America fighting for its life against the forces of American Jewry and their allies was the *sine qua non* of German propaganda; however, the translation of this image into an active policy was quite different from the realities of German activities in the German-American community. Compare Hitler's statement concerning the number of Germans living in America in "Rede Hitlers vor der deutschen Presse, 10. November 1938," *Vierteljahrshefte für Zeitgeschichte,* 6 (April 1958), 191, with the data in A. E. Frauenfeld, "Amerika, das Massengrab der deutschen Auswanderer," *Zeitschrift für Politik,* 30 (Winter 1940).

[35] Gottfried Feder, ed., *Das Programm der N.S.D.A.P. und seine weltanschaulichen Grundgedanken* (Munich, 1932), p. 42.

German anywhere and everywhere, and not countries and con-
tinents, climate and environment, "but blood and race determine
the German mentality." [36] It became the moral and national duty
of the Third Reich to "awaken" and "enlighten" all Germans to
the responsibilities imposed by blood and ancestry.

From the beginning of the Nazi regime, the combined forces of
State and Party were mustered in a gigantic effort to "keep awake
in our German racial comrades abroad the love for their Fatherland. It is a national duty to make them understand the events in
the new Germany." [37] Undoubtedly, the effort was prompted in
part by selfish national interest and, for some Nazi planners, had
nothing to do with race. But to dismiss racial politics as revolutionary clamor would be to minimize the profound impact Hitler's
ideas had on German foreign policy.[38]

In a study of Nazi Germany's efforts to make contact with Germans in the American hemisphere, Alton Frye cited eight agencies
that served as vehicles for racial politics. Some of these predated
National Socialism and, like the DAI, had been engaged in the
study of *Deutschtum,* while others were Nazi creations. Of special
importance was the Volksdeutscher Rat (VR—Ethnic German
Council), which was created by the Führer's deputy, Rudolf Hess,
in the fall of 1933. Theoretically, it had jurisdiction over all "unofficial organizations active in ethnic German questions." [39] Hess

[36] Ernst-Wilhelm Bohle addressing a meeting of the Auslandsorganisation,
Nuremberg, Sept. 11, 1936, as quoted in *The German Reich and Americans of
German Origin,* ed. Charles Burlingham (New York, 1938), p. 26.

[37] A. E. Martin, director of the Central Office for Foreign Cultural Broadcasts, in *Wir Deutsche in der Welt* (Stuttgart, 1936), pp. 191–193.

[38] A list of German agencies dealing with the ethnic German question can
be found in T-81/419/5165490–5.

[39] Jacobsen, *Nationalsozialistische Aussenpolitik,* pp. 160ff. Among the im-
portant leaders of the VR were Karl Haushofer and his son Albrecht, Her-
mann Ullmann, Hans Steinacher (also head of the VDA), Hans Helferich, and
Rudolf Pechel. The VR was replaced by the Volksdeutsche Mittelstelle (VoMi
—Ethnic German Office) in 1936, and Hess named SS *Obergruppenführer*
Werner Lorenz as its leader on January 27, 1937. Whereas the creation of
VoMi centralized agencies dealing with race and resettlement questions, the
Auslandsorganisation continued to handle foreign political matters involving
NSDAP people outside Germany. See Karl Dietrich Bracher, *The German
Dictatorship: The Origins, Structure, and Effects of National Socialism,* trans.
Jean Steinberg (New York, 1970), pp. 322–323.

hoped that some semblance of unanimity would emerge from the conflicting interests of various competing Nazi agencies. The VR, however, did not end the interministerial chaos. It has been suggested that perhaps Hitler did not at first want the VR or any other agency to assume total control over all decisions related to the ethnic German question and preferred overlapping and duplicate jurisdictions until he could personally take control of the development of German foreign policy. The creation of the Volksdeutscher Rat, moreover, came at the very time when the leaders of the NSDAP's foreign-policy section were attempting to place all overseas German matters under their control.

Several months after Hitler's appointment, Hess delegated a large measure of his responsibility for the overseas German community to his protégé, English-born Ernst-Wilhelm Bohle (the son of a German professor in Cape Town). At first, Bohle was the leader of the Abteilung für Deutsche im Ausland der NSDAP (the Party's Section for Germans Living Abroad). This group was superseded by the Auslandsorganisation der NSDAP in 1934, and Bohle was selected as its *Gauleiter* (the AO was considered a territorial unit of the NSDAP).[40] When Bohle was placed in charge of the Abteilung für Deutsche im Ausland, the office had over 150 overseas Party groups under its control, including one in the United States with several hundred members. During the next six years the competent and indefatigable Bohle followed Hitler's policy of "coordination" by bringing all agencies engaged in the manipulation of ethnic German groups under his sway, and on January 30, 1937, the AO was given an independent position in the Foreign Ministry (later that year Bohle was also named State Secretary in

---

[40] "Die Auslandsorganisation der NSDAP (5.8.1933)," in Jacobsen, pp. 126ff. The forerunner of the Auslandsorganisation, the Auslandsabteilung der NSDAP (Foreign Section of the NSDAP), was founded on May 1, 1931. A second agency, the Abteilung für Deutsche im Ausland, was created in 1932 and shared many responsibilities with the Foreign Section. In March 1933, the Abteilung für Deutsche im Ausland replaced the Foreign Section, and on April 26, 1933, Ernst-Wilhelm Bohle replaced Dr. Hans Nieland (who became the police president of Hamburg) as the head of the organization. Bohle was officially designated leader of this agency on May 8, 1933. In 1934, he became the head of the Auslandsorganisation.

the Foreign Ministry). In 1936, Bohle outlined his view concerning the Nazi concept of "transnationalization" (*Umvolkung*) when he told an audience, "Today our fighters are often defending desperate outposts," armed with the faith that National Socialism "can prepare the way for a cohesive Germandom." [41] At the Party Day celebration in Nuremberg in 1936, Hess told an assembly of representatives of the Auslandsorganisation that Hitler was a "godsend to the German people." He emphasized that National Socialism was a powerful cultist movement and that every German had certain "God-given" responsibilities to the race. According to his perverted logic, if a German did not fulfill these obligations he was committing treason not only against his own people, but also against Providence. Therefore, he concluded, it was Germany's solemn and unalterable duty to unite the world-wide German community.[42]

In spite of the Party's seemingly inelastic view of the world and its penchant for racial arithmetic, it was realistic enough to realize that the treatment of the ethnic German question would have to vary from country to country. The Party's pragmatism was obvious during the first years of the Nazi regime, when Hitler and his foreign-policy planners were not quite sure of the immediate direction Germany would take and wanted to retain normal—or traditional—diplomatic relations with other nations. These considerations did not, however, rule out the possibility of working with existing overseas Party groups if they could be used to create a favorable image of the New Germany. The Party's branch in the United States was used for this purpose. The presence of an extremely small cohesive pro-Nazi organization in America, as well as the Party's assumptions about Americans of German extraction, prompted the NSDAP to give qualified support to a handful of Party stalwarts in the United States who promised to unify their racial brothers into a political force and at the same time correct the American image of the new Germany.

There was, however, a fundamental difference between the Ger-

[41] Bohle, as quoted in *Völkischer Beobachter*, Sept. 12, 1936.
[42] Address by Hess, Sept. 1936, in *Der Parteitag der Ehre* (Munich, 1936), pp. 124ff.

man Foreign Institute's and the Party's ideas regarding the problem of reinvigorating American *Deutschtum*. On the one hand, the DAI's researchers believed that the revival might be accomplished through indigenous German-American organizations. On the other hand, the Party's planners for America maintained that German-America could be unified through the use of the existing Party structure. What emerged from these two seemingly irreconcilable points of view were two distinctly different phases of penetration into the internal affairs of the United States. Nevertheless, a common core of shared beliefs concerning Americans of German ancestry remained. In the end, both attempts failed completely, partly because of the gradual breakdown of diplomatic relations between Washington and Berlin and partly because of the internecine conflict that plagued the entire history of the Nazi movement in America.

In a larger sense, Germany's abortive efforts in America constituted a personal failure for Hitler and for those who welcomed National Socialism as a new and distinct form of ethnology. They, like other racists of that era, failed to avoid what David H. Fischer has cautioned contemporary historians against: "the fallacy of ethnomorphism," which he defined as "the conceptualization of the characteristics of another group in terms of one's own." [43] The elevation of Hitler's personalized and subjective view of world-wide *Deutschtum* to the status of dogma and its translation into an active foreign policy was ethnomorphism carried to an extreme. During the early formative years of the Nazi regime, the Party's foreign-policy planners assumed that overseas Germandom would respond to Germany's overtures because ancestral and *völkisch* ties were stronger than place of birth, process of acculturation, or assumed nationality. There was much evidence to support the contention that American *Deutschtum* had made great contributions to the development of the United States. But to conclude that German-Americans would unite on the basis of race and cultural oneness was a profound misreading of the political and cultural realities of American society. Many high-ranking members of the

[43] *Historians' Fallacies: Toward a Logic of Historical Thought* (New York, 1970), pp. 224–225.

Auslandsorganisation and the diplomatic elite were keenly aware that such theories were flights into fantasy, but few of these men ever criticized the Party's American policy—even the handful that considered the reclamation of Germandom in the United States a worthwhile undertaking, merely a revival of the *Kulturpolitik* of a former era. Too few fully realized that the study and pursuit of ethnology had degenerated into a vulgar mysticism and would eventually lead to the irrevocable defeat of National Socialism.

PART

II

GERMANY'S
INVOLVEMENT IN
THE UNITED STATES,
1923 - 1935

CHAPTER 3

The Years of Waiting, 1923-1932

"When we think of Weimar," writes Peter Gay, "we think of modernity in art, literature and thought; . . . we think of *The Threepenny Opera, The Cabinet of Dr. Caligari, The Magic Mountain,* the *Bauhaus* and Marlene Dietrich."[1] The Republic's cultural and intellectual productivity is legendary. To be sure, large segments of republican Germany's population welcomed neither its birth nor the emergence to prominence of those Gay refers to as "the outsiders": Jews, Socialists, and innovators in the arts. Many Germans learned to live with Weimar, so to speak; they were the "rational republicans"—*Vernunftrepublikaner.* Many others of their countrymen never accepted Weimar. For these people, the Republic's departures from cultural tradition were symptomatic of all its evils: inflation, civil strife, political murders, chronic unemployment, and the assumption of important positions in public life by individuals whom many considered "outsiders." Unable to adjust to the markedly different milieu of the postwar period, many Germans decided to emigrate to the United States. What started as a trickle of emigrants in 1919 turned into a flood within the next ten years. Approximately 430,000 Germans arrived in the United States between 1919 and 1933.[2]

There were fundamental differences between these migrants and the 5,500,000 of their ancestors who had arrived earlier: the later migrants left a Germany that had just lost a war resulting in 1,-800,000 Germans dead and 4,000,000 wounded; most of those who

[1] Gay, *Weimar Culture*, p. xiii.   [2] See Appendix I, below.

arrived later were proletarians or recently proletarianized members of the middle class. Bitter and disillusioned, many immigrants believed that America could provide them with the security their homeland could no longer offer.

Not all these immigrants came to the United States to put down permanent roots. Some were self-proclaimed émigrés from Weimar who hated the Republic and its leaders and lamented Germany's fate; some were members of Adolf Hitler's infant Nazi Party; some were right-wing German nationalists; many came to the United States for the express purpose of raising money for German causes. Initially, most of these men did not intend to remain in America, but their situation changed drastically in January 1933, when Hitler was appointed Chancellor and they became the nucleus around which Germany hoped to build a pro-Nazi German-American political movement.

Although the NSDAP did not consider transforming German-America from a shattered and disunited ethnic community to a political bloc favorably disposed to Germany's aims until some time after the Hitler victory, one member of the German immigrant community, Edmund Fürholzer, attempted to unite his German-American cousins long before the NSDAP attempted to do so.[3] Before emigrating to the United States in December 1926, Fürholzer had served as the business manager of the extreme right-wing group in Bavaria, the Reichslandbund. He arrived in New York City penniless.[4] He did, however, have one major asset: he knew how to manipulate people. During the years between 1926 and 1928, he made the acquaintance of a number of men in New York's predominantly German-speaking Yorkville section. Yorkville, also known as Germantown, was a fifty-square-block area in Manhattan's East Eighties. It was dotted with dance and beer halls, in which Fürholzer's new friends huddled together and bemoaned the fate of Germany and German-America. Although history has for-

[3] Edmund Fürholzer's papers, NSDAP records, T-81/186–189.

[4] Fürholzer arrived in the United States in December 1926. Before he left Germany, he was accused of stealing funds from the Reichslandbund. See George Messersmith to Fürholzer, March 26, 1931, T-81/188/339123; Otto Jürgens to August Jürgens, Nov. 21, 1926, T-81/188/339097.

gotten most of their names, they were middle-class café owners, agents for German import-export houses, and proprietors of fashionable restaurants and exclusive delicatessens. Like most of their middle-class counterparts in Berlin or Cologne, they were not usually extremist in their political views. But they were not republicans either. Significant to Fürholzer in his relationships with these men—many of whom had belonged to the National German-American Alliance and had joined one or more German groups after the war—was their belief that Germany had been tricked into defeat by traitors at home and by a world of enemies abroad. During the 1920's, this view of Germany's fate was the "correct," or national, interpretation, and it was shared by large segments of the German population in Germany and overseas.

Sometime in 1927, Fürholzer, sensing his friends' dismay, suggested that together they might start a German-language newspaper to "tell the real story" about Weimar and the hated Treaty of Versailles. The following year, a new newspaper, the *Deutsche Zeitung*, appeared on newsstands in Yorkville, in competition with the extremely popular *N.Y. Illustrierte Zeitung.*[5] During the first months of its existence, the *Deutsche Zeitung* was unsuccessful, and publishing expenses mounted. But later that year, Fürholzer and his friends had an unexpected windfall when they found a wealthy patron in Colonel Edwin Emerson.

The Colonel, as he was known to his associates, later became an outspoken supporter of Hitler and the leader of the Nazi-sponsored Friends of Germany (Freunde von Deutschland) organization in New York City. He was born into a well-established Saxon family in 1869. Shortly afterward, his family emigrated to the United States. After graduating from Harvard in 1891, he served as personal secretary to Andrew White, the first president of Cornell University, who was later appointed American ambassador to Berlin (1897–1902). He was a correspondent for *Harper's Weekly* and covered the exploits of Teddy Roosevelt's Roughriders during the

---

[5] This *Deutsche Zeitung* should not be confused with a newspaper of the same name published by the Friends of the New Germany in the next decade. For a short time he worked as a free-lance writer for a Yorkville scandal sheet, *New Yorker Spaziergänge* (T-81/187/337860).

Spanish-American War. With the outbreak of the European war in 1914, his journalistic interests took him to the Balkans, where he covered the German offensive of 1915. Shortly after America entered the conflict, he was captured by the Turks and turned over to the Germans. He spent the rest of the war in a prison camp, where he collaborated with his captors, with whom he obviously sympathized. While a prisoner of war, he edited the *Continental News*, an English-language paper carrying pro-German propaganda aimed at English prisoners. Upon his return to America in 1918, he surrounded himself with men of similar sympathies, men who did not believe Germany was responsible for the war. He and Louis Ewald, Willi Borutta, Dietrich Wortmann, and J. Achelis—all established members of Yorkville's society—published several articles condemning the Versailles settlement and the "November criminals." Convinced that newly arrived German immigrants shared his views, Emerson gave a sizable though undetermined amount of money to keep the *Deutsche Zeitung* alive.[6]

The influx of new capital was not enough to keep the paper going, and it ceased publication with the onset of the Depression. If Hitler had not come to power four years later, the activities of these men and the publication of the *Deutsche Zeitung* would perhaps not be worth serious attention. After 1933, however, the Nazi Party tried to unite German-America for its purposes; the paper's articles and attempts to make contact with German organizations in New York and elsewhere are harbingers of Nazi activities of the following decade.

Articles in the newspaper by hack writers like Johannes Büch-

[6] Emerson published several books in the 1920's: *War and Peace, Both Sides of the War, History of the Gutenberg Bible,* and *The Adventures of Theodore Roosevelt* (translated into German by Fürholzer). Emerson was not a colonel; the designation was an affection he seems to have acquired during the war. Bibliographical information on Emerson can be found in "Colonel Emerson," T-81/188/339100–101; and Ludwig Lore, "Nazi Politics in America," *The Nation,* 137 (Nov. 20, 1933), 617. The evidence, though fragmentary, suggests that the German consulate in New York gave limited financial support to the paper (Fürholzer to the German consulate, n.d., T-81/188/338821–22). The DAI requested copies of the paper for its files (Fritz Wertheimer to Fürholzer, Nov. 20, 1928, T-81/188/338806–7).

ner, Walter Blank, and Hans Kraus had the characteristics of incipient Nazism in their indictment of the "November criminals"
and condemnation of Bolshevism. Copies of the newspaper and re-
prints of some of its articles were sent free of charge to German-
American organizations considered by Fürholzer and Emerson to
be mildly sympathetic to its views. Some recipients of this unso-
licited literature returned it to the offices of the *Deutsche Zeitung*,
while others wrote back that they not only endorsed the paper's
work but also hoped that German-America could be revitalized
into the political force it once was.[7]

Encouraged by the response, Fürholzer and his supporters devised a bizarre plan to reunite German-Americans politically. On
the pretense that the paper was insolvent and on the verge of extinction, Fürholzer wrote the chairman of the New York State Republican Committee in October 1928 and solicited twenty thousand dollars. In return, he promised to deliver German-American
votes on election day. After reminding the chairman that he was a
"staunch Republican" and had organized a "Germanic Group for
Herbert Hoover" earlier that year, he claimed that Americans of
German extraction would rally behind the Republican nominee for
president because they had not forgotten how he had fed Germany
during the dark days following the World War; how Woodrow
Wilson had tricked Germany into a dishonorable surrender; how
Wilson had placed "spies in the homes of *good* [German-] Americans"; and finally, how greatly indebted Germany was to the Republican Party for helping to prevent America's acceptance of the
Treaty of Versailles. Fürholzer believed that these factors would
make any German-American think twice before voting for the
"anti-German Versailles Democrats." [8] Since the letter was written
just four weeks before the election, it is doubtful that Fürholzer
could have united all German-American societies into a political
bloc. Although his offer to work for Hoover's campaign was rejected by the New York State Republican Committee, many of his

[7] Mimeographed letters to ninety-six German-American organizations, summer 1928, T-81/188/338315–18. Cf. "Subscription Lists," *ibid.*

[8] Memorandum, n.d., T-81/188/338822–3.

ideas were accepted by that party's New York State committee four years later.[9]

Fürholzer's desire to see Americans of German extraction united into a political force was never satisfied. But the farfetched interpretation of Germany's recent history he and his associates outlined in the ill-fated *Deutsche Zeitung* was geared to the newly arrived German immigrant and did produce some tangible results. The little newspaper brought together a group of men who, when Hitler was appointed Chancellor, would be openly sympathetic to his cause. More important, the *Deutsche Zeitung* made connections with a handful of old and well-established German-American organizations receptive to the paper's right-wing interpretation of Germany's destiny. Information derived from these contacts would be used by the NSDAP in years to come. The name Edmund Fürholzer became synonymous with extreme right-wing German political causes in the émigré community of Yorkville and, like many of its members, he joined the New York City unit of the overseas National Socialist Party in 1931.

There was, however, a fundamental difference between Fürholzer and those German nationals who considered themselves émigrés: while he labored under the impression that German-America could be a political force in American politics and hoped to unite it, the émigrés huddled together for security, lamented Germany's misfortunes, and cared little about Americans of German ancestry. Fürholzer was well aware of their attitudes toward German-Americans. In September 1930, he wrote Adolf Hitler that he was pleased to see the interest the Party was taking in foreign matters and suggested that if the NSDAP hoped to make inroads into the German-American community, it should send to America materials printed in English and English-speaking representa-

[9] From 1929 to 1931, Fürholzer was a contributor to the *Yorkville Observer* (Mirabeau Herrschaft, editor). He also worked as a "special researcher" for the *Brooklyn Daily Eagle* (T-81/186/336688; 339097). On his activities in this period (his marriage, troubles with the Labor Department, a court case involving embezzlement, and financial problems), see T-81/186/338353; 338808ff; "Expense Book" (1928), 338305.

tives.[10] (Because of the internal problems the Party was facing at the time, it is doubtful that Hitler ever saw the letter.) The note implies that a cleavage was developing between men like Fürholzer, who wanted to approach native German-American organizations, and the émigrés, who did not. Instead of working with, and perhaps even joining, any of the hundreds of already existing German-American associations, these expatriates preferred to stay apart and, in some cases, to form their own groups. This tendency was partly the result of the "generation gap" between these people and the millions who arrived before the Great War. The chief difference between those who formed groups in the 1920's and those of the previous generation who managed to fit into existing cultural organizations is in the fact that some of the new arrivals had witnessed Germany's defeat personally and had come to believe that they had been forced to leave their homeland. Furthermore, many Americans of German ancestry, after the wartime period of supernationalism, simply wanted to be Americans; even though a number of prewar groups re-emerged in the 1920's, they tended to be cultural rather than political.

One example of the separatism advocated by some German nationals in America was the formation of the National Socialist Teutonia Association (Nationalsozialistische Vereinigung Teutonia).[11] Teutonia was the first full-fledged National Socialist organization on American soil. Its leaders published a party newspaper, sent money to the NSDAP in Munich, and attempted to proselytize the immigrant German community. Teutonia was one of thirty-odd or-

[10] Sept. 16, 1930, T-81/188/339707–8. It is clear from the documents that Fürholzer wanted the NSDAP to designate him its American correspondent. After the advent to power of the National Socialists, Fürholzer became a representative of the German news service, Transocean, which was founded after the British cut Germany's Atlantic cable in 1914. In the 1930's, Germany's major news service was the Deutsches Nachrichtenbüro (DNB).

[11] There have been several earlier studies of the Teutonia Association. Of special importance are the relevant sections in Smith's *The Deutschtum of Nazi Germany and the United States.* Jacobsen, in *Nationalsozialistische Aussenpolitik,* pp. 528–530, based much of his study of the group on Smith's findings, which outlined the broad contours of Teutonia's history.

ganizations with extreme right-wing leanings founded by émigrés between 1922 and 1933. As early as the fall of 1922, a local cell of the NSDAP was founded in the northeast section of The Bronx (New York).[12] In retrospect, the Teutonia Association seems to be the most important pro-Nazi group organized in America during the pre-Hitler years. It was the forebear of the first Bund, the Friends of the New Germany (Bund der Freunde des Neuen Deutschland, 1933–1936), and its lively successor, Fritz Kuhn's American German Bund (Amerikadeutscher Volksbund, 1936–1941).

The Teutonia Association was founded in Detroit on October 12, 1924.[13] The organizers—referred to in the next decade as the "old guard" from Detroit—were Friedrich (Fritz) Gissibl and his brother Peter, Alfred Ex, and Frank von Friedersdorff. These men proved to be diligent and dedicated workers for the Nazi cause in America. Several of their number returned to Germany in the next decade and were rewarded with positions in the Party structure.

[12] Application of Franz Westerdorff to Zentrale der Kameradschaft-USA, Nov. 1939. Some explanation of the Zentrale der Kameradschaft-USA is in order at this juncture. This organization was founded in Germany in 1938 by Fritz Gissibl, who served as the Bund leader of the Friends of the New Germany in the 1930's. The Kameradschaft was located in the German Foreign Institute headquarters in Stuttgart (House of Germanism) and was loosely affiliated with the DAI and the AO der NSDAP. Its functions were to help resettle members of the American Nazi movement who had been repatriated by Germany or had returned to Germany on their own in the late 1930's and to perpetuate the memory of the Nazi movement in the United States by unifying former Bundists, many of whom were naturalized Americans. In all, an estimated 450 to 500 Bundists returned to the Reich and belonged to Kameradschaft branches (after 1941, it was renamed the Amerikadeutsche Kameradschaft) in Braunschweig, Frankfort, Hanover, Düsseldorf, Leipzig, Hamburg, Stuttgart, Berlin, and Munich. The applications for membership in this group are rich in data concerning the origins of the Bund and the fate of many of its members. See Papers of Zentrale der Kameradschaft-USA, membership records, T-81/139–140/175985–177114; 144/183963–184204; "Mitgliederliste der Kameradschaft-USA, 25.5. 1939," T-81/143/180029ff. On the founding of the group, see Arthur Smith, Jr., "The Kameradschaft-USA," *Journal of Modern History*, 34 (Dec. 1962), 398–408.
[13] Walter Kappe, ed., *Kämpfendes Deutschtum: Jahrbuch des Amerikadeutschen Volksbundes auf das Jahr 1937* (New York, 1937); Otto Lohr, "Deukschrift für Atlas," 1938, T-81/620/5415464.

Fritz Gissibl had arrived in the United States on December 1, 1923, four months before his twenty-first birthday. Several months later, his brothers Peter and Andreas joined him. Fritz had been too young to serve in the war but old enough to appreciate the magnitude of Germany's defeat. Like many young men of his age and generation, he believed that the war had been lost because of the treasonous activities of the Jews and Marxists at home. Gissibl, a Nuremberger by birth and a member of a lower-middle-class family, thought of himself as a member of the "lost generation." Though the Teutonia Association cannot be compared with the infant NSDAP, there is a striking similarity in the youthfulness of the groups' members: Gissibl's age (he was twenty-one in March 1924) was representative of the ages in both groups.[14]

During the summer of 1925 Fritz Gissibl befriended a young man of similar background and frame of mind, nineteen-year-old Walter Kappe, who had arrived in the United States in March of that year. Kappe, who would later serve as the Bund's national editor, was a man of great energy and talent. As is the case with the Gissibl brothers, it is not clear why he left Germany. He was not avoiding arrest after Hitler's ill-fated *Putsch* in November 1923, as some anti-Nazis contended in the thirties. Fritz Gissibl did not join the NSDAP until October 1926, although Kappe had been a Party member since 1923.[15]

It was no accident that Teutonia was founded in Detroit, for this city showed in microcosm what was happening to many American

[14] For biographical data about Friedrich (Fritz) Gissibl see Appendix III, below; "Kameradschaft-USA," T-81/141/179577 (G); and "Politischer Lebenslauf des Parteigenossen Fritz Gissibl, 5. März 1938," prepared for the Personnel Division of the SS, Fritz Gissibl Folder, Berlin Document Center, Berlin. On his early membership in the NSDAP, see T-81/142/179978. Gissibl's NSDAP number was 45,200. See also "Statement of Fritz Gissibl," in *NP*, p. 73. On Alfred Ex, see T-81/144/178307. Brief biographical accounts of other members can be found in Propaganda and Related Materials, German-American Bund, 1926–1942, containers 1–39, RG 131.

[15] Walter Kappe, DAI, Personnel Papers, T-81/349/5078211ff (K). After 1933, many Bundists tried to enhance their standing in the eyes of their comrades by stating that they were with Hitler on the night of the abortive *Putsch* in November, 1923. In point of fact, only one member of the Bund was anywhere near Hitler on the fateful night, Josef (Sepp) Schuster. See note 18, below.

cities in the 1920's. Already known the world over as the automotive center of the United States, the city epitomized the rapid industrialization of the era. But mass production resulted in temporary technological unemployment for many workers.[16] This situation was partly alleviated by the creation of semiskilled and unskilled assembly-line jobs, which were easily filled by American and immigrant laborers. The largest employer in the city was Ford Motor Company. When the Depression of 1929 came, Ford, like many other producers, was forced to curtail operations. Among the first to be dismissed were the last who were hired, who in many cases were already despondent German immigrants. A handful of them, some in quest of security, others because of a genuine belief that their problems had been caused by a Jewish-capitalist plot, joined the infant Teutonia organization.[17]

While Teutonia did not exhibit any sign of growth until the effects of the Depression were felt in the community of German nationals, its organizational structure and *Weltanschauung* were formed by the end of the decade. The man primarily responsible was Josef (Sepp) Schuster.[18] He was born near Dachau, Germany, in October 1904 and joined the NSDAP before he reached his eighteenth birthday. As group leader of the Party's Fifth SA Company in Munich, Schuster took part in Hitler's November *Putsch*. After the ill-fated night of November 8–9, 1923, he fled across the border to Austria, where he worked as a baker's helper until his return to Germany one year later. Finding the Party disorganized and himself unemployed, he left for the United States in October 1927. On his arrival he went directly to the Midwest, where he met Gissibl and Kappe and joined their group.[19] By 1932 the group had

[16] Hicks, *Republican Ascendancy*, p. 110.

[17] Chapter 5, below, examines the Bund's ideology in detail.

[18] "Bericht über Pg. [party member] Josef (Sepp) Schuster," enclosed in a letter from Schuster to Rolf Hoffmann of the Amt Auslandspresse (Overseas Press Office), April 4, 1936, T-81/26/23820. See also "Schuster Biographie," T-81/139/177680, and Josef Schuster, "Personelfragebogen," June 15, 1937, Josef Schuster Folder, Berlin Document Center.

[19] "Bericht über Pg. Josef (Sepp) Schuster."

branches in Chicago, Los Angeles, New York City, and Cincinnati, and claimed a membership of over five hundred.[20]

Teutonia's "ideological" pronouncements were shaped by the adjustment of the evolving National Socialist political ideology to the exigencies of a new environment. The group's leaders outlined their views in handbills, pamphlets, and in their newspaper, *Vorposten*, subtitled *News of the German Freedom Movement in the United States*. Because of a lack of funds and capable literary talent, Teutonia's publishing record was spotty, and the writing was crude and ungrammatical. In the German language it admonished newly arrived Germans to join the "National Socialist Freedom Movement." After telling its readers that their problems had begun when the Fatherland was tricked into signing the armistice by "international Jewry," the paper usually proceeded to "tell the truth about Germany." Echoing Hitler's contemptuous views of the Weimar "system," the editor, Walter Kappe, painted the picture of a dishonored and disgraced Fatherland in the hands of "Eastern Jews" and communists controlled by "Jewish Moscow." In Germany, however, the teachings of one man, Adolf Hitler, were germinating, and soon the "real German man" would come to power and make short shrift of the Republic, the Jews and communists, and those responsible for 1918. When the "movement" (*Bewegung*) would finally eject the "outsiders," a new Germany would be born and rise to power, causing the rebirth of the world-wide German community. Teutonia's mission was to transplant the "National Socialist idea" to America—not to all America, not even to all Ger-

---

[20] It is extremely difficult to determine the exact number of members in the Teutonia Association. The estimate of five hundred is based on statements made in letters written by former Bundists in the Kameradschaft-USA collection. At this stage in the Bund's history, most members of the Teutonia Association were *not* members of the NSDAP. In the late 1920's, there was a cell of the German Nazi Party in New York, which was not related to Teutonia. As will be seen, this cell was later designated by the NSDAP as its American unit, Gau-USA. It would appear that the cell had about two hundred members ("Kampferlebnisse der alten Garde der NSDAP: Schneider, USA," *NSDAP Hauptarchiv* Collection, reel 27, folder 531, Hoover Institution, Stanford, Calif.).

man-America, but according to Kappe, to newly arrived German national elements living in the United States.[21] The last point is of cardinal importance. Initially, Teutonia's leaders did not envision any future for National Socialism in the United States. Accordingly, they regarded America as a temporary home for new arrivals from Germany, a refuge from the Weimar Republic. These men were firmly committed to National Socialism in Germany and believed in Hitler's inevitable victory. They hoped to return to Germany upon Hitler's advent to power and share the fruits of victory.[22]

Teutonia, then, was considered by its leaders as a temporary organization meant to house displaced Party members, disenchanted immigrants, and self-proclaimed émigrés from Weimar. From the extent of its purchases—a printing press, an assortment of Nazi paraphernalia (badges, uniforms, and so forth), a two-family Victorian house for its Chicago Branch—and from the contributions it sent directly to Hitler, it would seem that Teutonia had financial resources besides its nominal membership dues. The truth is that the organization's income came directly out of the pockets of members employed by the large industrial corporations in Detroit.[23] Teutonia's willingness to send some of its surplus funds to the NSDAP was implicit in a post card sent to Fritz Gissibl by Hitler in April 1925, thanking him for a generous birthday present. "If the affluent ones among the Germans and Germans in foreign countries would sacrifice in equal proportion for the movement,"

[21] Copies of *Vorposten,* handouts, and other materials distributed by the Teutonia Association can be found in "Deutschtum im Ausland," Sect. XVI, reel 35, folders 694, 695, 696, *NSDAP Hauptarchiv Collection.* See "Aufruf— an Deutschen in Amerika!"; address by Fritz Gissibl, "Hakenkreuz oder Sowjetstern," March 30, 1931; and Hitler Birthday Issue, April 20, 1931, folder 696.

[22] Fritz Gissibl returned to Germany in 1936, Sepp Schuster in the same year, and Walter Kappe in 1937. For additional details see Appendix III, below.

[23] After the rise of Hitler and the subsequent emergence of a small following in the United States, it was rumored (especially in Jewish circles in New York) that Henry Ford contributed to the infant American Nazi movement. The rumor seems to have had three bases: (1) Ford published the "Protocols of the Elders of Zion" in the *Dearborn Independent;* (2) many members of the

wrote the future Führer, "Germany's situation would soon be different." [24] Although the Gissibl brothers and their followers were by no means affluent, they had great enthusiasm for the Party and sent an undetermined amount of money to the NSDAP during the next eight years. One contribution of five hundred reichsmarks was used to defray travel expenses of SA men to the 1929 Party Day.[25] As late as 1932, Goebbels sent a long letter to Teutonia thanking the members for their numerous donations to the Party.[26] These contributions indicate the group's zealous belief in Adolf Hitler's movement; they fully expected, when their unchanging confidence in Hitler was finally justified, that they would share in his triumph upon their return to Germany.

After Hitler gained total control of the German Nazi Party in the spring and early summer of 1930, a period followed in which "intraparty differences were submerged in the expectation of coming power." [27] The converse occurred in the United States; Teutonia was still a long way from being a duplicate of the NSDAP in microcosm. Its leaders continued to view it as a transient rather than permanent group. Under the leadership of Fritz Gissibl, the Teutonia Association found new recruits in the German emigrant community, most of whom had backgrounds similar to those of Kappe,

---

Teutonia Association were employed by Ford Motor Company (for example, Fritz Kuhn, leader of the Amerikadeutscher Volksbund, who was employed as a chemist); (3) an NSDAP fund raiser, Kurt Lüdecke, approached Ford for money (he was rebuffed). Ford's anti-Semitism in the early 1920's has been well documented; however, there is absolutely no evidence to connect Ford with the Teutonia Association or any other Nazi group. Several illuminating examples of these charges against Ford can be found in the Noah Greenberg Collection, Archives, YIVO Institute. On Lüdecke and Ford, see Kurt Lüdecke, *I Knew Hitler* (New York, 1937), pp. 182ff. On the validity of Lüdecke's book, see *Vierteljahrshefte für Zeitgeschichte*, 3 (1955), 117.

[24] Adolf Hitler to Fritz Gissibl, May 20, 1925, T-81/144/183160.

[25] München Hauptquartier der NSDAP to Fritz Gissibl, n.d., T-81/144/183165.

[26] Joseph Goebbels to the Teutonia Association, 1932, T-81/144/183162–3; Goebbels to Andreas Gissibl, July 13, 1928, T-81/144/183164. Andreas' name appears on several documents of this period. After 1929, there is no mention of him; perhaps he returned to Germany.

[27] Joseph Nyomarkay, *Charisma and Factionalism in the Nazi Party* (Minneapolis, 1967), p. 103.

Schuster, and the Gissibl brothers. Between 1924 and 1930, the group encountered no opposition from other Nazi-oriented organizations, but the situation changed dramatically in the summer of 1932. In part, the crisis that Teutonia faced was prompted by events in Germany and by the Depression, which had altered the lives of the so-called émigrés from Weimar as well as of most Americans.

Now that a Nazi victory seemed possible, Teutonia's leader, Fritz Gissibl, wanted to present his group to the Munich headquarters of the NSDAP as the only genuine Nazi organization in America. Some members of the Party in the United States, however, correctly pointed out that Teutonia had never been designated as a unit of the NSDAP. Opposition came from members of the NSDAP living in the United States who had never joined Teutonia and had congregated in highly disorganized Party cells in cities with large German immigrant populations.

Never numbering more than two hundred before 1933, these Party members asserted that their cells represented the nucleus of a genuine Party structure, while Teutonia's membership was composed largely of non-Party people.[28] Shortly after the creation of the NSDAP's Foreign Section in May 1931, members of a New York City cell wrote to Dr. Hans Nieland, the leader of the agency in Hamburg, that they, not the Teutonia Association, should be selected by the Party to form a Nazi organization. In a swift move that was to have serious implications for Gissibl and his followers, Nieland, ignoring Teutonia, placed the unofficial New York Nazi cells under the control of the Foreign Section of the NSDAP and designated them the Nationalsozialistische Deutsche Arbeiterpartei, Ortsgruppe New York (National Socialist German Workers' Party, New York Unit); the membership referred to the unit as Gauleitung-USA (Department Headquarters, USA) or simply Gau-

[28] One way of determining if a member of the NSDAP belonged to one of the Party's overseas branches is to compare assigned Party numbers. After the creation of the Auslandsabteilung, Party members living overseas received new numbers. Party member Christoph Klausfeldner joined the NSDAP in 1921 and was assigned Pg. 4112; in 1931, while in the United States, his number was AA 195,221 (AA indicates Auslandsabteilung). See "Liste der Parteigenossen aus USA," 1935, T-81/147/18588–791.

USA. By June of that year, local branches of the group were founded in Seattle, Detroit, Chicago, and Milwaukee.[29]

Nieland's decision threw the Teutonia group into a state of complete disarray. Not only had he dismissed Teutonia as the potential base on which a Nazi organization in America could be built, but he also engendered a situation that caused Party members in the organization to withdraw from Teutonia, since they wanted to be part of the officially designated Nazi group, Gau-USA. As far as Gissibl was concerned, he had two options: he could convert Teutonia into a branch (*Stützpunkt*) of the newly created Gau-USA, or he could forcibly take control of Gau-USA's national headquarters in Yorkville. He rejected the first alternative; after seven years of serving Hitler's cause he felt he deserved more than the leadership of a Party local. Gissibl waited six months. Then, after hearing through the Nazi grapevine that the New York group was in a chaotic state, he decided to act. In order to determine whether a coup was possible in New York City, Gissibl sent his close friend and fellow Party member Heinz Spanknöbel to New York in late March 1932.

When he emigrated to the United States in 1929, Spanknöbel was thirty-six years old.[30] Like many of his confederates in the Teutonia organization, he worked for Ford motors until he was dismissed in 1930 when the effects of the Depression hit Detroit. Unable to find a job to his liking, he decided to work full time for

[29] On the early growth of Gau-USA, see Martha Schneider, "Ortsgruppe Chicago," 1932–1935, T-81/140/185886; and Alfred Erinn to Hans Nieland (Hamburg, Germany), Feb. 2, 1931, T-81/147/197889; NSDAP Ortsgruppe New York to Propaganda Section (NSDAP), June 15, 1930, *NSDAP Hauptarchiv* Collection, reel 35, folder 581, Hoover Institution. Although the members referred to their group as Gau-USA, this was incorrect according to Nazi usage. A *Gau* was the largest territorial administrative unit of the NSDAP. At the head of each *Gau* was a *Gauleiter* (for example, Ernst-Wilhelm Bohle was the *Gauleiter* of the Auslandsorganisation, which was independent of *Gaue* inside the Reich). In keeping with the Nazi administrative structure, the Nazis in America used the same designations. In order of administrative command, the United States was divided into departments (*Gaue*) and the appropriate subdivisions: region (*Gebiet*), district (*Kreis*), unit (*Ort*), branch (*Stützpunkt*), cell (*Zelle*), and the lowest, block (*Block*).

[30] Spanknöbel to Kameradschaft-USA, March 11, 1939, T-81/139/176387; see also Appendix III, below.

Teutonia and concurrently joined the NSDAP. Spanknöbel, a violent and impetuous man, was not the best choice for a fact-finding
mission that might determine the future of Teutonia.

When he arrived in New York, he found that the rumors of internecine quarreling were true. The current victor in the struggle was
Karl Neumann, who had just outmaneuvered Hans Stolzenburg as
the leader of Gau-USA. Neither Stolzenburg nor Neumann had
been recognized by Nieland as the leader. In early April, Neumann moved the headquarters from one section of Yorkville to another. What he created was a third group, since both the New
York branch of Teutonia and the officially designated Gau-USA
claimed to be legitimate Party organizations. The time seemed
right for Teutonia to assert its claim that it was the only cohesive
Party organization in the United States. Then came bad news from
Nieland's office in Hamburg. In an effort to end the intraparty
bickering, Nieland had appointed Paul Manger, an unemployed
janitor and NSDAP member, as the official leaders of Gau-USA.
Realizing that Manger's appointment had ruined Teutonia's hope
of taking over Gau-USA and that any move in this direction would
end Gissibl's chances of leading the entire movement, Spanknöbel
left New York for Detroit in the fall of 1932 to report his findings
to Gissibl.[31]

Meanwhile, in New York, the news of Manger's appointment
temporarily put a stop to the ambitions of those who wanted to
lead the infant American Nazi movement. Even Neumann decided
to rejoin the ranks, and Gau-USA stabilized itself. Regular meetings were held every Saturday night with eighty to ninety members attending. Since "the majority of the Party members were unemployed," many decided to conserve their funds by living
together. But as the effects of the Depression became more severe,
attendance at regular meetings in New York dwindled to less than
forty-five, and the group became disorganized amid constant bickering and recrimination. According to Neumann, those who remained active were hard-core Party members. These men had little

[31] Karl Neumann to Rolf Hoffmann, Jan. 23, 1934, T-81/27/24505–8. Neumann joined the New York branch of the NSDAP in August 1931, less than a
month after he arrived in America. On Paul Manger, see Appendix III, below.

else to do with their time and worked for the Party without monetary compensation.[32] In spite of their scanty financial resources, the group had a newspaper, *Amerika's Deutsche Post,* which was owned by one of the members of the group. Although there is no definite evidence to indicate that the NSDAP underwrote the newspaper, it did receive most, if not all, of its articles from Nieland's office in Hamburg. In general, most of these materials had appeared first in Party publications—*Der Angriff* and later the *Völkischer Beobachter.*[33]

Although *Amerika's Deutsche Post* claimed that the movement had a large following, the year 1932 appears to have been a disaster for the nascent Nazi movement in America. Had Hitler not come to power in the following year, the American unit of the NSDAP would undoubtedly have collapsed. In retrospect, it appears that 1932 was of paramount importance for the future history of the Bund movement. After Spanknöbel reported his findings to Gissibl, Gissibl decided to declare Teutonia defunct, and many of its members joined their fellow Nazis in Gau-USA. Why Gissibl did this is not clear; perhaps he suspected that once he and his comrades fell into line with the demands of the German NSDAP and demonstrated that the now defunct Teutonia Association could have been the nucleus around which the Party could have built a Nazi movement, Nieland would re-examine the situation. At any rate, the result was the absorption of Teutonia's membership by the American unit of the NSDAP. Gissibl and Spanknöbel assumed the leadership of branches in Chicago and Detroit, respectively.

The center of Nazi activity in the United States now shifted decisively to New York City, which was the home not only of Gau-USA, but also of an American branch of Germany's largest veterans' organization, Der Stahlhelm.[34] New York City also had

[32] Neumann to Hoffmann.

[33] Requests for literature are scattered throughout Rolf Hoffmann's papers (Amt Auslandspresse, T-81/25, 26, 27).

[34] German veterans of World War I founded an American branch of the Stahlhelm in the mid-1920's. In November 1933, Georg Schmitt was selected to coordinate the Stahlhelm with the Party organization in New York. As will be seen, few, if any, groups resisted. The subjugation of the Stahlhelm in Ger-

over a hundred other German immigrant associations and the old and well-established United German Societies of Greater New York, or UGS. The UGS included almost all the pre-1917 organizations of Americans of German extraction. Without Gissibl's knowledge, Heinz Spanknöbel was planning to turn his back on his Teutonia friends. He intended to return to New York and attempt to take over the leadership of the UGS. Hitler's assumption of power at the start of 1933 gave him the opportunity.

The year 1932 was also of pivotal importance because the NSDAP now began to consider Gau-USA a permanent rather than transient group, which prompted Gissibl, Kappe, and Schuster to stop considering America as only a temporary home.

The 1920's offered a preview of the direction Nazi activities in the United States would take in the next decade. Men like Edmund Fürholzer and Colonel Edwin Emerson hoped to unite German-America into a political force by conjuring up memories of the excesses committed againt them during the war. Throughout the campaign of 1932, Fürholzer worked for the Republican National Committee and gave a series of speeches in New York State on behalf of the incumbent. Hoover's opponent, Franklin D. Roosevelt, was portrayed as the "new Wilson," the man who had "utterly ruined Germany—with the result that they (THE NOVEMBER CRIMINALS) ruined the whole world." Wilson's former adviser Colonel House, now an associate of the Democratic nominee, was condemned as a man moved by a "pathological hatred of anything German," and German-American voters were reminded that "only the dumbest of animals would elect their own butcher." [35] With an

---

many came in April 1933, when Franz Seldte placed the group under the jurisdiction of the SA. On the American branch of the organization, see the *New York Times*, November 9, 1933; and Heinzpeter Thümmler, "Die Auslandsorganisation des Stahlhelm im Dienst der Faschistischen Propaganda (1934/5)," in *Der deutsche Imperialismus und der Zweite Weltkrieg*, (East Berlin, 1961), II, 283–302.

[35] "Warum stimmen wir Bürger deutschen Stammes wiederum für Herbert Hoover," Republican Foreign Language Bureau (M. W. Tuthill, director), T-81/187/336715–23. In the campaign of 1932, the New York State Republican Committee (Naturalized Citizens Division) engaged Fürholzer as a speaker

eye on the future development of Nazi German activities in the United States, Fürholzer attempted to penetrate the German-American community, but to little avail. Only when he and men like him received NSDAP and subsequent German support would their efforts bring tangible results. In the next decade, there would be a concentrated effort to make inroads into the amorphous community known as German-America. Fritz Gissibl and his friends were still thinking of unifying German nationals. In the last months of 1932, any hope of achieving unity was still a dream. But during the new year, with Hitler in power, the Nazi Party and its allies in the United States would attempt to transform this dream into a reality, and America would shortly find a well-structured unit of a foreign political party on its soil.

---

to German-American groups in central New York State ("Expense Voucher, November 1932," T-81/188/338405). Fürholzer returned to Germany in 1933 or 1934. On his activities in the Far East in the middle of the decade, see Weinberg, *Foreign Policy of Hitler's Germany*, pp. 341–342.

CHAPTER 4

The End of the Long Wait: Hitler Comes to Power

In the weeks following the torchlight parade that welcomed Hitler in 1933, clandestine Party members and opportunists, unemployed workers and wealthy industrialists, emerged as outspoken supporters of the new government. The development of a strong backing occurred not only throughout Germany, but also in countries with large populations of natives descended from Germans and of German nationals. In America, the pro-Nazi activities of a handful of Germany's nationals soon became an internal and diplomatic issue. Although the United States and Germany enjoyed good relations during the 1920's and early 1930's, the period following the change of leadership in both Berlin and Washington was characterized by mutual hostility and distrust.[1] At the root of much of this tension were the Bundists, who were initially selected by the NSDAP to propagate Hitler's supranational racial doctrines and help reverse what Nazi propagandists called "the Jewish image of National Socialism" in America.

For six months after Hitler's appointment as Chancellor, there was little outward change in diplomatic relations between America and Germany. The post of American ambassador to Berlin went to William E. Dodd, a Jeffersonian scholar with a traditionally liberal political background. "The German post," according to Dodd's biographer Robert Dallek, "was one of Roosevelt's early unconventional strokes." [2] Roosevelt, the new President, understood that Na-

---

[1] The best account of German-American diplomatic relations is Arnold Offner's *American Appeasement*. See also Weinberg, *Foreign Policy of Hitler's Germany*, ch. vi.

[2] Robert Dallek, "William E. Dodd and George S. Messersmith: Berlin and Vienna, 1933–1939," paper delivered at the American Historical Association

tional Socialism represented the antithesis of democracy, and he wanted a man who "would naturally act as a standing example of American liberalism in Berlin." [3] The new President also hoped that Dodd might establish contact with the more moderate elements, the traditionalists, in the Wilhelmstrasse so that he would be in a position to counteract any threat to normal diplomatic relations.

In March, the German ambassador to the United States, Friedrich Wilhelm von Prittwitz-Gaffron, resigned; his resignation was "the only possible means of stemming the tide of National Socialism." [4] He was replaced by the former Chancellor of Weimar Germany and one-time president of the Reichsbank, Hans Luther. Hitler appointed Luther just when the new administration in Washington and many business leaders with extensive economic interests in Germany were becoming concerned about the revolutionary aspects of National Socialism. In a parallel move to allay American fears that the new regime in Berlin might drastically alter Germany's economic relations with the United States, Hjalmar Schacht, president of the Reichsbank, visited the United States to participate in preliminary bilateral talks concerning the World Economic Conference.[5]

---

eightieth annual meeting, San Francisco, Dec. 1965, pp. 1–2, and *Democrat and Diplomat.*

[3] Dallek, "William E. Dodd and George S. Messersmith," p. 8. Dodd remained at his post from June 13, 1933, to December 29, 1937. He was replaced by Hugh Wilson.

[4] Prittwitz-Gaffron to Foreign Minister Neurath, March 11, 1933, *DGFP*, C, I, 147–148. On the reaction in the State Department, see *PRDR*, 1933, II, 187ff.

[5] An account of the circumstances surrounding Luther's appointment can be found in Graf Schwerin von Krosigk, *Es geschah in Deutschland* (Tübingen, 1952), pp. 123–130. Luther's autobiographical accounts, *Politiker ohne Partei* (Stuttgart, 1960) and *Vor dem Abgrund, 1930–1933: Reichsbankpräsident in Krisenzeiten* (Berlin, 1964), shed no light on this period. Weinberg has written that Hitler sent Luther to Washington as a consolation prize "after forcing his resignation from the Reichsbank" (*Foreign Policy of Hitler's Germany*, p. 32). On the early formative years of Nazi foreign policy, see Günter Schubert, *Anfänge nationalsozialistischer Aussenpolitik* (Cologne, 1963). On Schacht's visit to the United States, see Gerhard Weinberg, "Schachts Besuch in den USA im Jahre 1933," *Vierteljahrshefte für Zeitgeschichte*, 11 (April 1963), 166–180.

Once in Washington, Schacht, who had helped save the mark during the disastrous inflation ten years before and whose outward appearance epitomized the old Germany, energetically insisted that the Hitler government wanted to continue the excellent diplomatic and economic relationship that existed between Germany and America despite the problems regarding payments. When questioned by American diplomats about Hitler's and the Party's overt anti-Semitism, Schacht attributed it to revolutionary propaganda and dismissed violent outbursts of anti-Semitism as transient. In spite of his cordial reception and the expressions of understanding he received from some quarters, Germany's financial expert soon concluded that neither the American government nor its people were in any way sympathetic to the new regime. How could they be, he asked in a memorandum, when they "saw in the motion picture theaters marching, uniformed columns of Nazis"? [6]

Clearly, Schacht overemphasized the extent of American hostility; anti-German or anti-Nazi feeling was not widespread in 1933. Most Americans exhibited little interest in foreign events; they were primarily concerned with the new administration's efforts to pull the nation out of the economic morass. America's Jewish population, however, became extremely concerned about the turn of events in Germany, especially about the fate of German Jewry. The Jews, who were among the more recent groups to migrate to the United States, now numbered several million; the majority were concentrated in the Northeast. The Nazi seizure of power made

[6] Schacht to Foreign Ministry, May 6, 1933, *DGFP*, C, I, 392. On his report to Hitler, see Memorandum from Minutes of Conference with Ministers, May 26, 1933, p. 487. In April 1933, Roosevelt sent Samuel R. Fuller, Jr. (Fuller was an old friend of the President, who had known him since his days at the Navy Department) on a fact-finding tour of Germany. Fuller met with Schacht, who assured him that Germany did not intend to make any changes in the economic relationship between the two powers; moreover, Schacht felt that Hitler's anti-Semitism would ebb. Commenting on the NSDAP's legal revolution, Schacht said that the "Hitler movement is not an autocracy, but the most perfect form of Democracy." Fuller reported to the President that he believed that anti-Semitic persecutions would continue and that Hitler would probably start a war in the future (memorandum of a conversation with Schacht at the Reichsbank, April 24, 1933, submitted to Roosevelt May 11, 1933, President's Personal File, 2616, FDRL).

them, as well as Germans and Americans of German extraction, more conscious of their ethnic identity. Although American Jewry had experienced anti-Semitism in the past, the Party's racial anti-Semitic writings seemed especially ominous. Finding their coreligionists in Germany the objects of racial antagonism and organized economic and legal discrimination, many Jews made their indignation known. After much discussion and with some reluctance, the leaders of New York City's Jewish community decided upon a counterboycott of German products to retaliate the Nazi-organized boycott of Jewish businesses in Germany. Using the motto "Don't Buy German Goods," the leaders of the American Jewish Congress and the B'nai B'rith urged their fellow Americans to support the counterboycott, maintaining that economic pressure on the unstable German economy was the only pressure to which Hitler would respond. Unfortunately for German Jewry, the spreading boycott did not curb Hitler's anti-Semitism; instead it reinforced Hitler's belief that Jews controlled the world economy.[7]

Even though the counterboycott initiated by the Jews did not seriously damage trade relations between the two nations, the fact that it was undertaken as an expression of moral indignation against Nazism was interpreted by the new regime in Germany as symptomatic of America's failure to comprehend National Socialism.[8] The renowned German chemical works I. G. Farben hired a

[7] On the development of the counterboycott, see Gottlieb, "The First of April Boycott and the Reaction of the American Jewish Community," pp. 516–556; and Samuel Untermeyer, *Nazis against the World: The Counterboycott Is the Only Defense against Hitlerism's Threat to Civilization* (New York, 1934). Opinions of Jewish leaders during this period can be found in the *Jewish Daily Bulletin* (New York). Washington's response to, and eventual handling of, the Jewish issue in Germany was criticized in the 1930's; historical judgments have also been critical. See David Wyman, *Paper Walls: America and the Refugee Crisis, 1938–1941* (Amherst, Mass., 1968); and Henry Feingold, *The Politics of Rescue: The Roosevelt Administration and the Holocaust, 1938–1945* (New Brunswick, N.J., 1970).

[8] Erich Kordt, *Wahn und Wirklichkeit: Die Aussenpolitik des Dritten Reiches* (2d ed.; Stuttgart, 1948), p. 141. Hitler's reaction to the counterboycott can be found in *The Speeches of Adolf Hitler, April 1922–August 1939*, ed. Norman H. Baynes (London, 1942), I, 728–729. Secretary of State Cordell Hull wrote the Foreign Ministry that the counterboycott would cease when its leaders were convinced that the National Socialists would tone down their ra-

public-relations expert in the United States to help brighten Germany's tarnished image. Germany's new leaders were rapidly concluding that similar steps had to be taken to make National Socialism more palatable to the community of nations. Thus, as the summer of 1933 approached, Germany launched a propaganda campaign aimed at North America.

All government agencies with offices in the United States were requested by the Ministry of Propaganda to prepare for a propaganda drive. Of the countless people who became involved in this project, a handful were designated as organizers of the campaign. At the German consulate in New York, for example, Consul Hans Borchers and his superior, Consul General Otto Karl Kiep, welcomed the start of Germany's public relations activities as the only means of offsetting the negative picture of Hitler's Germany which, they claimed, Americans were getting from the press. Kiep, who had held his post since 1931, had acquiesced in the National Socialist assumption of power and, though not a member of the NSDAP, was unwilling to follow in Ambassador Prittwitz-Gaffron's footsteps. Hans Borchers was appointed after January 1933 with Party instructions to Nazify the consular service in the eastern part of the United States. In fact, the man he replaced at the New York consulate—Paul Schwarz, a Jew—was the first casualty of the appointment in 1933.[9] West of the Mississippi, the Nazification of the

cial practices (memorandum by Cordell Hull, Sept. 21, 1933, *PRDR*, 1933, II, 357–359). In general, the items most affected by the counterboycott were inexpensive retail items (toys, clocks). As will be seen, the counterboycott had its greatest impact on German- and German-American-owned stores in Yorkville and other German neighborhoods in New York. The Jewish-initiated boycott had no impact on corporate relations with Germany. In fact, the United States increased its dollar-value import of German products (from $69 million in 1934 to $91 million in 1937); the decline began in 1938 (Offner, *American Appeasement,* p. 63). See also Gabriel Kolko, "American Business and Germany, 1930–1940," *Western Political Quarterly,* 15 (1962), 713–728.

[9] Technically, the Nazis did not take over the Consular Service until the Foreign Ministry was thoroughly integrated into the Third Reich (Joachim von Ribbentrop was named foreign minister on February 4, 1938). In reality, the Consular Service was "Nazified" by late 1933. Members of the diplomatic corps with Jewish or other undesirable backgrounds were forced to resign their posts. Borchers joined the NSDAP in January 1936. After the war, he told interrogators that Bohle had threatened to dismiss him from his post if he did not join the Party (RG 59, "Borchers Interrogation," I, 195–199). See also Appendix III, below.

consular service was carried out by the professional diplomat Wilhelm Ernst Tannenberg, who, like Kiep, was a well-known figure in Washington diplomatic circles.[10] As a result of the untiring efforts of Tannenberg, Kiep, and Borchers, the German diplomatic corps in the United States conformed to the wishes of the new leadership in Berlin. The Party found also that the heads of several major steamship lines favored the project, especially Captain Friedrich Carl Mensing of the New York office of the Hapag-Lloyd Lines.[11] Such men became the nucleus of the German propaganda network in America.

Germany's efforts to improve the image of National Socialism began in May 1933, when the recently appointed Minister of Propaganda, Joseph Goebbels, ordered Kiep to hire a public-relations firm. With an initial allowance of five thousand dollars, Kiep enlisted the support of Edmund Furhölzer's old friend Colonel Edwin Emerson; the well-known controversial Germanophile George Sylvester Viereck; the less conspicuous General A. Metz, American representative of the association of German chemical industries (Interessen-Gemeinschaft der Chemischen Industrien Deutschlands, or IG); Willi von Meister, American representative of Durnier Motor Works; Adolf Scheurer, director of the American office of Hapag-Lloyd Lines; and the World War I propagandist Frederick Franklin Schrader.[12] Kiep engaged the public-relations firm of Carl Byoir and Associates, which had offices near the German consulate in lower Manhattan.

When Kiep had found a group of supporters, he notified Prit-

[10] RG 59, "Tannenberg Interrogation," III, 571–577.

[11] RG 59, "Borchers Interrogation," I, 194.

[12] T-120/4614/269150–162. Schrader had been active in German causes during World War I and into the 1920's. In the 1920's, he published *The Germans in the Making of America* (New York, 1924), in which he attributed to the German-Americans an extraordinary role in the building of the United States. In the middle of the next decade, Kuhn's Amerikadeutscher Volksbund published another of his works, *The New Germany under Hitler* (New York, n.d.). On Viereck, see Frye, *Nazi Germany and the American Hemisphere*, pp. 42–44, 49, 51–52, 161–162; O. John Rogge, *The Official German Report* (New York, 1961), pp. 130–172; and Niel Melvin Johnson, "George Sylvester Viereck: Pro-German Propagandist in America, 1910–1945," Ph.D. dissertation, University of Iowa, 1971. On Viereck's correspondence with the Nazis, see "Propaganda Geschäfte," T-120/4614/24704–24707; and Kipphan, *Deutsche Propaganda*, pp. 103–108.

twitz-Gaffron's replacement, Hans Luther, of the project. But Luther had his own plans. He had already been contacted by the secretary of the Carl Schurz Foundation, Wilbur Thomas, who, to promote good relations between the two nations, proposed to start a magazine called *Germany Today—American Magazine of Goodwill.* Not a pro-Nazi organization, the foundation, like the Steuben Society, attempted to make a clear distinction between being pro-Hitler and being pro-Germany. As far as Luther was concerned, this distinction was not an academic one, since he believed that most Americans, including the Jews, were distinguishing the Nazis from the great majority of the German people.[13] Acting on this belief, he endorsed Thomas' suggestion, and by the end of the year Germany was underwriting the publication with more than ten thousand dollars a year.[14] Luther's action did not, however, keep him from working with the pro-Nazi element in New York. In the early autumn of 1933, Luther arranged through one of Emerson's many friends, Herbert Houston, for the Macmillan Company to publish *Germany Speaks,* a collection of statements on "the Jewish question" by Germany's new leaders.[15]

Although Kiep felt that Germany's public-relations campaign was moving in the right direction, he needed more of a commitment from American citizens to propagandize for Germany. Kiep found a propagandist in the unscrupulous Colonel Emerson. After Hitler's appointment as Chancellor, Emerson had befriended Paul Manger and Karl Neumann, the leaders of the local Nazi unit in Manhattan. Undoubtedly, they welcomed Emerson's friendship and his connections with members of the Yorkville establishment in the United German Societies and on the German-American Board of Trade. Emerson, too, welcomed this relationship with Manger and Neumann and soon became the self-appointed, unofficial American adviser to Gau-USA. Finding that a handful of American citizens had joined the group, Emerson suggested that their continued presence might be unconstitutional. But Emerson

[13] Luther-Kiep Correspondence, T-120/4614/269180–185. Cf. Frye, pp. 33–36.
[14] Kiep to Edwin Emerson, Aug. 18, 1933, T-120/4614/269164.
[15] Memorandum by Kiep, n.d., T-120/4614/269171–3.

was far less concerned with legality than with becoming the leader of what he envisioned as an American counterpart of the Nazi local, which would publicize the Nazi cause and help correct the image of the New Germany. The Colonel's plans coincided with Kiep's. In March 1933, Emerson led a handful of Americans out of the local Nazi group and founded a new organization, the Friends of Germany (Freunde von Deutschland). Subsidized by the Nazi Party through the German consulate in New York (and housed in the same building, the Whitehall Building, at 17 Battery Place in lower Manhattan), Emerson's group brought together a number of pro-Nazi sympathizers; more important, the NSDAP now had a foothold, however precarious, in the German-American community in Yorkville.[16]

Kiep hoped that the Friends of Germany and Gau-USA would propagandize for Germany, but neither the consulate nor the Foreign Section of the NSDAP was able to exert any control over the Nazi local. By the summer of 1933 a chaotic situation had developed. For example, a group of Party members in the New York division of Gau-USA, claiming that Paul Manger was an ineffective leader, left to form a new organization, the Swastika League.

Dissension in the ranks of the infant Nazi groups was not confined to New York City. Across the Hudson River, in Union City, New Jersey, a Party member and nonunion bricklayer currently working as a stock clerk in a toy store in the Richmond Hills section of Queens, New York, made his bid for the leadership.[17] Now that Hitler was in power, rebellious Party members tried to take control of the fortunes of the officially designated group, Gau-USA. Almost daily, newspapers in New York City carried stories of intragroup fighting. The most tangible results were to place Germany and the pro-Nazi groups in a bad light and to neutralize the effects of the so-called public-relations program. In an effort to avoid fur-

[16] Kiep to Emerson, Sept. 15, 1933, T-120/4614/269217; 269150–164. The executive committee included Emerson (chairman), Dr. John Hooing, Lt. Col. Henry Torney, Joseph O'Donohue, Frederick F. Schrader, P. Bigelow, and M. E. Griswold (T-81/27/24001; 24507). O'Donohue met with Hitler on August 2, 1933, and discussed the counterboycott.

[17] *New York Times*, March 23, 1933; E. Röll to Rolf Hoffmann, Feb. 2, 1934, T-81/27/24498–9.

their bad publicity, the Foreign Section of the NSDAP cabled Paul Manger on April 16 and instructed him to disband Gau-USA.[18]

Germany's decision to abandon its unit in the United States was prompted by several factors. Gau-USA had become a liability to Germany and, of course, to Kiep and Emerson; certainly it did little to prevent the continued development of anti-Nazi feeling in New York. More important, the rebellion-ridden Nazi local stood in the way of Kiep's and Emerson's plans, and they wanted it eliminated. After all, they reasoned, why continue to support a handful of Party members at the very moment when a genuine pro-Nazi German-American group had come into existence? Obviously, the repudiation of Gau-USA was one means of reversing or at least stemming the tide of anti-Nazi sentiment and also permitted the Foreign Section of the NSDAP to coordinate its activities with Kiep and Emerson. The decision also reflected a drastic reorganization of the overseas apparatus of the NSDAP. Shortly after Paul Manger was notified, Rudolf Hess attempted to make the Party's overseas branches more responsive to the needs of the NSDAP and the responsibilities of power, factors which were not of cardinal importance during Hitler's struggle for the control of Germany and of Party groups overseas. As one of his first steps, he replaced Nieland with Bohle in mid-April and designated him leader of the Abteilung für Deutsche im Ausland on May 8, 1933. Bohle's appointment was a major turning-point in the Party's relations with the Nazis and pro-Nazi sympathizers in America.[19]

One man viewed the dissolution of Gau-USA as a unique oppor-

---

[18] Karl Neumann to Rolf Hoffmann, Jan. 24, 1934, T-81/27/24507. Kiep, at the German consulate, was concerned by the unfavorable publicity Germany was receiving in the American press and believed that the Nazis in America further tarnished Germany's image. As will be seen, the Nazis would eventually disavow the Bund in an effort to correct the damage done by the Bundists (Kiep to Foreign Ministry, n.d., T-120/4616/269120). New York columnist Henry Paynter published a series of exposés of Nazi activities in the *New York Evening Journal*. Like most anti-Nazis in this period, he exaggerated the extent of Nazi activities (clippings, Greenberg Collection, III, items 768–980. Archives, YIVO Institute).

[19] Jacobsen, *Nationalsozialistiche Aussenpolitik*, pp. 90ff. On the reaction in the Bundist community, see Gustav Guellich to Rolf Hoffmann, Aug. 8, 1933, T-81/27/24294–7.

tunity to rebuild the now defunct Nazi group and join forces with Emerson's Friends of Germany. Shortly before Hitler assumed the chancellorship, Heinz Spanknöbel, Fritz Gissibl's old friend and one-time member of the Teutonia Association, returned to Germany. While there, he managed to gain access to Hess's inner circle. Hess, who had not bothered to check Spanknöbel's exaggerated claims that thousands of Americans of German extraction were waiting for Berlin to initiate a genuine American Nazi movement, one that would serve as an umbrella group for the several disparate pro-Nazi cells and Emerson's organization, gave Spanknöbel permission to form a new organization. Armed with Hess's blessing and a document authorizing him to form a new group, Spanknöbel returned to the United States sometime in May 1933.[20]

Upon his arrival in New York City, Spanknöbel set up temporary headquarters in Yorkville. Careful to avoid the discredited Paul Manger, he personally got in touch with members of the NSDAP in the New York area and told them of his plans to form a new organization, composed of German nationals and Americans of German ancestry, which would be under the clandestine control of the Nazi Party. Throughout May and on into the summer, Spanknöbel worked with the personnel at the German consulate, Fritz Gissibl and the "old guard" from Detroit, Paul Manger's former followers, and many new-found friends. By July 1933, the Friends of the New Germany (Bund der Freunde des Neuen Deutschland, or FONG) had come into existence. To be sure, it had no control over the former membership of Gau-USA, let alone Emerson's Friends of Germany. Thus, there were now two Bunds, Emerson's group (for Americans of German background) and Spanknöbel's. Spanknöbel's aim was to combine the groups.

Spanknöbel believed that force, or the threat of force, was the only means of crushing any potential opposition to his rule.[21] On May 28, he appointed his old friend and former SA man Sepp

[20] Heinz Spanknöbel to German Embassy, Aug. 8, 1933, T-120/4616/269189.

[21] Understandably, Fritz Gissibl felt he had been betrayed by Spanknöbel. On the struggle between the two men, see "Zur Tagung der Ortsgruppenleiter am 28./29. und 30. Juli," T-120/5177/455049; see also T-120/4616/269190.

Schuster as the leader of FONG's fighting division, the Ordnungs-Dienst (OD—Uniformed Service), which had originally been organized as an adjunct of the Teutonia Association in the 1920's and integrated into Spanknöbel's group.[22] Schuster reorganized the OD after the model of Hitler's Sturmabteilung (Storm Troopers), copying its uniforms and even adopting its song.[23]

> Up, up for battle, we are born to battle,
>   Up, up for battle for the German Fatherland,
> We are sworn to Adolf Hitler,
>   And to Adolf Hitler we extend our hand.
>
> Firm stands a man, as firm as an oak,
>   Braving every storm as well as he can,
> Maybe on the morrow we will be a corpse,
>   And to Adolf Hitler we extend our hand.
>
> Up, then, for battle, all you brown batallions,
>   The Third Reich, our goal shall ever be;
> The World War's departed, all of these two millions,
>   Are forcing us to battle and to gain a victory.

Throughout June and on into July, Spanknöbel's henchmen coerced the last remnants of the Teutonia Association, Gau-USA, and the Swastika League into joining the Friends of the New Germany. His greatest asset, however, was not the group's counterpart to the Sturmabteilung, the OD, but the news that Hess had hand-picked him. Most obedient Party and non-Party members accepted his appointment as the will of the Führer. In general, he entrusted the process of "coordination" to time-tested Party members. In Cincinnati, for example, the job was given to his friend Christoph

[22] Schuster to Rolf Hoffmann, April 14, 1936, T-81/26/23820. During this period, the Bundists used the initials OD and SA interchangeably. Schuster also copied the NSDAP's arbitration tribunal (Untersuchungs- und Schlichtungsausschuss, USCHLA) in order to maintain discipline; that is, he used it as a purge instrument. (In the 1920's, Hitler appointed Martin Bormann's father-in-law, former major Walter Buch, as the head of the NSDAP's arbitration tribunal.)

[23] Sworn statement of OD man Richard Werner before U.S. district attorney for the Southern District, New York, as quoted in "Evidence," 1942, p. 32, available in the collection of the ADL.

Klausfeldner, one of the "old fighters" from the early years of the Nazi movement in Germany. Klausfeldner had been a member of the militant Rossbach Freikorps (one of many paramilitary and *völkisch* groups founded after World War I, the Rossbach Free Corps derived its name from its leader, former Lieutenant Gerhard Rossbach) and, at the age of seventeen, personal courier for the notorious Jew-baiter Julius Streicher, editor of *Der Stürmer* ("The Attacker"). Klausfeldner brought all the dissident Nazis in that city under Spanknöbel's control in a matter of days.[24] The splintering of the American Nazi group in the crucial years 1932–1933, made Spanknöbel's task an easy one. Thus, by the middle of July, he held the allegiance of all Party members, including the disenchanted Gissibl brothers; the one-time editor of Teutonia's newspaper, *Vorposten,* Walter Kappe; the former leader of Gau-USA, Karl Neumann; and one of the cofounders of the Teutonia group, Alfred Ex.

Confident that the group would mushroom into a viable movement of German-Americans subsidized by the Nazi Party, Spanknöbel announced that FONG would hold its first national convention in Chicago in late July. At a two-day meeting beginning on the twenty eighth, the members of FONG—who now called themselves the Bundists—sat obediently as they listened to their Führer, the thirty-nine-year-old former photoengraver Heinz Spanknöbel. At the opening of the meeting, Spanknöbel announced that the National Socialist movement in the United States and Canada had officially begun. The movement, he added, had one purpose: to unify the millions of Germany's racial comrades who had emigrated in the eighteenth and nineteenth centuries to North America. In order to accomplish this end, the North American continent had been divided into three administrative departments (*Gaue*), one each for the East, Midwest, and West, with a *Gauleiter* at the head of each department. The leadership of the Western Department went to Robert Pape, of the Midwestern to Fritz Gissibl, and of the Eastern to Hans Stolzenburg. There was a separate

[24] Klausfeldner headed the local until 1936. Until his return to Germany in 1938, he worked as an agent for the German consulate in Cincinnati (T-81/140/177791).

administrative region for Canada, under Hans Strauss. In addition, Spanknöbel announced that he had changed his title from Führer to Bundesleiter (literally, "national leader"), since there could be only one Führer, Adolf Hitler. The group was to be an image of the Nazi Party, administered on the *Führerprinzip* ("leadership principle"). Thus, six months to the day after Hitler was appointed Chancellor, a genuine Nazi movement in America came into being. More important, the administrative structure created by Spanknöbel would remain unaltered throughout the entire history of the Bund.[25]

Now that the Bundesleiter was firmly in control, he turned his attention to the reorganization of the group's publishing section. In a confidential letter to Hitler's close associate Ernst ("Putzi") Hanfstaengl, Charles Pichel, a pro-Nazi self-appointed observer of American affairs, wrote that there was only one pro-Nazi German-language newspaper in New York, Friedrich Heiss's *Amerika's Deutsche Post*, which had been the newspaper published by Gau-USA. Pichel claimed that Heiss, the leader of a splinter Nazi group, was "incompetent and indifferent to the cause which he should sponsor [and that] the great FAULT of the Party in New York has been its [*Amerika's Deutsche Post*'s] refusal" to carry any

[25] Heinz Spanknöbel, "Das Deutschtum Erwacht!" *Das neue Deutschland,* Aug. 31, 1933, p. 1. On arrangements for the convention, see sworn statement of Hermann Schwinn (West Coast leader of the Friends of the New Germany and the Amerikadeutscher Volksbund), *Schwinn* v. *U.S.,* C.C.A. 9th 112F (2d) 74, affirmed 311 U.S. 616. The group in Canada seems to have broken away from the Bund in 1934. In the middle of the decade the Deutscher Bund, Canada, was formed. Materials pertaining to this group can be found in Rolf Hoffmann's papers, T-81/25–27. A brief outline of the organizational structure of the Friends of the New Germany is in the first "leadership command" issued by Heinz Spanknöbel, August 7, 1933, T-120/4616/269190. According to the "leadership principle," the will and the decisions of the leader are absolute and are implemented by "leaders" at every level of the organization or movement down to the cell, the lowest level of the Nazi administrative structure. After 1936, it was widely believed in America that Fritz Kuhn took his orders from Hitler through the intermediary of the Auslandsorganisation; thus the leadership principle had international implications. A systematic discussion of the leadership principle is in Bracher, *German Dictatorship,* pp. 47, 92, 148–149, 340–350.

of Hitler's addresses in English.[26] The situation was soon rectified, when Kiep, who was already subsidizing several other projects, lent his support to Spanknöbel, and the EFDENDE Publishing Company was organized. On August 1, two FONG newspapers, the *Deutsche Zeitung* and *Das neue Deutschland,* appeared on news stalls in Yorkville. Each included a section in English called "German Outlook," which was prepared by Colonel Emerson after he ceased publishing his newspaper, *Die Bruecke,* in July 1933. Both newspapers were edited by Walter Kappe, the talented former editor of Teutonia's publication, *Vorposten.* By October, the group was publishing newspapers in Philadelphia, Detroit, Chicago, and Cincinnati.[27]

[26] Charles Pichel to Ernst Hanfstaengl, July 15, 1933, T-81/27/24114a. Pichel was a self-appointed observer of American affairs—according to himself, a world citizen dedicated to "the study of the world and its people." Claiming that he was the director of the American Heraldry Society, he requested Hanfstaengl to appoint him liaison man between the Americans and Hitler. The Germans dismissed him and other self-appointed observers as cranks. According to one of Pichel's reports, Hermann Göring was the adopted son of Dr. Hermann Epenstein, a Jew.

[27] Memorandum by Kiep, n.d., T-120/4616/269215. On Kappe, see Appendix III, below, and T-81/27/25533. On publications in other cities, see Appendix IV, below, and E. Mueller to Rolf Hoffmann, Oct. 30, 1933, T-81/27/24764. On Hoffmann's office supplying the Bund with literature to be published in its newspapers, see Kate MacLeod to Rolf Hoffmann, Jan. 14, 1934, T-81/27/24669; and Werner Haag to Rolf Hoffmann, Jan. 26, 1934, T-81/27/24330. Hess's designation of the Bund as an outlet for Nazi literature can be found in Hess to Kiep, telegram, Sept. 1, 1933, T-120/4616/269197. On the NSDAP's subsidizing the project, see Kiep to Foreign Ministry, Sept. 18, 1933, T-120/4616/269169; and Spanknöbel to Hoffmann, Sept. 13, 1933, T-81/27/23982; 24327. During this period, four newspapers were published: *Deutsche Zeitung,* a biweekly from August to December 1933, which in 1934 became a weekly; *Das neue Deutschland,* published irregularly during the same period; *Die Bruecke,* published by Emerson's group, March–July 1933; and *Amerika's Deutsche Post,* founded in Queens, New York, by Friedrich Heiss in 1924. Heiss's paper, which had served as the organ of Gau-USA in the New York area and had been subsidized by the consulate, found itself in serious financial trouble after the consulate transferred support to the *Deutsche Zeitung.* Since the consulate would no longer support Heiss, he threatened to blackmail German authorities. Although Borchers urged the Foreign Ministry to provide funds in order to quiet Heiss, it did not, and the issue simply died. See Frye, *Nazi Germany and the American Hemisphere,* p. 50.

On August 25, 1933, Spanknöbel sent a cablegram to Hess requesting a letter to confirm his designation as "the sole leader of the Nazi Party in the United States." His request was prompted by increasing opposition to his leadership.[28] One man who opposed Spanknöbel was Edwin Emerson, whose determination to lead the movement was as great as the Bundesleiter's. As the leader of the Friends of Germany, Emerson maintained that his group was potentially a genuine American Nazi organization, since its membership consisted of American citizens. Furthermore, he insisted that only through an Americanized organization could Germany hope to make National Socialism comprehensible to most Americans. Although the subsequent history of the Bund movement was to validate Emerson's argument, Spanknöbel had no desire to share his power, let alone to turn the leadership over to Emerson. More important, the consulate, while still underwriting Emerson's group, was solidly behind Spanknöbel.

But Spanknöbel could ill afford to oust Emerson from the presidency of the Friends of Germany; Emerson enjoyed the backing of too many businessmen in Yorkville and also had Kiep's ear at the consulate. In an effort to ward off a collision with Emerson, Spanknöbel offered him the presidency of the hastily created American section of FONG. In effect, Spanknöbel offered Emerson a merger, with Emerson retaining the nominal leadership of the Americans in the group. Much to his surprise, the Colonel accepted. Any further challenge to Spanknöbel might be interpreted as a violation of Party discipline and could result in the loss of the consulate's support.[29]

Emerson wanted to be the leader of the Bund organization. As far as he was concerned, the Party had appointed the wrong man at the wrong time. Emerson believed, correctly in this case, that American susceptibilities would be offended once it was discovered that a member of the German NSDAP was at the helm of the Bund. He also felt that the Bundesleiter's tactics were alienating the very people with whom the Party should be working—the German-Americans, not the German nationals. He also believed that

[28] Rudolf Hess to Heinz Spanknöbel, Aug. 25, 1933, "Evidence," p. 72.
[29] Rolf Hoffmann to Heinz Spanknöbel, Sept. 19, 1933, T-81/27/24109.

the floodgates of criticism would soon open, and the anti-Nazi ac-
tivists in the Jewish community in New York would have the evidence needed to make a case against Nazi German activities in
this country. Thus, by accepting Spanknöbel's offer of a merger he
believed that he would be in a position to take over the organization.

In September 1933, criticism came from still another quarter,
Rudolf Hess's office. On September 19, Rolf Hoffmann, an assistant
in the Party's Overseas Press Office, asked Spanknöbel whether
"the American section is a separate organization or whether it is
working with your movement." [30] Spanknöbel replied that the
entire organization was open to all who wanted to join as "an expression of their sympathy to Hitler." [31] In a second letter to Hoffmann, Spanknöbel betrayed himself by indirectly suggesting that
the inclusion of non-German American citizens was not in keeping
with the *völkisch* orientation of the NSDAP. "We have admitted
members of non-German nationality," he wrote, "which is surely
necessary considering the special conditions in the USA." [32] The
evidence, though scant, suggests that Hess wanted the group to remain an organization for German nationals and Americans of German extraction, thus retaining its purely *völkisch* identity. For
Spanknöbel, who had so methodically built up a Party structure in
the United States, his own recent activities proved a mistake. But
for the moment Spanknöbel believed that he had the complete
support of the NSDAP. On the evening of September 10, 1933, he
donned his Nazi uniform and left the Bundesleitung in Yorkville to
preside over the group's first "German Evening"; he did not know
that it would be his last major function as Bundesleiter of the
Friends of the New Germany.

Followed by an entourage that included his OD troopers, his
personal bodyguard, members of the Friends of the New Germany,
and invited guests, Spanknöbel boarded a German steamer, the
S.S. *Resolute,* in New York harbor for what was later described by
a United States government investigator as "a thoroughly German-

[30] *Ibid.*
[31] Heinz Spanknöbel to Rolf Hoffmann, Sept. 1933, T-81/27/23988.
[32] *Ibid.,* Sept. 21, 1933, T-81/27/23981.

Nazi evening from beginning to end." [33] After a brief speech by
Spanknöbel and group-singing of "Deutschland, Deutschland über
Alles" and the "Horst Wessel Lied," formality was abandoned, and
a night of beer-drinking began. For the former photoengraver from
Magdeburg, now Bundesleiter, the evening represented more than
a mere celebration; Spanknöbel remarked that it was like a "religious experience." The "spirit of the new Germany" seemed for the
first time to be entering the hearts of German nationals overseas.
As far as Heinz Spanknöbel was concerned, a full-fledged Nazi
movement on American soil now seemed within the realm of possibility.[34]

The relative ease with which he had brought members of the
NSDAP and Emerson's followers under his sway had encouraged
him to think in terms of a greatly expanded movement. During the
summer of 1933, Spanknöbel had cultivated some of Emerson's
friends, who for the most part were sympathetic to the Nazi cause.
Representing all segments of the German-American community in
the New York metropolitan area, some of these men were the
respected leaders in the United German Societies and the German-American Board of Trade. Such acquaintances sharpened
Spanknöbel's awareness that outside the newly arrived immigrant
community there were hundreds of large and well-established German-American organizations; in fact, the UGS, which served as an
umbrella organization for hundreds of such groups in New York,
claimed a membership of almost ten thousand. But he did not delude himself into thinking that the UGS was pro-Nazi; on the contrary, he was well aware that a handful of German-Jews and several important Roman Catholic families were urging the group to
take an anti-Nazi position. The German-Jews were led by the
UGS's treasurer, Fritz Schlesinger, and by Robert Rosenbaum, the
leader of the German Israelite National Guard. But Spanknöbel

[33] "Evidence," p. 72. Like some other German seamen, those on the S.S.
Resolute belonged to the NSDAP. The merchant marine later constituted a
separate administrative division of the Party's Auslandsorganisation (RG 59,
"Bohle Interrogation," I, 82–83). See also Ernst Hamburger, "A Peculiar Pattern of Fifth Column: The Organization of German Seamen," *Social Research*,
9 (Nov. 1942).

[34] "Am Bord SS Resolute," "Evidence," pp. 72–73. It is likely that Captain
F. C. Mensing (attached to the New York office of Hapag-Lloyd and AO representative in New York) arranged for the festivities.

was impatient, and believing that he alone was the executor of Hitler's will in the United States, he attempted to coerce the UGS into joining forces with him.

What journalists of the period dubbed the "Spanknöbel Affair" began on a summer afternoon in 1933 with the arrival of Heinz Spanknöbel at the office of the *New Yorker Staats-Zeitung und Herold* at 22 North Williams Street in lower Manhattan. The paper's publishers were Victor and Bernard Ridder, sons of the famous publisher Hermann Ridder, after whom the city of New York had recently named an experimental public school. The elder Ridder, who had died in 1915, had been active in German-American affairs and was a lifelong independent Democrat. In 1886, he founded the *Catholic News;* in the next decade he bought the *New Yorker Staats-Zeitung* from Oswald Ottendorfer and forged it into the largest German-language newspaper in the United States. After his death, his sons continued to publish both newspapers. Moreover, they also continued their father's excellent relationship with the Roman Catholic archdiocese, especially with Patrick Joseph Hayes, the archbishop, who was elevated to cardinal in 1919. At the time the Bundesleiter arrived at the Ridders' office, the brothers were counted among the elite New York families.

Spanknöbel asked to see either of the brothers, and when Victor appeared, told him that the paper had to publish material favorable to Hitler and Nazi Germany. Ridder, who had neither condemned nor condoned Nazism, was flabbergasted by the order and asked to see proof of this demand. Spanknöbel reached into his pocket and pulled out the document signed by Rudolf Hess investing him with the leadership of the Nazi movement in America. "This," he retorted, "is .my authority to act for the German government with respect to matters involving Germans and German-Americans in the United States." Ridder, unimpressed, threw him out of his office and then phoned the police.[35]

[35] The discussion of the Spanknöbel Affair is based on several sources: *U.S.* v. *Heinz Spanknöbel,* Civ. C 95–936, FRC; statement of Victor Ridder before a hearing committee, *NP*, pp. 112–117, 408–411; an exposé by Henry Paynter, *New York Evening Journal,* fall–winter, 1933–1934; and the Greenberg Collection, items 768–980, Archives, YIVO Institute. Cf. Rogge, *Official German Report,* pp. 17–22, and Ludwig Lore, "Nazi Politics in America," *The Nation,* 87 (Nov. 29, 1933).

Rebuffed by the editor of the nation's most prestigious German-language daily, Spanknöbel turned his attention to the UGS. On Monday evening, September 18, the UGS met to discuss plans for the annual German Day celebration to be held on October 29. A gala parade was being planned to commemorate the two-hundred-fiftieth anniversary of the arrival of the first German settlers in America. With the help of Emerson's pro-Nazi friends in the UGS, Spanknöbel managed to get his name on the agenda. Moreover, he packed the meeting hall with Sepp Schuster's OD men. The lines were now set for a showdown between the pro- and anti-Nazi elements in the UGS. During the meeting, Spanknöbel's supporters chanted, "Out with the Jews, out with the Jews," and the Bundesleiter threatened to use a blackjack on anyone who did not agree with him.

Outraged by such tactics, the representatives of four German-Jewish groups left the hall and withdrew from the UGS. The remaining sixty-six representatives were asked to vote on two key questions: whether to seat Spanknöbel on the UGS board of directors, and whether to invite Ambassador Hans Luther to speak at the German Day festivities. Both questions were answered in the affirmative. Believing that he had the representatives behind him, Spanknöbel asked for a vote on a resolution stating that the "official German flag [which would include the Swastika] and the Austrian flag" would be raised on German Day. On this question, Spanknöbel failed to get a majority vote. A second meeting was called for the following Monday, September 25.

In the week preceding the second meeting, the "flag issue" became crucial, since the German Day activities were scheduled to climax in the Manhattan Armory, a United States government military installation. An affirmative vote on this question would have meant that the UGS endorsed Nazi Germany; furthermore, the Nazi flag would be flown over a United States government building. On the Friday before the scheduled meeting, six non-Jewish groups withdrew from the UGS, and the entire board of directors resigned, with the exception of Heinz Spanknöbel. Alone on the board, he ordered the next meeting to take place in a popular meeting place in Yorkville, the Turnhalle. To Spanknöbel's surprise, the Ridder brothers, Schlesinger, and Rosenbaum appeared at the Monday meeting. The Ridder brothers were hooted out of the hall after they tried to announce that the UGS was being used by Hitler's agents. Finally, after the UGS treasurer, Schlesinger, resigned and Rosenbaum, of the German Israelite National Guard, was ejected from the Turnhalle, Spanknöbel called the question. The result was a foregone conclusion: the Nazi flag was to be raised.[36]

In the days following, complaints started to come into Mayor John Patrick O'Brien's office, and Samuel Untermeyer, a well-known lawyer active in city politics, brought them to his attention. If Spanknöbel's militancy had ended at this point, it would have been difficult to build a case against him. But he was starting to behave as if he were living in Berlin. In early October, he allegedly had his OD men paint swastikas on the doors of a number of Jewish synagogues in Manhattan. Angered by these acts of organized anti-Semitism and outraged by Spanknöbel's tactics at the UGS meeting, the mayor suggested to the Reverend William Popcke, the pastor of the Zion Lutheran Church, who represented the reconstituted UGS, that German Day activities be canceled; if not, he would have them stopped. On the twenty-fourth, O'Brien met with Popcke, Spanknöbel, and other representatives of the UGS. They argued that the mayor would be violating the organization's constitutional rights if he called off the observances. In the meantime, Congressman Samuel Dickstein, chairman of the House Committee on Immigration and Naturalization, had requested the Labor Department to order the deportation of Spanknöbel on the ground that he had not registered with the State Department as an agent of a foreign nation. O'Brien, who seems to have had prior knowledge of Dickstein's request, asked his guests to meet with him the following day. Somehow, Spanknöbel had gotten word of Dickstein's actions, and on the twenty-fifth, only Popcke appeared at the meeting. He told the mayor that he could not locate Spanknöbel; more important, some members of the UGS had decided to withdraw Spanknöbel's name from the list of speakers scheduled to appear on German Day and had ousted him from the group.

On Thursday, October 26, the UGS canceled its plans for Ger-

[36] *New York Evening Journal*, Nov. 3, 1933; Greenberg Collection, item 792.

man Day. Meanwhile, Spanknöbel went into hiding at the Hotel George Washington. On October 29, the day he was scheduled to address participants in the now canceled German Day activities, he secretly left the country on the S.S. *Europa*. While Spanknöbel was crossing to Bremen, a New York grand jury indicated it intended to investigate the Friends of the New Germany. Four days before that announcement, the Justice Department, acting on a complaint from United States Attorney George Z. Medalie, issued a warrant for Spanknöbel's arrest. The warrant charged that Spanknöbel was an unregistered foreign agent. And, on November 20, Samuel Dickstein's committee commenced preliminary hearings on Nazi activities in the United States.[37]

Spanknöbel's actions constituted a tactical mistake of major proportions. As Emerson had predicted he would, he antagonized the very people he should have been courting: the Ridder brothers and most of the non-Jewish members of the UGS, many of whom had not taken a public stand on the turn of events in Germany. More-

[37] Although the UGS canceled German Day, the Steuben Society of America sponsored a similar function on December 6, 1933. The major speakers were Ambassador Luther, Theodor Hoffmann, president of the Steuben Society, and Professor Arthur Remn, of Columbia University ("Der 'Deutsche Tag' in New York," clipping, German-American Bund Folder, Wiener Library, Institute of Contemporary History, London). The NSDAP's *Völkischer Beobachter* hailed the event as the start of a new day for Americans of German ancestry: "Grosse Deutschtumskundgebung in Neuyork, 25 000 Deutsch-Amerikaner grüssen die Heimat" (Dec. 10, 1933). A copy of the program can be found in container 17, RG 131. The indictment against Spanknöbel charged that he had not registered with the State Department as an agent of a foreign power, as prescribed in the Registration Act of June 17, 1917, and asserted that he was working "against the peace of the United States" (C 95–936, FRC). O. John Rogge, one-time special assistant to the United States attorney in charge of the wartime sedition cases, has written that Spanknöbel returned to Germany and became a general in the SS (*Official German Report*, p. 126). He returned, but there is no evidence that he became a general. The claim probably stems from wartime propaganda. Spanknöbel left the United States on the S.S. *Europa* (not the S.S. *Deutschland*, as claimed by some authors). The State Department notified the Foreign Ministry about the indictment; after some discussion with the Germans, the case was shelved but not dropped. Upon his return to Germany, he remained in the Party but never again held a post. (Spanknöbel to Kameradschaft-USA, March 11, 1939, T-81/139/176387). On Spanknöbel after his return to Germany, see Chapter 13 and Appendix III, below.

over, the Ridder brothers' articles about the Turnhalle incident put
the Bund in a highly unfavorable light in the eyes of some fifty
thousand readers. The Bundesleiter's behavior played right into
the hands of New York's Jewish leaders and journalists, who gave
it a maximum of news coverage. Dickstein, who had been collecting evidence for a congressional investigation of Nazi activities in
the United States, had to wait until January 3, 1934, the opening
day of the new Congress, to introduce a resolution authorizing the
formation of a special committee to probe into Nazi propaganda
activities in the United States. In March, Congress passed the resolution and provided funding for a House special committee to investigate un-American activities.

Reverberations were felt even in President Roosevelt's inner circle. On October 20, Harold Ickes, the Secretary of the Interior,
recorded in his diary that Frances Perkins, the Secretary of Labor,
had told him a "long, circumstantial and lurid story" of German intrigue. Germany, according to the account, had "several hundred
big men over here who have systematically joined the German societies, the control of which they are rapidly taking over." [38] Although the story had little basis in fact, it indicates the way the
Spanknöbel Affair was magnified. Inadvertently, Spanknöbel gave
the organizers of the boycott of German goods, Samuel Untermeyer, and Samuel Dickstein support for the allegation that Hitler
had sent hundreds of Nazi agents to the United States. As 1933
ended, hundreds became thousands. In New York City, the public's
imagination transformed German waiters and beer-hall owners into
Nazi spies. The Spanknöbel Affair gave Germany exactly the kind
of adverse publicity it least desired. Many large metropolitan dailies pictured Hitler as a contemptible demagogue, the leader of a
world-wide Nazi conspiracy bent on dominating the world.

Ironically, the entire episode might have been avoided. On September 23, two days before the second meeting of the UGS at the
Turnhalle, the Foreign Section of the NSDAP revoked Spanknöbel's
credentials and appointed the founder of the Teutonia Association,
Fritz Gissibl, to replace him as Bundesleiter. Although the news

[38] Harold Ickes, *The Secret Diary of Harold I. Ickes; I: The First Thousand
Days, 1933–1936* (New York, 1953), pp. 111–112.

could not have reached Spanknöbel before the second UGS meeting, there is no evidence to suggest that the recall was prompted by Spanknöbel's actions at the first UGS meeting, on the eighteenth.[39] Since the details of Spanknöbel's activities did not raise a storm of protest until the first week in October, it cannot be argued that the NSDAP was thoroughly dissatisfied with the Bundesleiter's recent work, even though Hess might have been dismayed by the revelation that non-Aryans were in the Friends of the New Germany. The decision was made for other reasons.

On May 24, 1933, Hitler had met with propaganda chief Goebbels and had placed him in charge of all overseas propaganda. In the ensuing months, Goebbels initiated many structural changes in Germany's propaganda network. On September 20, three days before the recall of Spanknöbel, Goebbels issued a document outlining his views on how the Nazi penetration of the Western Hemisphere could best be accomplished. The document, entitled "General Instructions for German Agents in North and South America," did not mention the Bund movement or Spanknöbel's name. Implicit in Goebbel's communication, however, was a condemnation of FONG's activities.[40]

Goebbels maintained that the World War had thoroughly crushed the German-American community and that Americans of German extraction had not yet "recovered full consciousness." The aim of German propaganda, he argued, was not forcibly to unify German nationals living in the United States, but to give German-Americans the impetus to come together voluntarily, and to reawaken their feeling of *Deutschtum*. Accordingly, the German element in America should not be bombarded with Nazi literature; racial awareness would have to be achieved by means of a "well-

[39] German Foreign Ministry to consulate (New York), Oct. 11, 1933, T-120/4616/269244.
[40] The document appears in translation in an article by Ernst Kris, "German Propaganda Instructions for 1933," *Social Research*, 9 (Feb. 1942), 46–81. Goebbels denied the authenticity of the document on November 18, 1933. The Alfred Hugenberg publishing house in Germany offered a reward of fifty thousand reichsmarks to anyone who could prove the authenticity of the so-called September instructions. On their use as a historical source, see Alton Frye's comments in *Nazi Germany and the American Hemisphere*, p. 21n.

camouflaged German propaganda network." Once German-Americans regained an awareness of their racial ancestry, he concluded, they would doubtless reassert themselves politically. Thus, just when Heinz Spanknöbel was inadvertently sabotaging Germany's aims in the United States, Goebbels was outlining a "grass roots" approach designed to achieve racial unification through infiltration and subtle propaganda.[41]

By the fall of 1933, then, two alternative—though not necessarily contradictory—methods of approaching Americans of German ancestry had emerged. On the one hand, men like Bohle, Hess, and Hoffmann hoped to create a German bloc in America favorable to Nazi Germany by using a broadly based, German-sponsored party or bund movement. On the other hand, Goebbels discounted the need for either a political party or a bund movement and favored a well-organized but camouflaged propaganda campaign directed at thousands of German-American organizations throughout the United States. Heinz Spanknöbel was a casualty of a realignment of Nazi policy in America. After his removal and the ensuing exposé of his activities, the NSDAP placed its hopes in a member of the Bund's old guard, Fritz Gissibl, a trusted Party stalwart who could be counted on to carry out the still vague policies of his superiors in Germany.

[41] Kris, "German Propaganda Instructions."

CHAPTER 5

The Friends of
the New Germany

Heinz Spanknöbel left a dual legacy. He provided the Bund movement with a nationwide structure and filled key party positions with trusted and dedicated National Socialists. His methods, however, combined with his activities in New York City, engendered internal confusion at Bund headquarters in Yorkville and gained for the American Nazi group unfavorable publicity. But Spanknöbel's questionable methods ought not to obscure the importance of his organizational abilities. Though his name was later expunged from the official history of the organization, the debt his successors owed to him cannot be overemphasized.

Before leaving the country, Spanknöbel even managed to hand-pick a successor, Ignatz Griebl, a clinical surgeon attached to Harlem Hospital, in New York City, and a member of the UGS.[1] With Griebl's appointment, the Bund entered its most troubled period. For more than a year, the group was shaken by intraparty revolts and splintered by secessionist movements. Journalists of the day and even the Bundists themselves did not believe that the organization could survive the confusion. But predictions of the movement's downfall were premature. The internecine fighting that followed Griebl's appointment was confined to the departmental headquarters in New York. Other regions experienced a period of stability and growth during the same period, beginning in the fall

[1] On Ignatz Griebl, see Appendix III, below. In the late 1920's, he was active in the UGS and was a close friend of the Reverend Popcke, of the Zion Lutheran Church. See also the *New York Times*, Nov. 21, 1933; and Ladislas Farago, *The Game of the Foxes* (New York, 1971), p. 20.

of 1933. In spite of the intraparty chaos, the Friends of the New
Germany spread to a dozen new cities and four new party newspapers appeared. In retrospect, it is clear that this was the gestation
period for the successor to the Friends of the New Germany, Fritz
Kuhn's Amerikadeutscher Volksbund which was founded in the
second half of the decade.[2]

Unaware of the movement's advances outside the New York metropolitan area, Bund member Karl Neumann wrote, "It is such a
pity that at the very moment when Germany is being reborn the
N.Y.C. Bund is in such a pitiful state." [3] Men like Neumann feared
that the movement was being undermined by dissension. Not all
the Bund's problems were internal. It will be recalled that after the
Spanknöbel Affair, Congressman Samuel Dickstein of New York
had opened preliminary hearings on Nazi activities in the United
States. In addition, the Spanknöbel incident had prompted the Justice Department and a New York grand jury to look into the
group's activities. Elisabeth Muller, a member of the Monticello,
New York, branch, commented, "The whole state is composed of
Jews and it is just like war-time—Germans are once again mis-
trusted." [4]

Bundists in New York City believed that the Jews were "out to
get them." Samuel Untermeyer, they argued, was instrumental in

[2] Fragmentary materials dealing with the organization's growth are in containers 5–37, RG 131. Of special importance are containers 6 (Detroit locals)
and 15–37 (New York and Newark, New Jersey). At this stage the group had
an estimated five thousand to six thousand members. This estimate is based on
the identification numbers assigned to new members after they entered the
Bund. Upon entering Kameradschaft-USA, former Bundists were required to
fill out an application form. They were required to enter the year they entered
the Friends of the New Germany or the Amerikadeutscher Volksbund and
their assigned registration numbers. See "Applications for Admittance,
1938–1941," in files of Kameradschaft-USA, T-81/140–142.

[3] Karl Neumann to Rolf Hoffmann, Jan. 23, 1934, T-81/27/24508.

[4] Elisabeth Muller to Rolf Hoffmann, Nov. 1, 1933, T-81/27/24761. The
staff at the German consulate in New York shared Muller's anxieties and also
likened the period to World War I; they hoped that New York Jewry's anti-
Nazi sentiment would not spread to other segments of the population (Kiep to
Foreign Ministry, Oct. 20, 1933, T-120/4616/269263–4). It is clear from the
papers of the consulate in New York that its staff had access to the transcript
of the proceedings of the Dickstein hearings *before* publication. Copies of gal-
ley proofs can be found in Kiep's papers, T-120/4616/269338ff.

furthering the counterboycott of German products, and Congressman Dickstein had threatened to put a stop to the supposed sedi-
tious behavior of the Bundists. Furthermore, the Bundists maintained that President Roosevelt was being advised by "court-Jews";
for example, Spanknöbel wrote Griebl that he had left the United
States because he could not bear the thought of being tried by
Jewish judges.[5] To add to the Bundists' fears, rumors were being
circulated in the immigrant German community: It was said that
the newly elected mayor of New York, Fiorello H. La Guardia, was
an "undercover agent for the Communists" who intended to appoint anti-Nazi Jews to high positions in the city administration;
that Joseph Goebbels was going to visit New York in an attempt to
unite the Bund movement against the Jews; and that Hitler's close
associate Ernst Hanfstaengl would shortly be selected as the new
Bundesleiter. The Bundists, in short, feared that the Jews would
use their influence to foment anti-German feeling and that the
NSDAP could do little to help the Bundists. Although many of
these suspicions were not without substance, some of the group's
troubles were caused by the changing international climate and
the Party's re-evaluation of the American situation.[6]

The dislocations that followed the Spanknöbel Affair may be explained in part by the uncertain international situation created by
Hitler's announcement on October 14 that Germany would leave
the League of Nations and had withdrawn from the disarmament
conference in Geneva, which had aroused mistrust of the new regime in world capitals, including Washington. Furthermore,
American diplomats registered a series of complaints about
Spanknöbel's activities with officials at the Foreign Ministry in
Berlin. Washington contended that since Spanknöbel was a German national, Germany was responsible for his actions. Moreover,

---

[5] Heinz Spanknöbel to Ignatz Griebl, letter in *New York Times,* Oct. 31,
1933. Griebl's wife, Maria, refused to be questioned by U.S. Attorney George
Z. Medalie before a federal grand jury; she claimed that as "an American citizen I have the right to be questioned by a gentile district attorney or judge."
Medalie was Jewish (Rogge, *Official German Report,* p. 21).

[6] Rolf Hoffmann Papers, Oct.–Nov. 1933, T-81/27. On Hanfstaengl, see
Charles Pichel to Rolf Hoffmann, Nov. 19, 1933, T-81/27/24558–9. Cf.
T-120/4614/269660–664.

Germany was responsible for the actions of members of the
NSDAP living in the United States. The Foreign Ministry expressed agreement and in October informed Ambassador Dodd
that, after a discussion with Bohle, it was decided that Party members in the Bund would confine their activities to the nonpolitical
arena, that only German nationals would belong to the Nazi Party,
and that the leadership of the Bund would go to an American citizen.[7]

The decision to give the leadership of the Friends of the New
Germany to an American citizen was a compromise between the
more traditionally oriented diplomats in the Wilhelmstrasse and
the Party's foreign-policy planners. The traditionalists maintained
that the NSDAP's support of a Nazi organization on American soil
was a diplomatic liability that would lead to a rift between Washington and Berlin. Hess and Bohle, on the other hand, argued that
a strong, Americanized pro-German movement in the United States
would be a boon to German-American diplomatic relations. Hess
contended that the one way to correct Germany's deteriorating
image in America was for Berlin to support the Bund. Hess did
not, however, challenge the Wilhelmstrasse's allegation that the
Bund was a disruptive factor in German-American relations. He
agreed that the Bund in its present state was a liability; but he
claimed that the entire overseas German community lacked organization and direction because too many government agencies and
Party ministries were competing for control of ethnic German affairs. The result was confusion, as evidenced by the history of the
Bund. In a belated effort to rectify this situation (which was by no
means confined to the United States), Hess created the Volksdeutscher Rat on October 27, 1933, and placed Karl Haushofer at
its head. In theory, this new coordinating body had jurisdiction
over all matters relating to Germans living overseas, with the ulti-

[7] Memorandum of Senior Counselor A. Fuehr, Foreign Ministry, Oct. 16,
1933, *DGFP*, C, II, 5–6; dispatch to consul general (New York), Oct. 16,
1933, T-120/4617/269246. In a telegram to Kiep, Fuehr stated that the activities of Party members in the United States were "downright dangerous"—
reflecting the Foreign Ministry's view of the Bund and Nazi German activities
at this juncture (telegram no. 109, Oct. 19, 1933, T-120/4617/269243).

mate decision-making power resting with Hitler.[8] The traditionalists in the Wilhelmstrasse argued that the Ethnic German Council should serve as an advisory rather than a policy-making body of the Foreign Ministry. In an effort to avoid further alienating Germany's traditional instrument of foreign policy, Hess temporarily accepted the Foreign Ministry's arguments.

Germany's decision to "Americanize" the Bund suggests that the NSDAP wanted to disassociated itself, at least temporarily, from the overseas group. Meanwhile, Hess and his subordinates could formulate a concrete policy concerning its future and the degree of German involvement. Hess, then, was able to placate both the traditionalists at home and irate members of the State Department in Washington.

Heinz Spanknöbel's appointment of Griebl suggests that the disgraced Bundesleiter believed that the American government would tolerate a pro-Nazi movement if it were directed by an American citizen. Griebl was a naturalized citizen of German birth. Thus he also had the qualifications specified in the Foreign Ministry's memorandum to Dodd. He counted among his closest friends some of the leaders of the prestigious United German Societies of Greater New York. Nevertheless, Spanknöbel's choice of a successor was a major miscalculation: Griebl did not receive Hess's approval. Hess wanted the Bund to "Americanize," but only along the lines dictated by the Party. Besides doubting Spanknöbel's judgment, Hess questioned whether Germany could control Spanknöbel's appointee; in late 1933, the coordination of all foreign activities under the NSDAP was of cardinal importance. Instead of accepting the deposed Bundesleiter's choice as a *fait accompli*, Hess asked Bohle to select Spanknöbel's replacement. It seems that the Party had other plans for Griebl. He was later recruited by the German spy net-

---

[8] Record of a decision by Rudolf Hess, Munich, Oct. 27, 1933, *DGFP*, C, II, 49. On the negative reaction of the Foreign Ministry, see Memorandum to Various Departments by the Foreign Ministry, Nov. 17, 1933, *DGFP*, C, II, 136, and D, VIII, doc. 523, n. 2. A history of the Volksdeutscher Rat can be found in Jacobsen, *Nationalsozialistische Aussenpolitik*, pp. 160ff; on the relationship of the VR to other State and Party agencies, see p. 185.

work and allegedly became a transmitter of classified American defense secrets.[9]

It will be recalled that Fritz Gissibl was the NSDAP's choice to be the new Bundesleiter. When he assumed the leadership, he was still a German national and a Party member—in direct contradiction to the Foreign Ministry's promise to Dodd. Gissibl managed to circumvent the stipulation about citizenship in a manner that became a model for other Party people to follow. The NSDAP suspended Gissibl's membership in the Party so that it could claim he had withdrawn. It was to be reactivated when he returned to Germany in the spring of 1936. Gissibl also began naturalization proceedings, although he never had any intention of completing the process. Through such devious tactics, Bohle and Hess could claim that an "American" was leading the Bund and that German nationals holding Party membership had withdrawn. During the two-year period following Gissibl's appointment, about three hundred Party members followed this route.[10] For the moment, at least, Hess and Bohle had resolved a twofold problem: they had quieted the diplomatic furor aroused by the presence of a Nazi organization in the United States, and they had "Americanized" the Friends

[9] It is clear from Fritz Gissibl's correspondence that he had little use for Griebl and made his feelings clear to Nazi officials. See T-120/5177/455040; 455044–5; 455047. According to Farago (*The Game of the Foxes*, pp. 20–26), Griebl offered his services to Goebbels in a letter dated March 3, 1934. Later that year, Griebl was recruited by the Abwehr (the intelligence section of the German armed forces) and undertook several espionage missions in America. An affirmation of Gissibl's appointment was made February 13, 1934 (NSDAP to German Embassy, Feb. 13, 1934, T-120/4616/269421–22).

[10] Schatzmeister Schneider (AO) to Reichsschatzmeister Schwarz, "Ruhen der Mitgliedschaft für Parteigenossen in USA, 2. März, 1935," T-81/146/185108–110. Cf. "Mitglieder der Kameradschaft mit amerikanischer Staatsangehörigkeit," Sept. 28, 1939, T-81/142/179962–180020. It should be added that many Bundists did withdraw from the Party; it is not known how many. Gissibl told the McCormack-Dickstein Committee that he had withdrawn from the NSDAP (statement of Fritz Gissibl, *NP*, pp. 62ff). During the next six years, several hundred members of the Bund completed the naturalization process. In 1942, the United States government initiated denaturalization proceedings against Fritz Kuhn and nineteen of his followers. (See Chapter 13, below, and Justice D. J. Bright, "Opinion," *US* v. *Fritz Julius Kuhn and Nineteen Other Cases*, Civ. 18–415, FRC.)

of the New Germany. Ironically, Samuel Dickstein, Samuel Untermeyer, and the New York grand jury became unwitting catalysts
of a major shift in Nazi policy toward the Bund.

Gissibl's appointment unexpectedly found the Bund with two
Bundesleiters, Gissibl and Griebl. Gissibl claimed that he was the
duly appointed leader and that his opponent had neither the credentials nor the authority to command. In turn, Griebl insisted
that his appointment, conferred by Spanknöbel, was valid. Griebl's
case was weak, but he had no desire to relinquish the position to
Gissibl. His supporters included the "remaining close friends and
supporters of the notorious Heinz Spanknöbel," many of whom
feared that they too would lose key positions in the group should
Gissibl assume the leadership.[11] By the end of October, the division in the New York City section of the Bund was becoming all
too apparent. But Gissibl was determined to prevent an intraparty
power struggle, which could result in more unfavorable publicity
and, perhaps, in the creation of two competing bunds.

In late October, Gissibl left New York for Chicago.[12] There is
reason to believe that before leaving, he met with his trusted advisers, and perhaps even with representatives of the consulate, to
plan a smear campaign designed to discredit Griebl. In short
order, Gissibl's followers circulated a rumor that Griebl was married to a Jewess. (Actually, he was married to a Catholic, the
former Maria Ganz, an Austrian nurse he had met while serving on
the Italian front in the World War.) Within days, the rumor grew:
not only was Griebl married to a Jewess, he was also a Freemason,
a Catholic, and a Communist. Within a few days, pressure was
brought to bear on Griebl, and he was forced to relinquish his position. In light of Griebl's future service to Germany, the rumor
campaign may have been nothing more than a smoke screen to
push Griebl underground so to speak. At any rate, for the NSDAP
and Bund members in the United States, Fritz Gissibl was the
Bundesleiter of the National Socialist German Workers' Party in

[11] Charles Pichel to Rolf Hoffmann, Nov. 26, 1933, T-81/27/24557.
[12] Rolf Hoffmann to Fritz Gissibl, Oct. 21, 1933, T-81/27/24234.

the United States.[13] With Gissibl in command, the NSDAP wanted a clear statement of the Bund's purposes and aims. For months the Hamburg office of the Party's Overseas Press Office had been asking the Bund to send a Party program. Finally, on November 16, 1933, an eleven-page document outlining the underlying principles of the movement was mailed to Rolf Hoffmann.

For the first time in its history, the Nazi movement in America had been forced to ask itself, What does the Bund movement stand for? Although in each phase the Bund has issued countless pamphlets, handbills, leaflets, and newspapers that indicated its aims and purposes, the document "Das neue Deutschland—Was geht es uns an? ("The New Germany—Why Is It Our Concern?") was the first explicit declaration it issued.[14] This statement claimed that the Bund was a defensive movement organized by concerned German nationals to protect themselves from the Jewish-Bolshevik menace and to inform the American public of events in Germany. The document justified the Bund's formation on the ground that the daily press was in the hands of "eastern Jews" who were fabricating lies about Hitler and distorting the significance of the New Germany. The first purpose of the Friends of the New Germany, therefore, was to provide the American people with an objective look at Hitler's Germany, to expose American Jewry as the tool of Moscow, and to protect the German and German-American community.

In a broader sense, the group's purpose was to awaken American *Deutschtum* to its blood-dictated responsibilities. The author of the

[13] The smear campaign was quite effective. Proof of racial purity was a prerequisite for entrance into the NSDAP. About similar smear campaigns, see Karl Neumann to Rolf Hoffman, Feb. 2, 1934, T-81/27/24498; and Charles Pichel to Hoffmann, Feb. 2, 1934, T-81/27/24554–6.

[14] Hans Winterhalder, "Das neue Deutschland—Was geht es uns an?" Nov. 1933, T-81/27/24732–41. Winterhalder was born in Germany in 1894 and entered the United States in 1929. As early as September 1933, Rolf Hoffmann had requested Spanknöbel to send a party platform. After Gissibl took over the group, Hoffmann requested him to send a program. On October 31, 1933, Gissibl wrote Hoffmann, "Our program has not been published. . . . Please be patient." It seems that Gissibl had nothing to do with its ireparation, since it was mailed from California (T-81/27/24110; 24234; 24235).

declaration of principles, Hans Winterhalder, declared that a large majority of the American people were part of a world-wide Aryan community; that is, the Germans and the Anglo-Saxons were united through blood. Despite the size of "racially correct America," however, the United States was controlled politically and economically by six hundred thousand Jews and *Mischlinge* (literally mongrels, or people of mixed blood—in Nazi usage, the offspring of marriages between Jews and Christians). The problem faced by the Bund was to reverse this imbalance by awakening Americans to their racial-political responsibilities.[15]

The author of the Bund program constructed his argument on the premise that political and economic power had to be commensurate with the historical contribution of a racial group to the development of a nation: since the Germans had made extraordinary contributions to America's growth and constituted at least a third of the population, they were entitled to a greater share of the political and economic power. History and destiny, therefore, demanded that they organize to obtain what rightfully belonged to them. Moreover, since American *Deutschtum* had resisted the forces of cultural amalgamation and had remained racially pure, they were the only racial group fit to rule. They alone had successfully resisted conforming to the Anglo-Saxon model, with its emphasis on the melting-pot philosophy (which this document labeled a Jewish invention; "melting pot" connoted cultural, not racial, amalgamation). Thus, although the author conceded that Anglo-Saxons were the racial counterparts of Germans, he barred them from entering the movement under present circumstances. To be sure, the fates of both groups were linked, and both shared the common goals of ousting the Jews from their entrenched positions and of awakening all Americans to the Jewish-Bolshevik menace. Should they fail, the Jews and their still unawakened allies, the millions of downtrodden Blacks, would consolidate their power, Bolshevize the nation, and convert it into a vast Jewish citadel.

This remarkable document was more than a summation of the Bund's previous propaganda activities; it was an outline of the

[15] "Das neue Deutschland—Was geht es uns an?"

future direction of the movement. Racial anti-Semitism, racial-politics, the Jewish-Communist equation, the specter of the Black terror, and the vague and still undefined argument for what some Nazi racial theorists called "minority group rights" became permanent features of the Bund's *Weltanschauung.* Although future Bund leaders and propagandists would redefine and manipulate this core of beliefs, the organization's ideological orientation remained essentially unaltered for the next five years. Thus, not only had Heinz Spanknöbel structured the Bund on the national level by the fall of 1933, but the group's ideological bent also was fixed by then.[16]

Admittedly, the document was a propaganda piece. But it digested the views of most Bundists, and it served as a guideline for the organization's propagandists. At the same time, it quieted Hoffmann, who wanted a statement of purpose. At this stage in the group's development, its leaders were under no delusions concerning the Bund's appeal; Fritz Gissibl and Walter Kappe were well aware that the Friends of the New Germany was made up of German nationals and that most German-Americans were wisely eschewing involvement. In New York City, the center of the movement, Spanknöbel's poorly timed and ill-conceived attempt to take over the old-line German-American societies did little to endear the Bund to Yorkville's notables. In the months that followed his clash with Victor Ridder, the Bund floundered; decisions were made as *ad hoc* responses to unexpected situations.

In the late fall and early winter of 1933, the Bund experienced a turn in its fortunes. With the help of Colonel Emerson and his friends at the German consulate, the Bundists became involved with the German-American Business League (Deutschamerikanischer Wirtschaftsausschuss, or DAWA). Actually, DAWA was an organization created by German-American businessmen to counteract the Jewish boycott of German-made products marketed in their stores; only in 1935 did it become a permanent subdivision of the Bund. The staff at the consulate and Emerson felt that the

[16] Other examples of propaganda distributed by the Friends of the New Germany can be found in containers 17, 37, 159, and "Scrapbooks," in Records and Papers of Deutsches Haus, containers 1–24, RG 131.

best way to involve the Bundists was as "sandwich men" and bully boys in the struggle against New York Jewry and its anti-Nazi allies; on the other hand, the Bundists viewed their involvement with DAWA as a means of expressing their obsessive anti-Semitism in concrete action and of effecting a new beginning in their relationship with Yorkville's German community.[17]

Prior to Hitler's take-over, most members of Yorkville's business community were small proprietors, lower-class and middle-class owners of specialty shops in Manhattan's East Eighties. In general, they catered to German-speaking customers, and their stores carried such items as *Apfelmus* (applesauce) and *Wurst* (sausage). In Yorkville and across the East River in Ridgewood and Richmond Hill, Queens, they represented to the German community a little of the old country. With the start of the boycott, some small shopkeepers joined the Bund; others remained aloof from the Bund but joined DAWA, which they viewed as a protective shield against the damaging boycott. Members of the League displayed its seal on their shop windows, organized their own boycott of Jewish-owned businesses (which were usually on the same block), circulated several commercial bulletins, and distributed handouts urging Americans to "Buy German" and "Patronize Aryan Stores Only." But most of the hard work was reserved for Bundists, who served as sandwich men, walking up and down the streets of New York with heavy advertising boards hung from their shoulders, one before and one behind. The message was simple: "Tell me, where

[17] In Yorkville, there was also the German-American Board of Commerce (founded in the 1920's), which was involved in the boycott. It published the *German-American Economic Bulletin* and the *German-American Commerce Bulletin*. By the middle of the decade, consulate personnel had taken charge of the Board of Commerce. A list of DAWA-affiliated stores, "D.A.W.A. Christmas Trade Guide," can be found in container 210, RG 131. "Program of D.A.W.A. Sponsored Anti-Boycott Meeting," Oct. 11, 1934, also lists members (container 17). See also "Correspondence of the German-American Board of Trade," containers 215–222. On the role played by the German consulate, see T-120/5179/456189 and T-120/1141/442089–91. On DAWA's role in the German Day, 1934, activities, see "German Day/Deutscher Tag 1934, October 6. Festprogramm," *NSDAP Hauptarchiv* Collection, 35, folder 696. Among the speakers at this program were Consul Hans Borchers and the German author Hans Grimm. Grimm's address was later published in his *Amerikanische Rede* (Munich, 1936).

do you shop and we'll tell you who you are!" [18] "Boycott the Boy-
cotters!" became the motto they hoped to see adopted nationally.
In some sections of the city, DAWA enjoyed initial success. But
the group's objective—to offset economic losses—suffered a
series of setbacks when some Bundists attempted to convert
DAWA's activities into virtual shakedowns of Jewish shop owners,
who called the police.

At any rate, the League responded to an immediate economic
need and provided the Bundists with an opportunity to work with
some of the very people they had offended during the Spanknöbel
Affair. Then, too, the involvement with DAWA gave the Bundists
an air of respectability and permitted them to represent themselves
as defenders of the small German businessman, who, they argued,
was being subjected to unjust discrimination. In April 1934, the
Bund published an open letter to President Roosevelt, asking him
to condemn the counter-boycott: "We ask with all due respect to
you, the President of the United States, to take whatever steps in
your power to prevent the continuation of this boycott which we
feel is an insult and humiliation to all loyal Americans of German
origin." [19] The Bundists saw themselves and those they assumed to
be their cousins, the German-Americans, as victims of Jewish invidiousness and racial discrimination. Together with racial anti-
semitism, the theme of the "persecuted minority," apparent in
DAWA and Bund literature, became the staple of the Nazi viewpoint in America.[20]

Throughout late 1933 and on into 1934, members of the Bund
carried on propaganda about the plight of the businessmen and
made firmer the group's ideological orientation. The Americanization of the group envisioned by the NSDAP meant an adjustment
of Nazi ideology to what the Bundists considered the realities in
American life. The Bundists were obsessive anti-Semites and saw
the Nazi swastika as a race symbol, not a Party emblem.[21] Never

[18] *Deutsche Zeitung*, May 19, 1934, p. 3.

[19] *Ibid.*, April 4, 1934, p. 2; Feb. 24, 1934, p. 5.

[20] "Fragmentary Records of the German American Bund," container 159, file
2, RG 131.

[21] *Deutsche Zeitung*, Aug. 4, 1934, p. 8. See also Edwin Emerson, "Lest Us
Forget," *ibid.*, Dec. 8, 1934.

again, wrote the national editor of Bund publications, Walter
Kappe, would the German element in the United States conform to
the dictates of the dominant Jew-ridden Anglo-Saxon culture: "To
give America our souls, as many of our fellow countrymen have
done, nobody can ask of us; to become German-American *mongrels,* who do not know where they belong, nobody can ask of us;
WE ARE AND REMAIN GERMANS. GERMANS *IN* AMER-
ICA." [22]

Those Americans who had German blood were expected to think
of themselves as Germans *in* the United States and to drop the hyphen forever. In this assertion lies the key to the ideological evolution of the Bund since the founding of Teutonia in October 1924.
Before Hitler's appointment as Chancellor, NSDAP members and
Teutonia's old guard in America had geared their appeal solely to
newly arrived Germans. After January 1933, and especially after
Spanknöbel was appointed Bundesleiter and Emerson assumed
control of the group's American section, the efforts of the Bund
were directed not only at disenchanted German immigrants but
also at Americans of German ancestry. In accordance with the dictates of National Socialism, the Bund's mission was to make all
Americans of German extraction aware of their Germanness and
their obligation to Germany. Walter Kappe maintained that German-Americans need not feel that they were compromising their
allegiance to the United States, "because one can be a good American and also be a good German." [23] But in spite of Kappe's assertion and Berlin's constant reiteration that "National Socialism was
not an article for export," [24] the Bund demanded of its members
complete acceptance of its aims and of the foreign and internal
goals of German National Socialism. These supranational demands
were, according to Samuel Dickstein and some of his colleagues,
incompatible with American citizenship.

At this stage, the Jews held a special place in the Bund's fixed
view of the world. Since many Bundists were recently arrived Ger-

[22] Walter Kappe, "America and WE," *ibid.,* n.d., clipping, Greenberg
Collection, Vol. IV, Archives, YIVO Institute.

[23] Walter Kappe, "Unsere Aufgabe in Amerika," *Das neue Deutschland,*
Oct. 16, 1933, p. 3.

[24] "Der Nationalsozialismus in Deutschland ist kein Exportartikel."

man nationals who had settled in New York, they believed that
that city represented in microcosm the whole of the United States.
Although most of New York's several million Jews were members
of the lower middle class or struggling factory workers in the gar-
ment and other industries, the Bundists always singled out a handful of wealthy Jews as representatives of the "cunning race." Invariably, the Jews were depicted as loud, pushy, money-grubbing
tools of Moscow who had an innate hatred of the Germans. The
caricatures in Bund literature dehumanized the Jews. Relying on
existing stereotypes, Bundists portrayed Jews as short and stocky,
with bulging eyes—a people motivated by lust, greed, and a desire
for money. Although the Bundists continuously maligned Justice
Louis Brandeis, Henry Morgenthau, and the President's other
"Jewish friends," they reserved a special hatred for Congressman
Dickstein. The New York congressman was depicted as the incarnation of evil—a Satanic Bolshevik who, as one Bundist wrote,
"was a loud-mouthed Jew with a talent for making the *Goyim* [a
derogatory word used by some Jews to connote supposed "non-
Jewish" attributes] Jew-conscious." Dickstein was America's number one "German hater." [25] This willful dehumanization of the Jews
took on a particularly insidious turn after the start of the McCormack-Dickstein investigation into the Bund's internal affairs in
1934. Each issue of the Bund newspapers carried a section entitled
"Hebraica," which reflected Nazi humor: "What is the main characteristic of the Jewish exodus from our Germany? A bad smell!
No wonder they had to leave!" [26]

Thus, the ideology of the Friends of the New Germany was a
copy of that of the Nazi Party, adapted to a new environment. Its
long-range purpose was to unify German-America along the lines
outlined in the document sent to Rolf Hoffmann to produce a

[25] *Deutsche Zeitung,* Jan. 4, 1934, April 14, 1934; "Dickstein," *Das neue
Deutschland,* Sept. 16, 1933; "Das Deutschtum Erwacht!" *ibid.,* Aug. 31,
1933. Dickstein was the archetype of evil—"Dickstein means business and
he is out to get us," wrote Bundist Gustav Guellich to Rolf Hoffmann
(T-81/27/24275–83). Cf. papers of German consulate, New York, fall–winter
1933–1934, T-120/4616/269495ff.
[26] *Deutscher Beobachter,* Nov. 20, 1934. The paper's motto—"Für ein ei-
niges Deutschtum in Amerika und der Heimat"—was adopted by Fritz Kuhn
as the official motto of his group.

"united Germandom" (*Einigung des Deutschtums*) that would counteract and eventually replace the Jews and Marxists who were running the nation. Its immediate goal was to combat the unfavorable impression of the New Germany that Americans were getting from those who "rake the gutters for filth to fling at the Germans." [27]

From its inception, the Bund maintained a party press to disseminate its views. Beginning with the first edition of the *Deutsche Zeitung* (not to be confused with Fürholzer's German-language paper of the same name published in the late 1920's) to the last edition of Fritz Kuhn's *Deutscher Weckruf und Beobachter*, later in the decade, Bund newspapers received some of their copy directly from Germany.[28] Under Kappe's guidance, the *Deutsche Zeitung*'s message was made to conform with the views outlined in Hans Winterhalder's document. The *Deutsche Zeitung*, which first appeared on the newsstands in Yorkville in late August 1933, made no attempt to compete with other German-language publications for circulation. In fact, although the group had the avowed purpose of unifying the German-American community, the newspaper was at first distributed only in German immigrant sections. It was more widely distributed when Kappe adopted the dual-language (English-German) format of Colonel Emerson's defunct newspaper, *Die Bruecke*, which had gone out of circulation in July 1933.

The *Deutsche Zeitung* described itself as "A Fighting Paper for Truth and Right—A Bridge between the United States and Germany." The paper's editors claimed it was the defender of Germany's interests in America and the official transmission belt of Nazi ideology to Americans of German ancestry. Almost every issue published an exposé of the supposed enemies of the Third Reich. Kappe requested and received news items, cartoons, comic strips, and photographs, as well as articles, from the Overseas Press Office. The materials selected for the newspaper were character-

[27] *Ibid.*, Dec. 1, 1934, p. 4.
[28] Kiep to Foreign Ministry, Aug. 18, 1933; telegram to Kiep, Sept. 1, 1933, T-120/4616/269169; 269197. On the financial problems of the *Deutsche Zeitung*, see Frye, pp. 53–54.

ized neither by subtlety nor by any attempt to disguise their place of origin.[29] There were two distinct types of articles: one attempted to tell the truth about the German situation, to combat the lies in the world press; the second attempted to frighten German-Americans and German immigrants into joining the Bund movement.

It is clear from letters written by members of the Friends of the New Germany that the Bundist version of the truth about Adolf Hitler and National Socialism did not in itself attract readers of the *Deutsche Zeitung* to the group. The lure of racial exclusiveness and the promise of a regenerated German-America had to be supplemented with something else. During the formative years of the movement (1933–1935), the Bund's propagandists attempted to revive or stimulate the lurking fear, felt by some Americans of German extraction, of a possible revival of the World War period's nativism, or "pure Americanism." [30] This time, however, the propagandists predicted that anti-German feeling would be more violent, because the Jews and *Mischlinge* controlled Washington. The activities of Congressman Dickstein and the initiation of the boycott intensified this fear. The Bund's chief propagandist, Walter Kappe, predicted that anti-German activity would have two distinct phases. First, the Jews would use their influence in Washington to initiate an investigation of the Nazi propaganda network in the United States. At this juncture, he said, Americans of German ancestry would be branded as agents of a foreign power bent on destroying the American system of government. Once that phase of anti-German activity was over, the government would label all Germans potential traitors and take steps to deport them. Kappe concluded that the only way for German-Americans to insulate themselves from the predicted "Jewish pogrom" was to flock en masse to the Bund movement, since the organization was prepared to defend and protect the race. Only a "united Germandom" could

[29] Walter Kappe to Rolf Hoffmann, Jan. 19, 1934, T-81/27/24669. Much of the material was translated into English by Colonel Emerson, who was paid by the German consulate (T-120/4614/269217–8; 269417). Topical articles in other Bund newspapers included "The Survival Prospect of the Jewish Tribal Group," *Deutscher Beobachter,* July 18, 1935; and "Christianity and Sterilization," *ibid.,* June 6, 1935.

[30] Kiep to Foreign Ministry, April 18, 1933, T-120/4616/269120.

combat and destroy those who were bent on the destruction of the German people, that is, the Jews and the Communists. Kappe reiterated Hans Winterhalder's assertion that Anglo-Saxons would eventually see the merits of racial politics and join the Germans to establish a new America—an America based upon the teachings of Adolf Hitler. It was the Germans, however, who were destined to reinvigorate and cleanse the United States, as Hitler had reinvigorated Germany.[31]

I. Meeting of the Friends of the New Germany: (1) George Froboese, (2) Fritz Gissibl, (3) Hermann Schwinn, (4) Fritz Julius Kuhn. (National Archives.)

In their attempts to frighten German-Americans, Bund propagandists capitalized on anti-Negro sentiment as well as on threats of Jewish revenge. In an article entitled "Black Danger—The Red Plague," Negroes were portrayed as black parasites, given to rapine and lust and bent on the defilement of the pure Germanic race. The Negroes' natural allies were the Jews, who were attempting to

[31] *Deutscher Beobachter*, Dec. 1, 1934, p. 2.

transmit Bolshevism to the millions of downtrodden blacks. The anonymous author concluded that the Jews were using the un-tapped reservoir of Blacks to consolidate their political and eco-nomic control of the United States.[32] Compared with the quantity of virulent anti-Semitic propaganda issued by the Bund, diatribes against the Negroes were limited in number during these years. Surprisingly, the Bundists did not fully exploit America's racial problem until the late 1930's; their energies were directed against the Jews.

In addition to National Socialist ideology, each issue of the Bund's newspapers carried news of new party branches and cells, sports news from Germany, timetables and program schedules for New York City's German-language radio station, and announce-ments of Bund functions. On May 10, 1935, for example, the *Deutscher Beobachter* informed its readers that Julius Streicher's *Der Stürmer* was on sale in Yorkville, and that three of the latest films from Germany (*Der erste Mai 1934, Der Tag von Potsdam,* and *Königin Luise*) would appear shortly in the New York area.[33] Thus, the press was used to recruit the rank and file. In addition, the Bund's leaders used other methods. During the Chicago re-cruiting campaign in November and December 1933, for example, cultural rather than strictly political propaganda was used.[34] On November 16, the Second German and American Book Exhibition opened at the establishment of Scheun & Co., book distributors. This exhibit of the latest books from Germany had been organized jointly by Peter Gissibl (Fritz's brother) and the consul general in Chicago. Displays were carefully arranged to include works with both political and nonpolitical themes: Hitler's *Mein Kampf* was balanced with W. Reinhardt's *The Life of George Washington* and W. Langewiesche's *The American Adventure;* F. Schulz's *The De-*

[32] "Schwarze Gefahr—Rote Pest (Negerproblem)," *ibid.*, Aug. 15, 1935, p. 1; Julius Streicher, "Das Geheimnis des Blutes," *ibid.*, Dec. 8, 1935.

[33] Motion pictures were provided by the German consulate in New York City (German Embassy to consulate, April 14, 1934, T-120/4616/269762). A limited number of copies of Streicher's *Der Stürmer* and the Party's *Völkischer Beobachter* were on sale on newsstands in Yorkville in the 1930's.

[34] "Aufruf an die Deutschten in Amerika—Auch ich habe meine Pflicht getan?" handout, n.d., *NSDAP Hauptarchiv* Collection, 35, folder 396.

cline of Marxism was flanked by *The Amateur Photographer* and
Dessoir's *Collection of German Songs and Piano Music*.[35] After examining the books, each visitor was given a pamphlet with a greeting from Joseph Goebbels on its cover. Inside was a list of the
books on display. Visitors were requested: "Vote for the Book You
Liked Best." They were also invited to a Bund meeting the following week. Thus, in addition to capitalizing on fear and stressing
the merits of National Socialism with its emphasis on *völkisch*
unity, Bund propagandists used a variety of cultural attractions to
rekindle the feelings of *Deutschtum* among those whom Kappe
called the lost generations of Germans.

A small but cohesive Nazi movement had come into being by
January 1934. The movement's unwavering support of Germany, insistence that Germans in the United States would be victimized by
Jewish intrigue, and efforts to dehumanize world Jewry have been
well documented. But who were the Bundists? Were they, as Dickstein and several popular magazines asserted, social outcasts,
thugs, and misfits, or were these epithets the result of wishful thinking, of a highly subjective interpretation of a seemingly irrational
movement which had been carried by German nationals and members of the NSDAP to America?

During these early years, the Bundists did not keep an elaborate
dossier on each member and, therefore, did not leave much documentation. Between 1933 and 1935, membership fluctuated between an estimated five thousand and six thousand. During this
period, the leadership and rank and file were composed of several
distinct types of Germans: German nationals who were members of
the NSDAP, German nationals who were not members of the
NSDAP, naturalized Germans, and native-born Americans of German extraction. The first group provided the nucleus around which
the Bund was built. The NSDAP's initiation of suspended membership accelerated the tendency for Party members to become leaders in the movement.[36] In April 1934, for example, of twenty-six

---

[35] "The Second German and American Book Exhibit, Scheun & Co., November 16–December 26, 1933" in correspondence between Scheun & Co.,
the German consulate (Chicago), and Peter Gissibl, T-81/394/513464ff.

[36] See note 10, above.

men who had suspended membership in the NSDAP, not one attained a position lower than that of commander in the group's fighting division (OD). Moreover, most—if not all—Party members who had held leadership positions in the Teutonia or Gau-USA remained in the new Bund, as is evident from a comparison of NSDAP records with membership lists of the Bund and from the testimony of individual Bundists. Exactly how many NSDAP members held concurrent membership in FONG is unknown, but one list compiled in the mid-1930's listed several hundred names. Admittedly, this was a partial listing, since it included only those who had been "suspended" from the NSDAP.[37]

German nationals who had arrived in the postwar period and were not members of the NSDAP and recently naturalized citizens born in Germany made up the most important part of the membership of FONG, the rank and file. A generous estimate would place their number at four thousand or five thousand. The lines of demarcation between these categories are blurred. Many of them had started on the road to naturalization or were already American citizens when they entered the organization.

The rank and file were remarkably similar in place of origin, age, purpose, and vocational background. In general, those who had arrived in the United States during the 1920's were Catholics from the German states of Baden, Bavaria, and Württemberg. Most of these men and women had intended to make America a permanent homeland; but with the re-emergence of Germany as a world power and the development of what they believed was the beginning of an anti-German campaign, many decided to return home in the late 1930's. These people, the *Rückwanderer* (returnees), belonged to the Bund until they left America. Upon their arrival in Germany, they joined Kameradschaft-USA, founded by

---

[37] "Liste der Parteigenossen aus USA," and "Parteigenossen in USA, welche aus der NSDAP austraten, um im Bund 'Freund des neuen Deutschland,' weiterhin tätig sein zu können," in files of Reichsschatzmeister der NSDAP, Schwarz, T-81/148/185888ff. This roll deals with the NSDAP court trials and hearings requested by members of the Bund upon their return to Germany. Members with "suspended membership" wanted their original NSDAP numbers, since a low number was a prestige symbol indicating one had joined early.

Fritz Gissibl after his return to Germany in 1936 to accommodate returning Bundists.[38] Their applications for membership in Kameradschaft-USA give ample evidence of similar biographies and characteristics. When the data for two hundred returnees were compared with materials compiled by the House Committee to Investigate Un-American Activities, the Justice Department, and a study sponsored by the American Council on Public Affairs, remarkably consistent pictures of the German nationals and recently naturalized citizens in the Bund emerged. Clearly, this methodology is a sociological short cut, and the findings are by no means conclusive about the membership of the Bund. But for the time being, the limitations imposed by insufficient documentation preclude the possibility of making a more systematic study.[39]

In an article entitled "The Genesis of Fascism," George Mosse maintained that fascism was a "movement of youth." [40] The cadres of the Belgian Rexists, the Italian *fasci,* the German SA, and the Iron Guard were composed of men in their early twenties and thirties; and although the contemporary picture of Hitler and Mussolini is of old and broken men, this image was born during World War II. We tend to forget that Hitler was forty-four in 1933, and that Mussolini was thirty-nine when he became Prime Minister. These relatively young men were epitomes of the entire movement: Nazism and fascism at their inception were movements of youth, especially in the United States. In 1924, for example, the founders of the Teutonia Association were in their early twenties.[41] Ten years later, the mean age of the German nationals and recently natural-

[38] Arthur Smith, Jr., "The Kameradschaft-USA," *Journal of Modern History,* 34 (Dec. 1962), 398–408.

[39] Folders of Zentrale der Kameradschaft-Stuttgart, T-81/139–140/175985–177114; 142/180242ff; 144/183963–184204; Donald Strong, *Organized Anti-Semitism in America* (Washington, D.C., 1941); membership materials in German-American Bund Collection, RG 131; information available in the collection of the ADL.

[40] George Mosse, "The Genesis of Fascism," *Journal of Contemporary History,* 1 (1966), 14–26.

[41] Fritz Gissibl (b. 1903), Walter Kappe (b. 1905), Josef (Sepp) Schuster (b. 1904), Paul Manger (b. 1897), Heinz Spanknöbel (b. 1893).

ized Bundists was thirty.[42] Moreover, these Bundists had been in the United States less than eight years.[43]

Almost all of the future returnees were unmarried when they left Germany, a fact which may be explained by the unprecedented social and economic dislocations they had experienced in the immediate postwar period. At the time of their repatriation, most of the subjects were married and had at least one child.

Why they joined the Bund movement in the United States is part of a larger question. For over three decades scholars have been dissecting the so-called fascist mentality in an effort to discover why people gravitate to the extreme right of the political spectrum. Why did one individual join a right-wing extremist group while another did not? In an attempt to find an answer to this question, scholars have focused on the National Socialist experience in Germany, not only because of the availability of materials, but also because of a fascination with the brutality Nazism unleashed. Most researchers explain the Nazi and fascist phenomenon in historical and political terms. In fact, the impression they convey is that the age of fascism was the inevitable product of easily identifiable antecedents and preconditions in European civilization. Many students of the period agree that fascism had disparate roots that can be traced to widening fissures in the groundwork of European life before 1914. The World War all but destroyed the rationalistic-optimistic certainty of the previous century and made credible the warnings of the prophets of doom. The muddled thinking of the Social Darwinians and neo-Hegelians resulted in solutions to the general European *Angst* similar to those offered by ideologues after 1918. Young extremists, eschewing a bourgeois value system

[42] The statistical data apply to the German nationals and recently naturalized citizens in the organization. Moreover, the analysis dealt only with those Bundists who returned to Germany (*Rückwanderer*) in the late 1930's and joined Kameradschaft-USA. For the purpose of this study, the dossiers of two hundred of these Bundists were selected from the Kameradschaft-USA papers (mean date of birth, standard deviation, 5.019; mean: April 1899. "Mean" refers to an arithmetic mean; standard deviation—SD—is a measure of·variability).

[43] Mean date of entry into the United States, SD, 1.7; mean: June 1925.

but keenly aware of middle-class society's longings, offered, as an antidote to uncertainty, a spiritual revolution and the promise of stability. Thus emerged a hybrid of extremist thought made up of varied ingredients, which for some achieved final expression in *Mein Kampf.* Although this particular interpretation is widely accepted, it is important to study fascism and National Socialism in specific manifestations, since it is improper to generalize from the European experience when examining Nazism in America.[44]

The information recorded in the *Rückwanderer* occupational and employment histories provides much insight into motivational factors. Most Bundists were not bureaucrats, corporate managers, or alienated intellectuals: only six of those whose applications were reviewed can be considered professionals by either American or European standards.[45] More than half of the returnees had been trained as skilled industrial workers or artisans before emigrating to America. The range of vocational skills was great; among them were locksmiths, bakers, carpenters, printers, electricians, glassmakers, and toolmakers. Unfortunately, the skills of many of these men had been rendered obsolete by the new industrialism of the postwar world; in fact, only three with specialized skills were able to pursue their chosen vocations in the United States.[46] The remainder of the skilled workers were forced to take jobs unrelated to their training. The three who were able to find work related to their vocational backgrounds lost their jobs with the onset of the Depression. Like many of their compatriots in Weimar Germany, these future Bundists must have feared further proletarianization, with the consequent loss of traditional industrial prestige. After 1931, over 90 per cent of the skilled potential returnees were forced to take service jobs (as waiters, dishwashers, gas-station attendants), when such employment could be found.

When the employment histories of the skilled workers are compared with those of the unskilled and semiskilled, it seems that

[44] Introduction, S. J. Wolfe, ed., *European Fascism* (London, 1963).

[45] The six professionals in the sample were Wang (professor), Behrmann (orthopedist), Groll (chemist), Frölich (journalist), Erich (music teacher), and Schwell (M.D.).

[46] Laumer (brewer, Pabst of Milwaukee), Rentsch (piano maker, Steinway, New York), Bauer (master machinist, General Motors).

those with little or no job training fared better than those with skills during the Depression. The evidence, though by no means extensive, suggests that, unlike the skilled German national, the unskilled immigrant was willing to take even the lowest position on the industrial ladder.

By 1930, two-thirds (126) of those who would become *Rückwanderer* were employed. In the spring of 1933, three years later, 162 were out of work. This fact can be explained, in part, by the pattern of resettlement followed by the German nationals. In general, most tended to gravitate to cities with large German-speaking populations. Those cities—Detroit, Chicago, Milwaukee, Pittsburgh, and New York—served as the home bases for some of America's largest industries. Ford, General Motors, Pullman, and other mammoth corporations epitomized the rapid industrialization of the decade, which had created thousands of semiskilled and unskilled assembly-line jobs easily filled by American and immigrant labor. After 1929, these companies were forced to curtail production, which meant the dismissal of many workers. The already despondent German national who had left Germany for America in search of a modicum of economic security was hurled into unemployment and further insecurity.

The Bundists, then, were hit hard by the Depression. Unquestionably, there was a correlation between the individual Bundist's economic problems and his anti-Semitism. The evidence points to one conclusion: many nationals and recently naturalized Americans were anti-Semites and incipient Nazis before they left Germany for America in the 1920's. Many had been members of the Freikorps; others had demonstrated against the Kurt Eisner regime in Bavaria or had fought the alleged Communist threat. After 1929, the Bundists attributed their misfortunes to the "ubiquitous Jews," who, according to the Nazis, were responsible for the world's ills. In short, the preconditions for organized anti-Semitism were already present in the German immigrant community before the Depression struck.

Racial purity and a desire to achieve a Nietzschean ecstasy— important ingredients in German National Socialism—were not of cardinal importance to the Bundists. Most of them seemed to have little use for the cult of the superman; their decision to join the Bund was motivated by fear—fear of the Jews, of the Communists, and of further proletarianization or unemployment. Germany's re-emergence as a world power and the Nazi Party's declared war on the Jews made the Bundists highly susceptible targets for racial-political propaganda. Many believed that American Jewry was plotting to take over the United States and involve the nation in a war with Germany. The boycott of German products was decried as an example of Jewish control over American economic life. Bundist Michael Schrick believed that the counterboycott was "an organized plot of international Jewry working with Moscow to strangle Germany." [47] Another Bundist, Henry von Holt, told a government investigator that the counterboycott had cost him his job, and he thought that the Bund could exert pressure on Washington to counter Jewish influence.[48] Not only the boycott, but also the increasing influence of Jews in American life—especially in the arts and the entertainment industry—was considered by the Bund as an element of a Jewish-Communist plot, hatched in Moscow, to dominate the United States. This belief in a conspiracy betrays the Bundists' failure to understand the mechanics of the political structure; nevertheless, the Jewish-Communist equation was used to explain the social and economic problems of the era and was accepted as gospel in the Bund community.[49] This doctrine, coupled with the conviction that the Jews would use their influence to foment an anti-German pogrom in retaliation for Hitler's treatment of German Jewry, gained wider circulation after Congressman Dickstein started preliminary hearings on the Bund's activities in 1933.

The coalescence of these recurring themes can best be illustrated by Bundist Otto Decker's answers to a government investigator's questions about why the Bund was organized:

A. Well, it was mainly organized to vote against the boycott of German products.

[47] Michael Schrick to Kameradschaft-USA, April 1, 1938, T-81/142/179581; 179581–2.
[48] Statement by Henry von Holt, U.S. v. *Holt,* C 18-394, FRC.
[49] F. Attig to Kameradschaft-USA, March 1939, T-81/141/179287.

Q. By whom?

A. By the Jews.

Q. Did they [the Bundists] have any other reason for organizing?

A. They were under the impression that lies were [being] spread about Germany. They wanted to overcome that.

Q. At the time the Bund was organized was it anti-Communistic?

A. Yes, [it] always has been.

Q. Would you consider the Bund as being anti-Semitic?

A. [Yes] . . . that's the way the thing started—the Bund was against the boycott and the Bund blamed the Jews for the boycott, that they did not want to trade with Germany.[50]

The only way he himself could help Germany, concluded Decker, was to join the Bund. Decker's testimony exemplifies the viewpoint of many of his cohorts. Many Bundists did not consider themselves hard-core National Socialists; rather, they were convinced that they were good Germans who had the duty to combat the lies and accusations circulated by the Jews against their fatherland.

By the time Germany hosted the Olympic Games in 1936, the argument that there was a distinction between a "good German" and a Nazi had become more and more indefensible. Nevertheless, in writing about the Bundists, it is necessary to distinguish between those who succumbed to the Bund's propaganda and those who, like Fritz Gissibl, had joined the Nazi Party in the preceding decade. Some members of the Bund were hard-core Nazis, Jew Baiters and anti-Communists. Dr. Albert Schley, for example, had fought against the Communists in the Ruhr before emigrating to America in 1925; Schley joined the Bund in order to continue the fight against world Communism.[51] Another Bundist, Henry Baumgartner, recorded in his diary that he joined the movement in order to express his hatred of the Jews; in his opinion, the "only ones who have any ideas here [in America] are the Jews and their ideas are vile, mean, and malicious." [52]

[50] Record of sworn statement of Otto Decker (b. 1886, Weimar; entered the United States 1910) in Portland, Ore., June 23, 1941, Department of Justice and Immigration and Naturalization Service, file 235-4093, German-American Bund folder, ADL.

[51] Schley, application to Kameradschaft-USA, 1941, T-81/141/179156.

[52] *Baumgartner* v. *U.S.*, 322 U.S. 665, decided June 12, 1944, p. 670. The

A small number of Bundists in the period of 1933 to 1935 were either Americans of German extraction or naturalized Americans who had emigrated before 1900. Bund records suggest that they accounted for no more than 10 per cent of the membership. Although some of them were in complete accord with the Hitlerian viewpoint, the evidence strongly suggests that they succumbed to FONG's propaganda. There seems to be a relationship between their experiences during the World War and their conception of the Bund as a protective organization. The case of Georg W. Krause was typical.[53] Krause emigrated to the United States in the 1890's and settled in Wisconsin. Like many of his fellow immigrants, he insisted that his American-born daughter have some knowledge of the German language. Since German was not taught in her school, Krause demanded that she speak German at home. In 1910, he became an American citizen. By 1917, he owned a small but prosperous farm. America's entry into the war changed Krause's life dramatically. "Along with Americans who had been in America for 150 years," Krause related to a friend, "we were hounded by the police and persecuted by our neighbors." In spite of his repeated protestations of loyalty to the United States, Krause claimed that he was accused of sympathizing with imperial Germany. At the war's end, Krause thought of returning to his native Germany but decided to remain in the United States. Fifteen years later, Krause, fearing a revival of anti-German sentiment, joined the Bund, hoping that it would protect him from the indignities he had purportedly suffered during the war.[54]

Were there many Georg Krauses in the Friends of the New Germany? This will remain an unanswerable question as long as information about the membership of the Bund remains privileged. But whether the Bundist was the owner of a small delicatessen in Yorkville, a toy store in Ridgewood, Queens, or a paint shop in Chicago, whether he was a music teacher in St. Louis, or a welder at

Supreme Court reversed the decision to denaturalize Henry Baumgartner *et al.* See Richard Polenberg, *War and Society: The United States, 1941–1945* (Philadelphia, 1972), p. 49; and letters by Bundist Hans Zimmermann and Carl Nicolay, 1940, T-81/140/177106; 147/185980ff.

[53] Georg Krause to Kameradschaft-USA, n.d., T-81/144/183138.
[54] T-81/144/183144.

the Ford plant in Michigan, he gave his allegiance to Nazism and ultimately to Adolf Hitler. Upon entry into the group he took the following oath:

I herewith declare my entry into the LEAGUE OF THE FRIENDS OF THE NEW GERMANY. The purpose and aims of the LEAGUE are clearly known to me and I obligate myself to support them without restriction. I acknowledge the "Leadership Principle"; *I do not belong to any secret organization of any kind (Freemason, etc.). I am of Aryan descent, free of Jewish or colored racial traces.*[55]

No matter what excuse he later used to justify his participation, he joined because he wanted to join. There is little evidence to suggest that anyone was ever coerced into joining. Admittedly, in places like Yorkville, where numerous shops were owned by German nationals or Americans of German extraction, there must have been some social and economic pressure. But in the last analysis, each Bundist exercised his own freedom of choice.

Moreover, most of the Bundists were obsessive anti-Semites, and their hatred of the Jews clouded their judgment: the machinations of the Jews became the only acceptable explanation for their plight and for the Bund's manifold problems. This tendency to see the world as they wanted to see it became especially apparent after Fritz Kuhn was selected as Bundesleiter in the mid-1930's. If the Bund had a problem, a Jew had to be behind it. The Jews were viewed as the incarnation of evil and of modernism. Hard-hit by the Depression and predisposed to attribute their plight to a conspiracy, the Bundists demonstrated their belief in the Hitlerian cosmology by joining the Nazi movement in the United States. Violently anti-Semitic and anti-Communistic, these men were transplanted National Socialists who, unlike many of their fellow countrymen in America, refused to accept personal disappoint-

[55] Application form, FONG, container 159, RG 131; my italics. Members of the organization were also required to take an oath of fidelity to Hitler: "I solemnly swear fidelity to my leader, Adolf Hitler. I promise Adolf Hitler and everybody designated by him, known to me or to be known to me, through his credentials, the respect and absolute obedience, and to fulfill all orders without reservation and with my entire will, because I know that my leader does not demand anything from me illegally" (*New York Post*, March 24, 1937).

ment. They lashed out at the Jews, and by doing so, lessened their own sense of failure. The German nationals in the American Nazi movement should therefore be considered fascists. Although the membership increased and by 1938 included several thousand Americans of German extraction, the nucleus around which the group was constructed remained constant—German nationals and recently naturalized citizens of the United States.[56]

These findings cannot be used to generalize about the members of other right-wing and pro-Nazi groups that sprang up in America in the 1930's. Eugen Weber cautions against placing the non-German American right in the framework of the Western European fascist experience. The North American experience was "radically different from those in the rest of the world. . . . The call for domestic conformity, predominant in the United States, is only an incidental part of more positive European platforms which stress the dynamic potential of national unity rather than the mollifying aspects of conformist security." [57] But the differences between members of the American radical right and the German element in the Bund should not obscure a shared attitude: the assumed enemies of the people were held responsible for the social and economic dislocations of the interwar years. The problem that confronted Bundesleiter Fritz Gissibl and later Fritz Kuhn was how to make the National Socialist viewpoint acceptable to millions of German-Americans who had already dropped their hyphens and wanted to be known simply as Americans.

[56] With the exception of the last leader of the Bund, Gerhard Wilhelm Kunze (b. 1906, Camden, New Jersey), most, if not all, of the Bund officials were born in Germany and emigrated to the United States in the 1920's.
[57] Eugen Weber, "The Right: An Introduction," in *The European Right: A Historical Profile,* ed. Hans Rogger and Eugen Weber (Berkeley, Calif., 1966), p. 12. See also Daniel Bell, ed., *The Radical Right* (New York, 1964).

CHAPTER 6

Hubert Schnuch, Ph.D., and the Collapse of the Friends of the New Germany

No sooner had Fritz Gissibl ousted his opponent, Dr. Griebl, and consolidated his control over the Friends of the New Germany than Samuel Dickstein introduced a resolution calling for an investigation of Germany's activities in the United States. Shortly after it received congressional approval in March 1934, John McCormack of Massachusetts was selected to chair the committee. The irascible Dickstein agreed to serve as cochairman; he was not given the chairmanship because several of his colleagues felt that the selection of a Jew to investigate Nazi activities in America might serve to discredit the proceedings.[1] The House's passage of the "Dickstein Resolution" was applauded by many people, regardless of their political, regional, or ethnic affiliation, as the first concrete, though indirect, step taken by the United States to condemn Nazi activities in America. Dickstein (whose parents brought him to America to escape anti-Jewish pogroms) saw the passage of the resolution as a chance to crush all Nazi-inspired activities. Shortly after the resolution was approved, Dickstein told an interviewer that he wanted to eradicate all traces of Nazism in the United States. All Bund activities, past and present, were to be carefully scrutinized by the committee, and "as many Bundists as time would permit" would be subpoenaed.[2] The Congressman's public

[1] Walter Goodman, *The Committee: The Extraordinary Career of the House Committee on Un-American Activities* (New York, 1968), p. 10. The committee met in executive session from April to July and opened public hearings in July 1934.

[2] Dickstein to editor of *Jewish Daily Bulletin,* interview, March 21, 1934, clipping, Greenberg Collection, II, item 963, Archives, YIVO Institute.

statements created considerable apprehension in the Bundist community and among some German diplomats; his detractors referred
to him as the "irascible Jewish wirepuller." Bundists dreaded ap-
pearing before the McCormack-Dickstein Committee (the "Jewish
Inquisition" it was labeled by the *Deutsche Zeitung*). Shortly after
the committee began its investigation, representatives of the German Embassy in Washington informed the Bundists that the Ge-
stapo had requested the German consuls to transmit to Berlin the
testimony of every Bundist who appeared before the McCormack-
Dickstein probers; to be sure, the information compounded the
Bundists' fears.[3]

Dickstein's disdain for the Bundists who appeared before him
was undisguised. He not only intimidated several witnesses but also
accused them of treasonous activities. By the late summer of 1934,
many of Dickstein's former supporters in Congress and some civil
libertarians were charging that his tactics violated witnesses' constitutional rights. Some congressmen went so far as to accuse their
New York colleague of using the Nazi issue as a political spring-
board. Despite his questionable methods, the evidence he accumu-
lated indicated that Nazi Germany was giving financial and
ideological support to a Nazi organization in the United States. By
the time the committee's findings were made public in February
1935, many of its conclusions, based on documented evidence of
German subversion, were already familiar to many Americans, for
the press and the radio had carried detailed accounts of the hearings.

[3] The Bundists' hatred of Dickstein needs little amplification. See Gissibl's
correspondence with Rolf Hoffmann, T-81/27/24275–83. Staffers at the German Embassy in Washington dismissed the resolution as a "Jewish publicity
stunt." As the next chapter shows, Kiep and Luther, however, tried to foster a
more sober appraisal of the situation. On the embassy's views, see German
Embassy to Hans Dieckhoff, Feb. 22, 1934, T-120/4616/269495. On the
transmission of testimony, see T-120/4616/269780ff. Germany's number-one
Jew-baiter, Julius Streicher, asserted that the hearings were the start of a
Jewish plot aimed at the destruction of the German-American community. According to Streicher, the kidnaping of the Lindbergh baby in 1932 was part of
this plot; the Jews, not Bruno Hauptmann, murdered the child and used his
blood in the Purim ceremony (Streicher, "Der jüdische Ritualmordschlächter,"
as quoted in "Wie das Hakenkreuz in Amerika arbeitet," *Die neue Welt*, June
13, 1935, clipping, German-American Bund folder, Wiener Library).

The German government responded to the committee's allegations by disclaiming any knowledge of the activities of its nationals. The Party was accused of supporting a branch in the United States and revealed as a potential threat to America's internal security. Each session of the committee threatened Berlin with exposure of its diplomatic treachery and participation in international subversion. Shortly after the committee's report was made public, Party officials in Germany were forced to grapple with the basic question: Was the existence of a Nazi movement in America advantageous to Germany in achieving its goals in America? Although variations of this question had been casually discussed previously by Party and State officials, they were now discussing it in earnest. Finally, after nearly two years of intra-Party debates, high-level ministerial conferences, and several attempts at making the Bund more acceptable to American authorities, Germany decided in November 1935 to forbid its nationals (including those with "first papers," which declare the intention of becoming American citizens) to be members of the Friends of the New Germany. Well aware that the group's leaders and most of the rank and file held German citizenship, Berlin hoped that their speedy withdrawal would accelerate the collapse of the organization.

The history of this decision began shortly after the recall of Heinz Spanknöbel in September 1933, when some members of the diplomatic staff in the Wilhelmstrasse urged the Party to abandon the Bund completely. Much to the chagrin of the traditionalists in the Foreign Ministry, Hess asked Bohle to appoint Fritz Gissibl as Spanknöbel's replacement. The appointment of a known Nazi sympathizer not only broke the promise the German Foreign Ministry had made to Ambassador Dodd, but also placed the Bund on a collision course with the movement's opponents in the United States. The selection of Gissibl days after the end of the Spanknöbel Affair and at a time when it was still fresh in many memories, gave Dickstein and the anti-Nazis exactly the ammunition they needed. Once the committee began its probe into Nazi activities, the German government tried in vain to rectify its mistake. In their efforts, Party and State officials compounded the error; the result was unmanageable deceit. Hess and Bohle soon realized that they had made a blunder in appointing Gissibl, a Nazi of long standing and a founder of the Teutonia Association, as Bundesleiter. They reasoned, however, that removing him at this time would give credibility to the suspicions of those who maintained that Gissibl was subject to orders from Berlin. So instead of recalling Gissibl and appointing a substitute, once again Bohle tried to allay American hostility and also continue Party involvement with the Bundists: on February 16, 1934, Bohle ordered all Party members out of the Bund and sent each member a circular forbidding him to carry on propaganda activities among American citizens.[4] Clearly, this order was nothing more than window dressing. In the winter of 1934, Hess and Bohle were still hoping that the Bund would develop into a far-reaching American Nazi movement. Subsequent events have demonstrated that the noxious activities of the Bundists, not the protests launched by the Americans, finally convinced them of the uselessness of such an undertaking.

As was to be expected, Hess's decision was not well received by the Bundists. Their personal letters written during this period reveal that they felt the Party had betrayed them. Although in the ensuing weeks the Party made it possible for NSDAP members to belong to the Friends of the New Germany clandestinely, many Bundists simply left the organization in disgust. Between February and June of 1934, membership in some sections of the Northeast dropped at an alarming rate.[5] These unsettling events led some Bundists to conclude that they must disengage the group from Nazi German control and change its policies: "Americanization" became the watchword. "It is impossible to build a permanent organization in New York State," wrote Bundist Karl Neumann to Rolf Hoffmann, "since the state is controlled by the Jews." Only when an American citizen assumed the leadership of the group, he concluded, could the movement fulfill its purpose.[6] In spite of Neu-

---

[4] The decision was announced on February 1, 1934, and went into effect on the sixteenth ("Rundschreiben Bohles an alle Parteigenossen in USA vom 1. Februar 1934," T-120/4614/269422; NSDAP [AO] to German Embassy, Feb. 13, 1934, T-120/4614/269421–22).

[5] Gissibl-Hoffman correspondence, spring 1934, folder 34, T-81/25/22186ff.

[6] Feb. 22, 1934, T-81/27/24500. Neumann's letter indicates how little some Bundists knew about their group's relationship with Germany. Neumann

mann's timely suggestion, the Party remained intransigent, refusing to replace Gissibl with an American of German parentage or even a naturalized American. Party membership was still considered the criterion for loyalty.

Daily newspaper accounts of the Bund's problems and discussions of anti-Nazi activities published elsewhere did much to publicize the Friends of the New Germany. Early in March, the American Jewish Congress decided to take advantage of the growing anti-Nazi sentiment in the nation. On the seventh, in conjunction with the American Federation of Labor, it conducted a mock trial of Adolf Hitler in Madison Square Garden. The program was entitled "Civilization against Hitlerism." Judge Samuel Seabury served as counsel for Civilization. Before an audience estimated at twenty thousand the case against Hitler was presented to "Justices" Alfred E. Smith, Fiorello La Guardia (then mayor), Millard Tydings, and Raymond Moley. Hitler was branded an "Outlaw of Humanity" and his supporters both in America and abroad labeled barbarians.

The State Department had tried unsuccessfully to stop the trial. Secretary of State Cordell Hull viewed it as a provocation that could result only in the further disruption of German-American diplomatic relations. In a letter to Samuel Untermeyer, Hull stated that although he realized that the government could do little to stop the trial without violating the First Amendment, he thought it would be best to postpone it indefinitely. Several hours after the justices issues their verdict against Hitler, Germany's foreign minister, Constantin von Neurath, registered strong protests with Dodd in Berlin and Hull in Washington.[7]

---

instructed Hoffmann to "tell Heinz Spanknöbel to appoint an American to lead the organization."

[7] Cordell Hull did not want the "mock trial" to take place, fearing that it would endanger German-American relations; but he could do little to stop it without violating the First Amendment. Jay Pierrepont Moffat, chief of the Division of Western European Affairs in the State Department, expressed the feelings of many of his colleagues when he wrote: "The whole proceedings seemed an *opera bouffe* affair with the evidence introduced by Germans under concealed names, by Communist editors, or stewards and waiters on transatlantic ships" (Nancy Harvison Hooker, ed., *The Moffat Papers: Selections from the Diplomatic Journals of Jay Pierrepont Moffat, 1919–1943* [Cambridge, Mass., 1956], p. 109). On preparations for the trial, see the *Jewish Daily Bul-*

The foreign minister's protestations were as insincere as the Party's efforts to disassociate itself from the Bund. State Secretary of the German Foreign Ministry Bernhard von Bülow wrote in a letter to the German Embassy in Washington on March 10 that the Foreign Ministry and the Party were annoyed at not having received more information about the trial beforehand; Bülow believed that Germany would have used this information to advantage by creating a diplomatic incident.[8]

The McCormack-Dickstein Committee's first formal session opened several weeks after the mock trial. Dickstein had a flair for the sensational and managed to capture newspaper headlines with unproved generalizations about the Bund. He made exaggerated claims: that every German seaman was a spy, that Germany was smuggling arms into the country, and that the Bund had a membership of over twenty thousand in the New York metropolitan area. Any criticism of Dickstein's methods or statements evoked the displeasure of many anti-Hitler groups and patriotic organizations, as well as the Congressman's wrath. The public's support of Dickstein did not go unnoticed by the German government. "We must not pass over the matter here with complete silence," wrote Bülow in response to one of Dickstein's allegations, "but produce a little bit of the 'people boiling over with indignation' so that we have a cause for complaint against the U.S.A."[9]

Although Germany's leaders disclaimed any responsibility for

---

letin, March 6, 1934. On Germany's pretrial protests, see Luther to Foreign Ministry, March 3, Hans Heinrich Dieckhoff to Luther, March 5, Luther to Foreign Ministry, March 5, Bülow to German Embassy, March 8, *DGFP,* C, II, 552–554, 557, 565, 574; Neurath to Dodd, in memorandum by Neurath, March 5, Dodd to Hull, March 8, 1934, *PRDR,* II, 512–515. In an effort to soothe ill feeling between the two powers, Dodd met with Hitler on the day of the trial (Offner, *American Appeasement,* pp. 82–83). Among those present at the trial were Al Smith, Judge Samuel Seabury, Raymond Moley, Mayor Fiorello La Guardia, and Woodrow Wilson's last Secretary of State, Bainbridge Colby, who presided over the meeting.

[8] Note by Bülow, March 22, 1934, T-120/4616/269492. On Ambassador Hans Luther's concern over Dickstein's growing influence, see T-120/4616/269486–99.

[9] Note by Bülow, March 22, 1934, T-120/4616/269492.

the actions of its nationals in the United States, the Foreign Ministry's denials became less convincing as the hearings progressed. Sergeant Gottlieb Hass of the New York National Guard told the committee that Bundists and members of the American division of the German veterans' organization, the Stahlhelm, were encouraged by the Party to join the National Guard. Hass reported that 20 per cent of his company were members of the Bund and that they had joined the National Guard so that the Bundists could use its training camp at Peekskill, New York.[10]

In June 1934, attempting to determine the extent of anti-German sentiment in America, Hess sent Hitler's former confidant Ernst Hanfstaengl on a fact-finding tour. Putzi, as he was affectionately called by friends, could not have been a poorer choice to send on such a mission. He had been expelled from the United States because of a purported connection with the sensational Black Tom munitions explosion in New Jersey in July 1916. Moreover, most American newspapers led their readers to believe, erroneously, that Hanfstaengl was Hitler's chief adviser. When he reached Ellis Island in New York Harbor, several New York newspapers suggested that he should be barred from the country as an undesirable alien. His unfriendly reception was an embarrassment for Germany.

Not long after Hanfstaengl's arrival, Hitler purged the SA during the "Night of the Long Knives." The murder of SA leader Ernst Roehm and other Party and non-Party people was detailed on the front pages of most American newspapers, confirming for many Americans the suspicion that National Socialism was a new form of barbarism. By midsummer of that year, Germany's prestige in the United States fell to a new low. This was underscored when Harvard's president, James Conant, refused to accept a cash gift from Hanfstaengl to his alma mater, explaining that Harvard College could not take a donation from a man who repre-

---

[10] *New York Times,* June 6, 1934, p. 8. On the Bund's absorption of the Stahlhelm in other cities, see memorandum by consul, Cleveland, Ohio, 1935, T-81/395/5136139–140.

sented a nation bent on destroying scholarship and academic freedom.[11]

Shortly after Conant's public condemnation of Nazi Germany, Hanfstaengl may have met with Bundesleiter Gissibl. The evidence, though fragmentary, suggests that Hanfstaengl was instructed by Hess to order Gissibl to appoint an American citizen to lead the Bund movement. By this time Hess too believed that with an American at the head the arguments of the anti-Bund forces would be muted. A month before Hanfstaengl arrived in the United States, however, Gissibl had already selected a naturalized American of German birth, Reinhold Walter, a Bundist of long standing but not a member of the NSDAP. Gissibl never intended to make Walter's political functions commensurate with the impressive title of Bundesleiter. But Walter was not content to play the role of Gissibl's front man, and in early May 1934 he attempted to lead an intragroup revolt against Gissibl. Gissibl responded to Walter's challenge by ousting him from office before he could command a following.[12] Thus, at the time of the alleged Hanfstaengl-Gissibl meeting, Fritz Gissibl was still leader of the Bund organization. Quick to realize that his continued occupation of this post might endanger the existence of the group, Gissibl turned for help to an old Bundist friend from the 1920's, Hubert Schnuch.

Schnuch, who had been a member of the old Teutonia Association, was an atypical Bundist.[13] His friends from Detroit and

[11] On Hanfstaengl's trip, see newspaper clippings, June–October 1934, Greenberg Collection, items 1200–1300, Archives, YIVO Institute. Dr. Conant's statement can be found in the *New York Times*, October 4, 1934. On the German Embassy's concern about Hanfstaengl's reception, see Luther to Foreign Ministry, June 1934, T-120/4616/269660–4. Cf. Hoffmann to Gissibl, June 18, 1934, T-81/27/24331.

[12] The exact date of Walter's ouster is not known. After the rift, Walter threatened to blackmail Gissibl. He claimed he had several "secret letters" written by Gissibl and threatened to turn them over to Dickstein. He never did. On Walter's testimony, see *NP*, pp. 176ff. Gissibl's view can be found in "Bericht über die Ereignisse in New York, Dezember 1934," roll 35, folder 696, *NSDAP Hauptarchiv* Collection.

[13] A biographical sketch of Schnuch can be found in Appendix III, below, and the *Deutsche Zeitung*, July 7, 1934, p. 14. Several of Schnuch's personal letters are in Fragmentary Records of the German-American Bund, container

Chicago—the Gissibl brothers, Kappe, Schuster (the so-called old guard)—had devoted their lives to the Bund and the Nazi cause; for them, disseminating Hitler's views was a way of life. Unlike these men, Schnuch did not channel all his energies into the movement; instead, he pursued an academic career. Born in Aachen in 1892, he emigrated to America in 1913, only to return the following year. He served in the imperial German army and upon being mustered out joined a Freikorps company, a paramilitary unit in Wesel, a small town near the Dutch border. After his brief experience in the Freikorps, Schnuch found employment with the German branch of the International Harvester Corporation. After two years as a salesman for that firm, he made his way back to the United States. Upon his arrival in New York in 1923, Schnuch, a *Gymnasium* graduate, taught his native language at the Berlitz School. Six years later, he moved to Chicago, where he met the Gissibl brothers and joined the Teutonia Association.

At this juncture Schnuch's life changed direction. Without giving up his involvement with the Teutonia Association, he enrolled in a Ph.B. (Bachelor of Philosophy) program at the University of Chicago. In 1931, he was awarded that degree and immediately started work toward a master's degree at Miami University in Oxford, Ohio, which he completed the following year. Shortly afterward Schnuch began doctoral studies at Yale University and in 1934 received a Ph.D. in Germanic languages. Fritz Gissibl, who was searching for a respectable and acceptable leader of the Bund, found his man in his old friend Dr. Hubert Schnuch, whose credentials were impressive.

In June 1934, Gissibl offered Schnuch the leadership of the Bund. Gissibl made it clear that the position was merely ornamental and that he would continue to control the Bund from behind the scenes. Schnuch acquiesced and assumed the titular leadership in the summer of 1934. The Party quickly approved Gissibl's selection. Berlin could finally claim that an American citizen was di-

136, RG 131. Schnuch's doctoral dissertation was entitled "Lautlehre der Mundart von Kornelimünster" ("Phonetics of the Dialect of Kornelimünster" —a village near his native Aachen).

recting the Friends of the New Germany. In an effort to give publicity to the fiction of Schnuch's leadership, Gissibl scheduled a
Bund convention for June 30 to July 3 in Chicago. The purpose of
this national meeting, the second in the Bund's brief history, was
twofold: to pretend to elect a new leader of the Friends of the New
Germany and to demonstrate to the public that the group had
been "Americanized," however belatedly.

The much publicized convention utilized all the trappings of democracy and aped the fanfare and artificiality of American political conventions. On a stage draped with American and German
flags, among pictures of Paul von Hindenburg, Franklin Roosevelt,
and Adolf Hitler, Fritz Gissibl resigned from his post and suggested that the delegates (who represented Bund locals from coast
to coast) elect a member of the old guard, Hubert Schnuch.
Schnuch was the only candidate, and his election was assured. But
Gissibl was crafty, and he was well aware that both officials in
Washington and members of the German-American community in
New York were watching the proceedings in Chicago. Democratic and parliamentary procedures were followed. The title
Bundesleiter—obviously "un-American"—was dropped in favor of
the more American-sounding president. In keeping with the organization's new orientation, President Schnuch's election was made
public on Independence Day, July 4, 1934.

Gissibl was a plotter. In order to avoid a repetition of the Walter incident and to ensure Schnuch's compliance with his wishes,
Gissibl had himself elected leader of the Bund's Midwestern Department, appointed OD chief Sepp Schuster *Gauleiter* of the Eastern Department, requested Walter Kappe to stay on as the organization's national editor and chief propagandist, and retained an
old friend, Hermann Schwinn, as leader of the Western Department.[14] Thus, by the summer of 1934, old fighters from the movement's early formative years in Chicago and Detroit had emerged
to assume positions of leadership.

[14] *Deutsche Zeitung*, July 7, 1934, p. 1. On Schnuch's early membership in
the Teutonia Association and the consulate's reaction to his appointment as
the new Bund leader, see Hans Borchers to Foreign Ministry, July 7, 1934,
T-120/4616/269842–5. On the new appointments, see T-120/4616/269844.

Unlike Gissibl's first puppet, Reinhold Walter, Schnuch quickly adjusted to the arrangement and enjoyed the newly acquired publicity. Just one day after his election he was subpoenaed to appear at the McCormack-Dickstein hearings. On July 9, he boasted to Dickstein that he was the president of the American Nazi movement and proudly asserted that he had ultimate decision-making power. Dickstein accepted these assertions at face value and proceeded to inquire into the movement's anti-Semitism, which the fiery congressman equated with un-Americanism. When asked by Dickstein if a Jew could join the organization, Schnuch leaned back in his chair and with a smirk on his face replied, "Not even if he was in America since Columbus' day." His remark did little to appease the already infuriated Dickstein; more important, such comments did not help to correct the public's image of the Bund. In the ensuing months, Gissibl kept his appointee out of the public eye. As a result, President Schnuch did not reappear publicly until the annual New York German Day activities in October.[15]

In addition to publicizing the New Germany, the purpose of German Day 1934 was to offset the disaster of the previous year. It will be recalled that the actions of the man whom the press dubbed "the notorious Heinz Spanknöbel" had forced the United German Societies of Greater New York to cancel the celebration. Endeavoring to avoid a similar situation, Gissibl assiduously planned a program designed to demonstate to the American public that the Bund's and German-America's first loyalty was to the United States and to emphasize that the Friends of the New Germany, under Schnuch's leadership, had been Americanized. He also took great care to create the impression that the Bund was only one of many German-American organizations taking part in the festivities. In the weeks prior to German Day, many organizations which had formerly eschewed the Bund for a variety of reasons began to coordinate their activities with those of that group.

This meant joining DAWA. It also meant presenting a united front on German Day. Consequently, included among the sponsors listed in the "Deutscher Tag, 1934, Festprogramm" were J. A.

[15] *New York Times,* July 10, 1934. Schnuch's testimony can be found in *NP,* pp. 176ff.

Henckels Cutlery Corporation, Schlitz Brewing Company, Telefunken Records, and several German steamship lines.[16]

The festivities were organized jointly by Gissibl and Hans Borchers, Kiep's replacement, consul general in New York. Germany spent a large amount of money advertising the event in Bund publications in New York and its environs. The advertisements stressed that the Bund was an American movement organized and directed by naturalized Americans; they also claimed that the Bund maintained no connections with Germany or the Nazi Party. At a rally at Madison Square Garden on October 6, Schnuch told a crowd estimated at twenty-one thousand that the German element in America should assert itself politically and culturally but within the framework of the American system of government. The next speaker, Consul General Borchers, reiterated Schnuch's remarks and brought "greetings from the old German homeland." Finally, in keeping with the Bund's new image, the rally closed with a chorus of "The Star-Spangled Banner." [17]

German Day 1934 was a mixture of nostalgic songs, veiled Nazism, and frequent references to loyalty to the United States. More important, Gissibl's reorientation of the Bund encouraged some German-Americans to join. Between October 1934 and March 1935, the movement nearly doubled in size. Several factors account for this growth. The fact that an American citizen was in command enabled some native German-Americans and naturalized German nationals to overcome their reluctance to join the organization. Furthermore, many of the new recruits saw the McCormack-Dickstein Committee as a harbinger of approaching anti-German-American feeling; apparently, the detailed news coverage of the hearings did more to recruit new members than did the entire Bund propaganda campaign. During the winter of 1934–1935, racial pride seemed far less important to many Bundists than their fears of persecution, however unfounded.

The Bund was encouraging not only individuals but also small

[16] "Deutscher Tag, 1934, Festprogramm." The program was sponsored by DAWA in conjunction with thirty-four German-American organizations in the New York metropolitan area. The theme was "The Political Awakening of Germany."

[17] *Völkischer Beobachter,* Oct. 20, 1934.

German-American social, sport, and cultural organizations to affiliate with it. In New York City alone, there were several hundred
such organizations under the umbrella of the United German Societies of Greater New York. The UGS, which had been factionalized almost to the point of extinction because of the Spanknöbel
incidents the previous year, would no longer support the small
Vereine. Unable to align themselves with any other major organization, dozens of these groups had to disband because of a lack of
funds from a parent sponsor or because they were torn apart by
the Jewish question. After German Day, the former leaders of some
of these organizations approached Schnuch for help, and an agreement was worked out that enabled these groups to reconstitute
themselves as affiliates of the Bund. In the winter of 1934–1935
more than a score in New York City alone joined forces with the
Bund, raising the group's national membership to about ten thousand.[18]

The Bund's rapid growth puzzled many people. Reports of the
movement's expansion infuriated Dickstein, and he responded by
purposely exaggerating its size and importance. By November
1934, Dickstein was claiming that the Bund had thirty to fifty thousand members. Despite the exaggerations, his efforts produced a
well-documented record of German intrigue in the United States.
But in spite of the organization's growth, neither the State Department nor the McCormack-Dickstein Committee took further action
against it, since the Bund was not found to be in violation of any
federal statutes. Dickstein and his friends were powerless. Although warrant had been issued for the arrest of Spanknöbel (who
had violated a 1917 statute that called for the registration of foreign agents), the law did not apply to Schnuch and his cohorts.

A reaction against the Bund came from an unexpected quarter
—Adolf Hitler. On October 31, Hitler met with the president of
the Steuben Society of America, Theodor H. Hoffmann.[19] Hoff-

[18] Most of these organizations were extremely small. In general, they were
the so-called Stadt-Vereine, named after German cities ("Hessen-Darmstädter
Volksfest"; Charles Pichel to O. Farmer, July 11, 1934, T-81/27/24548–50).

[19] Memorandum by State Secretary and Head of the Reich Chancellery to
Foreign Minister (Neurath), drafted on orders of the Führer, Nov. 2, 1934,
DGFP, C, III, 1115–1116.

mann told the Chancellor that the Bund's rapid growth and "un-American" activities had caused a deterioration of German-American diplomatic relations and confusion within the German community. In Hoffmann's opinion, most Americans believed that the Bund was controlled by Germany. He felt that Borchers' participation in the German Day activities only three weeks before had lent support to this allegation, and he urged Hitler to investigate. Hitler responded cautiously, expressing concern because German consuls had taken part in Bund functions. He reminded Hoffmann that the Party had given strict orders to all its members in America to refrain from all political activity and concluded the interview by assuring Hoffmann that neither the Party nor the State was in any way connected with the Friends of the New Germany.

After the interview, Hitler sent a memorandum to Rudolf Hess inquiring whether there was any substance to Hoffmann's remarks.[20] Bohle, responding for Hess, tried to dismiss the matter, claiming that Theodor Hoffmann found the Friends of the New Germany inconvenient for furthering his own plans. In addition, he stated that the Auslandsorganisation had ordered all Party members in the United States to withdraw from the Bund. "Absolute passivity towards the U.S.A.," Bohle wrote, "which had been most strictly observed by the Auslandsorganisation, is based on my view that at the present time any overt efforts made in the United States on the behalf of the New Germany are entirely pointless. . . . This would not be appropriate in all countries of the world, but in the United States the conditions are undoubtedly different." Bohle suggested that other agencies might be maintaining contacts with the Bund movement.[21]

Bohle's reply was deceitful and would not have been borne out

[20] Bohle to Hess, Nov. 16, 1934, *DGFP*, C, III, 1116.

[21] *Ibid.* State Secretary von Bülow attributed Hoffmann's negative criticism of the Bund to the growing rivalry between the Steuben Society and Schnuch's organization. It will be seen that Bülow's analysis proved correct (Bülow to Reich Chancellery, Nov. 6, 1934, *DGFP*, C, III, 1117). At this juncture, the Steuben Society had acquiesced, by silence, in the Nazi dictatorship. It was not until the anti-Jewish pogrom in November 1938 that the Society issued a statement condemning Nazi practices ("Statement by the Steuben Society," container 142, RG 131).

if an investigation had been undertaken; it may have been prompted by fear that the Führer might not approve of his close connection with the Bund. At any rate, by denying any connection between his agency and the Bund, Bohle in effect officially disengaged the Auslandsorganisation from the Bund. Hitler accepted Bohle's statements and dismissed the matter. In a letter to the Foreign Ministry, Hans Heinrich Lammers, State Secretary and Head of the Reich Chancellery, admitted that it was hardly possible to prevent "some contact" between Germany and the Bund. He suggested that Germany keep the channels of communication open, "if only for the sake of avoiding serious mistakes being made by the Association [FONG] or its local groups to which numerous *Reich* Germans [German nationals] belong, mistakes which might be harmful both to the aims of the Association and to German-American relations." [22] Apparently Lammers' statements reflected Hitler's desires and were communicated to the German Embassy in Washington. [23]

Theodor Hoffmann's protest underscored the Foreign Ministry's long-standing conviction that the Bund was a liability to the new regime. Instead of influencing public opinion in favor of Germany, the Bund had produced the opposite effect, not only by its candid pro-Nazi stand, but by precipitating the Dickstein investigation and consequently exposing Germany's propaganda network. Germany now desired to minimize its involvement with the Bund, but since the American phase of the movement was still in its infancy, the premature recall of the group's real leader, Gissibl, might sabotage his work and even destroy a movement that might someday be useful to Germany. Germany, in short, had modified its relationship with the Bund but had not relinquished the hope that Americans of German extraction might someday be unified into a political force. By January 1935, some German officials believed that the Americanization of the Friends of the New Germany had marked the beginning of an indigenous German-American movement.

But at the very time when the movement was on the verge of an

[22] Hans-Heinrich Lammers to Foreign Ministry, Dec. 3, 1934, *DGFP*, C, III, 1117.
[23] Foreign Ministry to German Embassy, Dec. 8, 1934, T-120/3302/270085.

era of sustained growth, a major intragroup revolt erupted. Unlike past episodes, which were mainly personality clashes, this struggle was never to be completely resolved; eventually, the conflict contributed to the collapse of the Friends of the New Germany and forced Germany to call for the withdrawal of its nationals and, in effect, to work to undermine the organization.

The proximate cause of the revolt was the Bund's unexpectedly rapid growth during the last months of 1934. Foreseeing a greatly expanded American Nazi movement, Bundist Anton Haegele rallied around him several dissidents and tried to wrench control from Gissibl, arguing that it was time for Gissibl and the old guard to step aside and for a new and creative leadership to take over.[24] Some dissidents maintained—correctly in this case—that Schnuch was Gissibl's puppet, that Gissibl was embezzling funds from the organization's treasury, and that he was not even a member of the Bund. The national editor, Walter Kappe, was labeled a thief and a liar who had been stealing funds since 1928. In sum, Gissibl and his entourage—Kappe, Schnuch, and Schuster—were denounced as traitors guilty of unpardonable crimes against the Bund. The solution offered by the dissidents was simple: the Bund's present leaders must be purged.[25]

---

[24] Fritz Gissibl, "Bericht über die Ereignisse in New York, Dezember 1934," roll 35, folder 696, *NSDAP Hauptarchiv* Collection. The leaders of the intragroup revolt were Ludwig Glasser, Gerhard Procht, Theodor Stroehlin, Reinhold Walter (the deposed Bund leader), Werner Brink, Walter Freund, Fritz Staatermann, Willie Meyer, Joseph Haubner, and Max Spohn. See New York consulate to Gustav Moshack (DAI), May 1935, T-81/394/5135027.

[25] *Deutscher Beobachter, Extrablatt,* Dec. 15, 1934. Gissibl dubbed the leaders of the revolt the "Kappists" (named after Wolfgang Kapp, who with General von Lüttwitz attempted to overthrow the Weimar Republic in 1920–the Kapp *Putsch*). The Kappists managed to gain control of the Bund's presses and published several special editions (*Extrablätter*), using the same masthead as the Gissibl factions. Since two editions of the *Deutscher Beobachter* were published simultaneously, the word *Extrablatt* distinguished between the two. The *Deutscher Beobachter* had replaced the *Deutsche Zeitung* as the Bund's official newspaper in the early fall of 1934. The name *Deutsche Zeitung* was assumed by a pro-German group in Brooklyn for its newspaper. See W. L. McLaughlin, "Apology to the Jews," *Deutsche Zeitung*, Nov. 17, 1934, pp. 1b–2b; and E. F. Grifat, "Unser Weg und unser Ziel," *ibid.*, Nov. 24, 1934, p. 1.

Haegele, the leader of the intragroup revolt, was a naturalized American who was born in Germany in 1896. At the Chicago convention he had been elected (more precisely, appointed) deputy Bundesleiter. Unlike Schnuch, Haegele was unwilling to obey Gissibl's orders; he wanted to direct the movement. The rebellion against Gissibl's behind-the-scenes leadership began in September 1934. Haegele rallied to his support all of Gissibl's enemies, including Reinhold Walter and a handful of Ignatz Griebl's remaining supporters. Bohle's assumption that the president of the Steuben Society, Theodor Hoffmann, found Gissibl inconvenient for the furtherance of his own plans proved correct. In early December, Hoffmann threw his support to the Haegele faction. By the middle of the month, Haegele and his followers took control of the movement's presses in New York City and published a manifesto entitled *The End of the Bund's Mismanagement.* But the insurgents failed to take control of the Bund's national headquarters (Bundesleitung) in Yorkville.[26] As long as Gissibl and Schnuch controlled the political heart of the organization, members in other cities were reluctant to side with Haegele. The rebels were further checked by their failure to gain the allegiance of Sepp Schuster's well-disciplined Ordnungs-Dienst (OD), the fighting arm of the Bund.

Although Haegele did not acquire many supporters, his faction still controlled the movement's presses and continued to publish the *Deutscher Beobachter.* Haegele claimed to be the new leader of the Bund and to have made inroads into the cadres of Schnuch's and Gissibl's followers. The situation became more confused when Gissibl's faction published its own editions of the *Deutscher Beobachter* and asserted that the revolt had been crushed. In January 1935, Haegele and four of his supporter—Willie Meyer, Werner Brink, Reinhold Walter, and Ludwig Glasser—proclaimed that

[26] "Das Ende einer Misswirtschaft," *Deutscher Beobachter, Extrablatt,* Dec. 15, 1934. After the break, Walter set up a new corporation, Zenger Press, Inc., and appointed Gerhard Schröder editor. See Walter—Rolf Hoffmann correspondence, T-81/27/23929ff. The Zenger Press collapsed in the late 1930's, and Walter turned to distributing Nazi progaganda in America—i.e., placing articles in German-American newspapers (*ibid.,* 1938–1939, T-81/31/28320ff).

they had wrenched control of the Bund from Gissibl and Schnuch and renamed the organization the American National Socialist Bund (Bund Amerikanischer Nationalsozialisten, or BANS).[27]

Haegele's bold assertion was a lie. His secessionist group was unable to recruit more than two hundred Bundists. In spite of his failure, Haegele's revolt against Gissibl's leadership cannot be dismissed as a weak attempt by one dissident and a group of disappointed party hacks to gain control of a growing organization. The insurgency was symptomatic of a disenchantment with the movement's leadership. The evidence suggests that a handful of Bundists wanted genuine reform and believed that Gissibl's, Kappe's, and Schuster's continued presence as leaders supported the widespread belief that the Bund was subservient to Germany. Haegele's attempt, however poorly organized, to oust these men revealed this feeling. Haegele argued that if the Bund had been led by American citizens from its inception, the Spanknöbel Affair and the Dickstein investigation could have been avoided. Reinhold Walter, who had been ejected from the Bund by Gissibl, underscored this point when he wrote in the *Deutscher Beobachter*, "It is high time for the 'German agents'—Gissibl and his clique—to return to Germany." Walter's correspondence with the Steuben Society's president, Theodor Hoffmann, suggests that if the insurgency had been a success, the society might have joined forces with Haegele and his supporters.[28]

The conflict between the two factions, labeled by the press the "Haegele-Schnuch Affair," was not only a struggle for the leadership. Haegele considered himself a reformer and argued that the or-

[27] The situation became more confused after Henry Woisin, treasurer of a branch of the Friends of the New Germany in New York City, sued Haegele for control of the group's presses. After a prolonged court battle, the presses were awarded to Haegele's faction. However, by this time Gissibl's group had purchased new printing presses and BANS was on the verge of collapse (*Henry Woisin* v. *Anton Haegele* [and nine codefendants], 1935, 7 vols., Legal Records of the German-American Bund, container 147, RG 131).

[28] Maude Le Hand to Reinhold Walter, n.d., T-81/36/32441. Kipphan maintains that the Haegele-Schnuch controversy lost the Bund much influence in the New York area. This was true in early 1935; after the appointment of Kuhn in late 1935, he managed to offset any losses the group might have suffered during the prolonged conflict.

ganization must conform to the realities of the American political system; unless it did, its enemies would destroy it. If one disregards the crude polemics the factions hurled at each other, two distinct arguments emerge. The Gissibl faction maintained that the Bund had evolved into a genuine German-American movement, though for the moment at least it could not sever all ties with the NSDAP, because it was unable to sustain itself financially. Haegele, on the other hand, argued that the Bund was subservient to the NSDAP and subject to the caprice of Party officials who knew little about the group's situation in America. He insisted that Gissibl had never conceived of the Americanization of the Bund as a step toward handing complete control of the movement to an American—which undoubtedly was what Berlin desired; Gissibl simply wanted to keep himself in power, even at the cost of destroying the Nazi movement in America and further tarnishing Germany's image.

Haegele's arguments were not completely fallacious. Since the Chicago convention, Gissibl had been trying to change the Bund's image and had been fairly successful, if rapid expansion and the group's success on German Day can be used as barometers. He had been forced into reorienting the Bund by the activities of the McCormack-Dickstein Committee and by his belief that the NSDAP intended to disassociate itself from the Bund in the not too distant future. After the July convention, Gissibl labored to create an American Bund movement, hoping to convince his superiors that if the organization were led by an American, it would grow and all criticism would cease. But the influx of Americans into the Bund brought further criticism from Dickstein and the anti-Nazis. By November 1934, Dickstein was claiming that the Nazis had infiltrated hundreds of long-established German-American associations. Ironically, the Bund's "new image" had produced an effect opposite to what Gissibl intended, and the group remained a thorn in German-American diplomatic relations.[29]

Anti-German sentiment became more conspicuous after the publication of the McCormack-Dickstein Committee's report in Febru-

[29] Memorandum by Hans Luther, April 8, 1935, *DGFP*, C, IV, 23–29.

ary 1935. The report was a massive indictment of the NSDAP which held it responsible for supporting a branch of the Party in the United States and accused it of aiding its nationals at the expense of the United States. Dickstein's findings, by providing support for the allegations of the liberal community, helped to make the word "Bund" synonymous with German intrigue and treachery. "All those elements which go to make up public opinion," wrote Ambassador Hans Luther shortly after the appearance of the report, ". . . are, however, outweighed by the predominantly hostile attitude toward the New Germany which has become established here, especially in the press." [30]

Thus, from the German standpoint, the Friends of the New Germany was now a major liability that contributed to the ill feeling between Washington and Berlin. At the beginning of the new year, 1935, Hess, Bohle, and the Foreign Ministry faced the problem of dissolving the Bund for the sake of better relations between America and Germany, and between Germany and the German-American community. Furthermore, the so-called Bund war had convinced them that FONG was unpredictable and unreliable— no matter how "Nazi-ish" its members were.

[30] *DGFP*, C, IV, 24.

PART **III**

THE FRITZ KUHN
YEARS, 1936-1939

CHAPTER 7

The Turning Point

Although Anton Haegele's coup failed and he mustered only a handful of recruits to his splinter group, the rebellion aroused much excitement within the Friends of the New Germany. Haegele's contention that Gissibl, Kappe, and Schuster were power-hungry was not unfounded. Gissibl, for example, had slandered Griebl, fired Walter, and would soon remove Schnuch. He had every intention of retaining the leadership. Undoubtedly, together with the McCormack-Dickstein probe, the Haegele-Schnuch (more precisely, Gissibl) struggle heightened the insecurities and anxieties of a usually fearful group. In times of crisis, members of foreign political groups share the same fear—of being abandoned to a real or imaginary foe in a hostile environment. But in times of relative quiet, although this apprehension is always present, anxieties are often sublimated into action, usually into preparations for the attainment of power. For the Bundists, power was to be assumed in the distant future—on *Der Tag*, the day they would oust the Jews and allies of the Jews from their entrenched positions and take control of the nation. Few, if any, Bundists thought this to be a realizable goal, however. The Bundists were not so naïve as to expect to sit in the White House. What Hitler and his entourage did in Germany was regarded as a miracle to be emulated but not duplicated. Clearly, the Bundists viewed their organization as a defensive group acting as a shield to protect them from the power they believed was held by American Jewry. Thus, when German State and Party officialdom began to question the propriety of supporting a group that was gradually eroding Berlin's position in America, Gissibl and his followers started to fear for their own fates.

The Bundists' fears were not without foundation. They believed that Samuel Dickstein and the "Jewish lobby" in Washington would use their influence to crush the Bund and all traces of Nazism at home. Admittedly, the tenor of the congressional probe had led the Bundists to the conclusion that if Dickstein had his way, they would be on the first boat to Germany. In essence, what the Jews were for Hitler, the Bundists would be for Dickstein. Such fears became more apparent by the middle of the decade. After all, they contended, Heinz Spanknöbel, the discredited Bund leader, had fled the United States in order to avoid being tried by Jewish Communist justices. Thus, as the winter of 1934–1935 approached, one topic dominated conversations among the Bundists —abandonment. Whether they were talking over a glass of beer in Ebling's Casino in The Bronx or Fesel's Pavillion in Suffern, New York, members of the group expressed the same anxieties. An aura of gloom had settled over the organization in the wake of the congressional probe. In the New York metropolitan area the situation became even more acute during the so-called Bund war, the Haegele-Schnuch controversy.

The Bund's footing was so uncertain and its members so depressed that most Bundists probably would have agreed with an observation made by Bundist Karl Neumann in early 1934. He wrote, "Sometimes I think during the night that if our Führer, Adolf Hitler, ever saw the mess in New York, he would cry." [1] Although the Gissibl faction had regained control of the New York unit in early 1935, some observers believed that the movement had been fragmented beyond repair, and that it was only a matter of time until it disbanded. "Even today," wrote German Consul Oskar Schlitter (New York) in mid-January, "the results of the quarrel are still unclear." [2] Undoubtedly, such comments from other knowledgeable members of the German diplomatic corps only helped to arm the Foreign Ministry's case against the group; moreover, negative criticism served to reinforce the long-held beliefs of the traditionalists in the Wilhelmstrasse. Before the year's end, Rudolf Hess was to find merit in their arguments and support a Foreign Minis-

---

[1] Karl Neumann to Rolf Hoffmann, Jan. 1, 1934, T-81/27/24507a.
[2] Schlitter to Gustav Moshack (DAI), Jan. 19, 1935, T-81/394/5135033.

try edict calling for the resignation of all German nationals from the Bund by December 31, 1935.

Germany's eventual disengagement from the Friends of the New Germany did not mean that the Party had despaired of unifying American *Deutschtum* or of propagandizing all Americans; disengagement did mean that Germany had dismissed Gissibl's political organization as the nucleus around which Americans of German extraction would group. Nor did the Foreign Ministry's and Party's decision preclude the possibility of Germany's giving material and ideological support to any viable indigenous pro-Nazi organization that might develop in America. As of December 1934, a grass-roots movement in German-America did not seem imminent. For the moment, at least, Germany wanted to rid itself of the harmful Bund movement.

The decision to frustrate the further development of the Bund had its roots in a long and complex history. The Spanknöbel Affair, the formation of the McCormack-Dickstein Committee, Theodor Hoffmann's complaints to Hitler, and, finally, the Haegele-Schnuch confrontation did little to endear the Bund to State and Party officialdom in Germany. The Bund stood as a major obstacle to Germany's entry into the German-American community; moreover, the Bundists did little to improve Nazi Germany's image in the eyes of many Americans. Even though Berlin repeatedly denied that it was behind the group, officials in Washington, members of the press, and of course the irascible Dickstein simply did not accept German assurances at face value. When, in February 1934, Bohle ordered all Party members out of the Friends of the New Germany and sent a circular to NSDAP people in America instructing them to refrain from all political activity, a copy of the circular fell into Dickstein's hands. It was like a godsend to Dickstein.

Especially disturbing to the old-line practitioners of foreign policy were the unsettling incidents created by the Bund. Ambassador Luther and his colleagues in Berlin, all of whom well remembered the debacle of less than sixteen years before, in 1934 had regarded Dickstein's probe as of little significance. With the start of the new year, they re-evaluated the degree of anti-German sentiment in America and were disturbed by what they discovered. Because of the distinction between State and Party in Germany, with respect both to responsibility and implementation of policy, invariably the Americans held the State, the traditional instrument of diplomacy, accountable for the activities of German nationals and their friends in the pro-Nazi Bund.

After the Haegele-Schnuch Affair convinced some Party people that a pro-Nazi political organization (at least one directed by the unpredictable Bundists) would not take root in American soil, Bohle and Hess concurred with the men in the Foreign Ministry. They did so for a variety of reasons. In the first years of the Nazi regime—that is, from 1933 to 1935—Hitler and his entourage craved respectability and recognition; the Bundists did little to help them gain such a status. Auslandsorganisation personnel, though by no means unsympathetic to the goals of a pro-Nazi movement in America, shared the popular American view of the Bundists as thugs recruited from the unemployable. This belief was also strong in the Foreign Ministry. Several years later, in 1938, Hans Heinrich Dieckhoff, the German ambassador to the United States and brother-in-law of Joachim von Ribbentrop, summed up what many high-ranking Germans had felt for years: the Bund movement was nonsensical, and its members were engaged in "conspiratorial child's play." [3] Although this was what one would expect from a professional diplomat who had firsthand knowledge of the Americans, it is clear that many old-guard Nazis also shared this view.

In light of the prehistory of National Socialism in the 1920's, such allegations against the Bundists seem inconsistent with Nazism's supranational goals. But the Nazi Party in 1935 was no longer a struggling extremist group; Hitler was institutionalizing his control of Germany, and he was attempting to move his nation to the center of the European stage. In June 1934, he had rid him-

---

[3] "Relations between the United States and Germany and the German-American element: Are we in a position to exert political influence on the German-Americans?" (memorandum, Hans Heinrich Dieckhoff to Foreign Ministry, Jan. 7, 1938, DGFP, D, I, 664–678). Dieckhoff had replaced Hans Luther in the spring of 1937. Several documents emphasize the evolution of German thinking on the situation in America. Of special importance are Luther to Foreign Ministry, March 22, 1934, DGFP, C, II, 653–655; Dieckhoff to German Embassy, March 20, 1934, C, II, 640–641; and Luther to Foreign Ministry, April 8, 1935 ("Animosity is primarily directed against us, especially in the State Department") C, IV, 23–27.

self of many of those who reminded him of his roots and of those who allegedly wanted to inhibit the institutionalization of the Nazi revolution; the Roehm purge was the turning point in Hitler's relationship with the old elite, especially the military. The Bundists presented a similar problem. Like Roehm's followers, they were unpredictable and had tarnished the image of the New Germany. By the winter of 1934–1935, Germany found it could no longer control the Friends of the New Germany. In essence, the group had become an inconvenient and troublesome burden. Hitler's continentalism notwithstanding, America's sensibilities had to be taken into account.

Anton Haegele's attempted takeover of FONG was a crisis in the State's and the Party's relationships with the group. It fostered a feeling in Berlin that something would have to be done to retard the Bund's growth. But what? Bohle tried to wash his hands of the problems by not answering incoming mail from the Bundists. Throughout the controversy, some concerned Bundists petitioned Bohle to intervene in the conflict; but their pleas for help only brought them further frustration and compounded their fears of being abandoned. Unwilling to get involved, Bohle forwarded their letters to other agencies engaged in propaganda work in the United States; perhaps he hoped that the correspondence would be lost in the labyrinth of bureaus created by the Party. Some of their letters were sent to Rolf Hoffmann in the Overseas Press Office, others to the recently Nazified German Foreign Institute in Stuttgart. At first, staffers at the DAI did not know what to do with the mail arriving from America. Undoubtedly, no new directive had arrived at the DAI's House of Germanism. But as the volume of correspondence increased, it became clear to those involved in American work that certain of the Bund's functions were worth salvaging; others became convinced that Germany would have to work through the Bund if it ever hoped to gain access to some segments of American *Deutschtum,* especially in the Northeast.[4]

---

[4] Kipphan, *Deutsche Propaganda,* pp. 36ff. The Deutsches Ausland-Institut's relationship with the Bund has been overemphasized by Smith in *The Deutschtum of Nazi Germany.* As will be seen, the DAI unwittingly inherited some of the Bund's problems. Its involvement with the Bund, however, in no way equaled the involvement of the Party with the Friends of the New Ger-

The man most responsible for furthering these views was Gustav Moshack, who had joined the DAI in the late 1920's and was attached to its immigration research department, which helped locate employment for German nationals residing abroad. In the spring of 1934, Moshack's duties were enlarged to include what may loosely be called research. In May, he arrived in the United States to take a firsthand look at the German-American community. At this juncture, the Bund was still considered part of this community, and Moshack became acquainted with some of the group's officials. During his several months' stay, he discovered that the Friends of the New Germany was not at death's door; he even found that Fritz Gissibl was in the process of incorporating many small native German-American groups into its structure.[5]

One such organization was the Germanic Bund, a Los Angeles-based pro-Nazi group.[6] Structurally and ideologically, the Germanic Bund was a duplicate of the Friends of the New Germany. In the summer of 1933, its leader, Ernst Rheydt-Dittmar, had begun an active recruitment campaign on the West Coast. In an effort to heighten his group's appeal and attract members of the German-American community, he organized an after-school German-language program for children. Jealous of its growth and widening appeal, the local branch of the Friends forced Rheydt-Dittmar to join forces with it. In July 1934, he wrote Moshack that the Germanic Bund had been dissolved; two months later he asked Moshack to help salvage the Germanic Bund, to extricate it from

---

many. Of special note are Heinz Kloss's comments in "Die 'Amerikaarbeit' des DAI im Dritten Reich." Kloss maintains, correctly, that Smith based part of his argument on the fact that Fritz Gissibl and Walter Kappe joined the DAI's staff after they returned to Germany. As will be seen, neither man held an important post (or was ever considered for one) at the Institute.

5 "Aufzeichnung über Moshacks Bericht über seine Reise nach den Vereinigten Staaten vom 24. August 1934," T-120/5177/455068. Moshack was head of the DAI's Stellenvermittlung section, which procured jobs for emigrants.

6 The Germanic Bund was affiliated with C. F. Fulliam's White Shirts and a section of William D. Pelley's Silver Shirts, both right-wing pro-German groups. In 1935, the DAI and other German agencies were attempting to work around Gissibl's organization. See invitations to the DAI-sponsored Stuttgarter Festwoche, Sept. 1934; Consul Wilhelm Godel to Gustav Moshack, June 26, 1935, T-81/396/5136325; and "Programm," T-81/462/5216587.

Gissibl's organization. From Rheydt-Dittmar's correspondence with Moshack, it is clear that Moshack would have liked to use the group to further the Institute's cultural work.[7] But Moshack had neither the power nor the authority to do so. If he had actively intervened in the internal affairs of the Friends of the New Germany, he would have become an advocate of decentralization at the very moment when Gissibl was attempting a union with German-American groups. Despite Moshack's refusal to intervene, calls for DAI intervention did not cease. The pace accelerated with the start of the new year. Bohle's rechanneling of the Bund's mail to the DAI and Moshack's befriending of many Bund and non-Bund people prompted Bundists to believe they had found in the DAI a new friend in Germany.

At no other time in the history of the Nazi movement in America do its links with Germany remain as elusive as in the winter of 1934–1935. This period was one of transition. Subsequent events point to the following conclusions. At the time of the Haegele-Schnuch controversy, the Bund's connection with the Auslandsorganisation was becoming increasingly weak. It will be recalled that following Theodor Hoffmann's meeting with Hitler, Hans-Heinrich Lammers, State Secretary and Head of the Chancellery, urged the Foreign Ministry to keep the channels of communication with German nationals in the Bund open, if only to avoid mistakes that might endanger German-American relations. In a parallel and unquestionably related move, Bohle had made a relatively minor Nazi agency, the DAI, answerable for the Bund. In the DAI's acceptance of a portion of the responsibility lies the key to the Bund's relationship with Germany during 1935 and 1936. Nazi officialdom had dismissed the Bund as the organization around which German-Americans would gather; it had not, however, ruled out the possibility that the Bund—perhaps under a different leader and after the initial American shock of having a pro-Nazi group on its soil had worn off—might prove a valuable asset for the implementation of Germany's evolving goals in America. The Party was

<hr />

[7] Rheydt-Dittmar to Gustav Moshack, Feb. 5, 1934, T-81/396/5137820–3; July 21, 1934, T-81/396/5137814; to W. Drascher (DAI), Feb. 2, 1935, T-81/396/5137835.

now in a position to meddle in the Bund's affairs with a degree of impunity. If the American government should claim that the Party was behind the Bund, Berlin was in a position to place the blame at the door of the House of Germanism, described in its literature as a privately subsidized institute.[8]

At the start of 1935 the correspondence between the Bundists and the Institute took a new turn. No longer were only minor Bund members calling for the Institute's intervention; now the leaders of Anton Haegele's splinter group BANS, and of the established group, the Friends of the New Germany, were joining in the call. In January, Reinhold Walter, one of Anton Haegele's supporters in the attempted coup, requested Moshack to designate BANS as the legitimate Nazi group. He asserted that the "new Bund" best served "German interests in the U.S.A." Despite his well-phrased arguments and a timely effort to present an embellished picture of the secessionist group, Walter's labors only brought him further frustration.[9] As far as Germany was concerned, Schnuch and Gissibl were still recognized as the legitimate leaders of the Bund.

Four months later, in May 1935, the vice-consul at the German consulate in New York wrote Moshack of a rumor circulating in the Bundist community that Schnuch intended to go to Germany to plead with the Party to end the "brotherly quarrel" which was weakening the movement.[10] It was not hearsay; in June, Schnuch announced that he intended to ask Bohle to intervene personally by declaring Haegele and Walter renegades. Fearing the consequences and realizing that BANS was on the verge of collapse, Walter broke with Haegele and called for the immediate end of the conflict. This is exactly what Schnuch—or rather Gissibl—had been waiting for, a virtual statement of defeat. Dismissing Walter's

[8] Hans-Adolf Jacobsen has shed much light on the mysteries of Nazi administrative structure in the realm of foreign affairs. See "Zentralisation der Volkstumspolitik," in *Nationalsozialistische Aussenpolitik*, pp. 214, 233, 245. The actual role of the DAI in the formation of German foreign policy was minor, and it had little or no authority. It is therefore not surprising that Bohle shifted part of his one-time responsibility for the Bund to the DAI.

[9] Reinhold Walter to Rolf Hoffmann, Jan. 14, 1935, T-81/27/23929–35; Kurt Hoeher to Walter, Jan. 21, 1935, T-81/27/23924.

[10] Vice consul (New York) to Gustav Moshack, May 1935, T-81/394/5135027.

bid for reconciliation, Gissibl arranged Schnuch's trip to the Reich.[11]

Accompanied by Fritz Gissibl's brother Peter, Schnuch arrived in Stuttgart on August 16 and met with Moshack at the Institute. Schnuch was cordially received. Moshack listened patiently as he outlined the history of the struggle. Unfortunately for Schnuch, Moshack informed him that there was little he could do to resolve the conflict, let alone commit the resources of the State or the Party to support a movement that was a proven liability. After the meeting, Moshack wrote Consul Oskar Schlitter that the Bund president had made an excellent impression on him; admittedly, he concluded, Schnuch might be a suitable Bundesleiter, but there was little the DAI could do to resolve the group's manifold internal problems.[12]

During the ensuing weeks, the Party kept its contacts with the Bund to a minimum; except for supplying Nazi literature, it stopped furnishing material and moral support. During this crucial period Moshack prepared the groundwork for what he later called the "new approach" to American *Deutschtum*—that is, an attempt to penetrate the German-American community by working in areas outside New York City. In late August, Moshack journeyed to Bad Kissingen for a meeting with Hans Borchers, who was in Germany to attend the *Reichsparteitag* scheduled for September. Fresh from the United States and well aware of the Bund's internal problems, Borchers told Moshack that although the Schnuch-Haegele controversy was confined to the New York metropolitan area and represented no real threat to the movement as a whole, the conflict epitomized the disunity of the German-American community. Part of the blame rested with the American press; it had so thoroughly publicized the Bund's internal problems that most German-Americans interpreted the "Bund war" as a harbinger of the inevitable collapse of the organization.[13]

[11] "Das Ende des Bruderstreits?" *Deutscher Beobachter*, June 13, 1935.

[12] Oskar Schlitter to Gustav Moshack, n.d., T-81/394/5135022. On the meeting between Moshack and Schnuch, see T-81/394/5135019ff.

[13] Gustav Moshack to Hans Borchers, Sept. 27, 1935, T-81/394/5135015. This was not the first meeting between the two men; they had met while Moshack was in the United States in 1934.

Borchers' assertions were well founded, though they were based on information he could not reveal to Moshack, whom he might have suspected of trying to take control of the propaganda network in the United States. As a member of the consular staff and consul general in New York, Borchers was in contact with Ambassador Hans Luther in Washington and with the Wilhelmstrasse. He consequently knew that from the outset of the Nazi regime, his superiors disapproved of the Party's continued involvement with the Bund. Despite their wishes and, at times, with the blessing of the Party, his presence in New York had led him to become involved in the Bund's internal affairs. From time to time the warring factions asked him to intervene in the internecine struggle that was sapping the group's strength; furthermore, German nationals bombarded him with questions regarding their status in the group. The Bund and the Bundists, in short, had become a troublesome problem for Borchers. Now that he was aware that the Party viewed the Bund as a liability, he started to disengage himself from the movement.

Borchers' views were shared by Ambassador Luther. Since the outcry that followed his attendance at the German Day activities in 1934, the ambassador had remained aloof from the Bund. In his opinion, the Bund was the Party's mistake and his own misfortune, because he was held liable by Congressman Dickstein and some State Department officials for the group's activities. Luther had long believed that Germany's designation of the Bund as an outlet for Nazi propaganda was a serious but not irreversible error. Now that the Bund had shown its inability to improve the image of the New Germany, Luther felt that the Party should be willing to re-examine its relationship with the consular service and the Bund and should designate the service as the chief American outlet for Party literature. The summer of 1935 seemed an auspicious time for his bid.[14] He made his request in a long communication to the Reich Ministry of Propaganda, in which he wrote that he was convinced that Americans of German ancestry would respond only to cultural rather than to political stimuli. This opinion, he added,

[14] Hans Luther to Ministry of Propaganda, June 28, 1935, DGFP, C, IV, 381–382.

had been reinforced when he toured the United States and spoke with members of the consular service, who were in close contact with American *Deutschtum*.[15]

Although Luther did not mention the Friends of the New Germany by name, he indicated that its existence had impeded Germany's efforts to make contact with the German-American community. One of the principal reasons for the ineffectiveness of cultural propaganda was the "total suspension of the remittance of freely disposable funds to the Embassy and the Consulates, to be applied in the sphere of art, music, films, radio, and sport." The American people "possess a culture of their own only in embryonic form." But "the cultural life of these people is still predominantly rooted directly in Europe." During the World War, he maintained, the German element had been forcibly Americanized and had never fully recovered its Teutonic orientation. Because of Hitler's rise and the consequent National Socialist revolution, many Americans were beginning to appreciate the health and strength of a reinvigorated Reich. If German cultural work in America was "kept unpolitical and place[d] its main emphasis on the preservation of the language," it would not only preserve the distinctiveness of the German element but would also make Americans see the worldwide benefits of Germany's spiritual rebirth. Somehow, he concluded, educated Americans would have to be shown that German, not French, was the language of the cultivated and urbane; once convinced of the superiority of German *Kultur*, a more sympathetic view of Nazism would naturally follow. Finally, German-America must be reanimated, "to strengthen it internally and to unify it externally, to awaken a cultural consciousness and a cultural urge." [16] To implement his proposals, Luther requested that funds be placed at the disposal of the Embassy.

Luther's letter arrived at the Foreign Ministry at an auspicious time. Reich officials had begun to believe that the time had come to reverse, or at least offset, the damage done by the Bundists; the time also had arrived to accelerate the collapse of the Bund movement. Throughout the spring and into the summer of 1935, predic-

[15] *Ibid.*, C, IV, 384–389.   [16] *Ibid.*, C, IV, 389.

tions of the group's demise came from many sources, all of which contended that as a consequence of Dickstein's hammer blows and the organization's internecine quarreling the Bund would soon die.[17] What was meant to be the final blow came on October 11, 1935, when the Foreign Ministry called for the immediate withdrawal of all German nationals from the Bund, including those with first naturalization papers. Unlike the previous decree (which called for the resignation of all Party members from the Bund), this edict was meant to be obeyed: German nationals were warned that if they remained in the Bund, they would have their passports confiscated and might forfeit their German citizenship. The ministry meant business, and the decree was implemented by the consular staff in the United States. Bohle's superior, Rudolf Hess, who was instrumental in formulating the order, reasoned that since all the leaders of the Bund were German nationals, the departure of these men would create a vacuum that could not be filled and would thus speed the collapse of the Friends of the New Germany.[18]

When the Bundists learned of this decision, a wave of panic, disgust, disillusionment, and fear swept the Bund movement, strongly recalling the days following the Spanknöbel incident. The lurking fear of being abandoned that preyed on the consciousness of every Bundist took on new force. But the Bundists' feeling that they had been sacrificed for the sake of improved diplomatic relations between Berlin and Washington was not evident in their letters to Nazi agencies; on the contrary, they believed that they were the victims of a well-organized plot concocted by members of the consular staff in America. This explanation of the Bund's fate was outlined by Peter Gissibl in his long and lucid account of the group's activities in Chicago to Rolf Hoffmann. Fritz's brother wrote that the October decree was implemented in the Midwest by Consul Jaeger, who was attached to the consulate in Chicago. Upon receiving a copy of the Foreign Ministry's order, Jaeger summoned

---

[17] Oskar Schlitter to Gustav Moshack, Aug. 16, 1935, T-81/394/5135022; Sept. 16, 1935, T-81/394/5135015.

[18] The substance of the decree is in a letter from Peter Gissibl to Rolf Hoffmann, Nov. 1, 1935, T-81/26/23283.

Gissibl and his subordinates to his office. The consul told them that if German nationals did not immediately withdraw from FONG, he would see to it that they lost their citizenship and, by implication, become stateless persons. Gissibl, a member of the "old guard" from Teutonia days, was astonished by Jaeger's blatant refusal to appease or at least soothe the ill feeling that had developed as a result of the edict. A heated verbal exchange ensued; at the height of the argument Peter Gissibl informed Jaeger that Fritz Gissibl intended to go directly to Hess in an effort to have him reverse the decision. "If your brother goes to Germany," replied Jaeger, "he can expect to be thrown into a concentration camp." Disgusted and resentful, the Bundists left the consulate.[19]

According to Gissibl, the zeal with which Jaeger implemented the October edict was prompted by factors in no way related to the Bund's past or present activities. Gissibl claimed that Jaeger was an "incompetent and tactless man," a career opportunist who, like other members of the consular service, had been sending only derogatory accounts of the Bund in order to gain favor with their superiors at home. Men of Jaeger's ilk had for years been sabotaging the work of the Bund. "From other places," he concluded, "Berlin's *competent* authorities received reports of our work that created the impression that we were harming Germany's image in America." As a result, State and Party officialdom was now bent on destroying the only genuine Nazi group on American soil.[20]

Peter Gissibl's letters reveal the frustrations of a man who was witnessing the destruction of eleven years of hard work; they give evidence as well of a breakdown in communications between Germany and the Bundists. That Gissibl thought Rolf Hoffman, who was responsible for disseminating Nazi propaganda, was the man who could—"by means of your influential connections in Berlin" —rescue the Bund indicates how little he knew about Hoffmann's position in the Third Reich. In spite of his disdain for Jaeger and his obvious effort to disclaim any personal responsibility for the Bund's demise, Gissibl's contention that the consular staff had actively undermined the Bund's position was not without substance.

[19] T-81/26/23283–5.   [20] T-81/26/23284.

To be sure, the diplomatic corps and the Bund had once been close allies. In New York City, members of the consulate helped organize the Friends of the New Germany. Members of the consulate had lent support to Colonel Edwin Emerson and underwritten the Friends of Germany and later the Friends of the New Germany, participated in the German Day activities, channeled money into the Bund, and perpetuated the myth that Germany was in no way connected with the Bund movement. But they did so on orders from Berlin; in 1933 and 1934, Hess and Bohle believed that the Bund might prove useful, might become a viable political force. In spite of their optimism, the more conservative voices in the Party and the State predominated as the Bund moved from one crisis to another. The decree issued in October was welcomed by the traditionalists in the Wilhelmstrasse; it was also welcomed by men like Luther and Jaeger, who never shared Hess's optimism about the Bund.

Peter's brother Fritz refused to acquiesce in the decision. But unlike Peter, he did not register a complaint with a consulate official. In early November, he made a hurried trip to Berlin, where he made a desperate plea at the Foreign Ministry. Gissibl argued that the Friends of the New Germany had attempted to Americanize (he claimed that 60 per cent of the ten thousand members were still German nationals); that the organization had substantial financial holdings in real estate, camps, and newspapers; and that the enforcement of the edict would cause the group's collapse. Much to his chagrin, the order was not rescinded. His visit did produce one tangible result: it prompted representatives of the AO der NSDAP, the Foreign Ministry, the Ministry of Propaganda, and the Büro Ribbentrop (literally, Ribbentrop Office) to meet and discuss Gissibl's plea. Instead of reversing the decision, they reaffirmed it. The decree was modified only to permit German nationals to remain in the Bund until midnight, December 31, 1935, so that they could settle their affairs. As he had in his earlier dealings with Germany, Gissibl accepted the decision as the will of the Führer and returned to the United States to implement the order. On December 27, 1935, shortly after he returned to America, Berlin released the text of the discussions and a copy of the edict signed by Hess to the Associated Press.[21]

Germany hoped that the rapid withdrawal of German nationals from the Bund would accelerate the group's demise and permit Germany to bring about the unification of American *Deutschtum* without hindrance from the troublesome Bund. Subsequent events, however, would show the Germans that they had created an insoluble problem: The Bund did not collapse; in fact, the edict only prompted the Bundists to put their house in order.

The next year, 1936, witnessed the reinvigoration of the Bund, renamed the Amerikadeutscher Volksbund, under the leadership of a former chemist and long-time Party member, Fritz Julius Kuhn. Germany discovered that Fritz Gissibl's "Americanization" of the Bund had gone further than anyone had expected. For Berlin to begin extricating the German-American groups already under the Bund's influence would have meant the kind of involvement that Berlin had so strenuously labored to end in the late fall of 1935. The situation became more complicated when Kuhn demonstrated that he could attract Americans of German extraction to his organization.

The year 1936 marked the beginning of a massive propaganda campaign aimed at Americans of all regions and ethnic backgrounds, which continued unabated until America's entry into World War II. What the Germans called the "American Enlightenment" took several forms. On one hand, Germany increased the volume of Nazi propaganda sent to the United States and became the chief supplier of literature to most of the pro-Nazi and militant anti-Jewish and anti-Communist groups that had sprung up in cities throughout America. The chief beneficiaries were William Dudley Pelley, the Jew-baiting leader of the Silver Shirts; C. F. Fulliam, leader of the White Shirts; Dr. Otto Vollbehr, a close

---

[21] Memorandum of a meeting in the Foreign Ministry, Nov. 13–14, 1935, T-120/K1054/270567–270659; consulate general (New York) to Foreign Ministry, Jan. 24, 1936, T-120/2961/474509. The Büro Ribbentrop was a Party creation and assumed many of the functions of the Foreign Ministry. It was a "paradiplomatic" agency. See Bracher, *German Dictatorship*, p. 321.

associate of the anti-Semitic evangelist Gerald B. Winrod and publisher of *The Defender;* and the Germanophile George Sylvester
Viereck. Largely clandestine, such efforts were aimed at whipping
up native anti-Semitism and latent Anglophobia. On the other
hand, Germany placed greater emphasis than formerly on using
what might be called its legitimate outlets for propaganda dissemination. Among the most important were the German Library of Information in New York, the German Railroads Information Office,
the German Tourist Information Office, the Fichtebund, and the
VDA. The last agency, which had extensive contacts with a number of Americans dating from the pre-Hitler period, retained a full-
time representative, Günther Orgell, who lived on Staten Island
and had easy access to incoming German steamers.

In spite of its stepped-up efforts to make contact with Americans
outside the German-American community, the Party had not relinquished its desire to propagandize its racial comrades in
America.[22] This task was entrusted in part to the experts on America at the German Foreign Institute, who were working in conjunction with the consular service. The Institute's involvement with the
German-American community did not suddenly begin with Germany's disengagement from the Bund in December 1935. New,
however, was the increase in involvement in American affairs.
What Gustav Moshack aptly referred to as the "new approach to
American *Deutschtum*" began when he visited the United States in
May 1934.[23] At the start of his five-week fact-finding tour, he wrote
Hans Borchers that his aim was "to personally examine the situa-
tion in the U.S.A. and renew old acquaintances with German-
Americans and their organizations under the new conditions." [24]

[22] The German propaganda campaign in this country has been discussed by
Kipphan in *Deutsche Propaganda.* For the purposes of this study, the Nazi
propaganda offensive will be examined only insofar as it related to the Bund
organization. The records of the German Railroads Information Office and the
German-American Chamber of Commerce are in RG 131. To date, these records have not been explored by researchers.
[23] Hermann Rüdiger (DAI), "DAI: Vierteljahresbericht," Jan.–March 1936,
T-81/425/5172666.
[24] Gustav Moshack to Hans Borchers, May 12, 1935, T-81/394/5135047;
Aug. 14, 1935, T-81/394/5135045.

Moshack's visit merely served to reinforce his long-held views concerning the most expeditious way to approach the German-American community. After he returned to Stuttgart, he told his colleagues that blatant pro-Nazi propaganda would avail Germany little in America. The New Germany had to be sensitive to the loyalties of German-Americans, and they must be approached cautiously, that is, on a cultural rather than a strictly political basis. Translated into an active policy, this meant getting in touch with the thousands of German-American *Vereine* and providing them with free films, literature, and guest speakers.[25] In a letter to Consul Wilhelm Godal in Denver, Colorado, Moshack asserted that if the DAI's "new approach" was to succeed, the tension between Washington and Berlin had to be eased; otherwise, any overtures would be suspect.[26]

Moshack maintained, correctly, that the Institute's best ally was the consular service, since the service enjoyed excellent connections with hundreds of well-established German-American groups. Since the mid-1920's, the DAI had gathered much of its statistical information about Americans of German descent from the consuls, who had long provided the names and addresses of newly arrived German nationals to the House of Germanism; they had also been supplying lists of recently organized German-American organizations found in the postwar period. Thus, when Moshack requested a consul in Cleveland to send a list of German-American organizations sympathetic to Nazi Germany, he was simply following a long-established practice.[27] When this information was correlated with existing information in the DAI's files, a reasonably accurate picture emerged of the political leanings of thousands of migrants who had left Germany since 1900.[28]

The DAI's efforts to unify the German element in America occurred in two distant stages. The first period, from about mid-1934

[25] Gustav Moshack, "Stuttgart und das Auslandsdeutschtum," address to DAI; Rüdiger, "DAI: Vierteljahresbericht," p. 5, T-81/425/5172666.

[26] Gustav Moshack to Consul Godel, Dec. 29, 1934, T-81/395/5136318.

[27] Consul W. T. Hinrichs (Cleveland, Ohio) to Gustav Moshack, Dec. 1934, T-81/395/5136139–40.

[28] Lists of Immigrants from southwestern Germany, 1935, VDA files, T-81/575 (entire roll).

to 1937, was characterized by the planners' mystical faith in their ability to create sympathy for Germany by rekindling the latent feeling of *Deutschtum;* the second period, from 1937 to 1939, had none of the optimism of the first. When the DAI's specialists on America—Heinz Kloss, Otto Lohr, and Gustav Moshack—began to realize that their efforts to propagandize American *Deutschtum* systematically were failing, they decided to work with two of the largest and best-established groups, the Steuben Society and the Carl Schurz Memorial Foundation.[29] In addition, they found that they had to include the reorganized Bund under Fritz Kuhn in their plans. In May 1938, it became obvious to Moshack that the ideal and the reality of the American situation were far apart; he confided to Consul Knopfel in Pittsburgh: "We always move in the wrong direction because we compare American *Deutschtum* with *Deutschtum* in other countries, and do not allow Americans of German extraction to remain part of the American nation, as it is and wishes to be." [30]

But in the Spring of 1936, Moshack and his co-workers believed they were moving in the right direction. They approached their task as one would a mathematical equation; after spending years researching the historical development of the German-American community and analyzing the information sent to them by consuls and other agencies, they believed that unification would automatically follow the translation of theory into policy. The first step came in the summer of 1936, when the well-known poet and story writer Karl Goetz made a fact-finding tour of the New World. Goetz, who was an expert on the history of German immigration, arrived in New York in June.[31] Several days after his arrival, he

[29] Steuben Society, "Ansprache Moshacks an die Mitglieder der Steubengesellschaft von Amerika," n.d., T-81/406/5150371. Cf. Kloss, "Die 'Amerikaarbeit' des DAI," pp. 14–17.

[30] Gustav Moshack to Consul Knopfel, April 29, 1938, T-81/396/5137020–1.

[31] Goetz was not a member of the DAI's staff; however, he was a close friend of the DAI's honorary president, Karl Strölin. In the mid-1930's, Goetz held two positions: he was a member of the city government of Stuttgart and the head of the VDA's Volksschularbeit. Among his writings about German immigration are *Brüder über dem Meer* and *Deutsche Leistung in Amerika* (Berlin, 1940). See T-81/144/183852–879. On the arrangements for his trip, see T-81/141/0179046.

delivered the first of five addresses to a crowd he estimated at seven thousand attending a German Day celebration in Hudson County, New Jersey. He told the audience, which included Bund units from North Bergen, Union City, Passaic, and Fairfield, that the German Foreign Institute and other agencies of its type had enjoyed a long and fruitful relationship with the German-American community. The DAI, he continued, though a private agency working independently of the Party, understood the needs of the Germans in the United States; above all, it appreciated their contributions to the historical development of this country, and although he was fully aware that they were Americans, he urged them to assert their *Deutschtum.* Finally, he reminded them that the "great work of Adolf Hitler" was spreading to Germans throughout the world and that they were part of the world-wide German community.[32]

As a result of his tour of the New York metropolitan area, Goetz concluded that the Bund was still quite active. He found that the group, far from being a moribund organization, had made inroads into many long-established *Vereine.* This meant that Germany might have to work with the Bund if it intended to penetrate the German-American community in New York and its environs.[33]

From New York, Goetz traveled to Philadelphia, where he addressed the United Swabian Societies under the leadership of Pastor Jaeger. Although the minister and his friends were "good people," Goetz reported in a letter to Strölin, he found "new and difficult problems in Philadelphia"; in fact, he confided to Strölin that during his address to a large audience (which he estimated at ten thousand), it exhibited little enthusiasm for the new Germany. Goetz, however, conveyed a different impression to Heinz Könekamp, who served as a liaison man between the DAI and the Auslandsorganisation: "Here in Philadelphia my work is going better

[32] "Goetz-Reise nach Nord- u. Mittel.- u. Südamerika, 1936/7; Briefe und Ausschnitte," Goetz Papers, T-81/583/5365950ff. For his itinerary, see Moshack to Consul Wendler, "Reiseplan von Karl Goetz," June 10, 1936, T-81/396/5136937. See also Goetz to Strölin, June 24, 1936, T-81/583/5365957.

[33] Goetz to Strölin, n.d., T-81/583/5365966–7; "Der Deutsche Tag von Hudson County," *Deutscher Weckruf und Beobachter* (New York), June 25, 1936.

than ever. I have had little sleep. In New York I gave five addresses; in Philadelphia, I spoke three times, once on a German radio station. Tonight, I will address the German Societies of Pennsylvania." [34] Apparently, Goetz did not want the Auslandsorganisation to suspect that there was lack of response to his fact-finding tour of the United States. But much to his chagrin, when he arrived in Cleveland, his somber appraisal of German-Americans' awareness of the new Germany was reinforced. "Our five representatives [members of the DAI *Verein*] in this city," he wrote Strölin on July 27, "have little or no influence." [35]

When Goetz went farther west, his spirits underwent a profound transformation, and his correspondence with Strölin reflects a renewed enthusiasm. Elated by the receptions he received from German-American groups, he reported to Strölin that he had finally "found a circle of friends in the United States"—real German men, individuals who had not been contaminated by materialism.[36] In Omaha, Lincoln, Kansas City, and Chicago he addressed scores of minor German singing groups, businessmen's organizations, and sport clubs. "The world is very small," he wrote Strölin in mid-August; "here in Lincoln, Nebraska, I found Volga Germans." [37] In the remaining days of his midwestern tour, Goetz met with leaders of the organizations and promised to have the DAI send them literature about their historical development.

Karl Goetz's trip was a major turning point in Germany's relationship with many German-American groups. It is difficult to estimate how many people he met or how many groups he addressed. But it is clear that Goetz appreciated the extent of German-America's efforts to maintain its *Deutschtum* by establishing clubs and organizations. He considered no group too small to visit. In Chicago, he met with the leaders of the fifty-man Schwäbischen Saegerbund; in Columbus, the Männereschor; in Detroit, the owner of Max Stephen's German Restaurant; in Kansas City, the Germania Männer Chor; and in Indianapolis, the Verband Deutscher Vereine. Most

[34] Goetz to Heinz Könekamp, June 24, 1936, T-81/583/5365970–1.
[35] Goetz to Strölin, July 27, 1936, T-81/583/5366021.
[36] *Ibid.*, Aug 8, 1936, T-81/583/5366064–66.
[37] *Ibid.*, Aug. 21, 1936, T-81/583/5366077.

of these groups had been founded in the nineteenth century, and although they were by no means overtly pro-Nazi, most of their leaders welcomed an opportunity to receive literature from Germany. Throughout the entire trip, Goetz carefully recorded the names of the leaders and members of each organization. Weekly, he sent this information to the DAI and the VDA. In the months and years that followed, these organizations were supplied with free film strips, guest speakers, and literature; many of their members took advantage of reduced-rate fares to Germany.[38]

Goetz's trip demonstrated the close relationship that had developed between the Institute and the consular service. Hotel arrangements were made by members of the consular staff, who also made advance contacts with the German-American groups in their areas. Germany's plans to create sympathy for the New Germany among the members of the hundred of *Vereine* that dotted America had taken shape. Over the next three years, Germany depended more and more on the consular service to measure the impact of its American work. The correspondence between the consulates and the planners for America at the Institute records the successes and the failures of their approaches to American *Deutschtum*.[39]

[38] It will be recalled that the DAI's representatives and members of its *Verein* had been sending monthly reports since the 1920's. These reports were received by members of the Institute's research staff; if a report was deemed essential to a current project, it was sent to the appropriate section. On cooperation with the consuls, see Goetz to Strölin, Aug. 7, 1936, T-81/583/5366064–6; T-120/5389/516103–636. In the late 1930's the DAI's American activities included the Sister Cities Project (an exchange program between Stuttgart and Chicago); the Black Forest Colony Project (the construction of a DAI camp near Port Jervis, New York; the land was purchased through the New York consulate, but the camp was never constructed); and an exchange program with a number of Lutheran colleges in Pennsylvania. See Otto Lohr, "Vorschläge für aktive Amerika-Arbeit des DAI, 28. April 1938," T-81/425/5172751–772; "Niederschrift über zweite Besprechnung der Amerika-Sachbearbeiter der DAI, 16. Mai 1938," T-81/614/5406522; "The Sister Cities Project," Moshack to Consul Baer, May 19, 1938, T-81/394/5134586–7; "Schwarzwaldstätt," correspondence of German consulate, New York, 1937, T-81/394/5134965ff.

[39] Goetz to Strölin, July 2, 1936, Aug. 8, 1936, T-81/394/5365978; 583/5366064–6; Moshack to Consul Wendler, June 10, 1936, T-81/396/5136937; Goetz Papers, T-81/583/5365983–88.

Always presenting himself as a German first and rarely mentioning the Jewish question, Goetz was well received by the German-American community. Even Bernard and Victor Ridder's *New Yorker Staats-Zeitung und Herold* commented that for the first time since Hitler came to power, a "representative of Germany spoke to us about our history" in America and described Goetz as a "researcher, teacher, editor, and storyteller." [40]

Obviously, the indefatigable Goetz was many things to many people. The response to his cultural (as opposed to a blatant racial-political) appeal prompted him to conclude that there were two distinct categories of German-Americans and that each would have to be approached on a different basis. First, there were the "real German men"—the Volga Germans and Pennsylvania Dutch —who should be held up to other German-Americans as examples of how *Deutschtum* could be preserved in an alien environment. Second, there were the members long-established German-American organizations, which were of two types: those that had come under the Bund's influence and those that had not. Goetz believed that Germany should work to prevent the still independent organizations from coming under the Bund's control. But Germany should not dismiss the Bund as unimportant in German-American affairs. In a letter from Seattle to Hans Borchers in New York, Goetz wrote, "In the middle of this bleak area stands the Bund! The American German Bund stands as an oasis in the desert." [41]

It is clear that while Goetz appeared to some German-Americans as a good German, he also presented himself to some Bundists as a stalwart Nazi. In places where he found the Bund to be a substantial force he met with its leaders, especially in New York and New Jersey. To be sure, all that Goetz promised the Bundists was a continued supply of Nazi literature; but this was enough, since he created a feeling within the Bund community that Germany had not forsaken it after all.[42]

[40] Address by Goetz, T-81/583/5365979–80; clipping, "Die deutschamerikanische Presse zu der Arbeit von Ratsherr Goetz," Goetz Papers, T-81/584/5366440.

[41] June 17, 1936, T-81/583/5365953–6.

[42] Amerikadeutscher Volksbund to Karl Strölin, July 29, 1936, T-81/583/5366026; Goetz to Borchers, June 17, 1936, T-81/583/5365953–6. On the

Goetz concluded his American fact-finding tour in October 1936. After a brief stay in New York's luxurious Waldorf Astoria Hotel, Goetz boarded a steamer for South America. En route he visited German groups in Mexico, Guatemala, the Canal Zone, Ecuador, Peru, Chile, Argentina, Uruguay, and Brazil.[43] Upon his return to the Reich in 1937, he reminded his superiors of what they already knew: Germany would have to work with the Bund if it ever hoped to make inroads into the German-American community.[44]

---

twenty-first, Borchers mailed Goetz a list of groups under the Bund's control (T-81/583/5365959–64).

[43] "Goetz Reise," T-81/583/5365951.

[44] "Aussprache Goetz mit Gauleiter," n.d., T-81/141/0178615–6.

CHAPTER **8**

The American Führer:
Fritz Julius Kuhn

In the years between Karl Goetz's tour of the New World in 1936 and the outbreak of the European war in September 1939, the DAI's president, Karl Strölin; experts on America Gustav Moshack and Heinz Kloss; and Hitler's adjutant Fritz Wiedemann were among the many Germans who visited the United States. They returned with the same story Goetz had brought back: the Bund had re-emerged as a factor in some German-American communities.[1] For those in Germany who had hoped to see the total demise of the Bund, their reports were unsettling, especially during the rapid deterioration in German-American relations following the American outcry against the Nazi anti-Jewish pogrom, the *Kristallnacht* ("Night of Broken Glass"), in November 1938 and the subsequent mutual recall of ambassadors. For members of Nazified German agencies and the Auslandsorganisation, the reports were disturbing, too, since they believed that the Bundists' raucous ac-

---

[1] The DAI's honorary president, Karl Strölin, arrived in New York on the S.S. *Deutschland* in October 1936. During his stay in New York, he addressed a number of German-American organizations and met with the new leader of the Bund, Fritz Kuhn. His interpreter was Gustav Moshack. Speaking arrangements were made by the Consular Service. Materials pertaining to Strölin's trip are in the DAI collection, T-81/394/5134626–994. On Kloss's visit to America (1936), see Heinz Kloss, "Die 'Amerikaarbeit' des DAI," pp. 7, 14–17; and yearly report of the DAI, 1936–1937 (Aug. 14–16, 1937), T-81/480/5238335–7. Hitler's one-time aide and former commanding officer, Fritz Wiedemann, made his first visit to the United States in November 1937; in March 1939, he was appointed Consul General in San Francisco. For Wiedemann's account of his first visit, see Fritz Wiedemann, *Der Mann—der Feldherr werden wollte* ([Dortmund?], Germany, 1964), pp. 217, 238ff.

tivities were sabotaging Germany's maturing propaganda campaign. But the Germans could not simply ignore the Bund. Far from being the indigenous German-American movement envisioned some years before, the Amerikadeutscher Volksbund (or simply the Volksbund) was directed almost exclusively by recently naturalized Americans or by German nationals on the path toward citizenship. This exclusiveness too disturbed the Germans, since Washington held Berlin responsible for the activities of its nationals who remained in the Bund in violation of the prohibition decided on in October 1935 and implemented two months later. But Berlin found irritating, above all else, the leader of the Volksbund, Fritz Julius Kuhn.

In November 1935, in the midst of the intragroup chaos engendered by the edict calling for the withdrawal of all German nationals from the Bund, Fritz Gissibl had designated Fritz Kuhn provisional Bundesleiter. Earlier, in September, Gissibl had taken complete control of the Friends of the New Germany and had himself elected Bundsleiter at the group's third national convention in Philadelphia (September 1–4). As in his other dealings with the forceful Gissibl, Schnuch simply withdrew from the picture. Obviously, Anton Haegele's poorly organized intraparty rebellion had a resounding impact on Gissibl, who did not want to see years of work go unrewarded. While in Germany in November, Gissibl had assured officials that he would oversee the exodus of German nationals from the Bund; he had also secured the Party's permission for the Bund to use the Nazi symbol after January 1, 1936.[2] Of course, Party and State officials believed that this was a small price to pay to be rid eventually of the Bund; little did they suspect that the heyday of the Bund movement was shortly to begin —the Fritz Kuhn years, 1936–1939.

Unlike Schnuch, Kuhn did not like to be called president; he maintained that this designation sounded too American, too democratic, and he dropped it in favor of the old title, the more Nazi-sounding Bundesleiter. Although a minor change, Kuhn's revival of the old title suggests the direction of his thinking during the form-

[2] Consulate general (New York) to Foreign Ministry, Jan. 24, 1936, T-120/2961/474509.

ative years of the Volksbund. He believed that fascism and National Socialism were being hailed—or feared—as the waves of the future. "By 1936," writes George Mosse, "a fascist Europe seemed within the realms of possibility—this even before Germany came to exercise its dominance over the movement." [3] This belief gave Kuhn's Volksbund its momentum. In flattering English and in German, Bundesleiter Kuhn loudly proclaimed to audiences in Madison Square Garden, in the Yorkville Casino, in Hermann-sohn's Park in Oakdale, California, and in the German-American Bund Home in Union City, New Jersey, that National Socialist Germany pointed the way to America's future. This bold assertion was echoed by his followers and repeated by native American fascists, including the fundamentalist evangelist Gerald Winrod and Lawrence Dennis, whose book *The Coming American Fascism* appeared in 1936.

On the other hand, Kuhn could not have appeared at a more auspicious time for the enemies of fascism and Nazism in the United States. The sight of thousands of his followers singing "Deutschland, Deutschland über Alles" in New York's Madison Square Garden helped to coalesce anti-German feeling. For many Americans, Kuhn represented the essence of un-Americanism: his thick foreign accent, his Nazi-style uniform, his repeated statements of allegiance to Hitler, and above all, his apparent misuse of his recently acquired American citizenship. By 1937, Kuhn accomplished what Samuel Dickstein, Samuel Untermeyer, John McCormack, New York Jewry, and a host of other Americans had failed to do in the years immediately following Hitler's consolidation of power: he made numerous Americans aware of the fascist challenge.

The Kuhn years were not characterized by major changes in the Bund's structure or ideology. The organizational pattern set down by Heinz Spanknöbel in the summer of 1933 and the ideological orientation outlined by propagandist Walter Kappe remained relatively unaltered until the fall of 1938. In the twenty-three Bund commands issued by Kuhn to his followers (between October 28,

[3] George Mosse, "The Genesis of Fascism," *Journal of Contemporary History*, 1 (1966), 14.

1936, and September 8, 1939), the Bundesleiter stressed that he was simply picking up where his predecessors had left off: "Today I know better than ever before the direction in which our Bund must go. I know that it is not only important to continue our work; I understand that the American German Bund is called to assume the political leadership of the German element in the United States." [4]

Although he made few changes in the appearance the group presented to the public, Kuhn infused a new ingredient into the movement—sensationalism, which was merely an extension of his personality. His demeanor was distinctive. The Bund's propagandists made every effort to publicize his activities. In contrast, former leaders Griebl the physician, Schnuch the academic, Gissibl the master organizer, and Spanknöbel the one-time photoengraver had been colorless men. Kuhn consciously aped Hitler's manner. Like the German Führer, he regarded himself as a great man, a man chosen to unify his racial brothers in America. He was rarely out of uniform. His black leather jack boots apparently fastened to his six-foot frame, his thinning hair slicked back over his broad head, his legs apart, and his thumbs fixed in his Sam Browne belt, Kuhn loudly proclaimed himself the American Führer. Perhaps his appearance and his flamboyant style help to explain why so many persons thought him more a buffoon than a leader. At any rate, unlike his predecessors he created a powerful cultic organization, making his name synonymous with the group. In consequence, during the Fritz Kuhn years the American Nazi Bund changed from a factionalized and ineffective group to the instrument of an active movement.

By nature an egoist, Kuhn did little to keep his personal life secret. Much to the annoyance of many of his close associates (and his wife and two children), Kuhn often appeared at nightclubs along Broadway and in beer halls in Yorkville with his girl friends, one of whom was a former Miss America. Kuhn was known

[4] Bund Command I, Oct. 28, 1936. The Bund commands were issued in German. After the United States government seized the Bund's records in 1941, the commands were translated into English. Copies of the translations are available in the German-American Bund collection, ADL.

to some people more as a man about town than as the leader of the Volksbund. During his trial for the theft of Bund funds in November 1939, the chief prosecutor, Assistant District Attorney Herman J. McCarthy, produced several "Dear Fritzi" letters, which revealed his relationship with another woman, Mrs. Florence Camp.

Other documents revealed that Kuhn was an excellent businessman. Many of his detractors claimed that he was a big-time racketeer and that if the movement shook off its ideological guise, a full-blown money-making operation would come into view. There was substance to this allegation, as his trial and conviction (Kuhn was sentenced on December 5, 1939, to serve from two and a half to five years in Sing Sing) would later indicate.[5] For example, between 1936 and 1938, Kuhn created, reorganized, or incorporated six independent corporations: the German-American Business League, the A. V. (American Volksbund) Development Corporation, the A. V. Publishing Company, the Prospective Citizens' League, the German-American Settlement League, and the German-American Bund Auxiliary. Kuhn served either as president or as a member of the board of directors of all these. Kuhn the businessman managed to transform the Bund from a debt-ridden group dependent upon Nazi German support into self-sustaining, money-making operation.[6]

Kuhn's insatiable desire for publicity catapulted him into the national limelight. After 1936, much literary and journalistic activity in America was devoted to exposés and stories detailing ever aspect of the alleged Nazi-fascist threat. Writers for popular magazines sometimes claimed thay had the "inside story" of Kuhn and his movement. Their articles were a reflection of the public's desire to know more about fascism and about what one writer referred to as the "new barbarian invasion." Among popular treatments of the

[5] Kuhn's trial and conviction are discussed in detail in Chapter 12, below.

[6] Kuhn created an elaborate corporate structure and served as the president or director of each of the above-mentioned corporations. His office was at 178 East 85 Street, in Yorkville. A detailed examination of the Bund's corporate and financial structure can be found in Commissioner of Investigation William B. Herlands to Mayor Fiorello H. La Guardia, "Report of the [New York] City Emergency Tax Investigation of the German American Bund and Related Groups and Concerns," May 17, 1939, City Document MR-9026, available in the collection of the ADL.

American fascists and Nazis were the writings of George Seldes, Leon Turrou, and Harold Lavine; in the early forties appeared Martin Dies's *The Trojan Horse in America* and John Roy Carlson's sensationalistic best seller, *Under Cover: My Four Years in the Nazi Underworld.* In addition, the movie industry dramatized the plight of fleeing refugee intellectuals and depicted the machinations of spies and saboteurs at home and abroad. Regardless of the format, each production carried the same message: Nazism was a spreading malignancy, and its leaders were sadists and murderers. For some Americans, Chaplin's *The Great Dictator* summed up what Nazism was all about. Such films, shown in movie houses throughout the country, were accompanied by weekly newsreels depicting the Volksbund's much publicized summer camps, youth rallies, and battles with various anti-Nazi groups. The unintended result of this publicity was to attribute to the Bund a far greater influence than it actually exerted.[7]

Reports of the Bund's activities were not confined to America. Most foreign news stories—especially in Germany and England—tended to exaggerate the size and scope of the Volksbund's activities. The German press invariably emphasized Kuhn's difficulties with American authorities and the House Committee to Investigate Un-American Activities under the chairmanship of Martin Dies. Kuhn and his followers were depicted as innocent victims of Jewish harassment; editorializing about Kuhn's conviction in December 1939, one German paper commented that international Jewry always got its way. England's interest in the Bund—and American fascism in general—was more complex. The British press found America's tolerance of the Bundists unintelligible, a warning to Britons to beware of the followers of Sir Oswald Mosley, leader of the British Union of Fascists and National Socialists. Writing in the *Daily Herald* (London), A. P. Luscombe Whyte warned his fellow Englishmen:

Do you remember Sinclair Lewis's novel about a man who created a Fascist organisation and eventually made himself Dictator of the United

---

[7] An extensive bibliography was compiled by Thomas Huntington in 1940: "The Trojan Horse Bibliography," *Bulletin of the New York Public Library,* 44 (Oct. 1940), 741–744.

States, with all the brutality and bestiality that we have read about in real life?

Twitting Americans for their complacent "it can't happen here" attitude toward Fascist dictatorship, he gave his novel that title.

Now read this article, bearing in mind that there are 1,600,000 Germans naturalised in the United States, and millions more with German blood.[8]

The newspaper coverage and newsreel footage afforded the Bund initially aided the movement but eventually harmed it. The Kuhn technique involved the use of elaborate fanfare and regalia, gross exaggerations of the size and importance of the organization, and bellicose denunciations of "non-Aryan America." Many of Kuhn's flights of fantasy ("I have hundreds of thousands of followers") and half-truths ("I have just spoken with the Führer") were skillfully exploited by his enemies. One was Martin Dies of Texas, who was loathed not only by the Bundists but also by the Roosevelt Administration, New Deal liberals, and a host of other people and groups he labeled un-American. After his appointment to the chairmanship of the House Committee to Investigate Un-American Activities, Dies attempted to compile evidence against Kuhn and all "enemies of Democracy." The Dies committee hearings were forerunners of the McCarthy investigations of the 1950's. As sensational as Kuhn's verbal exchanges with committee members in August 1939 were the revelations of other Bundists and of captains of German steamships, waiters, and nineteen-year-old Helen Vooros, who revealed that she had been sent to Germany by the Bund for training in the Hitler Youth Movement and implied that the Bund was not without homosexuals.

Dies was not alone in his pursuit of Kuhn. In New York City, Thomas Dewey, a young investigator and prosecutor of grafters and racketeers, attempted to obtain an indictment against Kuhn and his fellow Bundists. In addition, New York State Senator John McNaboe held several days of sensational hearings in June 1938. In the West Virginia House of Representatives, Jennings Randolph introduced a bill calling for the immediate deportation of all

[8] "It Might Happen There," June 13, 1938 (clipping, German-American Bund folder, Wiener Library, Institute of Contemporary History, London).

Bundists. Many men made their own names and Kuhn's well known through their efforts to incriminate the American Führer.

Some journalists of the day viewed the Bund as part of a well-organized conspiracy—the "Nazintern"—aimed at overthrowing the American government. The spy scare had precedents in recent American history. In no way did it reach the intensity of the "pure Americanism" campaign directed against the German-American community during the Great War or the Red scare of the early twenties. The ill repute of Kuhn's Volksbund was part of a larger picture involving the reaction generated by the gradual breakdown of diplomatic relations between Berlin and Washington. Although the mutual recall of ambassadors after the anti-Jewish pogroms of November 1938 was a result of Germany's racial anti-Semitism, the Bund's growth and the presence of an outspoken supporter of Nazism on American soil accelerated the hardening of anti-Nazi sentiment. Before Kuhn's ascendancy over the Bund, anti-Nazi feeling had been confined mainly to metropolitan areas with large Jewish populations; furthermore many Americans had made a clear distinction between Nazis and Germans. But as Americans watched internal developments in Germany, Mussolini's invasion of Abyssinia, the incorporation of Austria into a new German empire, the final dismemberment of the rump Czech state just six months after the Munich Conference, and Franco's attainment of power in Spain, the argument that fascism and Nazism were not for export began to lose its earlier force. In consequence, numerous Americans transferred their disdain of Hitlerism and fascism to Kuhn and the Bundists, who, they argued, were preparing a Trojan horse. But in contrast to the period 1914 to 1918, disdain for *the* Germans was never transferred to the German-American community, whose members appear to have been either totally disinterested in, or, in many cases, opposed to the Bund and to Hitler's racial nationalism.

Of course, the man who was supposedly building a Trojan horse was Fritz Kuhn. Who was this man who would sit in Broadway nightclubs listening to what he degraded as "Negroid jazz", who viewed himself as a carrier of Nazism to the American shores, who was considered by Berlin to be a pathological liar, and who was

II. Lieutenant Fritz Julius Kuhn during World War I. (National Archives.)

charged with embezzling over fourteen thousand dollars from the organization he had molded into a viable force in some American cities? Kuhn was born in Munich on May 15, 1896; he would die there fifty-five years later after being sentenced to ten years in prison as a minor war criminal by a Bavarian de-Nazification court. After the outbreak of war in 1914, he joined a Bavarian infantry unit and served as a machine gunner in France. Following the collapse of the German army in November 1918, he returned to his native Munich. At the age of twenty-two he had no occupation —other than soldiering—and little promise for the future. He joined a Freikorps company under the leadership of Major-General Ritter von Epp, Ernst Roehm's former commanding officer and an early follower of Hitler. As a member of Freikorps Epp, Kuhn fought against the Communists and Socialists in his native city. Like many other members of the Free Corps movement, he joined the NSDAP in 1921. But unlike many extremists of that era, Kuhn had a vocational education at a university. In 1921, he enrolled at the University of Munich, where he studied chemical engineering.

Two years later, in 1923, Kuhn left his native land and migrated to Mexico. There was nothing extraordinary about this decision. Dislocations engendered by the war and disastrous inflation prompted many young Germans to migrate to the New World. But why Kuhn chose Mexico is uncertain; it is likely that he realized that the Obregón and, after 1924, Calles regimes would welcome skilled European workers and technicians. There is no evidence to support a statement Kuhn made in the late thirties that he was at Hitler's side during the Beer Hall *Putsch* and was forced to emigrate. Kuhn worked as a chemist for four years in Mexico. Three days after his thirty-first birthday, he entered the United States at Laredo, Texas. After a brief stay in New York, he moved to Detroit. Kuhn claimed that he worked for Ford until 1935, although the company has no record of his employment. But it is certain that he lived in Detroit and that he became a naturalized citizen on December 3, 1934, just one year before he was designated provisional leader of the Bund movement.[9]

[9] While in Mexico, Kuhn married. His wife, Elsa, was born in Lichtenburg, Germany, in January 1898. Kuhn met her while a student at the University of

Kuhn was not a member of the Teutonia Association. He did not join the local branch of the Friends of the New Germany until the summer of 1933. His early membership in the NSDAP, his university education, his service in a Free Corps company, and the Bundists' realization that he was a powerful and skillful organizer won him an appointment as a local leader of the Bund. Two years later, he was selected to be *Gauleiter* of the midwestern department of the Bund. His organizational talents and other impressive qualifications did not go unnoticed by Fritz Gissibl, who was searching frantically for a suitable successor after he returned from Berlin in late 1935. If there was a victor in the Haegele-Schnuch conflict, it was Fritz Kuhn.

Kuhn was fully aware that the "Bund war" had destroyed the movement's chain of command; he also realized and used to his advantage the fact that the controversy was confined to the New York metropolitan area. Throughout the dispute, Kuhn steadfastly maintained his loyalty to the established organization and thus assured Gissibl that the struggle would not spread to the Midwest. In March 1935, Kuhn felt strong enough to assert himself on the national level. Representing the Midwestern Department, he attended a Bund meeting at Camp Deutschhorst, in Sellersville, Pennsylvania, which came at a time when the movement's survival was in doubt. Kuhn presented himself to the delegates as a man who stood above the internecine struggle and called for the immediate reconciliation of the warring factions. He was instrumental also in the drafting of a new constitution, which reaffirmed the "leadership principle"—the complete submission of members to the

Munich. In the mid-1930's, the Kuhn family (a son, Walter, b. 1927, Mexico City, and a daughter, Waltraut) lived in Jackson Heights (Queens). Kuhn filed for naturalization on June 28, 1934, in the United States District Court, East District, Michigan. He received his certificate of naturalization on December 3, 1934. Materials on Kuhn's background are in "De-Naturalization Proceedings, Fritz Kuhn and Nineteen Other Cases," Civ. 18–415, FRC; *Hearings,* Appendix VII, pp. 62–63; and *People* v. *Kuhn,* 5 vols., Legal Records of the German-American Bund, containers 48–49, RG 131. On Kuhn's membership in the NSDAP, see "Maschinegeschriebener Bericht, *Amerikadeutscher Volksbund,*" T-120/3010/487076–88. Kuhn's written and spoken English was extremely poor. He seems to have learned English by translating scientific articles ("Chemistry Notebooks, 1929," container 142, RG 131).

decisions of the Bundesleiter. Clearly, this meeting was a turning point in Kuhn's career; his attempt to resolve the seemingly insoluble struggle was given much publicity in Bund publications. Thus, when Gissibl announced his successor later that year, his selection of Kuhn was no surprise to the Bundists.[10]

Immediately after his appointment as Gissibl's successor, Kuhn began to fortify his position. He understood thoroughly what the Bund war had done to the movement; the vagaries of Bund politics had brought him to power. Above all, he wanted to end the intra-party warfare and convert the Bund into a genuine German-American organization. In December 1935, attempting again to reconcile the two factions, he offered a general amnesty to Anton Haegele's supporters; the only stipulation was that they must agree to the leadership principle, must submit to all his decisions. Haegele rejected Kuhn's overture; his followers, who never numbered more than two hundred, used the amnesty to speed the collapse of the splinter group.

The appointment of Kuhn coincided with the wave of panic that swept over the Bund in the winter of 1935–1936, and Kuhn used the coincidence to his advantage. The call for the withdrawal of all German nationals from the Friends of the New Germany, the congressional hearings, and the ramifications of the struggle in New York served to make those Bundists who stayed in the movement more submissive than before. In consequence, Kuhn was able to implement major organizational changes with ease. In keeping with the leadership principle, Kuhn made himself absolute leader of the movement. He immediately took personal charge of the Uniformed Service (Ordnungs-Dienst), which he called his SS, and reserved the right to appoint and dismiss the National OD Leader (Landes OD-Führer). He also made each member of the OD take an oath of fidelity to him. Membership in that group was increased to no less than 10 per cent of the total membership of the Volks-bund.[11] Three years after these changes were implemented and at

[10] "Evidence," pp. 12, 16n; Deutscher Beobachter, Dec.–Jan. 1935–1936.

[11] "Organization Structure and Rules for Membership, Order Division," container 15, RG 131. In early 1936, the OD uniform resembled the black SS uniform. Kuhn ordered several changes in the uniform—in his words, "to

the time when the Bund's overtly Nazi stance was under close scrutiny by federal and state authorities, some Bundists suggested that the OD be disbanded, if only to quiet their opponents. Kuhn felt otherwise and retorted that his authority rested on the existence of the OD: "Naturally, I cannot give you the assurance that I would ever acquiesce in such a desire, . . . but . . . the Bund stands or falls with the OD." [12]

III. The Uniformed Service (Ordnungs-Dienst), Eastern Department, of the Amerikadeutscher Volksbund, 1937. (National Archives.)

In January 1936, just one month after his appointment, Kuhn learned that Fritz Gissibl and Sepp Schuster would be returning to Germany in the near future. These men, the "old guard" from De-

make it more American looking." As of January 1937, the OD uniform consisted of "black long trousers without cuffs—black shoes, steel gray shirt with breast pockets, long black tie, Stark gray uniform jacket (the same cut as the American National Guard)" (Bund Command VI, Jan. 26, 1937, p. 1, ADL).

[12] "Evidence," pp. 24–25.

troit and Chicago, had welcomed the selection of Kuhn. They
believed that he would be able to mold the Bund into a powerful organization, so that their twelve years of work would have not been
in vain. Their decision to leave America was prompted by the
implementation of the October edict and the promise of employment upon their return to Germany.[13] Kuhn welcomed their imminent departure; unlike his predecessors, with Gissibl and Schuster
gone he would have the opportunity to plot his own course. The
unsettling events of the last two years had made an indelible impression on him: any member of the Bund might be a potential
enemy. Also, the old guard still enjoyed the respect and loyalty of
the membership. Gissibl was unscrupulous, as Kuhn was well
aware. Gissibl had engineered the fall of Bundesleiters Griebl and
Walter and had proved his ability to deal with dissidents.

Kuhn wanted his own circle of friends. Gradually a core of
trusted and dedicated followers began to develop. For Kuhn,
friendship was synonymous with dedication to the organization
and unwavering loyalty to him. Rarely if ever did Kuhn take into
his confidence persons outside the Bund. The people he selected to
direct the various departments, camps, local groups, corporations,
and numerous other activities numbered more than a hundred.
Often a leader of a national organization must assume that his subordinates are trustworthy. Kuhn found that he needed a circle of
confidants, men he could trust when he was on a national tour or
in Germany. He needed people to handle the day-to-day business

[13] Upon his return to Germany, Gissibl was considered for a position at the
DAI. Though never a full-time member of the staff, he worked with the leadership of the Institute and established the Kameradschaft-USA in 1938. He
also held a position in the Tarnungsverlag (Stuttgart), a Nazi publishing
house; in 1937, he was appointed SS *Hauptsturmführer*, and after 1941 he was
an SS *Obersturmbannführer* (SS number 309,051). See "Dienstaltersliste der
Schutzstaffel der NSDAP," Oct. 1, 1942, T-611, roll 1, p. 21. Gissibl was married in 1928 and later had four children. Schuster secured a position in the Nazi
Labor Front and worked with Kameradschaft-USA. Kappe remained in America
until 1937. Upon his return to Germany, he worked in the DAI's press division
(Heinz Kloss to the author, Jan. 18, 1972; Feb. 2, 1972). In the early 1940's,
he was recruited by Abwehr and helped train eight saboteurs who landed via
submarine in America during the war. Further details can be found in Eugene
Rachlis, *They Came to Kill* (New York, 1961).

of the Bund, to settle disputes, and to quiet potential dissidents; he also needed people who would not expose the Bund's inner machinations when testifying in state and federal investigations. During the early formative years of his leadership of the movement, the men he most relied on were Gerhard Wilhelm Kunze, a former chauffeur-mechanic from Camden, New Jersey; Hans Zimmermann, a German-born waiter and former member of Roehm's SA; Richard Schmidt, who had served as an engineer in the German navy and held the Iron Cross; Anton Fuchs, who would later serve in Rommel's Afrikakorps; Carl-Heinz Eymann, who returned to Germany in 1938 and was killed on the Russian front in August 1942; and Carl Nicolay, who served as the uncrowned poet laureate of the Bund.[14] All these men would eventually be rewarded with positions of relative importance.

Carl Nicolay was by far the most interesting member of the group.[15] Born in Baden in 1879, he left Germany for America twenty-four years later and settled in Brooklyn. He earned his living as a song writer, poet, and feature writer for several German-language dailies. He published his writings under the pseudonym "Wilhelm Meister." Nicolay found that the editors of the Bund's several newspapers welcomed his writings. In 1933, he joined the Friends of the New Germany. It was not, however, until Kuhn took over the leadership of the Bund that he was appointed to a minor position, as a youth leader in South Brooklyn. In spite of his unimportant post, Nicolay was given important responsibilities in the Bund's press and propaganda division. Although Walter Kappe was scheduled to return to Germany in 1936, he stayed in America one more year and remained at the head of the press division. He was replaced by Severin Winterscheidt, whom Nicolay served as an informal adviser and as a composer of songs and mottoes in ex-

---

[14] Information about Kuhn's relationship with his immediate subordinates is based on statements made by Kuhn during his denaturalization trial; data about the fate of these men can be found in the papers of Kameradschaft-USA, T-81/140–142.

[15] On Nicolay, see Nicolay to Rolf Hoffmann, May 30, 1939, T-81/25656–8; to Hoffmann, June 29, 1939, T-81/25654; to Hoffmann, Aug. 27, 1939, T-81/25664; application to Kameradschaft-USA and related letters, Aug. 1940, T-81/144/182658; Oct. 14, 1942, T-81/144/182652.

panding the ritualistic aspects of the movement. Kuhn was quick to appreciate Nicolay's talents and often called on him to substitute at speaking engagements. Thus, at nearly age sixty and after a lifetime of unrewarded work, Nicolay was at last recognized.

The Kuhn era began officially on March 29, 1936. On this date, the thirty-nine year old chemist from Munich was elected Bundesleiter at the first annual convention of the Amerikadeutscher Volksbund in Buffalo, New York. Obviously, his election merely formalized an existing state of affairs. He inherited the leadership of an organization with an elaborate national structure, which included fifty-five separate groupings in seven regions of the United States.[16] From a stage draped with German and American flags Kuhn announced to the delegates that he intended to continue Fritz Gissibl's Americanization of the Bund. Accordingly, he declared the Friends of the New Germany defunct.[17] The name of the old group, Kuhn explained, did not reflect the aims he envisoned. He asked the delegates to adopt a new title: Amerikadeutscher Volksbund (American German Bund), known to most Americans by its hyphenated name, German-American Bund. "This change," according to Bundist Severin Winterscheidt, "mainly has its origins in that the Bund leaders at this time stood on the standpoint that the *Friends of the New Germany* sounds too German and makes people shy away and keeps them back from joining the Bund; . . . in German it is called *Amerikadeutscher Volksbund* which means literally translated really American-German as distinguished from German-American."[18] During the preconvention discussions, Kuhn had maintained that the hyphenated term "German-American" implied that American citizens of German extraction had become Americans, that having forsaken their Germanness, they had

[16] "Organization of the German-American Bund, Division of the United States into Principal Jurisdictions," *Hearings*, Part IV, Appendix, pp. 1549ff. See also Appendix II, below.

[17] Seppl Popfinger, "Wie arbeitet die deutsche Freiheitsbewegung in Amerika?" *Westdeutscher Beobachter*, Feb. 7, 1936.

[18] Statement of S. Winterscheidt to Investigator Stine, Department of Immigration and Naturalization, 1940, "Evidence," pp. 9–10. See also *Deutscher Beobachter*, April 8, 1936. On the response of the consulate (New York) to these changes see Hans Borchers to Foreign Ministry, March 3, 1936, T-120/3010/486929–31.

been assimilated into the dominant Anglo-Saxon culture. Kuhn insisted that these Americans were "Germans *in* America," whether they had been in America for ten years or ten generations. For Kuhn and Nazi ideologues in Germany, this point was of cardinal importance: blood was stronger than citizenship or place of birth, and the dictates of blood could not be altered by history.[19] In October 1936, Kuhn told an audience:

If we prefer the term American German to the term German-American, we do so for the same reason for which former German-Russians called themselves Russian-Germans, . . . namely, for the reason that we are, first of all, Germans by race, in blood, in language. We belong to the great commonwealth of all German peoples on this earth. By obtaining other citizenship papers we have not lost our German character. We remain what we are: GERMANS IN AMERICA, AMERICAN-GERMANS, BECAUSE WE DID NOT BECOME AMERICANS.[20]

The events leading up to Kuhn's announcement that the Friends of the New Germany was defunct and had been replaced by the Volksbund came as no surprise to the German government. In the weeks preceding the December 31 deadline for all German nationals to withdraw from the old Bund, the consulate in New York found itself once again involved in the Bund's problems. Consulate personnel found their desks covered with queries from Bundists concerning the meeting of the deadline. Some Bundists argued that the deadline did not affect them, because Bundesleiter-designate Kuhn was forming a new organization. Staff members of the consulates and several consuls agreed in principle with this interpretation. Since no new directive was issued, the consuls did little to discourage German nationals from remaining in the movement. A possible exception was Consul Jaeger in Chicago, who, it will be recalled, had threatened Fritz Gissibl's brother Peter and wanted the Bund destroyed. At the Overseas Press Office in Munich,

[19] Kuhn outlined his views in *Awake and Act! Aims and Purposes of the German American Bund: An Appeal to all Americans of German Stock* (New York, 1936). Bund headquarters housed an extensive collection of books (about five hundred volumes) on the history of German-America, World War I, and Nazism. This collection is in twenty-one boxes in RG 131.

[20] Fritz Kuhn, "What Are WE?" *Deutscher Weckruf und Beobachter*, Oct. 7, 1936.

Rolf Hoffmann responded to one inquiry by writing, "We have little information about the new organization"—in effect, "If you stay
in, hope for the best." [21] Most German nationals (how many will
never be known) simply stayed in the movement and started naturalization proceedings. It was estimated that less than 10 per cent
obeyed the edict. (See Table 1.)

Table 1. Percentage of German nationals
joining and withdrawing from the
Bund movement, 1933–1940 *

Year	Per cent joined	Per cent withdrew
1933	16.67	00.00
1934	23.33	10.00
1935 †	26.67	10.00
1936 ‡	23.33	10.00
1937	6.67	13.33
1938	3.33	13.33
1939 §	0.00	43.33
1940	0.00	00.00

* The classification German nationals includes those Germans who had taken out first
papers toward American citizenship.
† In October 1935, a decree was issued calling for the withdrawal of all nationals, including
those with first papers.
‡ In March 1936, Kuhn proclaimed the formation of the Volksbund.
§ In May 1939, Kuhn was arrested and
charged with theft; in December, he was convicted.
Source: Based on two hundred Rückwanderer (returnee) applications to Kameradschaft-
USA. This material was processed by the IBM
Data-Processing Center, State University of New
York at Binghamton.

More important, Germany never carried out the threat to confis-
cate the passports of those German nationals who transferred their
allegiance to Kuhn. Since Germany had dismissed the Bund as its
major vehicle for penetration into the German-American community and since so many of its nationals had started naturalization

[21] Rolf Hoffmann to Oscar Pfaus, April 28, 1936, T-81/26/23705.

proceedings, Berlin did little to accelerate what it assumed would be the imminent collapse of the organization. By March, however, officials in Berlin began to realize that the Bund under Kuhn was far from dead. Instead of getting involved, officials in Germany followed a policy of benign neglect; now that Germany had severed most of its ties with the organization and Kuhn seemed to have things under control, this policy cost Berlin little. Kuhn, in turn, interpreted Germany's new stance as a sign that its leaders approved of his actions.

Kuhn circumvented the December 31 deadline by creating a theoretically separate but Bund-affiliated organization for German nationals, many of whom had started on the road toward American citizenship. Without Nazi Germany's knowledge, he encouraged its nationals to join a fictitious subdivision of one of the Bund's economic divisions, the Deutsche Konsum Verband (German Consumers' Cooperative). The VDA's representative, Günther Orgell, wrote Rolf Hoffmann from Staten Island, "American citizens have remained in the Bund and German nationals have been eliminated as of January 1; they have come together in the DKV Foederer Bund [the so-called Furthering Group]." [22]

Kuhn's deceptions continued, much to the annoyance and dismay of Reich officials. Several weeks before he convened the Buffalo convention, Kuhn replaced the fictitious subdivision with the Prospective Citizens' League, which was "open to all Americans and prospective citizens of Aryan blood, of German extraction, and of good reputation." Although this group would later serve to screen potential Bundists for membership in the parent organization, in 1936 its purpose was to house German nationals who had either started naturalization proceedings or had promised to do so. By June, Berlin accepted this arrangement as an accomplished fact and acquiesced, by silence, in the creation of the group. Many German nationals did become American citizens between 1936 and 1940. After 1938, several hundred returned to Germany. Some Bundists who stayed found themselves in trouble with Federal au-

[22] Günther Orgell to Rolf Hoffmann, Jan. 29, 1936, T-81/26/23664; consulate general (New York) to Foreign Ministry, Jan. 24, 1936, T-120/2961/474509.

thorities after the passage in June 1940 of the Alien Registration Act (commonly called the Smith Act), which was designed to strengthen existing legislation governing the admission and deportation of aliens; it also made it unlawful for any person to advocate or teach the violent overthrow of the United States government. The Nationality Act, also passed that year, made it possible to revoke the citizenship of naturalized Americans who retained allegiance to a foreign power at the time of naturalization. During World War II, Federal attorneys maintained that some Bundists had willfully deceived the government by attempting to secure naturalization although they had sworn allegiance to a foreign power. (See Table 2.) [23]

Table 2. Number of citizens and aliens in branches and units of the Amerikadeutscher Volksbund in New York and New Jersey (Eastern Department, Region I), 1936–1938

Place	Estimated no. of members	U.S. citizens	Aliens *
Clifton, N.J.	55	24	31 †
Manhattan, N.Y.	115	0	115
Rochester, N.Y.	16	4	12
Hudson County, N.J.	148	54	94
Newark, N.J.	101	17	84 ‡
White Plains, N.Y.	41	10	31
Brooklyn, N.Y.	474	140	334 §
Total	950	249	701

* Includes foreign nationals with first papers toward American citizenship.
† Includes two Austrian citizens.
‡ Includes one Russian national.
§ Includes one Austrian, one Swedish national, and one Czech (Sudetenland).
Source: Based on information available in the collection of the ADL.

[23] Even a cursory examination of the Bund's membership lists reveals that the leadership and most of the membership remained constant during the crucial transitional period, 1935–1936, and that the core of the organization consisted of recruits from the German-national community. On Germany's response to the changes in the Bund, see Hans Borchers to Foreign Ministry, March 3, 1936, T-120/3010/486929–31.

The Kuhn period, then, began with a lie. During the three years from 1936 to 1939, Kuhn managed to free the Bund from the internecine quarreling that had characterized its entire history, to locate new sources of income, and to propagate the belief that he enjoyed a very large following of German-Americans. His bombast, propensity for exaggeration, and lies were part of his technique. In all, he never had more than twenty-five thousand followers; even this estimate may be too high.[24] More important, the nucleus around which the Bund was built remained what it always had been: a core of transplanted Germans who trod the path toward citizenship only in order to stay in the movement. Whether his following was fifteen thousand or fifty thousand (as Dickstein later claimed) is immaterial; what is important is the belief shared by many Americans that the Volksbund was controlled from Berlin. As Germany prepared for war in the late 1930's and Hitler's speeches became more menacing, some Americans viewed the Bund as a potential fifth column. Others viewed it as a militant organization composed of Jew-haters and thugs. In consequence, when the Bundesleiter and his followers appeared in public, violence followed. Kuhn blamed the violence on the Jews, who, he claimed, had been "out to get" the Bundists since 1933. Kuhn also became a champion of the Bund's right to exercise its civil rights —an assertion later supported by the American Civil Liberties Union during one of the Bund's many bouts with the law. Protected at first by America's tolerance and Germany's silent acquiescence, Kuhn prepared his followers for *Der Tag*.

[24] It is extremely difficult to establish the exact size of Kuhn's organization. The membership lists, addressograph plates, and mailing lists in the Washington National Records Center (RG 131) are closed to public inspection, in accordance with the Administrative Procedure Act (5 U.S.C.A. 552). However, sections of the Bund's general records are open for inspection, in keeping with the National Archives' "limited access" qualification. The estimate of 25,000 members includes men, women, and children and members in the several subdivisions of the Volksbund. This estimate is based in part on the Bund's general records and on registration numbers uncovered by the author in the files of Kameradschaft-USA. The highest number uncovered was 17,981. On the identification of individual Bundists by registration numbers, see T-81/142/179781ff. Cf. Bell, *In Hitler's Shadow*, p. 22.

CHAPTER 9

The Amerikadeutscher Volksbund: The Nazi Party in Microcosm

The period between the world wars witnessed a continuous flow of emigrants and political refugees from one nation to another. Though by no means equal to the migrations of the previous century, the movement of people, especially pronounced after the signing of the several peace treaties in 1919 and the Bolshevik revolution and civil war in Russia, continued unabated into the next two decades. America, which closed its door to some nationals and opened it for others in the mid-1920's, continued to serve as a refuge for people with diverse backgrounds. It will be recalled that the Teutonia Association and later the Friends of the New Germany recruited their rank and file members from among the nearly 430,000 emigrants and self-proclaimed political exiles from the Weimar Republic. After 1933, the opponents of the Bund movement and of fascism in general gathered momentum from the refugees arriving from the Reich and other fascist nations. These men and women were living affirmations of Nazism's racial madness and of the modern totalitarian idea of freedom. After the *Anschluss* with Austria and the absorption by Germany of the rump Czech state in 1939, the number of refugees from National Socialism grew and included non-Germans.

The stories these people told shocked the sensibilities of many Americans. Germany's treatment of the Jews, political dissenters, and, after 1938, other national groups, did little, however, to stem the flow of American tourists visiting Germany. Americans were familiar sights in the Rhineland, at the Olympic Games in Berlin in 1936, or visiting the famed medieval walled cities of Nördlingen or

Rothenburg ob der Tauber.[1] Germans also visited the United States in great numbers.

Among the thousands who arrived was the well-known German propagandist Colin Ross.[2] Ross was a familiar figure in the Bund community. For years he had been a frequent contributor to the group's several newspapers and helped its propagandists formulate their views of America and its people. More by coincidence than design, Ross published his most widely circulated work, *Unser Amerika* ("Our America"), in 1936, the year Fritz Kuhn remolded the Bund into the Amerikadeutscher Volksbund. Unlike the highly specialized academic distortions prepared by researchers at the German Foreign Institute and other Nazified agencies, Ross's *Unser Amerika* was a crude propaganda piece. His description of a homogeneous German-America stood in sharp contrast to the realities of American life. In the opening chapters of *Unser Amerika,* Ross hailed the future arrival of a German Thomas Paine, a man destined to bring about the unification of Germany's racial comrades:

A man will rise and gather them, a German Thomas Paine. He will not found a new party, no association, no alliance, no union, but will comprise a matter-of-fact fellowship of all who are of German blood, as soon as they become aware of the fact that they are not Americans but "Amerikaner," people of German blood and American soil. They will

[1] Materials relating to the promotion of tourism can be found in RG 131: Records Relating to the German Railroads Information Office, Part I, press releases, 1932–1941; Correspondence to Promote Travel in Germany, Part II; The Olympic Games (1936), Part V; Promotional Material, 1929–1939, Part VIII.

[2] Dies pointed to Colin Ross as a shining example of a "leading Nazi" and "close friend of the *Führer*." Ross's influence on the German leader is questionable. His writings—*Unser Amerika* (1936), *Amerikas Schicksalsstunde* (1937), and "Amerika Greift nach der Weltmacht," *Zeitschrift für Geopolitik,* June 1939, pp. 416ff–accorded well with Hitler's evolving image of the United States. However, one cannot deduce that he had a direct influence on Hitler and, by inference, on German policy. Upon Ross's return to Germany, he discussed his American trip with Hitler. See Memorandum of a Conversation between Hitler and Ross, March 12, 1940, *DGFP,* D, VIII, 910–913. On the trip itself, see *Hearings,* VII, 42–53. On Ross's activities in the United States, see Hoffmann Papers, June 26, 1939, T-81/26/22873. See also Compton, *The Swastika and the Eagle,* pp. 11–13.

drop the hyphen that others have attempted to fasten on to them and no longer call themselves German-Americans, but simply "Amerikaner." [3]

Did the leader of the Volksbund, Fritz Kuhn, see himself as the new Thomas Paine, as the man destined to awaken German-America to its blood-dictated responsibilities? The answer is no. In spite of his rhetoric, his claim that he was a "historical personality," and his assertion that he was the leader of "united Germandom in America," the leader of the Volksbund was well aware that outside the Bund's youth camps and the enclaves of German nationals and recently naturalized Americans in Yorkvilles throughout the land, there existed little sympathy for him or his goals in the German-American community. From the formal beginning of the Kuhn era in March 1936, most German-Americans viewed him as they had Heinz Spanknöbel and Fritz Gissibl—as an interloper, an outsider. Kuhn was regarded as a rather silly imitation of the German Führer.[4]

The refusal of German-Americans to join ranks with the Bund en

[3] Colin Ross, *Unser Amerika,* as quoted in *Hearings,* VII, 46–47. This passage also appeared in *Kämpfendes Deutschtum: Jahrbuch des Amerikadeutschen Volksbundes,* 1937, the yearbook of the Bund. In *Unser Amerika,* Ross wrote:

America would have nothing
If we were not Amerikaner—
We, Amerikaner, we—!

A more concise statement of his views cannot be found.

[4] The correspondence between Rolf Hoffmann's Overseas Press Office and Americans of German extraction suggests that many of these people considered the Bund farcical. However, one cannot conclude that the same people felt the same about Hitlerism. In the 1930's, the novelist William Seabrook made a study of German-American attitudes toward Hitlerism: 70 per cent of those interviewed were indifferent; 20 per cent were anti-Nazi; 9 per cent were "pro-Nazi"; and 1 per cent were militantly Nazi (cited in Richard O'Connor, *The German-Americans,* p. 439). In general, O'Connor tends to minimize the importance of non-Bund-affiliated organizations, most of which acquiesced in the rise and spread of Nazism. Voting behavior and public-opinion polls have been used to examine attitudes within the German-American community (e.g., in Manfred Jonas, *Isolationism in America, 1935–1941* [Ithaca, N.Y., 1966]). In any case, it is clear from the Hoffmann Papers and the APA World War II Seized Enemy Records, RG 131, that thousands of Americans of German ancestry wisely eschewed all Nazi overtures while an equal number did not.

masse was a source of constant irritation to Kuhn. His resentment manifested itself in several ways. Bund Youth Leader Theodor Dinkelacker reflected his superior's disdain for the German-American community: "Proud is our youth, . . . and it will always look with disdain on those who shrink from the fight, who gather in little groups and small circles, and later belong to rabbit-raising clubs or bowling clubs." [5]

Kuhn became a notorious liar, since he had to perpetuate the hoax that the cadres of his followers had been recruited from the ranks of Americans of German descent; he lied to his friends, to his followers, and to German officialdom in Berlin. At first, in 1936 and 1937, Kuhn's willful deception was accomplished with great skill, so that many did in fact believe that he enjoyed a large American-born following.[6] His bombastic speeches, well-organized rallies, and often repeated assertion that he alone was capable of uniting German-America came at a time when many Americans believed that Hitler and his foreign followers and imitators were creating a fifth column. Kuhn skillfully manipulated this belief (which received even greater currency after the formation of the House Committee to Investigate Un-American Activities). As will be seen, he used the several Federal and state probes into the internal affairs of the Volksbund to further his own ends.

For the time being, Kuhn wanted Berlin's recognition as the American Führer. If Berlin accorded him this recognition, he believed, the German government would reopen the avenues of material as well as moral support. In light of Germany's decision to implement the prohibitions decided on in October 1935, which were meant to destroy Gissibl's organization, Kuhn's quest for recognition seems bizarre. But Kuhn, like his ideological mentor in Berlin, believed in "will" and the force of personality. To achieve his main goal, he believed he had to achieve several other goals: First, he had to convince German officialdom that the Volksbund was a new organization that was solving the problems Berlin had once found

[5] Theodor Dinkelacker, "Our Youth Movement," *Kämpfendes Deutschtum*, p. 6. In 1940, Dinkelacker returned to Germany and lived in Berlin (T-81/142/179625).

[6] Kuhn, *Awake and Act!*

objectionable and that had prompted it to break off contact. Second, he had to give the group a permanent status, which meant he had to work within, not against, the American legal system. Finally, he had to convince Berlin and his followers that he had created an all-encompassing movement, a microcosm of the NSDAP, with a social, political, and economic program and its own schools, camps, and means of self-support—a movement, moreover, composed of men, women, and children recruited from American *Deutschtum*. Only so, he reasoned, could he stop the complaints of the Foreign Ministry and Auslandsorganisation personnel.

Kuhn knew that if time was not on his side, America's tolerance of diversity was. A problem that confronted the McCormack-Dickstein probers, troubled State Department officials, and perplexed the Germans in Berlin was that the Bundists were not in violation of any existing Federal laws; at least, no existing statute seemed to apply to them. The accusation of un-Americanism was one thing; to prove it was another. It is noteworthy that Kuhn was removed from the American scene in December 1939 by convictions for larceny and forgery, not for un-Americanism. Only later, in 1942–1943, when new legislation was available, was the government able to denaturalize the fallen Bund leader. But when he took control, he was well aware that as long as he worked within the law he was untouchable. For example, nine months after the transformation of the old Bund into the Volksbund, Kuhn obtained from the State Department permission for German nationals working toward citizenship to remain in the Prospective Citizens' League in order to "prepare them for American citizenship." [7]

With the acumen of a corporation president, he incorporated several of the *ad hoc* groups he and his predecessors had created

[7] "Return of German Nationals to German-American Bund," Bund Command III, Oct. 30, 1936, ADL. Years later, in 1942, at a time when Kuhn was fighting to retain his American citizenship, he argued that he had always worked within the framework of the American legal system and that attempts to prove otherwise were ill-founded. He claimed, correctly, that the State Department had approved the reentrance of German nationals into the Bund, provided that they worked toward American citizenship (Kuhn to United States District Court, Southern District, Sept. 1, 1942, Civ. 18-415, FRC).

and thus gave each group permanent status. Properties purchased by the Bund and later converted into training camps—Hindenburg near Grafton, Wisconsin; Deutschhorst in Pennsylvania; Nordland in New Jersey; Sutter in California; Siegfried at Yaphank, Long Island; and Efdende North in Pontiac, Michigan—became independent divisions of the Volksbund. Kuhn eventually created a continuing, money-making operation, which was one of cardinal importance in light of Germany's new stance vis-à-vis the organization. Even if renewed support should not be forthcoming from Berlin, Kuhn believed he had placed the Bund in a position to survive the vicissitudes of German policy.[8] The Friends of the New Germany never enjoyed a debt-free status. Kuhn's Volksbund, on the other hand, was in debt only during the last three years of its existence, from 1939 to 1941. The resourceful Bundesleiter managed to develop new sources of income: membership dues, the marketing of Nazi paraphernalia and of Bund newspapers and books, the sale of summer cottages at Bund camps, and charges for advertising.

One was privileged to be a member of the Volksbund, and membership seemed costly, especially during the Depression.[9] When his followers argued that they had the right to attend major functions free of charge, Kuhn dismissed their complaints as latent "Jewish materialism":

For a Bund member, there is no such thing as a "right" to free admission for official attendance at assembly, nor a right to a refund for traveling expenses, or other expenses in connection with the official performance of his duties!

[8] The Dies committee probe revealed the Bund's organizational structure. (See Appendix II, below.) The financial records of the Bund are in RG 131, in more than fifty containers.

[9] The Bund's profits were derived mainly from advertising. The Volksbund's financial records for the period 1935–1936 reveal that some German-American businessmen, the Hamburg-American Line, and the German Railroads Information Office paid as much as two hundred dollars for an eight- to ten-line advertisement in Bund publications. See containers 15 (bank records, canceled checks, Long Island Division), 16 (purchase subscriptions), 136 (Fragmentary Records, "List of Firms and Individuals Contributing to the AV"), and 183 (financial records of A. V. Publishing Company), RG 131. On Germany's use of former Bund leaders Griebl and Walter as contact men to provide support for non-Bund-affiliated groups through the subterfuge of advertising in their publications, see Rolf Hoffmann's correspondence with Griebl (Jan. 1936) and with Walter (winter–summer 1936), T-81/27/23918; 23879; 23888.

In the Bund service is not compensated by favor or privileges. . . . It is only through a spirit of joyous self-sacrifice that we shall prevail; the Jewish spirit of materialism must not be permitted to enter the Bund or we shall be destroyed individually and collectively.[10]

Thus, sacrifice was equated with contributions, and thrift was labeled a Jewish invention.

Each member joining the Volksbund was required to contribute $1.50 to the propaganda campaign; an additional fee of $.20 was charged for a membership card. Every month Bundists had to pay $.75 for dues, making their checks payable to the German-American Business League (DAWA) or its president, Fritz Kuhn. Of the monthly dues, $.25 was retained by the National Executive Committee (headed by Kuhn), $.45 went to the local organizations, and $.05 was sent to the headquarters of the eastern, midwestern, and western departments. Only single women and the needy were offered reduced membership rates. Collecting about $9.00 a year per person for dues, the Bund, if it did in fact have twenty-five thousand members, derived a yearly income from dues of nearly a quarter of a million dollars, which was used to meet operating expenses and to purchase new properties. Kuhn also created a variety of accoutrements, and each member was required to wear appropriate uniform and insignia at all Bund functions. The prices ranged from $18.00 for the Ordnungs-Dienst standard to $.35 for the black chevron worn by a regional OD leader.[11]

[10] "Organizational Set-Up (Organic Structure)," 1939, *Hearings*, Part IV, Appendix, p. 1582.

[11] Money was collected from the membership on the local level and prescribed amounts were sent to the national headquarters in New York. Although $250,000 may seem excessive, it must be weighed against the Bund's outlays, including the purchase of properties (in 1937, for example, the Bund attempted to purchase a 178-acre tract in Connecticut) and the rent for fifty-eight branch offices. Leland V. Bell has shown that the DKV (German Consumers' Cooperative, replaced by the German-American Business League—DAWA—in 1935 or 1936; but after 1936, the abbreviations DAWA and DKV were still used interchangeably) grossed $63,343.08 between July 1937 and July 1938. However, its net profit for that period was only $920.41 (*In Hitler's Shadow*, p. 76). The DKV expense record (Manhattan office) for April 1939 lists outlays: "Salary, Max Rapp, Treas. $60 (plus $30 in petty cash), rent, $30; phone, $24; publishing expenses, $100 . . ." (financial records of DKV, statement from Manufacturers Trust Company, container 132, RG 131). On

Not only the Bund but also Bund-affiliated stores and individuals profited from the sale of these items. For example, Kuhn's friend Max Buchte, a custom tailor and the owner of a small shop in Queens, manufactured uniforms for Bund officials and members in the New York area; another close associate Karl Kienzler, the president of Kienzler and Schimpf, Inc., and the owner of an import house in the West Forties, had the exclusive franchise for the sale of Bund emblems, rings, pins, and other jewelry. Bund revenue was not derived only from the sale of paraphernalia and the collection of dues. The German-American Business League, Inc., sold certificates of membership to store owners, many of whom had been affected by the Jewish-initiated boycott and were hopeful that Bund members and German sympathizers would purchase from stores displaying DAWA or DKV stickers—"Patronize Aryan Stores Only" or "Buy German"—on their windows. With each purchase, consumers received Bund trading stamps, which were redeemable when making purchases in DAWA affiliates or in marks upon their return to Germany. The German-American Business League and the German-American Settlement League, which was the holding corporation for the camp at Yaphank, sold inexpensive bungalows built on Bund-owned property on Long Island and in New Jersey. These small and hastily built frame cottages (those at Yaphank were constructed along Hermann Göring Strasse) reverted back to the corporation upon the death of the owners.[12]

The resourceful Bundesleiter, furthermore, held the controlling

---

financial demands made on the membership, see Bund Commands VIII, IX, and XV, ADL. A secondary but by no means unimportant source of income was the sale of Nazi flags, jewelry, uniforms, and books. See "Statement Concerning the Financial Affairs of Max Buchte (Custom Tailor), Kienzler and Schimpf, Inc. (Importers of Nazi emblems)," Herlands, "Report of Tax Investigation," ADL. On the sale of books, see Rolf Hoffmann's correspondence with the Aryan Book Store and German House (California), T-81/29/26405ff; and Records of German House, boxes 1–21, RG 131. Some Bund officials supplemented their incomes by selling Nazi propaganda. See statement of Bundist Schwenk in *U.S. v. Fritz Julius Kuhn and Nineteen Other Cases*, 49 F., Supp. 407 (SDNY, 1943), p. 434.

[12] Herlands, "Report of Tax Investigation." See also containers 132, 171, 190, 194, 195, RG 131. On the sale of Bund properties, see statement of Hermann Hoeflich in *U.S. v. Kuhn and Nineteen Other Cases*, filed under Fritz Kuhn, Civ. 18-415, FRC

shares of stock in the A. V. Publishing Company, which had offices in the Bund headquarters in Yorkville. In theory, each administrative section of the Bund had its own newspaper: in Chicago, the *Deutscher Weckruf;* in Philadelphia, the *Philadelphia Deutscher Weckruf und Beobachter;* in Los Angeles, the *California Weckruf;* and in New York, the *Deutscher Weckruf und Beobachter*. In reality, each newspaper was a subsidiary of the New York publishing corporation. Although the Bund used its own presses, Kuhn often found it necessary to farm out publishing jobs to several of his friends. In New York, one of the chief printers for the Bund was Hackl Press, Inc., which was owned by Fred Hackl, the president and sole stockholder. Later in the decade, Kuhn used the John Willig Press on Staten Island. (Richard Mettin, treasurer of the A. V. Publishing Company, also served as the treasurer of Willig Press.) A substantial portion of the Bund's income depended on its publishing activities. Many German and German-American merchants advertised their products on the pages of the Bund's several newspapers, and for advertisements they paid dearly. One of the main reasons for the near collapse of the Friends of the New Germany during the Haegele-Schnuch conflict was that the Bund had to stop publishing its newspapers on a regular basis and, consequently, income from advertising stopped.[13] Shortly after Kuhn took over the leadership, the *Deutscher Beobachter,* the chief organ of the Friends, reappeared in New York City, only to cease publication in mid-December. Not until April 2, 1936, did the Volksbund resume publication, using the title *Deutscher Weckruf und Beobachter,* on a regular basis. By the summer of that year, Bund newspapers reappeared on newsstands in Chicago, Philadel-

[13] Financial records of A. V. Publishing Company, 1935–1936, container 183, RG 131. After the financial losses incurred as a result of the Haegele-Schnuch Affair, Kuhn tried to recoup by selling shares of preferred stock in the A. V. Publishing Company at 10 per cent of par value (dividend of 7 per cent). See "Purchase Subscriptions," container 16, RG 131. On the receipt of literature from Hoffmann's office, see T-81/26/22933ff; 29/26405ff. In 1943, the government lost its denaturalization case against Fred Hackl. The "Opinion," by Justice D. J. Bright, stated that the Bund's printer (Hackl) could not be held responsible for the content of the materials printed and the judge therefore argued against denaturalization (*U.S.* v. *Kuhn and Nineteen Other Cases,* Civ. 18-415).

phia, Milwaukee, Seattle, and Los Angeles, again providing income for the group. (See Appendix IV.) [14]

The Bund's publishing activities were not confined solely to the printing and distribution of newspapers. Under Kuhn's careful supervision, the A. V. Publishing Corporation marketed its own publications and Nazi literature published in Germany. Bundists were required to read (and buy) Hitler's *Mein Kampf,* Michael Fry's *Hitler's Wonderland,* and Hans Andersen's crude and violently anti-Semitic pamphlet, *Litvinoff.* The company published numerous pamphlets. Printed on inexpensive paper (which had the same odor as the paper used in comic books), these pamphlets outlined the purposes and aims of the Volksbund. Among the most popular were *Awake and Act!, The Snake in the Grass,* and *The Protocols of the Elders of Zion.* These books and pamphlets were sold at Bund meetings, on street corners in Yorkville and Jersey City, in Bund-affiliated and owned bookstores (for example, the Aryan Book Shop in California), and sent on request through the mails.[15] Thus, behind the façade of Kuhn's OD men parading through the streets of New York's Germantown or the Bundesleiter listening to jazz in a New York nightclub, were a multitude of interlocking corporations directed by Kuhn, who exerted one-man control over the operation, finances, and activities of a small corporate empire.

Kuhn's success was due in part to his adherence to the leadership principle—to his unlimited dictatorial control over the membership and his demand for unconditional loyalty. But he exercised control only over Fritz Gissibl's former followers, transplanted German nationals, veterans of the defeated imperial army, members of the Freikorps movement, Jew-haters, and a small number of Ameri-

[14] In the period 1936–1938, the Bund's official publication was the *Deutscher Weckruf und Beobachter;* this newspaper was distributed nationally. Newspapers published in other cities (*Philadelphia Deutscher Weckruf und Beobachter* and *California Weckruf*) were duplicates of the New York City paper except for an appropriate change in the masthead, local news coverage, radio program listings, and news of the Bund in the particular locale.

[15] Most of the books on the Bund's "suggested reading list for new recruits" were printed in Germany or written by Nazi sympathizers in America. Included were the writings of the Nazi sympathizer Edwin Schoonmaker. The Bund also published more than fifty song books, the *DKV Newsletter,* and *Junges Volk* (January 1937–December 1940), a magazine for young people.

cans of German extraction who saw in National Socialism a dynamic world view and a cure for America's ills. In order to disseminate his ideology, Kuhn had to make the Volksbund more
appealing to Americans of German ancestry. Somehow, he had to
balance *völkisch* nationalism with traditional cultural nationalism.
This balance was never achieved, and he continued to address his
fellow Germans, who seemed to experience National Socialism vicariously by participating in the Bund movement.

For them, Kuhn replaced the German Führer. But neither Kuhn
nor the Volksbund ever enjoyed the almost religious veneration
German National Socialism received. There was never a Fritz
Kuhn cult or a Kuhn mystique. The Bundesleiter lacked Hitler's
oratorical virtuosity and demagoguery. Few of his followers were
dazzled by his speeches; even fewer were inspired by this charla-
tan's pretentious statements, and his flattering and ungrammatical
English did little to heighten his appeal. Undoubtedly, Kuhn was
popular among some segments of his followers, but his popularity
was related to Hitler's and Germany's successes, not to his own.[16]
It is not surprising that the Bundists' favorite film was Leni Riefenstahl's documentary of the 1934 Nuremberg Party rally, *Triumph of
the Will*, a propaganda piece of the first order, which portrayed a
Germany most of Kuhn's followers did not know firsthand.

Kuhn attempted to capture the dynamic of German National Socialism by means of parades, elaborate uniforms, appeals to emo-
tional and violent irrationalism, slogans, catchwords, torch-lit rallies, the fostering of power worship, racist and crude Social
Darwinian theorizing, and militarism. Meetings invariably took
place at night and were characterized by feverish activity and
lengthy speeches. Night rallies in Bund camps and in Bund haunts

[16] The documents have yielded few favorable appraisals of Kuhn. In general, his followers regarded his work highly. As will be seen in subsequent
chapters, the revelations concerning his scandalous personal life and the
widely circulated rumor that he was embezzling funds from the organization's
treasury did little to endear him to his followers. People joined the Bund for a
variety of reasons; they did not join because of Kuhn's charismatic appeal. In
the summer of 1939, a Nazi sympathizer commented that the "Bund under the
leadership of Fritz Kuhn became extraordinarily aggressive in an entirely unfit
manner, . . . something like a beer club" ("Report of the *Schwaben* Society,"
enclosed in a letter from Karl Goetz to DAI, July 1939, T-81/141/183237).

across America were planned to appeal to what Kuhn considered the psychological need of his followers—the desire to experience National Socialism while living in the United States. Emphasis was placed on *völkisch* solidarity, and addresses were designed to heighten emotion. The unity and destiny of Aryan men, Kuhn told his followers, made them unique and separated them from the mongrel hordes—the Americans. For the disenchanted, union in the *Volk* compensated for feelings of inferiority. Kuhn hailed National Socialism as signaling the beginning of a new era for German man and the beginning of the end for world Jewry.

Not surprisingly, the Bund commanded its largest following in cities with large and influential Jewish populations and equally large German immigrant communities: for example, in New York and, across the Hudson River in New Jersey, in Union City, Passaic, North Bergen, Hackensack, Fairfield, and Newark.[17] In these densely populated and ethnically diverse areas where the Jews were workers or small shopkeepers, German nationals and Jewish immigrants had rubbed elbows since the turn of the century. Many neighborhoods were "Old World" in character, with Jewish bakeries and German delicatessens, corset shops, and beer halls, Hebrew schools and church schools. To the outsider German and Yiddish seemed to be the same language. Here the Jews were not large entrepreneurs but members of the working class and owners of small, even marginal, stores. To many Bundists they represented the cunning emancipated Jew, and many of Kuhn's followers saw themselves as the victims of their emancipation.

The Bundists' anti-Semitism and at times fanatical hatred of the Jews were tempered only in part by their experiences in the United States. Since most Bundists were German nationals or recently naturalized Americans, their anti-Semitism must be exam-

---

[17] It will be remembered that the heart of the Nazi movement shifted from Detroit and Chicago to New York in the winter of 1932–1933. The majority of Kuhn's followers were concentrated in the New York metropolitan area. The Eastern Department (the territory from Maine to Florida) included the New York area. The most important units in terms of membership were: Manhattan (James Wheeler-Hill, leader), Brooklyn (Karl Frick), Astoria (Hermann Schwarzmann), Lindenhurst, Long Island (V. Meyer), Bergen County, N.J. (Henry Siebert), and Passaic County, N.J. (Karl Wagner).

ined against the background of imperial Germany and the Weimar Republic. In general, rank-and-file Bundists brought from Germany a revulsion toward the commercial Jew; those who had served in the defeated imperial Army and later joined the Freikorps brought with them the so-called Freikorps mentality. They equated defeat with the alleged machinations of world Jewry and condemned the German republic as the exclusive preserve of the Jews and their socialist friends.[18] America in the depression years heightened their hatreds and fears. Whether each Bundist actually believed that the Jews were at the root of Germany's, America's, and their own misfortune does not matter; what is important was that the Bundists as a group acted upon these beliefs.

Kuhn had much in common with many of his fellow Bundists. He had been a front-line fighter during the war, served in the Freikorps, and had been an early member of the NSDAP. He told them that he understood their problems, that they were "heralds of the Third Reich," and that together they would preach the German world view "before the eyes of the world." After 1936, Kuhn tried to implement his beliefs by placing greater emphasis on ideological trends that were already present before he assumed control. Although anti-Semitic and anti-Black feelings were important ingredients and had been encouraged by propagandists since 1933, Kuhn's fanatical hatred of the Jews and the Blacks reached a new level after 1936. Echoing Adolf Hitler's, Julius Streicher's, and Alfred Rosenberg's views of world Jewry, Kuhn asserted that the Jews were social parasites, a primitive tribal people with no culture of their own. American Jewry was even more sinister than its racial brothers in other countries, since it had infiltrated every level of society under the guise of "Americanization"—the melting-pot philosophy. Until the election of Franklin D. Roosevelt, Jewish incursions had been gradual—the remaining untainted Anglo-Saxons

---

[18] Evidence of their views is extensive. Of special importance is the testimony of Bundists before the Dies committee and in the denaturalization cases, and the written statements of former Bundists in the Kameradschaft-USA collection, T-81/140–142. On the development of the Freikorps mentality, see Robert Waite, *Vanguard of Nazism: The Free Corps Movement in Postwar Germany, 1918–1923* (Cambridge, Mass., 1952).

had seen to that; but Roosevelt's election signaled the beginning of Jewish invidiousness.

Kuhn was at one with other extremist leaders and groups of that era—George Deatherage, Robert Edmondson, the Silver Shirts, and the Ku Klux Klan—in his view of Roosevelt and the New Deal; they all replaced the "N" in "New" with a "J," and the New Deal became the Jew Deal. They pointed to Roosevelt's Jewish friends and advisers—Louis Brandeis, Henry Morgenthau, Felix Frankfurter, Bernard Baruch, Herbert Lehman, and Samuel Rosenman —as evidence of a Jewish conspiracy. With horror Kuhn viewed the specter of Roosevelt winning a second term. A Roosevelt victory meant a Jewish victory: "His preference for the Jewish element and his placing of many Jews in public office is well-known. His racial policies are opposed to ours, not to mention the New Deal. . . . Under a new Roosevelt administration, Communist thought would make considerable progress." [19]

Kuhn's contention that the New Deal was a Jew Deal and that Roosevelt and his friends were tools of Moscow was not new. This contention had been circulated since 1933 by many groups that indiscriminately used "Christian," "Patriotic," "Defenders," and "National" in their names. To bolster his arguments, Kuhn circulated an up-dated version of the notorious *Protocols of the Elders of Zion.* The well-known forgery, which claimed that the Jewish elders were cornering the world's gold supply, was distributed by the Bund after its propagandists re-edited it to conform to an interpretation of the New Deal as a conspiracy. In 1938, the A. V. Publishing Company distributed another vicious attack on the New Deal and American Jewry, *What Price Federal Reserve? Read the Protocols of the Elders of Zion and Understand the New Deal.* Ac-

[19] Bund Command II, Oct. 29, 1936, ADL. Shortly before the election, Kuhn endorsed Alfred Landon: "The election of Landon is recommended from the German standpoint because it can absolutely be assumed that under his administration more favorable commercial relations with Germany would be effected" (*ibid.*). Kuhn refused to endorse William Lemke, a Republican who ran with Thomas O'Brien on the Union Party ticket, because the only thing German "about this man is his name." Moreover, Lemke was courting the followers of Dr. Francis E. Townsend, proponent of the old-age revolving pension; Kuhn wrote, "We can't subscribe to the communist ideas of a Townsend Plan" (*ibid.*).

IV. Bundesleiter Fritz Julius Kuhn in the late 1930's. (National Archives.)

cording to this account of the Roosevelt Administration, the proph-
ecy of the elders had been borne out; Roosevelt and the Jewish
"vampires, the parasitic swarm," had taken over the money supply
(the Federal Reserve) and were now preparing to take over the nation. This process could be reversed if Americans would only wake
up to the danger and follow Germany's example (the promulgation
of the Nuremberg Laws in September 1935) of "excluding the Jews
from national life." [20]

Kuhn also reserved a special hatred for what he dubbed the
"Jewish *New York Times*" and other "Eastern newspapers," which,
he maintained, controlled public opinion and viciously defamed
Hitler and National Socialism. Jewish control was not confined to
the press alone; Jews also controlled the radio and other news
media. The Jews, by promulgating the melting-pot philosophy in
the movies, on the airwaves, and in the newspapers, had made
America into a "cesspool of humanity." Jews were everywhere.
Kuhn pointed to racketeers, to Benny Goodman, Irving Berlin, the
directors at Twentieth-Century Fox and Paramount Studios. He
echoed what Hitler had written in *Mein Kampf* in the 1920's:

Was there any form of filth or profligacy, particularly in cultural life,
without at least one Jew involved in it? . . . If you cut even cautiously
into such an abscess, you found, like a maggot in a rotting body, often
dazzled by a sudden light—a kike! . . .

Hence today I believe that I am acting in accordance with the will of
the Almighty Creator: *by defending myself against the Jew, I am fighting for the work of the Lord.*[21]

Following the pattern established by Hitler and other anti-Semites,
Jew-baiting became the hallmark of the Bund: Charles Dawes became Charles Davidson, J. P. Morgan became J. P. Morganstern,
and Franklin D. Roosevelt became Franklin D. Rosenfelt. The
Bundesleiter claimed that eventually the Star of David would "be
stamped on Our New One-Dollar Bills, over the American Eagle."

[20] *What Price Federal Reserve? Read the Protocols of the Elders of Zion
and Understand the New Deal* (New York, 1938), container 90, RG 131.

[21] Adolf Hitler, *Mein Kampf,* pp. 57, 64. Kuhn's echoing of these words can
be found in *Das Programm und die Ziele: Eine Rede des Bundesführers Fritz
Kuhn* (Detroit, 1936).

The Bund's views were summarized when its national secretary, James Wheeler-Hill, told New York State Senator John McNaboe that a state of war existed between the Germans and the Jews.[22]

Though the Jews were allegedly disproportionately wealthy and influential, the Bundists understood that they were small in numbers. Therefore, in an effort to make his interpretation of recent American history believable, Kuhn placed emphasis on indigenous American fear of the Blacks. His hatred of the Jews was obsessive. There was an underlying theme of jealousy—the argument that the Jews "had too much." This was not true of the supposed allies of the Jews, the Blacks. Bund propagandists contended that until recently, the Blacks had had nothing and wanted even less. They were illiterate but physically strong and numerous. Black communities had been infiltrated by Jewish-Communist organizers, who promised them the full exercise of their civil rights in return for support in converting America into a Jewish citadel. Bund propagandists did not have to create a stereotype of the Black man in their effort to strike terror in the hearts of white America; they relied on existing dehumanized images. Accordingly, Black males were said to be sexually more potent and to "want" white women; Blacks were stupid, destined to engage only in menial labor; and Blacks were highly susceptible to Communism, which appealed only to the dregs of the earth (for example the "inferior" Slavs). As evidence of the Black man's innate inferiority, the Bundists cited "jazz" and the dances it accompanied, which they argued were present-day residues of an African background: "These jungle dances and the assortment of noises which go along with them . . . have been ushered out of Germany and declared unfit for the German race." [23]

In the Bund's portrayal of the Blacks and the Jews the Nazi viewpoint was readjusted to apply to special conditions in the United States. Thus, jazz was "Negroid" (and strictly forbidden at

[22] Testimony of James Wheeler-Hill before the McNaboe Committee, June 1938, State of New York, *Report of the Joint Legislative Committee*, Doc. 98 (New York, 1939).
[23] *Junges Volk*, Dec. 1938. On dancing at Bund functions, see "Basic Instructions for Unit and Branch Directorates," *Hearings*, Part IV, Appendix, p. 1496.

Bund functions), menial labor was "Black," capitalism was "Jew-ish," material gain at the expense of the movement was cited as ev-idence of "Jewish materialism," and, any questioning of the leader was construed to be an example of "Jewish cowardice."

It will be recalled that some ideologues in the Friends of the New Germany believed that American Jewry would relinquish its control when faced with a united German-American bloc. Kuhn was less hopeful. His attitude was a reflection of his derogatory es-timate of his Americanized racial comrades. He envisioned a cata-clysmic war between the racially pure elements and Jewish Amer-ica allied with the so-called lesser breeds of humanity. In short order, Jews would be ejected from their entrenched positions of power; if need be, they would be killed. Hermann Schwarzmann, leader of the OD in Astoria, Queens, New York, told a Bund gath-ering: "In all likelihood the day of trouble will come—*Der Tag*—with a financial crisis in Washington. Then will be the time to wipe out our enemies." [24] Related to this view was Kuhn's belief that time was running out for American *Deutschtum:* it was rap-idly undergoing Americanization, which he equated with racial death. World War I had quickened the pace of this process; the postwar period had been characterized by an acceleration of Americanization on every level. At times, Kuhn lamented the fate of German-America; he could not understand why it was severing ancestral roots in favor of Jewish materialism. This tragedy was be-coming more acute, since there was "no more immigration of new blood from Germany to freshen up the dying cadaver of German America." [25] Using Hitlerian invective, he dismissed most Ameri-cans of German extraction as Americans lost to Germany forever.

[24] On June 17, 1938, Schwarzmann told a crowd of Bundists: "There will be blood shed. It has to come, judging from the trends in the nation. When we understand how Germans handle their situation in Germany we shall know how to handle difficulties which shall arise in America. In all likelihood the day of trouble will come with the financial crisis in Washington, then will be the time to *wipe out the Jew pigs*" ("Evidence," p. 68—my italics). In *UA,* the phrase "Jew pigs" was replaced by "our enemies" (p. 93). This discrepancy and many others can be accounted for by the fact that the editors of the gov-ernment reports translated, polished, and rephrased statements made by mem-bers of the Bund. Schwarzmann's remarks were recorded verbatim.

[25] *UA,* p. 93.

Kuhn saw German-America's salvation coming through its children. The future of American *Deutschtum* rested with its youth:

The assimilation of the entire German-American youth with the Bund is the one aim we have set for ourselves, because we need the youth if our work is to be lasting.

Many an old fighter's arm has become lame in the struggle for unification, and young energies must take hold.[26]

In a major policy address at Camp Nordland, Kuhn outlined his somber appraisal of adult German-America. He asserted: "The youth is our great hope, the life line of our organization. Through them we must live for the future." And through the Youth Division, Kuhn and the Bundists vicariously lived National Socialism.[27]

The Youth Division was directed by Theodor Dinkelacker. Unlike others of the Bund's many subdivisions, the youth movement was separatist, kept apart from the mainstream of American life. According to Kuhn, German-America's young could be free from the sinister influences of "Jewish Americanization" only in their own schools and camps, where they would be prepared for *Der Tag* and schooled in National Socialism. "Our *camp*," Kuhn told an audience in Andover, New Jersey, "is designed principally to be a place which breathes the spirit of the New Germany. Conscious of this fact, the *camp* is dedicated to our youth. It is here that our boys and girls shall be educated; it is here where the spirit of camaraderie and the feeling of belonging to one community is to be inculcated into them; . . . it is here where they shall be strengthened and confirmed in National Socialism so that they will be conscious of the role which has been assigned to them as the future carriers of German racial ideals to America." [28]

[26] Theodor Dinkelacker, "Our Youth Movement," *Kämpfendes Deutschtum*, p. 6.

[27] *UA*, p. 98.

[28] *Camp Nordland*, pamphlet, July 18, 1937. The camps owned and operated by the Bund were organized as holding corporations. The "owners" of Camp Siegfried were the six directors of the German-American Settlement League; the German-American Bund Auxiliary operated Camp Nordland. On activities in the camps, see "Ein Sommertag in Camp Siegfried," German-American Bund folder, ADL; and "Nazi Military Training Camps in the United States," Dec. 1937, *ibid.* Nazi Germany's view of the benefits derived from camp activities can be found in S. Popfinger, "Sammellage 'Siegfried' der Freunde des neuen Deutschlands," *Westdeutscher Beobachter*, Feb. 7, 1937.

After 1937, the Bund published a magazine for youth, *Junges Volk,* which stressed the significant role played by the Germans in the historical development of the United States, vaunted German heroes, praised the Aryan race, degraded and dehumanized the Jews and Blacks as lesser human types, maintained that their public school teachers were communists, and lauded the new German world view. In spirit and structure, the youth movement was the image of Baldur von Schirach's Hitler Jugend (Hitler Youth). During the summer months, parents sent their children to the Bund camp nearest their homes. Divided into groups according to age and sex, youngsters and those in their early teens were required to don uniforms (brown oxfords, brown shorts, and tan shirts or blouses) and to learn the German language. Most of these children, according to Dinkelacker, were the sons and daughters of the old fighters in the movement (that is, of Germans who had emigrated in the 1920's). There were some children of American-born German-Americans in the Youth Division, but only a handful. For the members of the Dies committee and many adult Americans of the era, no single aspect of the Volksbund's manifold activities was so offensive and overtly "un-American" as the youth movement. People were appalled by the sight of children and young adults dressed in Nazi-style uniforms, wearing Sam Browne Belts and *"Blut* und *Ehre"* ("Blood and Honor") buckles, singing "Deutschland, Deutschland, über Alles." [29]

What the Dies committee called the four *H*'s—Health, Hitler, Heils, and Hatred—applied to camp activities. The camp song hailed the arrival of National Socialism:

Youth, Youth—We are the future soldiers.
Youth, Youth—We are the ones to carry out future deeds.

[29] Children of ages six to thirteen joined the Jungvolk; at fourteen, they also entered the Jungenschaft (boys) or Mädchenschaft (girls). In their late teens, girls could join the Women's Command. Boys exhibiting "a personality of strength and will" (*kraftvolle Persönlichkeit*) had the option of joining the Ordnungs-Dienst. In the summer of 1937, nearly two hundred children were registered at Hindenburg and twice that number at Nordland (*Hearings*, II, 1123ff, 1206–1207). See also "Welcome to Camp Siegfried on Long Island," container 121, and "Ledger Books Containing the Names, Addresses and Accounts of the Bund Youth Division," Jan. 1940–Dec. 1941, container 206, RG 131.

Yes; by our fists will be smashed whoever stands in our way.
Youth, Youth—We are the future soldiers.
Youth, Youth—We are the ones to carry out future deeds.
Führer—We belong to you; yes, we comrades belong to you.[30]

A week at camp (at a cost of five dollars) was filled with martial drills, indoctrination, hiking, and singing.

How many children participated in the movement is not known. It is clear from the public revelations of Bundists subpoenaed before the Dies committee that several youths were sent to Germany and passed their summers in the Hitler Jugend. Motivated by a separatism born of racial politics, the youth movement attempted to capture the minds of the young and to train them for *Der Tag.* The emphasis Kuhn placed on the young, who were impressionable and seem to have enjoyed their summers, amounted to an admission of defeat. He believed that because adult German-America had been "crippled by Americanization," the Bund's future had to depend on the young. But the youngsters in the movement were the children of the very people who made up the group's rank and file. Kuhn and Dinkelacker thought that at Camps Nordland, Siegfried, and Hindenburg they had created the spirit of German National Socialism. Surrounded by banners and with the band playing the German national anthem, they stood with their arms extended in a *Heil* salute reviewing marching columns of children. It was a world of fantasy, of make-believe, of play-acting, or so cynics asserted. The Bundists argued, in turn, that it was a very real world, since "National Socialism was a godsend for the German people" and the marching columns of children were the rulers of tomorrow.[31]

By the summer of 1936 Kuhn's ascendancy over the Bund move-

---

[30] *Junges Volk,* June 1937, p. 4.

[31] Some parents took advantage of reduced fares to send their children to Germany; others permitted their children to work on German steamers and thereby receive free passage. On the establishment of a connection between the Youth Division and the Hitler Youth, see Bundist Richard Aszling to Rolf Hoffmann concerning a visit to the Hitler Jugend headquarters, Dec. 1936, T-81/26/22999. On visits to Germany, see "Evidence," p. 87. Copies of Youth Division songs are scattered throughout containers 51–127, RG 131; photographs of Kuhn and Dinkelacker commanding their young troops are in container 16.

ment was complete. By June, many of the reforms outlined at the Buffalo convention were in effect. Membership was increasing, intraparty struggles had been resolved, new sources of income had been discovered, German nationals were remaining in the movement, and above all, Kuhn was their unchallenged leader. Much to Kuhn's pleasure and surprise, the July 16, 1936, issue of the NSDAP's official organ in Germany, the *Völkischer Beobachter*, commented, "Bundesleiter Fritz Kuhn is finally creating a permanent movement of German-Americans." [32]

There were still many unfinished tasks on Kuhn's agenda. The most important was to make himself appear as German-America's spokesman—in his own words, "to reach Germans of America through the mediums of flaming words and inspiring examples." Between January and August 1936, the Bundesleiter attempted to coordinate the activities of unaligned German and American organizations with those of the Volksbund. Fully aware that he could never gain the unwavering allegiance of most of these clubs and understanding that most hesitated to associate with a militant Nazi group, Kuhn did not believe he could exert direct control over them. As a result, he employed the technique of creating an appearance of unity among German-American and non-German groups. Translated into policy, this meant encouraging sport, singing, cultural, and other profascist clubs to appear publicly with the Volksbund. Often the Bundists marched side by side with Josef Santi's Liktor Assozion, John Finzio's Circolo Mario Morgantini (both groups were divisions of the Italian Black Shirts), the Ukrainian Brown Shirts, and with remnants of Pelley's Silver Shirts and Deatherage's American Nationalist Confederation. Kuhn's aim was to create the illusion that he was the bona fide leader of a united American *Deutschtum* and a leader who was able to work with other, non-German, fascist groups. In an effort to attract more German-Americans, Kuhn had to expand the Bund's social activities. He never attempted, however, to disguise the movement's Nazi orientation: all social functions were by definition

[32] "Die Lage des Deutschamerikaners," *Völkischer Beobachter*, July 16, 1936. Cf. S. Popfinger, "Wie arbeitet die deutsche Freiheitsbewegung in Amerika?" *Westdeutscher Beobachter*, Feb. 7, 1936.

ideological. The Bund's propagandists began to use social lures to attract new members.[33]

Certain German establishments became known as gathering places for the Bundists. One was Ebling's Casino, in The Bronx. Located on St. Ann's Avenue, not far from the Third Avenue Elevated, Ebling's had for years been patronized by Germans. Starting in the spring of 1936, Kuhn used the casino to attract new members. Every Thursday night at nine, the Bund held a "Beer Evening," and for those who did not like alcohol, a "Coffee Hour." Beverages and sandwiches were free, decks of playing cards were provided, and free movies were shown. On May 21, 1936, for instance, the Bund held a "Cultural Evening" at Ebling's. Following the showing of the German-produced film *Nationalsozialismus gegen Kommunismus*, Kuhn's friend Carl Nicolay (affectionately known as "Papa") gave a lecture on Nazi art and music.[34] Many Bundists brought their friends and family members to these functions, which seem to have been highly successful in attracting recruits.

Many young men in their twenties were attracted by the lure of the Bund's fraternal activities, which included an all-encompassing athletic program. By the summer of 1936, the Bund's two soccer teams, Hansa and Hamburg, had entered tournaments in New York State. There were also competitive tennis, hockey, swimming, and skiing teams. For the noncompetitive, the Bund sponsored skiing weekends in the Catskill Mountains.

[33] Materials concerning Kuhn's relationship with the Italian fascist organizations are available in the collection of the ADL; with Salvatore Caridi, president of the North Hudson County Chapter of Ex-Italian War Veterans, 1937, in *UA*, pp. 110–111, and "Evidence," pp. 89ff. The membership records of the Italian War Veterans Organization, U.S.A., are in the Seized Enemy Records Collection, containers 1–41, RG 131. See also Diggins, *Mussolini and American Fascism*, p. 105.

[34] "Amerikadeutscher Volksbund, Ortsgruppe Bronx: Das Programm für diesen Monat, Mai," enclosed in a letter from Carl Nicolay to Rolf Hoffmann, n.d., T-81/26/23637. In addition to "propaganda evenings," the Bund sponsored "educational and speaking evenings," "comradeship evenings," and "allegiance observations" (Hitler's Birthday, April 20; American Independence Day, July 4; German Day, in October; George Washington's Birthday, February 22; Potsdam Celebration, March 21).

While Kuhn labored to attract the sympathies of single young males, he also did much to recruit entire families. Bund propagandists emphasized that the movement was a family organization. It was not uncommon for a family to swim in the Verdome Pool in Manhattan on Friday nights, to rent a cottage at Camp Siegried or another camp during the summer months, and to take a boat ride with a Bund group on the Hudson River on a fall weekend.

In keeping with the Nazi viewpoint, the family was an indissoluble, organic unit, an image of the German state. Each member of the family had a prescribed role and function: father was destined to work, fight, and procreate; mother was to serve the family and state by keeping house and rearing children; and the children were to be educated in National Socialism and trained for their adult roles as members of an elite ruling class. Family education stressed a pseudoegalitarian leveling, a revolt against modernism, and health. Propagandists held out the lure of utopian *Volk* communities, the camps, where families could escape the pernicious influence of Americanization and experience the feeling of belonging to an exclusive racial community. It is not known how effective family recruitment was.[35]

The role assigned to women by the Bund reflected National Socialism's reactionary views. The so-called feminine occupations —housekeeping and motherhood—were not seen as degrading; on the contrary, the prescribed functions of women were historically determined and essential for the preservation of *völkisch* unity. The conception of woman's role was reflected in all levels of the Bund, and the organization remained male-oriented and dominated. The only woman who held a national office was Anna Rehfeldt, the director of the National Women's Command. Unlike other national leaders, she did not have a position on the Volksbund's National Executive Committee. Except for the film maker Leni Riefenstahl, the world-wide Nazi movement did not produce

[35] In 1936, Kuhn wrote, "We desire that the spiritual rebirth of the German people at home shall be transmitted spiritually to the Germans of America through the mediums of flaming words and inspiring examples" (*Awake and Act!*). Admittedly, Kuhn managed to transplant the structure of Nazism and its emphasis on order, dedication, race, courage, and militarism. He was unable to transplant the totality of the Nazi experience.

any women of note; the movement in America was no exception.[36]

To some extent, the expansion of the Bund's social programs accounted for its growth in 1936 and 1937. But there were other factors. The membership in some locals increased because of the incorporation of many small and relatively unknown organizations into the Bund. In New York City, for example, many small groups once affiliated with the United German Societies (which had been factionalized since the Spanknöbel Affair in the fall of 1933) joined ranks with the Bund in order to stave off bankruptcy or dissolution. Each new affiliate could retain its rituals and name. Although some of the societies had been founded before World War I (among them, Turnverein, 1854; Sängerbund, 1883; Hermannssöhne, 1890; and Andreas Hofer, 1897), most had been hastily organized to house German nationals during the crucial transitional period of the Bund's history. Many (including Bund der Sudetendeutschen in Amerika, A-D Nationalverband, and Kameradschaftsvereinigung) were Bund fronts and shared the Bund's offices at its national headquarters. Kuhn managed to join forces with many long-established *Vereine*.

Far more impressive was the number of front organizations he created, which seemed to justify his claim that he was the titular head of many German and German-American singing groups, veterans' organizations, and cultural societies. The fact that most were very small—each had less than a hundred members—did not concern Kuhn. For Kuhn, it was the image the Volksbund projected that counted. On paper, Kuhn had an impressive following.[37]

[36] Kuhn did not consider the leadership command of the National Women's Command (Landesfrauenführung, or LFF) as important as the Ordnungs-Dienst or the Youth Division. The LFF (headed by Anna Rehfeldt [*Bundesfrauenschaftsreferentin*] from September 14, 1937, to February 15, 1940) was not represented on the National Executive Committee, which, at least in theory, governed the Bund and included representatives of all divisions. Kuhn often said, "Women are in the special domain of women," and he meant it.

[37] In the late 1930's, the DAI prepared a list of *Vereine* housing German nationals. Although the unnamed author of the document exaggerated the number of German-national groups and included more than two score founded before 1900, a careful comparison of this list with the materials in RG 131 suggests that Kuhn had under his control more groups than had been suspected by Martin Dies or the Justice Department. A comparison of addresses reveals that many were front organizations (the Vereinigten Sänger moved

The creation and absorption of groups accounted for the Bund's immediate growth in 1936. Several organizations, however, had been affiliated with the Bund since the creation of the Friends of the New Germany in the summer of 1933. One was the American division, founded in 1931, of the Stahlhelm, (Steelhelmets), a right-wing German ex-servicemen's organization. In early 1933, the leader of the Stahlhelm, Franz Seldte, and his second-in-command, Theodor Düsterberg, capitulated to Ernst Roehm's SA. The subjugation of the Stahlhelm was a major victory for the NSDAP. Where Stahlhelm groups had been established outside Germany, their leaders usually joined ranks with the local Nazi groups. Since the founding of the Friends of the New Germany, units of the American branch of Stahlhelm had marched side by side with the Bundists. In fact, the relationship was so close that most members of the veterans' organization belonged to the Bund. In July 1936, Kuhn concluded that the distinction between the two groups was nominal; following the example established in Germany three years earlier, the Bundesleiter "ordered" all Stahlhelm units to integrate with the Bund. In a swift move, Kuhn created a veterans' division in the Bund and named it the Frontkämpferschaft. Every Stahlhelm group followed Kuhn's order except one in Detroit, whose leader, Rudolf Heupel, discovered that some of his comrades resented being associated with "Nazis and enemies of America." Heupel attempted to convince these men that the Volksbund was composed of "American citizens who were pledged to work with other groups toward the aim of preserving and strengthening the

---

from Manhattan to Ebling's Casino, which was The Bronx headquarters of the Bund, and the Bund der Sudetendeutschen in Amerika, the Deutscher-Kriegsbund, and the Kyffhäuser-Kameradschaft von Hindenburg shared the Bund's headquarters in Yorkville). Some of the groups on the DAI's list were anti-Bund but pro-Nazi. The Schwäbische Vereine, for example, had extensive connections with the VDA's representative in America, Günther Orgell (T-81/617/5411336). See DAI, List of German National Vereine in the U.S.A. (Los Angeles, Milwaukee, Hartford, New Haven, New Orleans, Portland, Rochester, N.Y., New York City, St. Paul, San Francisco, Spokane, Seattle, Chicago, Washington, D.C., Philadelphia, Baltimore, Pittsburgh), T-81/619/5414301–331. Cf. container 213, RG 131.

American system of government." Heupel's pleas for unity were in vain, and the Detroit unit chose to remain independent.[38]

The rapid absorption of the Stahlhelm and other national groups that had been founded since 1918 demonstrated that the Bund remained what it always had been—an organization composed of former German nationals, people who had firsthand knowledge of Germany's defeat and the dislocations that followed. Moreover, it underscored the absurdity of Kuhn's assertion that the Volksbund and been Americanized—a contention that was nothing more than propaganda aimed at deceiving both the American and the German governments. In an effort to accommodate German nationals who had been banned from participating in the Bund, Kuhn had created a large number of front organizations. Although it was unnecessary for these groups to retain their names after the establishment of the Prospective Citizens' League, Kuhn decided to prolong their fictitious lives.

Kuhn was not the type of leader who measured his strength by the number of new recruits for a given month. What counted was the impression the Bund projected. In creating the image he desired, Kuhn was a very effective leader. When detractors suggested that he had few followers or that he had created paper organizations, Kuhn pointed to a rally in Reading, Pennsylvania, where fifteen thousand had turned out, or to one in New York City, where twenty-two thousand people had packed Madison Square Garden to hear the American Führer speak.

[38] On the integration of the Stahlhelm, see Rudolf Heupel (leader of the Frontkämpferschaft des Amerikadeutschen Volksbundes) to consulate (Detroit), March 19, 1938, T-81/140/178028–30. Shortly after the absorption of the Stahlhelm, Kuhn created the Frontkämpfer-Führung (War Veterans' Command), an administrative subsection of the Bund. The Stahlhelm was not the only German armed forces veterans' group in the United States. In Pittsburgh, the Kyffhäuserbund was incorporated by Karl Schumacher in August 1937. Although it was not part of the Bund, most of its members belonged to the Volksbund; in fact, Kuhn considered it a "substitute organization." See Hearings, Part VII, pp. 75, 1102–1104; "Kyffhäuserbund und Hermannssöhne in die Kongress-Untersuchung verwickelt," Rochester (N.Y.) Abendpost, July 20, 1940, and T-81/619/5414301ff.

Thus, in less than six months, from January to June 1936, Fritz Kuhn accomplished what Reich officialdom believed impossible: he infused new life into the beleaguered Bund, and he did it with no help from Germany. Admittedly, Kuhn did not create the Volksbund; he inherited and remodeled a structure that had been created by Heinz Spanknöbel three years earlier. Kuhn's political and business resourcefulness notwithstanding, his greatest asset was Hitler's successes. For many Germans at home and abroad, Hitler was a twentieth-century Luther. In three short years, the German leader had brought about a national revival. The American Führer rode into the German national community on a wave that had started in Germany. Unquestionably, this was the key to his initial successes; it was also the key to his eventual downfall. Traditional American tolerance and indifference permitted him to gain some momentum; indifference soon turned to concern, and tolerance became intolerance. As Americans witnessed the revival of the Bund in juxtaposition with the events in Europe, they became convinced that Kuhn's Trojan horse was nearly completed. In consequence, many Americans were willing to believe Kuhn's exaggerated claims.

CHAPTER 10

Kuhn's Meeting with the German Führer: Summer 1936

The year 1936 was crucial in the history of National Socialism and international fascism. In March, German troops occupied the demilitarized Rhineland in violation of the accords reached at Locarno a decade before; much to Hitler's surprise, Germany's former enemies acquiesced in this action. The Treaty of Versailles had finally died. Less than three months later, Italian troops occupied Addis Ababa, an action hailed by Mussolini as the beginning of a revived Roman Empire. The success of Italian aggression brought about the collapse of the League of Nations as a political machine. In France, Léon Blum formed the first popular-front ministry on June 5, which led to the coalescence of anti-Republican forces. It was a turning point for the radical right in that nation. In the Third Republic, in the Balkans, in the Iberian Peninsula, and elsewhere in Europe and abroad, Hitler and Mussolini had their imitators. For these people and their followers the *élan* of Italian fascism and the momentum of German National Socialism gave promise of the emergence of a new world order.

The summer of that year began with the nomination of Franklin D. Roosevelt at the Democratic National Convention at Philadelphia on June 26; it ended with a spectacular display of Nazi pageantry at the annual NSDAP Party Days in the medieval city of Nuremberg. Fresh from an uncontested victory in the Rhineland, Hitler placed Germany on display before the world. In a well-timed effort to appease ill feeling, the Nazis played down their obsessive racial anti-Semitism and "entertained with a splendour that rivalled the displays of *le Roi Soleil* and the Tzars of Russia" as visitors flooded the Third Reich.[1] It was the summer of the German Olympics. Pensions and hotels were filled, and foreigners marveled at the newly constructed *Autobahnen* and government buildings in the capital city. Many returned home believing that the spirit of National Socialism was not merely the creation of propaganda. Much to the surprise and obvious pleasure of the German Führer, members of a French Olympic team paid homage to him as they passed the reviewing stand with their arms extended in *Heil* salute. Some occurrences were not soon forgotten by Germans or by visitors from North America: Hitler's predictable reaction to Jesse Owens' victory and the tea party given in honor of the Lindberghs at Tempelhof Airport by the Lufthansa Company. These events were given extensive coverage by the news media in the United States.[2] Many readers and radio listeners were, for one reason or another, neither disturbed nor interested. In early August, a much publicized incident aroused many Americans from their indifference: Fritz Kuhn's meeting with Adolf Hitler.

Throughout the spring and early summer, official Berlin had watched the turn of events in the Bund's fortunes. Neither the Party nor the State, however, made any moves to accord Kuhn political recognition, or for that matter, any other assistance. Germany's reasons for reluctance need no elaboration. Kuhn believed that the Reich would designate him the leader of a united Germandom in the United States, since he had proved himself, so to speak. Was this belief an example of Kuhn's ability to delude himself or was there some reason, perhaps an indication from a Reich official or agency, which prompted him to arrive at this conclusion? The only grounds for Kuhn's hopes were several minor articles about the Volksbund in the *Völkischer Beobachter* and Germany's un-

[1] Alan Bullock, *Hitler: A Study in Tyranny* (rev. ed.; New York, 1962), p. 355.

[2] William Shirer, *Berlin Diary: The Journal of a Foreign Correspondent, 1934–1941*, entry for July 23, 1936 (New York, 1942), p. 51. The German Railroads Information Office, German steamship lines, and German-American tourist agencies distributed several million pieces of literature advertising the summer Olympics; one report, dated June 15, 1936, stated that the Railroads Information Office distributed 1,201,750 leaflets ("Promotional Activities in Connection with the Olympic Games," in file "Oly. Bericht 1936," Records Relating to the German Railroads Information Office, RG 131).

willingness to take any action against its nationals who joined the Prospective Citizens' League in the first months of 1936.[3] There were, nonetheless several factors that Kuhn felt were working in his favor. First, now that Hitler had moved the Third Reich to the center of the European stage and was bolstering pro-Nazi movements on the Continent and elsewhere, the American Bund leader assumed that a newly reorganized Nazi movement might receive the same support afforded groups in other countries and, of course, the help given to the old Bund, the Friends of the New Germany. Closely related was Kuhn's conviction that since he had demonstrated that his organization could support itself and since he had freed the group from the internecine quarreling which had characterized its entire history, Berlin might re-evaluate its stance and throw its weight behind the Bund. Finally, Kuhn believed that German officials would have to deal with him if Berlin hoped to influence the German-American community in some sections of the United States, especially in New York and New Jersey. With these misconceptions uppermost in his mind, Kuhn assiduously prepared for a trip to the Reich.

Preparations for Kuhn's much publicized "Olympic journey" began in April 1936. Throughout the late spring and early summer, each issue of several of the Bund's newspapers advertised his forthcoming trip. Kuhn extended a personal invitation to all Bundists to join him; if they could not, he suggested they send contributions to a newly created Olympic fund. More than three thousand dollars was sent from locals across the land to the Bundesleitung in New York. Part of the fund was diverted and used to defray publication costs of the *Goldene Buch der Amerika-deutschten,* an elaborate leather-bound pictorial history of the Bund from its founding in 1924 that contained the signatures of six thousand subscribers. If he had the opportunity, Kuhn intended to present the "Golden Book" to the German Führer. By mid-June, preliminary plans were complete. On the night of the thirteenth, Kuhn told a group of well-wishers at a special benefit ball held at the Yorkville Casino that travel and hotel arrangements and tickets to all Nazi functions

[3] "Die Lage des Deutschamerikaners," *Völkischer Beobachter,* July 15, 1936.

had been secured, and that he, together with two hundred of his followers, would board the S.S. *New York* on June 23. Ten days later, the ship arrived in Hamburg.[4]

A tentative itinerary had been prepared by Kuhn's right-hand man, Carl Nicolay, with the help of Rolf Hoffmann, of the Party's Overseas Press Office. It is clear from "Papa" Nicolay's correspondence with Hoffmann that any exhilaration Kuhn might have felt was premature. When Nicolay requested a press pass—claiming that he would serve as the representative of the *Deutscher Weckruf*—Hoffmann wrote back that he would first have to receive permission from Goebbels' Ministry of Propaganda. Nicolay, in turn, got in touch with a Herr Voigt in that agency's American Section; Voigt never answered his several requests. Only after Nicolay arrived in Germany was he finally issued the much sought pass. Ostensibly of minor importance, the incident suggests that despite Kuhn's plans and high hopes, Germany did little to prepare for the arrival of the Bundists. Admittedly, Hoffmann had secured hotel and pension accommodations for the Bundists in Munich, Berlin, Stuttgart, Cologne, and other German cities. But Hoffmann, as well as several German travel agencies in New York, made reservations for thousands of visitors. By treating its members as individuals, Germany avoided giving official sanction to the Bund, making no distinction between Bundists and other visitors from North America and elsewhere. Once they disembarked from the S. S. *New York*, however, the situation changed dramatically. During Kuhn's stay in the Reich, he was feted and invited to Party functions. He met with representatives of several Nazi agencies and with four of his comrades, had an unanticipated audience with Hitler.[5]

[4] On arrangement for the trip, see Elsa Kuhn to Rolf Hoffmann, July 1936, T-81/26/23439; Rolf Hoffmann to Frontkämpfer Group (New York), May 4, 1936, T-81/26/23446; "Die Olympiafahrt des Bundes," *Kämpfendes Deutschtum*, 1937 (materials about the preparation of the *Jahrbuch* and the section on the Olympic Games are in T-81/394/5135800ff); *Deutscher Weckruf*, April–June 1936. Cf. Leland Bell, *In Hitler's Shadow*, pp. 39–42.

[5] Rolf Hoffmann to Carl Nicolay, June 15, 1936; Nicolay to Hoffmann, July 1936, T-81/26/23632, 23629. Voigt was a staffer in the American section of the Ministry of Propaganda.

When the Bundists arrived in Germany, the uncertainty they may have felt was immediately dispelled. Many of them, including the Bundesleiter, had never seen Hitler's Germany. This was the first time in thirteen years that Kuhn returned to his native land. After their disembarkation, Kuhn and his party visited several cities. On hand for their arrival in Berlin was Sepp Schuster, a member of the Bund's "old guard" and organizer of the organization's fighting division, the Ordnungs-Dienst. The fragmentary evidence suggests that Schuster, now a member of the Labor Front and enjoying a good standing in the Party, arranged for Kuhn and his entourage to march with Schuster's old unit from the early days of Hitler's struggle for power, the Fifth SA Company (it will be recalled that Schuster took part in the abortive *Putsch* in November 1923), down the Unten den Linden. It was August 2, 1936.

This date is of cardinal importance in the history of the Nazi movement in the United States. Undoubtedly, August 2 was the high point of Kuhn's turbulent and ill-fated career. Shortly before the procession started down the Unten den Linden, Schuster seems to have informed Kuhn that the marchers would stop in front of Hitler's chancellery and that the German leader would receive him. The unexpected had happened. There is no record of Kuhn's immediate reaction. Perhaps he thought to himself that this meeting would permit him to plead his case before Hitler and that the Führer would designate him the leader of American *Deutschtum*. As will be seen, nothing of the sort ever happened, despite Kuhn's later assertions to the contrary. At Kuhn's side during the reception was George Froboese, head of the Midwestern Department, who was to become the last leader of the Volksbund, a week before the Japanese attack on Pearl Harbor. Following the audience with Hitler, Froboese recorded what allegedly transpired and later published his account in the 1937 issue of the Bund's yearbook, *Kämpfendes Deutschtum:*

He [Hitler] shook hands with each of us, looked straight in our eyes and placed his hand on the shoulder of our Bund leader. . . . He asked us about our comrades of German blood across the sea, thanked us for our strong opposition to the immoral press and its infamous lies, and inquired in detail about the future plans of our Bund and our excursion through Germany. When our Bund leader mentioned our coming visit to Munich, the Führer took steps to ensure a warm welcome for the Bund in that city, where our movement had its beginning. The Führer thanked us for the presentation of the book of testimonials [the "Golden Book"] and for the accompanying donation [for the winter relief fund].

Hitler then bade them farewell and added, "Go over there and continue the fight." [6]

V. Fritz Julius Kuhn and four members of the Bund's Uniformed Service (Ordnungs-Dienst) meeting with the German Führer, August 1936. (National Archives.)

[6] *Kämpfendes Deutschtum*, pp. 55–56. During the preparations for his denaturalization trial, Kuhn told his attorney that Ambassador Dodd arranged for his meeting with Hitler. In light of Dodd's stance vis-à-vis the Nazi regime and his protests about Nazi activities in America, Kuhn's claim seems highly unlikely (Fritz Kuhn to Matthias Correa, Sept. 1, 1942, Civ. 18–415, FRC). Also with Kuhn during the meeting with Hitler were Rudolf Markmann (*Gauleiter Ost*), Carl Weiler (his position is unknown), and an unnamed fourth person (original photographs of Hitler-Kuhn meeting, container 38, RG 131). See Plate V. Kuhn's reaction to the meeting can be found in the *California Weckruf*, Dec. 10, 1936, and the *Deutscher Weekruf und Beobachter*, Aug. 13, 1936.

Hitler's reception of his imitator from America should not be construed as either a particularly dramatic gesture or a major departure from German policy toward the Bund. Between the start of the summer Olympics on August 1 and the conclusion of the games sixteen days later, the German leader gave audiences to several foreigners; in fact, on the morning after the Hitler-Kuhn meeting, the German Führer had a discussion with the former American ambassador to Germany (1925–1930) Jacob Gould Schurman. The Third Reich was on display, and the leadership took advantage of the propaganda value of playing host to thousands of important and unimportant foreigners. What was significant about the Hitler-Kuhn meeting was the excitement it aroused in the United States and the fact that Kuhn later used it to deceive his followers by making them believe he took orders from Hitler. It also reinforced the widespread belief that Hitler personally endorsed the Bund's activities and that the Party was still behind the movement. The truth is, Hitler never recommitted the resources of the State or Party. All Kuhn received were a pat on the back and a few trite remarks. He left the meeting—and Germany—in the same situation he was in when he arrived: Germany refused to throw its support behind him and designate him the leader of the German-American community.[7]

But for the millions of Americans who saw a widely circulated picture of the Führer shaking hands with the Bundesleiter on the front pages of many daily newspapers, it was another story. This picture enraged some Americans, and Kuhn's enemies cited the meeting as evidence that the Bundists were bent on undermining the Republic.[8] At first the Bund was dubbed the Nazi conspiracy —the "Nazintern"; later, after the fall of Spain to Franco's forces, the conspirators were called the Fifth Column. Needless to say, Congress' number one anti-Nazi, Samuel Dickstein, immediately

[7] Between August 1 and 14, Hitler had discussions with more than fifteen dignitaries and unofficial representatives of other nations, including the former American ambassador to Germany, Jacob Gould Schurman, and the Sudeten leader, Konrad Henlein.

[8] An excellent example of the way in which the photographs were used by American editors can be found in "Hitler Speaks and the Bund Obeys," *Look*, Oct. 10, 1938.

called for a renewed investigation of the reorganized Bund's un-American activities and its relationship with Berlin. Two years later the responsibility for the probe was delegated to Martin Dies, a controversial and at times flamboyant congressman from Texas. In 1942, in a letter to President Roosevelt, Dies summarized the belief that prevailed after Kuhn returned to America: "We have always believed that the German-American Bund was the spearhead of Hitler's attempted penetration into this country." [9] The coalescence of public opinion against Kuhn was swift. Following his meeting with Hitler, he could count among his foes not only outraged American Jews, but also some leaders of organized labor, liberals and conservatives alike, and countless Americans who viewed the Volksbund as a subversive and downright un-American group.

Hitler's willingness to meet Kuhn and the excitement it aroused also enraged some high-ranking members of Germany's diplomatic corps, who believed the meeting was a major miscalculation. They asserted, correctly, that the pictures of the Hitler-Kuhn meeting did little to assuage American ill feeling; they believed, too, that the meeting inadvertently reinvolved Germany with the Bund movement, since Kuhn, who was already known to them through his exaggerations and bombast, would use it to impress his unsuspecting followers and cite it as evidence of a personal relationship with the Nazi leader. When Hans Heinrich Dieckhoff replaced Hans Luther at the German Embassy in Washington in 1937, he told Hitler personally that the picture-taking ceremony was an irrevocable mistake.

Hitler expressed agreement. He had only seen Kuhn once, he said, and did not wish to see him again. But that once, Dieckhoff pointed out, had caused considerable excitement, since he [the Führer] had been photographed with Kuhn. That, retorted Hitler, was unfortunate but hardly his fault, since it was at the Olympic Games where one was photographed with all sorts of people.[10]

At the time, however, neither Kuhn nor those responsible for the meeting were aware that it would cause so much controversy. For

[9] Martin Dies to F. D. Roosevelt, Aug. 15, 1942, Official File 320, FDRL.
[10] RG 59, "Dieckhoff Interrogation," 251.

Fritz Kuhn, it was the reward for years of hard work. Hitler was a charismatic leader who had created a pseudo religion and enjoyed the veneration of millions of people. Kuhn, in turn, had assiduously cultivated and manipulated the Hitler cult in the United States and viewed himself as the American Führer. In his own eyes, Kuhn had finally arrived at the center of power.

The Olympic Games ended on August 16. Although many foreign visitors left Germany, an equally large number stayed and made arrangements to attend the Party Days (Reichsparteitag der "Ehre"), which began on September 8. Kuhn and his party visited several German cities and were invited by his predecessor, Fritz Gissibl, now a staffer at the German Foreign Institute, to a dinner held in their honor. "Papa" Nicolay found time to visit his brother Mannheim and to tour the Party's Central Archives in Munich.[11] For the most part, the Bundists spent their evenings renewing old acquaintances and eating and drinking in Munich's many beer halls. One evening in late August, they gathered in the Hirschbräu-keller in Munich with other foreign Party and non-Party people. Moved by the fraternalism of the occasion, Nicolay composed a song especially for this evening: "From the Hudson to the Isar, German brothers walk hand in hand with new hopes, . . . a new life and a renewed love of holy Germany." On an autographed copy sent to his friend Rolf Hoffmann, Nicolay wrote a dedication: "To the Führer of all Germans, of the holy Third Reich, and of the German *Volk*—Adolf Hitler, we thank you." After the Party Days in Nuremberg, the Bundists returned to Munich and, together with members of other foreign Nazi organizations, were given a reception at a restaurant, the Löwenbräukeller, a *Kameradschafts-Abend* ("Comradeship Evening") arranged by the Ortsgruppe Gabrielen-platz, a local group of the NSDAP. Here Kuhn had an opportunity to meet for the first time Nazis from Central and Eastern Europe

[11] Report of a meeting with Fritz Gissibl in "Tagung des Deutschen Ausland-Instituts in Stuttgart," Aug. 26, 1936, *Deutscher Weckruf und Beobachter*, Sept. 10, 1936; report of Rolf Hoffmann's meeting with Kuhn's wife, Elsa, at the Brown House, Munich, Hoffmann to Elsa Kuhn, Sept. 22, 1936, T-81/26/23436. On arrangements for the Party rally, see T-81/26/23439; on meetings with representatives of German agencies, see Carl Nicolay to Rolf Hoffmann, July 23, 1936, Sept. 18, 1936, T-81/26/23631, 23620–1.

and from South America.[12] The evening obviously made an indelible impression on the American Bundesleiter: like the founding of the Teutonia Association in 1924, the official founding of the Friends of the New Germany in July 1933, and the much acclaimed Buffalo convention in March 1936, *Kameradschafts-Abend* (September 19, 1936), received an honored place in the Amerikadeutscher Volksbund's "Dates to be Remembered."

Camaraderie was one thing; gaining the recognition Kuhn desired was another. Although Kuhn had an opportunity to plead his case before the man directly responsible for his appointment, Fritz Gissibl, and the representatives of other agencies, the impromptu discussions made him keenly aware that the break with the Bund effected nearly a year before, in October 1935, was permanent.[13] He received expressions of sympathy and the promise of an unlimited supply of propaganda material, but little else. In some respects, Kuhn's friend "Papa" Nicolay faired much better. Nicolay took advantage of the trip to visit friends and relatives, tour Germany, and compose songs and poems. A career opportunist who latched onto National Socialism late in life, Nicolay squandered the Bund's funds on entertainment and travel. He spent several evenings with Rolf Hoffmann at his home in Munich. On the other hand, Kuhn was rebuffed by those whose support he sought. Except for the consolation of his much publicized meeting with Hitler, he returned to the United States disappointed and frustrated.

Upon his return to America, however, he gave his followers no indication of his failures. In Bund Command I, issued in Detroit on October 28, he wrote:

> The high point of the trip naturally was the reception for us by the *Führer* of the German people, Adolf Hitler. And at this time I desire to thank all members of the Bund and friends of the organization in his name for the *Golden Book* and the gift of money.

[12] Carl Nicolay, "Isarstand," performed at the Hirschbräukeller, enclosed in a letter from Nicolay to Hoffmann, Aug. 30, 1936, T-81/26/23624; "Kameradschafts-Abend am 19. September 1936 im Löwenbräukeller, Programm," enclosed in a letter from Nicolay to Hoffmann, Sept. 1936, T-81/26/23619.

[13] See "DAI an Fritz Kuhn von 10. Juli 1936," T-81/394/5135828. Neither the DAI records nor the papers of the Amerikadeutscher Volksbund reveal that Kuhn received any further accommodations (e.g., financial backing).

I have spoken with several leading men and agencies concerning our work and our determination and our goals. I know today better than ever before, the direction in which our Bund must go.[14]

Kuhn then proceeded to outline a twelve-point program which he intended to discuss with department leaders. He called for the continuation of all projects that had been initiated since the Buffalo convention in March. Far more important was the statement that he knew "better than ever before the direction in which our Bund must go." What he had been unable to achieve by persuading the Germans, Kuhn now sought to accomplish by deceit: he began to lie to his unsuspecting followers about a relationship with the German Führer. During his remaining three years as leader of the Volksbund, he shrewdly manipulated the events of the summer of 1936 to enhance his own position. In 1937, for example, Kuhn told John C. Metcalfe, who joined the Bund under the alias Helmut Oberwinder in order to gather materials for several feature stories that appeared in the *Chicago Times:* "You see, I have a certain special arrangement with Hitler and Germany that whenever any of our groups have trouble with the consulates in their districts they are to report to me in full detail. I then take it up with the Ambassador and Germany is not to be troubled with this unless I get no satisfaction from the Ambassador." [15] He even asserted that Hans Luther had lost his post as ambassador to Hans Heinrich Dieckhoff in 1937 because Luther would not cooperate with him. With Dieckhoff in control, Kuhn said, "all new consuls are Nazis and are under special instructions to give us the fullest cooperation in every way." [16] The truth was, of course, that Kuhn never enjoyed a special arrangement with Hitler or the Party, and especially not with Dieckhoff, who was later instrumental in exposing Kuhn for what he was—a liar.

Nevertheless, a relationship did exist between the Volksbund and Germany. In no way, however, was it of the kind alleged by Martin Dies's House Committee to Investigate Un-American Activities. As far as individuals involved with the Nazi propaganda ma-

14 Bund Command I, Oct. 28, 1936, ADL.
15 "Evidence," p. 81.   16 *Ibid.*

chine were concerned, the Volksbund had value as an instrument for the dissemination of propaganda; often Goebbels' ministry compared its growth to that of the National German-American Alliance before World War I. Kuhn's involvement with Federal, state, and local officials, which ended in his arrest in May 1939 and the consequent withering away of his following, accorded well with the official Nazi image of the United States: Kuhn, the loyal German and good Nazi, was depicted as a victim of the sinister machinations of international Jewry. It was claimed that his arrest was a harbinger of things to come—the incarceration of German-America in "Jewish prisons." In brief, Kuhn and his followers served a useful function and lent support to the often repeated Nazi claim that America was becoming a vast Jewish citadel.

Despite such bold assertions, Germany never extended to Kuhn or the Volksbund the practical political support or recognition it had given to the Friends of the New Germany. After 1936, Germany's aim was to appease the ill feeling the Bund and internal events in Germany had aroused in the United States. It was no coincidence that 1936 witnessed the beginning of a major propaganda campaign aimed at the Americans. To accomplish this end, Berlin utilized almost every pro-German, anti-Communist, and right-wing organization to disseminate its viewpoint. From time to time, Germany used the Bund to hawk copies of *Mein Kampf* or to clip editorials favorable to the Reich from American newspapers. But Berlin never considered using the Bund to implement its significant goals in the United States and eschewed its overtures, preferring to work through outlets in both Germany and America for the distribution of propaganda. Among the more active agencies were the German Library of Information in Manhattan,[17] the German Foreign Institute, and Rolf Hoffmann's Overseas Press Office.

By far, Hoffmann's was the most skilled propaganda agency.[18]

---

[17] The German Library of Information was located in the same building as the German consulate. The first head of the library was Heinz Beller. After 1939, the library distributed *Facts in Review* and other newsletters (*Hearings*, Part VII, pp. 12ff). Other important Nazi publications distributed in America were: *News from Germany* (1937–1941), *News Flashes from Germany* (1939–1941), and *German Art and Culture* (1940–1941).

[18] Hoffmann's office supplied free Nazi literature to groups and individuals in places as far away as Madras (*Der Deutsche in Indien*), Bombay (*The

His staff answered requests for literature and wrote letters with a personal touch. Among the thousands of letters he sent, an excellent case in point is one to Joseph M. Reichle of St. Albans, Queens, New York:

> Thank you very much for your long letter of April 24th. I am highly pleased that you enjoy so much reading our "News from Germany." . . .
>
> It must be very difficult for you to find out the truth while the American press is publishing such horrible lies. However, I think it is only natural of our press to reply to the outrages of American journalists with defiance, though our expressions are certainly not half as strong as those used by the American press and even by American statesmen.
>
> Have you read the Führer's speech before the Reichstag? We all think that it was a masterpiece. The official translation will go forward to you together with the next issue of "News from Germany." Today I am having an article by Reichminister Goebbels, a booklet on the Jewish question in Germany, and a Party program sent to you under separate cover. I trust this literature will be of interest to you.[19]

Clearly, this propaganda offensive, which became more pronounced during the neutrality debates in the United States after the outbreak of hostilities in Europe in September 1939, did little to lessen the already existing American hostility toward Berlin and

---

Aryan Path), and Hong Kong. In the United States, recipients of materials from his office included the League for the Advancement of Aryan Culture (New York), the American Vigilant Intellectual Federation (Chicago), Nation and Race (Florida), and the Anti-Communist League of New England. Admittedly, these groups had little impact and small memberships; but what is striking is the number of these right-wing and pro-Nazi groups that sprang up in the 1930's. See Hoffmann Papers, T-81, rolls 25–27. From time to time Hoffmann requested one of these groups to send him copies of its publications. In April 1936, Hoffmann requested Kuhn to mail him copies of materials distributed by the Friends of the New Germany so that "future generations will have a glance at your struggle and your propaganda work in America" (Hoffmann to Kuhn, April 1, 1936, T-81/25/23443).

[19] Hoffmann to Joseph M. Reichle, May 10, 1939, T-81/29/25610. In March 1939, former Bund leader Reinhold Walter suggested to Hoffmann that too much time and money had been spent on distributing propaganda in New York City. "America," wrote the deposed Bundesleiter turned propagandist, "is not New York. . . . It has a hinterland." As a corrective, he suggested that Germany concentrate on the Midwest and the South, sections with deep-rooted antiurban feelings (T-81/29/26079–81).

gave support to the contentions of the isolationists as well as of the interventionists.

Thus, in spite of Kuhn's bold assertions and fraudulent claims, Germany viewed the Amerikadeutscher Volksbund as only one among many avenues for the dissemination of propaganda in the United States. It should be added, however, that members of the Bund did receive special treatment when they visited Germany and that one of the Volksbund's projects was supported with German money. The Bund's yearbook for 1937, for example, was planned with the aid of the DAI; membership in the Bund opened doors to certain government offices in the Reich; members of the movement's Uniformed Services (OD) were given free passage on German liners; and some of the leaders and members of the Bund's subdivisions (the women's and youth organizations) were given training in Germany. In contrast to the assistance given Gissibl's organization and before that, Gau-USA, the help afforded the Bund amounted to little. Preferential treatment was given because of the Party's commitment to racial politics, not to the Volksbund. As an organization, the Bund had discredited itself and was viewed as a troublesome problem by German officialdom; after 1936, it was regarded as only one of many pro-German organizations that sprang up in America during the 1930's. The Bundists as individuals, however, were seen by Party people as racial comrades in Germany's struggle against world Jewry, and for this reason the Party was not inclined to ignore them once they were in Germany.[20]

Kuhn was keenly aware of these contradictions. His failure to obtain a commitment of support and a thoroughgoing endorsement

[20] This distinction is of cardinal importance. The Party adhered to its commitment to supply the Bund with propaganda materials but supplied little else. Examples of German support after 1936 can be found in correspondence between the Bund's Press Division and Walter Kappe (DAI) concerning the planning of the *Jahrbuch* for 1937, T-81/394/5135804ff. See Carl Nicolay to Rolf Hoffmann, Oct. 5, 1936, on entree to Nazi agencies, T-81/26/23627; Richard Aszling to Hoffmann, concerning a visit to Hitler Jugend headquarters, Nov. 1936, T-81/26/22999; and "Statement of Identification for Bund Members Going to Germany," Bund Command V, Jan. 5, 1937. On free passage on German ships for members of the Ordnungs-Dienst, see *Hearings*, Document 1, Appendix IV.

from Hitler and the Party baffled him and became a source of resentment against those in Germany who were, in his opinion, "directly sabotaging my work." His dismay was reflected in a Bund
command he issued in the fall of 1937. Concerning the Volksbund's
collection of money for Germany's winter relief program, Kuhn
wrote:

It is strongly forbidden to send this money to the Consulate. The reason
for this is as follows: Every year the Bund has sent thousands of dollars
for the Winter Relief [Winterhilfswerk] to Germany, but has never received recognition of this, although other organizations have received
letters of praise. The cooperation of the Bund has never been acknowledged: the *Auslandsorganisation* always got the credit.[21]

Kuhn's bitterness and failure to comprehend why Germany refused
to designate him the leader of American *Deutschtum* quickly became a matter of concern to German diplomats. In November 1937,
Ambassador Dieckhoff, himself a seasoned diplomat and astute observer of American affairs, believed that "Kuhn's stupid statements
of friendship with Hitler" did little to help Germany's cause in the
United States.[22] Consequently, the more Kuhn exaggerated and

[21] Bund Command XV, Nov. 12, 1937. The Bund's winter relief program was
modeled after Germany's. The Bund's women's auxiliary collected money,
foodstuffs, coal, and medicine, which were shipped to families in Germany or
distributed to needy Bund members in America. The program also permitted
Bund members to designate recipients in Germany for direct cash donations
("Cash Records for Winter Relief, 1937–1938," container 131, RG 131). During Kuhn's denaturalization trial, he was accused of giving direct support of
Nazi Germany through the winter relief program. In response, he argued that
the program was in the same category as relief programs for refugees of the
civil war in Spain ("Statement of Fritz Kuhn," Civ. 18–415, FRC).

[22] Hans Dieckhoff to Hans-Georg von Mackensen (son of Field Marshal von
Mackensen; he was named State Secretary in the Foreign Ministry on March
24, 1937; he later served as ambassador to Italy, 1933–1943), Nov. 24, 1937,
DGFP, D, I, 651. As will be seen, Kuhn's behavior had so thoroughly alienated German officials that after 1938 they refused to receive him. The former
chargé d'affaires at the German Embassy in Washington summarized the prevalent feeling in Berlin: "We considered Herr Kuhn and his followers as a
small and rather ridiculous [group]" (Hans Thomsen to the author, April 4,
1968). After the war, Bohle tried to rationalize his early support of the Bund
by dismissing the organization as "impossible and stupid." However, Bohle's
claim, after the dissolution of Gau-USA, that the Auslandsorganisation maintained no connections with the Bund was a blatant lie (RG 59, "Bohle Interrogation," 110).

lied about his relations with Berlin, the more Berlin thought of publicly disavowing the Volksbund.

Continued rejection only caused Kuhn to redouble his efforts to maintain the illusion of Hitler's personal involvement with the Bund. In the spring of 1938, nearly eighteen months after his meeting with Hitler on August 2, 1936, Kuhn made a second trip to Germany. At the Bund's annual convention in September, Kuhn stood before his followers and reported on the outcome of this trip. After claiming that he had had a private meeting with Göring and Goebbels, he implied that his tenure as Bundesleiter had been re-affirmed by "someone" in Berlin: "I need also not tell you with whom I have spoken. . . . All that is my affair and likewise to be trusted to me by you. Either a confidence exists which gives me free action, or no such confidence exists, in which event you have the opportunity today to deprive me of this trust." He concluded by attempting to make a victory of defeat: "I give you my word of honor that a denial of our organization in Germany would have caused me to stand before you today and state: 'I can no longer undertake the responsibility of continuing the leadership of the Bund and herewith withdraw.' Then you would have perceived yourself that the continuance of the Bund would be useless." [23]

To be sure, by 1938 most German leaders involved in the making of foreign policy had little use for Kuhn's honor. On one occasion, Dieckhoff was so amazed by Kuhn's brazen statements about friendship with the Nazi elite that he wondered whether Kuhn might be telling the truth. To set his mind at ease, he requested the Wilhelmstrasse to investigate whether Göring and Goebbels had in fact received Kuhn. An investigation followed, and the ministry reported that the "natural conclusion is that Herr Kuhn was —as already on other occasions—consciously deviating from the truth in order to strengthen his position with his adherents." [24] This view of Kuhn was confirmed by a former German diplomat assigned to the embassy in Washington, who asserted also that Party officialdom considered the Volksbund a "small and rather ridiculous organization." Eventually, it was believed that Kuhn's fol-

[23] Minutes of 1938 Bund convention, in "Evidence," p. 79.
[24] Foreign Ministry to German Embassy, Dec. 15, 1938, *DGFP*, D, IV, 650.

lowing would wither away as it became aware of its leader's transparently false statements, since the help he was always talking about never arrived. As far as the diplomats were concerned, in essence the Bund in 1936 was not different from the Bund in 1933, and the Bundists were "the same people with the same principles and the same appearance." [25]

But the Bundesleiter's chicanery was not transparent to his followers after he returned from his first trip to Germany in the fall of 1936. They followed every detail of his trip, which was given full coverage in the organization's publications. Understandably, their leader's reception in Berlin and other cities, his meeting with the German Führer, and the much publicized march of a contingent of OD men down the Unten den Linden reaffirmed their belief that Germany considered the movement a viable force in American affairs.[26] This particular interpretation of the Bund's relationship with Berlin was strengthened within days after Kuhn returned to New York. In October, Ambassador Luther; Karl Strölin, the lord mayor of Stuttgart and honorary president of the DAI; and Avery Brundage, the pro-German president of the American Olympic Committee, spoke at the annual German Day festivities in Madison Square Garden. It will be recalled that exactly three years before German Day had created much controversy and had to be rescheduled. In the fall of 1936, however, the Spanknöbel Affair was a distant memory and many of the organizations that the first Bundesleiter had so thoroughly alienated were now in the Bund's orbit. German Day, 1936, was marked by the Volksbund's effort to demonstrate that it had created a united front within the communities of German nationals and German-Americans in the New York area and was working for the betterment of relations between Washington and Berlin.[27]

[25] Memorandum by Freytag (Foreign Ministry, Political Department IX, U.S.A.), Oct. 11, 1937, *DGFP*, D, I, 336. Cf. Bohle to Ernst von Weizsäcker, Oct. 3, 1938, D, IV, 26–27.

[26] Bund newspaper coverage of the summer Olympics was extensive. From time to time, Kuhn sent a "special report" to his followers. See *Deutscher Weckruf und Beobachter*, Aug. 17, 1936, p. 7.

[27] Details of Strölin's trip to America can be found in "Strölin Besuch," correspondence between consuls and DAI, T-81/394/5134626–994; on his visit to New York City, see Gustav Moshack to Strölin, n.d., T-81/394/5134626.

In Kuhn's absence, his able lieutenants had planned a gala celebration in conjunction with pro-German groups in the New York
area. More than twenty-two thousand people patiently listened to
a one-and-one-half hour address by Ambassador Luther, who was
described by one State Department official as a man given to "Teutonic blasts." [28] "Germany," Luther told the audience, "is rearming
not to make war, but to make peace secure," and he reaffirmed
Berlin's often repeated contention, "National Socialism is not an article for export." Strölin followed the same line of thought. Although he had considerable praise for the historical role played by
the German-American community and told an enthusiastic audience that he intended to tell Hitler and the German people that he
had found evidence of unity in American *Deutschtum*, his
comments reflected Germany's new decision regarding the Bund,
that is, to give verbal support without commitment.[29]

The presence of the German ambassador at the Bund-organized
function should not be construed as a departure from his past relationship with either the Bund or the German-American community. For political as well as "racial-political" reasons, Germany
wanted to retain its contacts with the German-American community, even if this meant limited and temporary relationships with
the Bund. In New York City, Germany had to work with the Bund
from time to time if it wanted to propagandize the old-line German-American groups. Luther, who was well aware that many
Americans believed that Germany was underwriting the Bund
movement, now had good reason to conclude that the Party had
abandoned its initially intransigent stand on the Bund. His
mention of what was rapidly becoming a Nazi adage—
Nationalsozialismus keine Exportware—was a subtle though firm
warning to the Bundists. Unlike AO chief Bohle during the early
formative years of the Nazi regime, Luther did not view German-

[28] Jay Pierrepont Moffat, entry for Sept. 10, 1933, *Moffat Papers*, ed.
Hooker, p. 101.
[29] "Anmerkungen zu dem Entwurf für die Rede des Herrn Oberbürger-
meisters zum Deutschtum-Tag in New York," in "Strölin Besuch"; *Deutscher
Weckruf und Beobachter*, Oct. 8, 1936, p. 3. On Luther's comments, see
Rogge, *Official German Report*, p. 120; cf. "Deutscher Tag in Neuyork: Eine
Rede Dr. Luthers," *Westdeutscher Beobachter*, Oct. 6, 1936.

America as an irredentist problem. Beginning in 1935, his correspondence with the Foreign Ministry was characterized by a sober
appraisal of American affairs. He reminded his superiors that isolationism was not an absolute given in America's relationship with
the world. In a prophetic letter to the Foreign Ministry, he wrote
that "people are above all concerned with German policy" and if
"Japan were to exploit the tense situation in Europe," American
isolationism would prove as ephemeral as it had been in 1917.[30]

Bund leader Kuhn failed to understand the wide gulf between
the ideal and the reality of Germany's relations with America. The
ongoing conflict between ideologues in the Party's foreign apparatus and the traditional diplomats in the Wilhelmstrasse was no
longer concerned with the Bund problem; here there was considerable agreement. But Americans believed that Germany's posture
toward the Volksbund had not changed. The several edicts and the
pledges given to American officials meant little. Given the pictures
of Hitler accepting the "Golden Book" from Kuhn, Kuhn's statements of friendship with the Nazi elite, children and adults parading in uniform, German officials (including the ambassador) participating in German-American rallies, and the flooding of the United
States with Nazi literature, what other conclusion could have been
arrived at? German activities did not seem contradictory and
added up to a meaningful program. Only in retrospect does Germany's relationship to the Bund become apparent and the contradictions in German policy become obvious.

[30] April 4, 1935, *DGFP*, C, IV, 23–27.

IV

TO THE
VERY END

CHAPTER **11**

The Betrayal

It is difficult to determine precisely when the Amerikadeutscher Volksbund began to decline. Since the founding of the National Socialist movement in America, the Bund had been an embattled organization. The intragroup quarrels in the pre-Hitler period, the unsettling events following the Spanknöbel Affair, the internecine struggles engendered by the ousting of Ignatz Griebl and Reinhold Walter, and the much publicized Haegele-Schnuch controversy were merely surface eruptions of inner tensions. The long history of inharmonious relationships within the several organizations known as the Bund was not the result of hairsplitting ideological arguments; rather, most of the stresses and strains were caused by deep-seated personal conflicts among Bundists. Kuhn's ascendancy over the movement in the early months of 1936 did much to close the fissures created by fear, distrust, and economic dislocation. Despite Kuhn's many personal failings, he managed to usher in a period of prolonged peace. But the restoration of harmony combined with the movement's sustained growth led to a series of new problems.

It will be recalled that the Kuhn era began at the very time the Party decided to alter greatly its commitment to the Bund. It was widely believed that the movement was on the verge of collapse. Much to the surprise of German officialdom in the Auslandsorganisation and the Foreign Ministry, the Bund survived and emerged reinvigorated from a period of prolonged turmoil. The evolution of the Bund from a badly factionalized organization into a revitalized stable political group had not been anticipated by Berlin or by its consular people in America. Germany found itself saddled with a foreign political organization it no longer found

useful. Although the Bund problem was of relatively minor importance when examined in the framework of the total configuration
of German foreign policy, it was nevertheless a problem and had
to be dealt with, some German diplomats believed. The Bund
question became even more burdensome when Reich officials came
to appreciate the extent of Kuhn's deceit and duplicity. His ill-conceived fabrications and bellicosity convinced the Foreign Ministry
that the Bund remained a major disruptive factor in German-
American relations, and if need be, the ministry would have to work
to destroy it. This opinion was not confined to the more traditional
diplomats; in spite of the dictates of racial politics, the Party also
welcomed the prospect of the Volksbund's destruction.

The more traditionally oriented diplomats, especially Hans Luther and his successor, Hans Heinrich Dieckhoff, were haunted by
the prospect of America's re-emergence from temporary isolationism. They were well aware that Hitler's estimate of the Americans
was distorted and potentially fatal to Germany; the nightmare of
another 1917 loomed large in their minds. Although neither Luther
nor Dieckhoff criticized the Führer publicly, their references to the
debacle of 1918 in their letters to the Foreign Ministry betrayed a
growing distrust of Hitler's ability to see the world as it really was.
On the other hand, the Party's officials and foreign-policy planners
were not greatly concerned about the prospect of America's entry
into a future European conflict. Adhering to a self-imposed and
confining mythology, they dismissed America as a distant Jew-ridden plutocracy incapable of waging a major war. Echoing the
views of the German leader, they had the capacity for self-delusion
and dismissed another 1917 as a remote possibility. It was in this
framework that those who shared Hitler's image of the United
States welcomed the prospect of a besieged Bund fighting for its
life against the alleged "German haters." The depiction of the
Volksbund caught in Jewry's vise gave credibility to the Nazi concept of America and its people. Therefore, it is not surprising that
the organization received more coverage in the German press after
the arrest and conviction of Fritz Kuhn in 1939 than in preceding
years.[1]

[1] Examples of German coverage of Kuhn's trial can be found in the *Völkischer Beobachter*, summer–winter 1939; publications of the VDA's informa-

The year 1937 marked the beginning of what may be termed the Bund's "time of troubles": the start of state and local investigations of its activities, resulting in the conviction of several leading Bundists; the renewal of a congressional probe under the chairmanship of Martin Dies; the replacement of Hans Luther by the more forceful Hans Heinrich Dieckhoff; and the rapid deterioration of German-American diplomatic relations, culminating in the mutual recall of ambassadors in late 1938. Admittedly, the Bund was by no means focal in the accelerated decline in relations. But the combined impact of these occurrences was overwhelming and fostered a spirit of fatalism within the Bund community. Some Bundists found the prospect of being cut off from Germany in the wake of local, state, and Federal investigations so awesome that they returned to Germany. It is difficult to determine exactly how many left the United States between 1938 and 1941; a generous estimate would be five hundred.[2] Those who remained were haunted by the expectation that their enemies—the Jews—would crush them and that there was little, if anything, Berlin could do to help. Several days before the German invasion of Poland, Bundist Carl Nicolay sounded a prophetic note in a letter to Rolf Hoffmann: "What will happen to us should war break out?" Naturally, the hardening of anti-German sentiment made the prospect of being trapped in the United States in the event of war with Germany more intense. By December 1938, the public reaction against Hitlerism became so widespread that even German diplomats could no longer dismiss it as the work of Samuel Dickstein and a handful of "Jewish wirepullers" in the Capitol.[3]

---

tion service, July–Aug. 1941; and the *Aussendeutscher Wochenspiegel*, 29 (Aug. 1941).

[2] Upon their return to Germany, many Bundists joined Kameradschaft-USA. One list, prepared in the fall of 1939, listed 452 returnees, of whom 116 held U.S. citizenship (T-81/142/180256–60). Another list prepared in December 1939 listed 334 returnees who held U.S. citizenship (T-81/142/180242). Kameradschafts-USA established branches in nine German cities. Sepp Schuster was the leader of the Munich branch, and Walter Kappe headed the branch in Stuttgart (see T-81/142/180235). See also "Liste der Parteigenossen aus USA," T-81/147/185887ff.

[3] Carl Nicolay to Rolf Hoffmann, Aug. 27, 1939, T-81/29/25664. The answer for Nicolay was to abandon his wife and two children and return to Germany in 1939. The phrase "Jewish wirepuller" at first referred to Samuel

The Bundists' and Germany's appreciation of the extent of anti-German sentiment and awareness that the widening rift between Berlin and Washington was not temporary became apparent in the late fall of 1938. On November 7, Herschel Grynszpan (Grünspan), a seventeen-year-old Jewish youth whose parents had been deported from Germany to Poland in a boxcar as part of the Nazi "Easter Exclusion Program" (the transfer to Poland of Polish Jews residing in Germany), entered the German Embassy in Paris and assassinated the third secretary, Ernst vom Rath. The diplomat was buried on the morning of the ninth—the fifteenth anniversary of the abortive Beer Hall *Putsch* in Munich. That night and throughout the morning of November 10, the Jews of Germany were subjected to the horrors of a vast and well-organized pogrom that has gone down in the history of the Third Reich as the *Kristallnacht* ("Night of Broken Glass").[4] The killing of vom Rath was used as a pretext for carrying out Göring's plan for the total exclusion of the remaining 250,000 Jews from the economic, social, and cultural life of Germany. Temples were wantonly destroyed, and stores were systematically looted by organized bands of Nazi hooligans. Jews were molested in the streets of Germany's major cities, and many native Jews were sent to concentration camps. In the face of these events, it became impossible for even the most credulous Jews in Germany and many foreigners to rationalize Hitler's anti-Semitic madness. In the wake of this unprecedented and savage pogrom, the German government promulgated a series of laws which severely restricted both emigration and the transfer or liqui-

---

Dickstein (see Memorandum by an Official in Department III, Foreign Ministry, Dec. 20, 1933, *DGFP*, C, II, 252–254). On American feeling about the Nazi government, see public-opinion polls cited by Jonas, *Isolationism in America*, pp. 210–215; and Sander A. Diamond, "The *Kristallnacht* and the Reaction in America," *YIVO Annual of Jewish Social Science*, 14 (1969), 196–208. In late 1938, German officials discussed the possibility of repatriating German nationals in the United States. In December 1938, the Foreign Ministry commissioned Otto Karl Kiep (former consul general in New York, 1931–1934) to go to America and explore the feasibility of such an undertaking. In January 1939, the proposal was dropped, and Kiep's assignment was canceled. See *DGFP*, D, IV, 651ff.

[4] Diamond, "The *Kristallnacht*," n. 1; Bracher, *German Dictatorship*, p. 367. "The Night of Broken Glass" refers to the breaking of more than seven thousand store-front windows of Jewish-owned shops and the total destruction of many of Germany's oldest synagogues.

dation of assets. The *Kristallnacht* pogrom spelled the end of German Jewry.[5]

The *Kristallnacht* had far-reaching ramifications for the United States. The declaration of open warfare against German Jewry came only five weeks after the Roosevelt Administration and numerous Americans had given a qualified endorsement to the accords reached at the Munich Conference. The prevalent feeling now was that Munich had incited rather than restrained Hitler. The editoral pages of most American newspapers registered a storm of protest. Anne O'Hare McCormick of the *New York Times* expressed the general feeling in early November:

It is difficult [to understand the events of November 9–10] because it is no longer a defeated nation, and the suffering they inflict on others, now that they are on top, passes all understanding and mocks all sympathy. The darkest day Germany experienced in the whole post-war period was not as dark as Thursday.[6]

So great was the outpouring of protest that, after years of wavering, the Steuben Society of America and the influential Ridder brothers condemned the Nazi dictatorship. Deeply concerned over the extent of the denunciations of Germany, Ambassador Dieckhoff reported to the Foreign Ministry that American Jewry was no longer alone in its fight against Nazism. Even those people who had maintained a comparative reserve toward the Third Reich were "now publicly adopting so violent and bitter an attitude against us" that the appeasement that was to follow Munich was in jeopardy.[7] President Roosevelt waited for the public outcry to so-

[5] On November 12, 1938, the German government levied a fine of one billion marks (about 400 million dollars) on the German-Jewish community (estimated at a quarter of a million, with another quarter million designated as *Mischlinge*). The fine was aimed at forcing the Jews out of Germany. It was also a ransom—Göring hoped that British and American Jewry would pay ("Stenographic Report of a Meeting on the Jewish Question," in *Nazi Conspiracy and Aggression* [Washington, D.C., 1946–1947], IV, 425–457; Raul Hilberg, *The Destruction of European Jews* [Chicago, 1967], pp. 23–28).

[6] "Nazi Day of Terror: A Threat to Civilization," *New York Times*, Nov. 12, 1938, p. 4.

[7] "Statement of the Steuben Society of America," Nov. 21, 1938, container 142, RG 131. On the Ridder brothers, see "The Foreign Language Press in America," *Fortune*, 22 (Nov. 1940), 90–93, 102. On Dieckhoff, see Dieckhoff to Foreign Ministry, Nov. 14, 1938, *DGFP*, D, IV, 639–640. Striking a pro-

lidify before taking a concrete step against Germany. On November 14, he ordered the American ambassador, Hugh Wilson, to return to the United States on the first available non-German ship.[8] The following morning, Roosevelt convened his five-hundredth press conference. Departing from established practice, he had an aide distribute copies of a prepared message:

The news of the past few days from Germany deeply shocked public opinion in the United States. Such news from any part of the world would inevitably produce similar profound reaction among Americans in any part of the nation.

I myself could scarcely believe that such things could occur in a twentieth century civilization. With a view of gaining a first-hand picture of the current situation in Germany, I asked the Secretary of State to order our Ambassador in Berlin to return at once for report and consultation.[9]

In a retaliatory move, Berlin recalled Dieckhoff on November 18; diplomatic relations would no longer be conducted on the ambassadorial level.[10]

Roosevelt's recall of Wilson was one way in which the President could express his moral indignation over Nazi racial practices and

phetic note, the editors of the *Christian Century* posed the question: "Suppose that, instead of subjecting the Jews to economic and social disadvantages, Nazi Germany should decide to massacre them?" (15 [Nov. 1938], 1422–1423). On the Bund's defense of Germany's contention that the Jewish question was an internal affair, see Joseph Goebbels, *The Grünspan Case*, pamphlet distributed by the Volksbund, container 37, RG 131.

[8] Cordell Hull to Hugh Wilson, Nov. 14, 1938, *PRDR*, 1938, II, 398–399.

[9] Samuel L. Rosenman, ed., *The Public Papers and Addresses of Franklin D. Roosevelt; VII: 1938—The Continuing Struggle for Liberalism* (New York, 1939–1941), pp. 596–597. The State Department had drafted a statement for the President; he felt it lacked force and changed certain key phrases (Hull to Roosevelt, Nov. 14, 1938, President's Secretary's File, Germany: Diplomatic Corres., 1933–1939, box 6, FDRL). Responses to Roosevelt's action can be found in *ibid.*, Germany, 1934–1938, 76C.

[10] After his recall to Germany, Dieckhoff was not received by Hitler. Even Ribbentrop kept him waiting two weeks. In mid-December he met with Ribbentrop, who reproached him for not adequately "counteracting Jewish influence" in the United States (RG 59, "Dieckhoff Interrogation," 254). After Dieckhoff's recall, diplomatic relations were conducted by the chargés in Berlin and Washington. On the role played by Hans Thomsen (chargé d'affaires, Washington), see Compton, *The Swastika and the Eagle*, chs. iv, v, and vii. Thomsen was recalled to Germany in 1941. See also Appendix III, below.

the German dictatorship. His use of the withdrawal as a means of condemning Nazism came at a time when anti-German sentiment had coalesced into a genuine, though passing, public reaction. Although Roosevelt did not break off diplomatic relations, the recall of the ambassador was interpreted by several German officials as a signal that the United States might pursue a more active role in international affairs. A little more than a year before the *Kristall-nacht,* on October 5, 1937, in Chicago, Roosevelt had made his widely acclaimed "quarantine-the-aggressor" speech, an address that suggested a possible route for future American foreign policy. The President's personal feelings notwithstanding, America was still far from participating actively in world affairs. At this juncture, Washington still thought in terms of using economic sanctions to curb the actions of potential aggressors. Germany's absorption of Austria into the Reich was followed by Washington's cancellation of the Austro-American trade treaty and the demand that Berlin assume Austria's debts. Another action was the blocking of the sale of huge quantities of helium to be used in German dirigibles.[11] These tactics, coupled with the recall of Wilson and a series of strongly worded protests to the Wilhelmstrasse about the treatment of American Jews in Germany during the *Kristallnacht* pogroms, were a source of serious though transient concern to the personnel in the Auslandsorganisation and other Nazi agencies. On the other hand, Dieckhoff and his colleagues at the Wilhelmstrasse did not dismiss anti-German sentiment out of hand. Following the recall of Ambassador Wilson, what can only be termed a wave of panic swept over the Foreign Ministry as its staff evaluated the possible impact of economic sanctions and the prospect of the mass expulsion of Germans from the United States.[12]

[11] Friedländer, *Prelude to Downfall,* pp. 6–9; Offner, *American Appeasement,* pp. 89ff. Another irritant to German-American relations was the "spy trial" in December 1938. Three men and a woman were arrested and convicted of conspiracy to steal military secrets (they were sentenced on December 2, 1939). One month later, two Germans (Schachow and Kuhrig) were tried and convicted of espionage in the Canal Zone (Frye, *Nazi Germany and the American Hemisphere,* p. 89).

[12] Memorandum on the Political Consequences of a Possible Rupture of Diplomatic Relations with the United States, Nov. 20, 1938, *DGFP,* D, IV, 644–648; Dieckhoff memorandum, Dec. 16, 1938, *DGFP,* D, IV, 652–654;

The spread of anti-German feeling seriously affected the Volksbund. The accelerated decline in German-American diplomatic relations was paralleled by a heightened concern among Americans
about the presence of a Nazi movement on American soil. In January 1937, Congressmen Samuel Dickstein and Adolph Sabath,
whom the Nazis labeled "the Jewish inquisitors," called for another
congressional investigation of the Bund and other "un-American"
organizations. Six months later Martin Dies submitted a similar
resolution and requested a hundred thousand dollars for an investigation. Several midwestern congressmen, who feared a renewal of
the "pure Americanism" of another era, opposed the resolution.
The resolution was debated but was of secondary importance during the first half of 1937 to Roosevelt's plan for reorganizing the
Federal judiciary and the discussion of the Ludlow resolution,
which called for a national referendum on a declaration of war. It
was not until May 26, 1938, that Congress authorized the formation
of the House Committee to Investigate Un-American Activities,
commonly known as the Dies committee, and allocated to it an initial sum of twenty-five thousand dollars.[13]

---

memorandum by Friedrich Stieve (Foreign Ministry), Dec. 19, 1938, *DGFP*,
IV, 657–659. In anticipation of a break in diplomatic relations and widespread anti-German activities, plans were made to move all secret files from
the German Embassy in Washington to Berlin (Hans Thomsen to Foreign
Ministry, Nov. 20, 1938, *DGFP*, D, IV, 648–649).

[13] An example of Germany's denunciations of Dickstein can be found in
"Abfuhr für den jüdischen Oberhasser Dickstein," *Westdeutscher Beobachter*,
April 10, 1937. Martin Dies's name first came to public notice after he announced that he wanted to probe into the affairs of Ogden Mills and the international bankers. By the end of the decade, he and Dickstein were regarded as the chief German haters by the Germans. However, Dies was much
more concerned with alleged Communist infiltration than with the Nazis. He
probed into Jewish and Black civil-rights groups, New Deal agencies, campus
activities, the CIO, and organizations with international connections. Members
of the committee were selected in June and included Arthur Healey (D.,
Mass.), Harold Mosier (D., Ohio), J. Parnell Thomas (R., N.J.), John Dempsey
(D., N.M.), Noah Mason (R., Ill.), and Joseph Starnes (D., Ala.). See August
Raymond Ogden, *The Dies Committee* (New York, 1944); William Geller-
mann, *Martin Dies* (New York, 1944); and Goodman, *The Committee*, chs. i,
ii.

The passage of Martin Dies's resolution accelerated the pace of existing state investigations and signaled the start of new probes into the Bund's internal affairs on the state and local levels. In New York City, State Senator John McNaboe conducted a series of hearings in June. In Riverhead, on Long Island, a local justice looked into the German-American Settlement League, which owned Camp Siegfried in Yaphank. In Manhattan, Mayor Fiorello H. La Guardia set into motion an inquiry into the Volksbund's financial dealings. In New Jersey, state officials probed into the affairs of the Bund to establish whether the group was violating any existing statutes. In Massachusetts, the legislature started to review alleged "un-Americanism" throughout the Commonwealth. The Bund's time of troubles had begun in earnest, and Kuhn, alarmed that the combined impact of these inquests might cost him his following, assured the Bundists that the law could not affect them.[14]

His optimism was not catching, and a gradual exodus from the Bund began in mid-1937. Complicating matters, a renewal of serious financial problems occurred in 1937. Revenue from advertising in the Volksbund's publications dwindled, because many merchants feared having their names associated with Kuhn's in the face of local, state, and federal pressure. The Bundesleiter tried in vain to counteract the loss of income with *ad hoc* measures. He urged his followers to collect old metal (tin, zinc, and copper), which he hoped to sell to junk dealers; to hold local fund-raising dances and concerts; to patronize only stores displaying the DKV sticker on their windows; and to find new sources of revenue from

---

[14] On the McNaboe investigation (June 1938), see State of New York, *Report of the Joint Legislative Committee,* Doc. 98; and Fritz Kuhn to John McNaboe, June 15, 1938, container 153, RG 131. On the Riverhead case, see transcript of proceedings, container 104, RG 131; on Camp Nordland, see "Preliminary Report of the State of New Jersey: Examination of Statutes Affecting the German-American Bund and Its Relationship to Existing Civil Rights Legislation," n.d., ADL; on La Guardia's action, see Herlands, "Report of Tax Investigation," pp. 1–2, ADL; on Massachusetts, see *New York Times,* Oct. 1937; on the impact of the FBI and Justice Department probe on the Bund, see Bund Command XVII (Feb. 17, 1938), XVIII (May 3, 1938), XIX (July 12, 1938), XXI (Oct. 8, 1938), ADL.

advertising.[15] These stop-gap measures were not enough. Reluctantly, Kuhn announced in November 1937 that "no local improvements, welfare work or any other dispensable undertakings are to be begun until the maintenance of the Bund *AS A WHOLE* is assured through campaign contributions."[16] Kuhn became increasingly defensive in public and predicted bleak days ahead. Anticipating the worst, he established a bail fund of fifty thousand dollars in late 1937.[17] In January 1938, Kuhn issued his annual report to his comrades and warned them to prepare for the worst:

The opponent has changed his tactics: we are being opposed by secret undermining work and lying whispering campaigns. I ask you my dear Bund members to have confidence and remain free from all doubt. We are conducting an honest and righteous battle for our old and new homelands. . . . May we never forget that we are a militant organization and that we shall remain fighting lies, slander, Marxism, and racially-foreign cliques until victory is ours. And so, with fresh courage and faithful cooperation we go into the year 1938.[18]

As Kuhn implied, he knew that the new year would bring further complications to his increasingly embattled movement. In the face of several concerted efforts aimed at permanently dismantling the Volksbund and in the light of developments in German-American relations, Kuhn had every reason to believe that Berlin would publicly repudiate the organization for the sake of better relations with Washington. Although the Reich had already extricated itself from the closeness that had characterized its association with the Friends of the New Germany and had reduced the aid given to the present group by Nazified agencies to the distribution of propa-

[15] Bund commands, 1937–1938. The financial records of the German-American Bund indicate that scores of businessmen extended credit to Bund locals. Although most of the unpaid bills were for refreshments (small items such as beer), these debts amounted to a large sum of money. Complaints from storekeepers and creditors can be found in container 142, and "List of Classified Ads and Bank Statements," container 209, RG 131. On the withdrawal of advertising, see container 137.

[16] Bund Command XV, Nov. 12, 1937.

[17] Until November 1937, the Bund had an established "fighting fund," which was used for bail money. The increase in the fighting fund to fifty thousand dollars is first mentioned in Bund Command XV, Nov. 12, 1937.

[18] "Annual Report for 1937," Bund Command XVI, Jan. 10, 1938.

ganda on a limited basis, it had never issued a thoroughgoing disavowal of the Bund movement. Admittedly, it is questionable
whether anyone in America would have believed such a declaration. Experience had taught the Germans that public rejoinders
had little or no impact; the United States placed little stock in
pledges originating in Berlin. Making matters worse, the Germans
had learned from their past dealings with the Bundists that they
were unreliable, and the Germans had little respect for Kuhn's
credibility. The time had arrived when only swift and resolute action would undermine the Bund movement.

The first warning came on March 30, 1937, when Hans Heinrich
Dieckhoff was appointed to replace Hans Luther as ambassador to
the United States.[19] Before his appointment, Dieckhoff had privately voiced concern over the deterioration in relations between
the two powers to his colleagues in the Foreign Ministry and to his
brother-in-law, Joachim von Ribbentrop. At the time of his arrival
in America his views were well known, and the appointment of a
nonideological and traditionally oriented diplomat to replace Luther was construed in some Washington circles as a sign that Germany had re-evaluated the worth of continued good relations with
Americans. Dieckhoff shared this belief; it proved a false hope. A
week before the *Kristallnacht* pogrom he told Roosevelt's friend
Under Secretary of State Sumner Welles that he considered his ambassadorship a failure. He had long believed that the Nazis had
been thoroughly corrupted by success—"L'appétit vient en
mangeant." [20] This view was reinforced in the weeks following the
wholesale destruction of the German-Jewish community in November 1938. Years later, after Germany's collapse in 1945, he told a

[19] Among historians there is considerable agreement that Dieckhoff tried to
ward off a conflict between the two powers. For a balanced treatment of unsuccessful efforts in this direction, see Manfred Jonas, "Prophet without honor:
Hans Heinrich Dieckhoff Reports from Washington," *Mid-America*, 47 (July
1965); cf. Compton, *The Swastika and the Eagle*, pp. 47ff.

[20] Welles memorandum, Nov. 11, 1938, *PRDR*, 1938, II, 446. Several examples of Luther's views (which indicate that Dieckhoff was not an innovator on
the American question) can be found in Luther to Ministry of Propaganda,
June 28, 1935, *DGFP*, C, IV, 384; and Luther to Neurath, April 8, 1935,
DGFP, D, I, 653. Dieckhoff's view of Luther can be found in RG 59, "Dieckhoff Interrogation," 247.

State Department interrogator that "from the German point of view, it [the diplomatic result of the *Kristallnacht*] was as though we had presented Roosevelt with a present on a silver platter." [21]

The "present" was, of course, the coalescence of anti-Nazi sentiment in America, which Dieckhoff believed Roosevelt had been patiently waiting for. Since the middle of the decade he had been convinced that war between the two powers was inevitable. This conviction dominated his thinking, and after he assumed the ambassadorship, he worked to prevent the outbreak of war. In a letter to Ernst von Weizsäcker, who was appointed State Secretary under Ribbentrop in April 1938, he wrote that he had much knowledge of America and its people.[22] This claim was justified, and unlike many of his colleagues, his views were not encrusted with the National Socialist cosmology. His diplomatic career began before the outbreak of the World War in 1914. Following service in the imperial German army as a cavalry officer, he rejoined the Foreign Ministry and was appointed counselor of embassy in Washington in 1922. He left this post in 1926 and was appointed to a similar position at the German Embassy in London. In 1930, he returned to Berlin and held two important posts at the Wilhelmstrasse until his appointment as ambassador in March 1937.

Although it can be argued that Dieckhoff hid behind the shield of traditionalism and does not deserve his anti-Nazi reputation, he did exhibit a spirit of ideological independence at a time when the Nazi regime was demanding stricter conformity from the traditional elite. In view of Hitler's opinion of Americans and in keeping with the Führer's contention that the United States was of minor importance in world affairs, a case could be made that Dieckhoff was sent into diplomatic isolation; many governments handle important but troublesome people in this way. For a time, it seems, Dieckhoff may have subscribed to this viewpoint. At his home in Lenzkirch in November 1945, Dieckhoff told an interrogator that Fritz Wiedemann, Hitler's aide-de-camp (1935–1939) and former commanding officer in the World War, had fallen into dis-

[21] RG 59, "Dieckhoff Interrogation," 250–251.
[22] Hans Dieckhoff to Ernst von Weizsäcker, Dec. 24, 1938, Dec. 30, 1938, *DGFP*, D, IV, 665, 667.

favor with Hitler and had been "sent into the desert": he had been appointed consul general in San Francisco early in 1939. A few weeks after Wiedemann returned to Germany in 1941, Hitler had sent him on a special mission to China—"a faraway post in exile." [23] Albert Speer later added some fresh details to the Wiedemann story. According to Speer, Wiedemann "kept urging Hitler to have talks with the Americans. Vexed by this offense against the unwritten law of the round table, Hitler finally sent him to San Francisco as German consul general. 'Let him be cured of his notions there.'" [24] Can it be argued that Dieckhoff was shipped off to Washington for the same reason? The evidence points to the opposite conclusion. At the time of Dieckhoff's appointment, anti-German feeling was running high in some circles in Washington. Dieckhoff, like Luther before him, represented the traditional instrument of diplomacy, and Berlin assumed that he would be well received upon his arrival in Washington. The fact that he was appointed in early 1937, a little less than a year before the Blomberg-Fritsch affair and Ribbentrop's elevation to the position of foreign minister on February 4, 1938, is also significant. Dieckhoff's was one of the last major appointments made by the Wilhelmstrasse while it still exercised a semblance of autonomy in conducting its own affairs.[25]

Arriving in Washington with an understanding of American anxieties about the turn of events in Germany and a deep commitment to his homeland, Dieckhoff did not subscribe to the Nazi contention that America was a Jewish-dominated plutocracy that was incapable of becoming involved in European affairs. More im-

[23] For a more detailed account, see RG 59, "Dieckhoff Interrogation," 248.

[24] Albert Speer, *Inside the Third Reich*, trans. Richard and Clara Winston (New York, 1970), p. 121. Hitler's feelings about Wiedemann have been known for some time. See Ulrich von Hassell, *Vom anderen Deutschland: Aus den nachgelassenen Tagebüchern, 1938–1944* (Zurich, 1946), p. 18.

[25] Compton, pp. 47ff. On the Blomberg-Fritsch Affair, see Bracher, *German Dictatorship*, pp. 393–394. Dieckhoff's comments after the war (Nov. 7–8, 1945) suggest that he viewed his term as ambassador as doomed to failure. But he accepted the Washington post and hoped that he could alter German foreign policy, could reverse the feeling in Berlin that "American opinion could be influenced via the German-Americans" (RG 59, "Dieckhoff Interrogation," 247).

portant, he dismissed the Party's propagandistic claim that a community of blood existed between Germans in the Reich and American *Deutschtum*. He concluded that any further intrusions into the internal affairs of the United States would only widen the already existing rift. Above all, the nightmare of another 1917 had to be avoided. Although he was never overtly anti-Nazi and served Hitler to the end, he did little to hide his opinions on the American question. To translate his ideas into practical policy, he had to convince Berlin to attempt to reverse the anti-German tide in America. He thought that the persons responsible for making and implementing policies concerning the United States had to compare the realities of American life and politics with the official Nazi version of the United States. To argue, for example, that all "German haters" were Jews was untenable. This may have been true in 1933 and 1934 but was certainly not in 1937. Berlin had to realize that anti-German feeling had penetrated many levels of American society and that it was in part a carry-over from World War I. He believed that many Americans thought that Nazi aggressiveness was an outgrowth of traditional German belligerence, an inbred *Angriffslust* (thirst for aggression), and tended to view all German actions as the result of this thirst. At the time of the *Anschluss*, for example, he considered it significant that the American press used the image of the "Prussian wolf" raging among the "Austrian sheep."[26] Compounding the problem of America's "traditional distrust" of the Germans was the widespread feeling that Berlin was supporting a "Nazintern" on American soil.[27] Dieckhoff did not suppose that anti-Nazi sentiment could be reversed overnight, but he felt that obstacles in the path of normal relations should be removed, if only to appease American sensibilities.

[26] Dieckhoff's reports from Washington are numerous and lengthy. Of special interest are: German Embassy to Foreign Ministry, Dec. 20, 1937 (Americans believe that the Germans had a "thirst for aggression"); Dieckhoff to Weizsäcker, March 22, 1937 (on the American reaction to the *Anschluss* with Austria); his dismissal as nonsense of the "Rechenberg thesis" that America was on the verge of collapse and communism would take hold, outlined in *Roosevelt—Amerika—Eine Gefahr* (*DGFP*, D, I, 642, 659, 661, 696).

[27] Dieckhoff to Hans-Georg Mackensen, Nov. 24, 1937, *DGFP*, D, I, 649; to Weizsäcker, Dec. 20, 1937, D, I, 658–661.

Among such obstacles were the Amerikadeutscher Volksbund and its leader, Fritz Kuhn.

The ambassador brought to Washington a contemptuous view of the Bund and Kuhn. In a letter to Hans-Georg von Mackensen dated November 24, 1937, he wrote, "Nothing has resulted in so much hostility toward us in the last few months as the stupid and noisy activities of a handful of German-Americans"; their efforts to wield American *Deutschtum* into a political force were "absurd." [28] Much to his annoyance, he was aware that some Nazi agencies, including the German Foreign Institute and the Volksdeutsche Mittelstelle (VoMi—Ethnic German Office) under SS *Obergruppenführer* Werner Lorenz, had retained limited contact with the Bundists in spite of existing prohibitions.[29] Sensitive to the demands of ideology, he understood that many Party people and several well-placed individuals in the Foreign Ministry were torn between the realities of foreign policy and racial-political needs and that they believed the Bund still had some value as a propaganda outlet. In a lengthy communication prepared in October 1937, the Foreign Ministry admitted that it knew of the presence of large numbers of German nationals in the Bund and that Kuhn's Prospective Citizens' League was a transparent front organization; at the same time, it asserted that Germany could not abandon these people to their fate. After the advent of Kuhn, the resolution of this dilemma had seemed to be to give the Bund what Berlin called "moral support" and to supply the Bund with propaganda. But in light of the spread of anti-German feeling in the United States, Dieckhoff questioned whether Germany could still afford to give moral support to the Bundists.[30] In December 1937, he wrote

[28] *DGFP*, D, I, 648–651. Dieckhoff's comments were made after a meeting with Jacob Gould Schurman, ambassador to Germany (1925–1930).

[29] Mackensen to Dieckhoff, Dec. 22, 1937, *DGFP*, D, I, 662. On VoMi, see "Die Volksdeutsche Mittelstelle unter SS-Obergruppenführer Lorenz (1937/8)," in Jacobsen, *Nationalsozialistische Aussenpolitik*, pp. 234–246.

[30] The American chargé d'affaires in Berlin, Prentiss Gilbert, met with Ernst von Weizsäcker (State Secretary, Foreign Ministry) on October 2, 1937. Gilbert protested the continued presence of German nationals in the Bund. He also asserted that many German nationals had taken out first papers and were therefore permitted to vote in several states, and since they were alleged to be controlled by Germany, the fact that they could vote was tantamount to med-

Weizsäcker that the American public was outraged at the news that representatives of more than a hundred German-American groups had attended the annual meeting of the German Foreign Institute. Germany could not be indifferent to public opinion in the United States: "I believe that we should remember that once before, only 20 years ago, the development of unfavorable public opinion in America proved fateful to us." [31]

His stay in Washington during the preceding decade had taught Dieckhoff that the Americans were a sensitive people who became enraged when anyone challenged their concept of a nation or interfered with the process of amalgamation. America was a new nation, a nation of minorities; he believed that after years of stress and strain an American nationality was finally emerging. For Dieckhoff, this meant that the Bund, with its appeal to the concept of ancestral roots, was striking at the heart of the concept of a nation. For this reason, it and other allegedly un-American groups were hated, feared, and investigated.[32] In January 1938, Dieckhoff summarized his views in a long and lucid communication to the Foreign Ministry headed: "Relations between the United States and Germany and the German-American element. Are we in a position to exert political influence on the German-Americans? The German-American Bund." [33] He began his analysis by reminding his superiors that relations between the two powers had declined markedly in 1937 after a long period of deterioration. Contributory factors were the Bund and Germany's ill-conceived efforts to unify Americans of German extraction. Such a policy, whatever its merits, was predicated on an erroneous assessment of German-America's position in the United States. During the final years of the imperial period, he recalled, Germany's leaders had made a similar and eventually fatal mistake when they equated German-America's

---

dling in the internal affairs of the United States (memorandum by Weizsäcker, Oct. 2, 1937, *DGFP*, D, I, 632–633; memorandum by Freytag, Oct. 11, 1937, *DGFP*, D, I, 636).

[31] Dieckhoff to Weizsäcker, Dec. 20, 1937, *DGFP*, D, I, 660.

[32] Dieckhoff to Mackensen, Nov. 24, 1937, *DGFP*, D, I, 650.

[33] Dieckhoff to Foreign Ministry, Jan. 7, 1938, *DGFP*, D, I, 664–677. Cf. Frye, *Nazi Germany and the American Hemisphere*, pp. 86–90; and Jacobsen, pp. 547–548.

pride in *Deutschtum* with political power. The truth of the matter was that this group of Americans had not formed a political monolith in 1917, and Germany could not expect it to do so in 1937:

Anyone measuring the political significance and power of the German-Americans by the enthusiasm which prevailed on the occasion of Prince Henry's [of Prussia, brother of Kaiser William II] visit in 1907 would have been deceived, just as today anyone would err in regarding the magnificent spirit which greets the colors of German Day celebrations in New York or Chicago or San Francisco as a criterion of the political influence of the enthusiastically cheering German-Americans. No, the German-American element had no political power, and will not have any because it lacks unity.[34]

The Bund, which tried to arouse sympathy for the ancestral homeland, had failed to muster support from the German-American community. As evidence, Dieckhoff cited the Volksbund's unsuccessful recruitment drives in Chicago:

There 700,000 are of German descent, in the broadest sense; of these about 40,000 are members of clubs of a definitely German character (athletic clubs, choral societies, German regional societies, etc.); of these, in turn, only 450 are in the German-American Bund, the only really politically minded organization which energetically stands up for Germany! In brief, 700,000, 40,000, 450! These figures hold good for most of the other sections of the country, and I feel that they speak volumes.[35]

"Things being as they are," he argued, "any attempt to urge or force any pro-German political activity on the German-Americans

[34] Dieckhoff, "Relations between the United States and Germany," *DGFP*, D, I, 670. Some consideration was given to forming an organization modeled after the Dante Alighieri Society, a cultural rather than strictly political group created by the Italians in an effort to propagandize the Italian-American community. In October 1937, Freytag (in the American Section of the Foreign Ministry) opted for the creation of the Immanuel Kant Society. It is clear from Dieckhoff's, Luther's, and others' correspondence that they believed the Italians had been successful and that they themselves had failed in America. The Italian efforts resembled the *Kulturpolitik* of the late imperial period, a resemblance Luther and Dieckhoff tried to impress on traditionalists in the Foreign Ministry.
[35] *DGFP*, D, I, 671.

VI. Presentation of Christmas presents to children of the Amerikadeutscher Volksbund, date unknown. (National Archives.)

would not lead to unification; on the contrary, it would, rather, intensify the existing differences." [36]

Invoking historical precedent, Dieckhoff asked the Foreign Ministry to recall that Chancellor Bismarck had never developed contacts with the Baltic Germans, because such a move would have endangered the Russo-German alliance; surely, America's good will should be as highly prized as Russia's had been. He urged his superiors—that is, all Germans responsible for American policy—to abandon their idealistic and unrealistic preconceptions of the members of *Deutschtum* in North America. These people were not comparable to the Germans in Central Europe, Eastern Europe, or

---

[36] *Ibid.* His realistic appraisal of the situation in America also meant an indirect though by no means less critical attack on Germany's racial-political diplomacy: "The mere transplanting of Reich-German concepts into the population of this country, with such a different mentality, is a futile undertaking, no matter how valuable these concepts are in themselves for the inner strength of a movement carried on by German people" (*DGFP*, D, I, 674).

South America. Because the passing of laws restricting immigration in the mid-1920's, the German element would soon be amalgamated ("The German element cannot last long"). In essence, German immigrants and their descendants had become Americans and wished to remain Americans. In fact, Dieckhoff contended, the reemergence of Germany in the 1930's had accelerated the melting-pot's work. Fearful of renewed anti-German feeling and because of the ongoing investigations of the Bund and related groups, many Americans of German ancestry had redoubled their efforts to conform to the dominant cultural norm. Consequently, Germany's and the Bund's efforts to propagandize them had been unsuccessful and had caused the hardening of anti-German feeling and prompted American *Deutschtum* to eschew German overtures. Dieckhoff concluded by urging Berlin to sever all existing ties with Kuhn's organization and to consider the possibility of a public disavowal if other tactics failed. And if some ties with the German-American community were deemed vital, they should be cultural links only. He reminded the ministry that for some time the Italians had used the Dante Alighieri Society to further their nonpolitical interests in America.[37]

Dieckhoff's scathing criticism of the Bund and of Party policy toward America since 1933 was received in Berlin on January 24, 1938. It could not have arrived at a more auspicious time. Since November, Hitler had been bent on a more aggressive and expansionist policy in Central and Eastern Europe. On Friday, November 5, Hitler had outlined his expansionist-imperialist plan for the reconstruction of the East at a secret meeting in the Reich Chancellery (recorded by his army adjutant Colonel Friedrich Hossbach). Present were Admiral Erich Raeder, Field Marshal Werner von Blomberg, General Werner von Fritsch, Hermann Göring, and Foreign Minister Constantin von Neurath. For nearly four hours, Hitler reviewed his years of work for Germany; he then turned to the future course of German foreign policy. Germany's problems could be solved in only one way: "There is only the road of force." This meant that the Austrian and Czechoslovakian problems might be solved in 1938. The group listened quietly; the generals and the

[37] *DGFP*, D, I, 664–677.

Foreign Minister were uneasy, reluctant to commit a recently re-
built but still weak Reich to war.

But Hitler had little patience for these vestiges of the old Germany. Minister of War and Commander in Chief of the Armed
Forces Blomberg and Commander in Chief of the Army Fritsch
formally lost their posts on February 4, 1938. Fritsch, who had
been falsely accused of homosexuality, was replaced by General
Walther von Brauchitsch. Blomberg was also scandalized. On January 12 he had been married in the presence of Hitler and Hermann Göring. Shortly after the marriage Heinrich Himmler and
Göring discovered in police records that Blomberg's wife had once
registered as a prostitute. His resignation came shortly after the
discovery. Instead of appointing a successor to Blomberg, Hitler
assumed the position of Commander in Chief of the Armed Forces.
He also created the High Command (Oberkommando der Wehrmacht, or OKW) under General Wilhelm Keitel. In a related move,
Foreign Minister Neurath was replaced by Ribbentrop on February 4. After forty years of state service, Neurath was named chief
of the Secret Cabinet Council, which was to help Hitler formulate
foreign policy; it never convened. Hitler's control over the military
and the foreign apparatus was now complete.[38]

The Dieckhoff communication must be examined against the
backdrop of these internal changes and tensions in the Reich.
When it arrived, the Foreign Ministry was in a transitional stage.
Neurath and many holdovers from the republican and imperial
governments were dismayed at the possibility of a renewed European conflict and the possible future involvement of the United
States. The flow of memoranda between Berlin and German diplomats assigned to the United States underscores this dismay.[39]

[38] The source materials concerning the Party's takeover of the Foreign Min-
istry and the preparation for expansion are abundant. See Bracher's comments
in *German Dictatorship*, pp. 307–308. On the steady decline of the Foreign
Ministry, see the appropriate sections in Jacobsen; and Gordon Craig, "The
German Foreign Office from Neurath to Ribbentrop," in *The Diplomats*, ed.
Gordon Craig and Felix Gilbert (Princeton, N.J., 1953), II, ch. xiii.

[39] On the Wilhelmstrasse's concern over possible American involvement in a
future European conflict, see memoranda and related material, Jan.–March
1938, *DGFP*, D, I, 667–679.

Dieckhoff was well aware that a conflict was brewing at home; he also knew of Neurath's concern (needless to say, he did not know the substance of Hitler's monologue in November) and most likely assumed that his suggestions would not be disregarded.

On January 26, 1938, just two days after his report arrived, a meeting was called to discuss it.[40] Present were Willy Grothe, *Gauamtsleiter* of the AO der NSDAP and a protégé of Bohle; Werner Lorenz, head of the Volksdeutsche Mittelstelle, which had worked with the Cultural-Political Section of the Foreign Ministry on matters pertaining to the ethnic German question; and Hans Wilhelm Freytag, the chief of the North American section of the political division of the Foreign Ministry.[41] At the outset, Grothe stated that Kuhn's organization had replaced the Friends of the New Germany and that the AO der NSDAP was well aware that both groups had created much excitement in the United States. Despite German admonitions that all German nationals must leave the group, Kuhn had "encouraged the membership of Reich Germans and Party members" in the organization. Grothe suggested that Germany reaffirm previous decisions and order all German nationals and Party members out of the Bund; this order, he concluded, should be announced by the official German news agency, the Deutsches Nachrichtenbüro (DNB), thus indicating to the

[40] Dieckhoff had called for a meeting on the Bund question in October 1937; the Foreign Ministry informed him that a meeting could not be arranged until January. In the meantime, Dieckhoff received assurances from the Auslandsorganisation and VoMi that they did not include the German-American community under their jurisdictions (memorandum from office of State Secretary, Dec. 17, 1937, *DGFP*, D, I, 657). On Wiedemann's visit, see Dieckhoff to Weizäcker, Dec. 20, 1937, *DGFP*, 658–661; and Wiedemann, *Der Mann— der Feldherr werden wollte*, p. 217.

[41] Memorandum of meeting, Jan. 26, 1938, *DGFP*, D, I, 685. Willy Grothe was considered by some Party personnel an expert on American affairs. In 1937, he was the director of Section VI of the Auslandsorganisation, Nordamerika, which in theory had jurisdiction over Party people in the United States. His expertise in American affairs seemed to stem from the fact that he had corresponded with members of the Teutonia Association and Gau-USA in the early 1930's. He joined the NSDAP in 1930 and served as a correspondent in Hans Nieland's Auslandsabteilung until it was dissolved. In 1934 he was appointed director of the section of the Auslandsorganisation which had jurisdiction over NSDAP members in Africa (before World War I, he had worked in Africa for twenty years as a representative of a German import-export firm).

Americans Germany's willingness to solve the problem. Freytag agreed and asserted that the cultural unity of five million Germans in America should not be jeopardized for the sake of five hundred Bundists. In addition, he agreed with Dieckhoff's suggestion that Germany should fall back on cultural activities similar to those of the Italians. There was much agreement among the conferees. But the Germans could not bring themselves to the point of publicly disavowing the Bund. In an effort to minimize the impact of Dieckhoff's report, Auslandsorganisation chief Bohle, who had also held a post in the Foreign Ministry since January 1937, agreed to help draft a statement ordering all German nationals out of the Bund. In a belated effort to placate the American government, Dieckhoff would inform Washington of this decision through diplomatic channels.[42]

The text of this draft statement was not what Dieckhoff wanted; it lacked teeth and merely reiterated previous edicts, which had had little or no impact. Much to the ambassador's annoyance, Berlin refused, as he had suggested, to withdraw the passports of German nationals who refused to comply. What he had wanted was a final and irrevocable break with the Bund, which meant a public disavowal and the severing of all connections, however limited. In light of the rapid deterioration of diplomatic relations with the Americans, he had little use for those who asserted that some ties with the Bundists should be retained, if for no other reason than that they had worked for the new Germany. Set them adrift, he requested, even if this meant ignoring them when they visited Germany. Even in Germany the Bundists were a menace. Several days before the high-level conference on January 26, he had sent additional evidence in support of his view that the Bund and the Bundists were a major cause for concern. In a memorandum to the Foreign Ministry he cited Peter Gissibl's recent trip to Stuttgart to visit his brother Fritz. Dieckhoff reported that Peter had given a talk at the DAI on January 14. Later in the day, he had held an in-

---

[42] *DGFP*, D, I, 686. After the meeting, a two-part memo was drafted: (1) Bohle called attention to the fact that Reich-Germans may not belong to the German-American Bund or any of its related organizations; and (2) Reich Germans must give up their membership in Bund-related groups (D, I, 687). See also D, I, 685–687, 692–693.

formal press conference and told reporters that the Bund was trying to unite the German-American population in Chicago. Dieckhoff, who had read the text of Gissibl's remarks in an American newspaper, was appalled. Gissibl's pretentious assertion that the Bund was making inroads in the Chicago area flew in the face of Dieckhoff's argument. The irate ambassador requested the Foreign Ministry to "get to him" before he further endangered German-American relations.[43]

Over the years Berlin had tried to placate the Americans by treating the Bund question as a legal problem—that is, by considering the presence of German nationals in the movement as criminal and in violation of some federal law. As far as Dieckhoff was concerned, it was not a matter of the Bund's legality or illegality. Kuhn had resolved the legal problem by the time he left New York to attend the Olympic Games in the summer of 1936. In response to a letter from the Foreign Ministry concerning this question, Dieckhoff reported that United States Attorney General Homer Cummings and FBI Director J. Edgar Hoover had conducted an investigation of the Bund's internal affairs and announced on January 5, 1938, that the group was not in violation of existing federal statutes.[44] Thus, far from posing a legal question the Amerikadeutscher Volksbund created a political problem, and Germany must acknowledge this distinction.[45]

An unnamed representative of the German Embassy in Washington arrived in the German capital several days before the removal of Blomberg and Fritsch and the Party's belated absorption of the Foreign Ministry. He immediately requested the government to re-examine its stand on the Bund question. On Thursday, February 3—one day before the reorganization of the military and the

---

[43] Dieckhoff to Foreign Ministry, Jan. 21, 1938, *DGFP*, D, I, 684. Gissibl's remarks were reported in the *Chicago Daily News*.

[44] In a memorandum to Mackensen, Dieckhoff commented: "The fact that no *criminal* derelictions can be imputed to the Bund in no way changes the *political* rejection of the Bund which is to be observed everywhere here" (Jan. 13, 1938, *DGFP*, D, I, 679). Dieckhoff was referring to a recent report in the *New York Times* (Jan. 6, 1938, p. 4) that the Justice Department had not found the Bund in violation of existing Federal statutes. Kuhn's response to the report was recorded in Bund Command XVII, Feb. 17, 1938.

[45] *DGFP*, D, I, 685–713.

appointment of Ribbentrop—he attended a meeting held under the
auspices of the Cultural-Political Section of the Foreign Ministry,
at which were Hermann Behrends, Werner Lorenz' subordinate at
the Volksdeutsche Mittelstelle; the Auslandsorganisation's Willy
Grothe; and representatives of the Ministry of Propaganda and the
political and intelligence divisions of the Foreign Ministry. The
prepared agenda included two items: a discussion of the draft
statement prepared at the January 26 meeting and a second discussion of Dieckhoff's report of January 7. Once more the conferees
agreed with the ambassador's assessment of the Bund's relative
worth as a political and cultural organization. Wasting little time,
Behrends called for the immediate removal of all German nationals
from the Bund and a complete break with that organization. He
added that if a new and thoroughly Americanized Bund came into
being at some future time, Germany should consider reopening the
question. Grothe expressed his agreement once more emphasized
the damaging effects of the Bund. In short order a consensus was
arrived at and the conferees turned their attention to methods of
implementation. They felt that they should not simply issue a
statement calling for the immediate withdrawal of all German nationals (as had been suggested at the previous meeting), but that
Kuhn had to be told personally that Germany would no longer tolerate the presence of its nationals in his organization, that the
group was forbidden to use the Party insignia, and that should he
venture a trip to Germany, he would be received only by the
director (or his designee) of the Volksdeutsche Mittelstelle. In addition, Kuhn was to be forbidden to discuss the Bund publicly
while in Germany. Behrends also agreed to instruct the DAI and
other Nazified agencies to sever any connections with the Bund,
however slight. Dieckhoff was instructed to call on Secretary of
State Cordell Hull and inform him of the decision, which he did on
February 28. The following morning, on March 1, the American
people read a formal DNB press release in their newspapers.[46]

[46] Meeting of Cultural-Political Section of Foreign Ministry, Feb. 4, 1938,
DGFP, D, I, 687–688. After Hess and Bohle gave their approval to this decision, Mackensen instructed Dieckhoff to withhold a public statement until all
Nazi agencies had made the necessary adjustments. In addition, he did not
want the American press to make any premature judgments on Germany's ac-

Kuhn had received word of the German decision on or about February 10; horrified by its goal of destoying his movement, he decided to make a personal appeal against the decree.[47] In late February, Kuhn disembarked in Belgium, rented a Ford automobile, and drove to Berlin.[48] There were no bands to greet him, no processions down Berlin's famed avenue, and no audiences with Hitler. The summer of 1936 was a distant memory. Much to Kuhn's dismay, the man he was told to see, Werner Lorenz of the Volksdeutsche Mittelstelle, sent Fritz Wiedemann in his place. Why Hitler's former commanding officer and one-time confidant was selected is not known. By nature a cautious man who shared many of Dieckhoff's feelings about the United States, Wiedemann had fallen into disfavor with Hitler. Kuhn, of course, was unaware of this and probably assumed that he was speaking with one of Hitler's closest advisers, who had shown some sympathy for the Bund while visiting the United States in November 1937. The two men met in late March. At the start of the meeting, Wiedemann told Kuhn that its purpose was to clarify Germany's relationship with his movement.[49]

In a manner resembling that of a naughty child asking a dis-

tion (*DGFP*, D, I, 691). Dieckhoff later told Secretary of State Hull that "the American Government and the American public would now realize what great pains we are taking to improve the evidently unsatisfactory relations between Germany and the United States" (D, I, 692).

[47] On February 28, Dieckhoff sent a letter to the Foreign Ministry addressed to Volksdeutsche Mittelstelle chief Werner Lorenz marked "urgent and very personal." The irate ambassador requested Lorenz to forbid Kuhn to see Ribbentrop's former assistant Heinrich Georg Stahmer (*DGFP*, D, I, 693). (On Stahmer, see Jacobsen, *Nationalsozialistische Aussenpolitik*, p. 278.) Dieckhoff stated that he had reason to believe that Stahmer had promised Kuhn renewed assistance via Fritz Gissibl's brother Peter, who was the head of the Bund in Chicago. Lorenz took the necessary precautions after he discovered that Stahmer had corresponded with Kuhn in 1937 (it seems that Stahmer was urging Kuhn to convert his group into a political organization). See Stahmer to Kuhn, Oct. 7, 1937, T-120/3010/487006; Nov. 20, 1937, T-120/3010/487036–8.

[48] On Kuhn's preparations for the trip, see car-rental information, receipts, American Automobile Association registration, container 142, RG 131.

[49] Text of conversation between Wiedemann and Fritz Kuhn, enclosed in a letter from Wiedemann to Freytag, April 7, 1938, *DGFP*, D, IV, 701–703. Wiedemann's autobiography, *Der Mann—der Feldherr werden wollte*, adds little to the story. See p. 217.

traught parent what he had done wrong, Kuhn said, "I am an American citizen. . . . I have the feeling that Reich German officials are opposed to the Bund. I wish to remove the obstacles, the causes of which are unknown and incomprehensible to me." Since he had always obeyed instructions sent from Berlin, he went on, he could not understand why Germany issued an order which was "tantamount to the destruction of the Bund." Still believing he could cajole Wiedemann into using his presumed influence to have the decisions reversed, he asked whether Berlin still attached any importance to his work in America. "If not, I shall dissolve it [the Bund]," Kuhn continued, "but I call attention to the fact that unification of German-Americans will never again be achieved." Then he said: "There is no ground for action against me personally. I have never claimed to have had a second conversation with the Führer in Berchtesgaden or even to have received instructions from him." Kuhn's monologue soon came to an end.

Wiedemann responded: "You are an American citizen, [so] I have no instructions to give you." Wiedemann then elicited a promise from Kuhn that their discussion would be kept strictly confidential and added, "Your conduct will determine my future attitude toward you." He then reminded Kuhn that any further questions had to be channeled through Lorenz' agency. More important, as far as Germany was concerned, the order calling for the withdrawal of all German nationals from the Bund was final. Kuhn, not Germany, said Wiedemann, was responsible for his own undoing: his methods, his lies, his violation of confidential conversations, and the fact that the Bund had contributed to a rift between Washington and Berlin had made this decision inevitable. In response, Kuhn said that he only wanted to "give the Bund an American tinge." At this point, Kuhn burst out: "We desire friendly relations with Reich-German officials, but the desire to understand us is lacking." Wiedemann replied: "The latter remark is a serious accusation, which I reject and which, besides, does not tally with the facts." Moments later the meeting ended. Wiedemann bade Kuhn farewell and reminded him to obey the law when he returned to the United States.[50]

[50] Conversation between Wiedemann and Kuhn, *DGFP*, D, IV, 701–703.

Bitter and disillusioned, Kuhn returned to New York. He had made no promises to Wiedemann since he had no intention of implementing Berlin's wishes. He had found ways to solve such problems in the past and intended to do so again. His methods were always the same—the use of the lie and the creation of auxiliary groups—and he knew that there was little that Berlin could do to stop him. Admittedly, German officials could revoke the passports of those nationals who refused to comply; but Kuhn was a gambler, and his bet was that the German nationals intended to remain in the United States. He also was sure that they would believe him and not Berlin. His reasoning was that the edicts and other official German statements would be published by the American press. But who would believe the "eastern Jewish press"? Certainly not the Bundists, who had been propagandized into believing that the press lacked any semblance of objectivity, since it was controlled by the German haters. The German nationals were receiving what they could only interpret as a series of contradictory signals—from Kuhn, the press, and Berlin.

But German authorities were aware that they were dealing with a liar, a leader fighting for his political life, and they intended to catch him at his own game. It was decided in February that the best way to handle the matter was through the consulates, since the consuls had immediate responsibility for the German nationals living in America. Anticipating that the Bundesleiter would dismiss the decree as a trick or minimize its importance, the consuls felt that speed was of the utmost importance: they had to get to the nationals before Kuhn did. While Kuhn was in Germany in late March and April, the consuls told Reich Germans that they had to withdraw from the Bund. In substance, their reason was that Kuhn had discredited himself by exaggerating the importance of Germany's relations with the Bund and had consequently created a host of problems for them. The consuls advised the nationals to get out of the Bund while the going was good. The preceding year's gradual trickle of Bundists from the movement developed into a flood. Exactly how many withdrew is not known; it is known, however, that several hundred nationals returned to Germany by the end of the year.

Despite efforts to discredit Kuhn, Germany's worst fears were realized. On May 3, just a few days after Kuhn returned to New York, the Bundesleiter issued a command that called for the reorganization of the movement. The Prospective Citizens' League, created to house German nationals who intended to become American citizens, was not discontinued; on the contrary, he ordered all nationals in the Bund to take out first papers toward citizenship and insisted that "every foreigner is duty bound to become a citizen if he has been or intends to be in this country for many years." He added, "No foreign government can or will oppose this." For those who did not want to become citizens, a new subdivision was created as a refuge, the Sympathizers of the German-American Bund.[51] The purpose of this group was transparent and needed no explanation. In Bund Command XVIII, he informed his comrades: "This group includes those persons who sympathize with our struggle and work and who express this sympathy by paying regular donations of money. They are not members of the Bund or the Prospective Citizens' League. Any worthy Aryan can become a member. . . . Nationality plays no role thereby." Although he forbade members of this subdivision to take part in the Bund's regular functions, wear the Bund insignia, or belong to the Ordnungs-Dienst, he also said that its purpose was to "grasp those persons who because of any political or economic reason cannot become members of the Bund but who nevertheless desire to support our causes." [52]

Did the Germans encourage Kuhn's duplicity, or was Kuhn acting on his own? This question is of cardinal importance because of the allegations made by Martin Dies and Germany's highly suspect efforts to appease ill feeling in the United States. Admittedly, in the late 1930's Germany channeled money and propaganda through its embassy, the consulates, the German Library of Information, the German Railroads Information Office, Transocean

[51] Bund Command XVIII, May 3, 1938. Kuhn did not encourage members of the Prospective Citizens' League to withdraw; however, he did prohibit them from holding any office of higher rank than schooling leader, DKV office administrator, cultural adviser, or youth leader. On the structural changes in the Bund after Kuhn's return to the United States, see *ibid.*

[52] *Ibid.*, Part III.

News Service, and the American Fellowship Forum to a host of Nazi front organizations, isolationist groups, and private individuals working for the German cause. In light of Germany's outright contributions to numerous organizations, its relationship with the Bund was of no consequence after March 1, 1938. At most, Kuhn's group received a very limited supply of Nazi literature from Nazi agencies that attempted to circumvent the interdict in mid-1938.[53] By 1938, Germany had established enough outlets for its propaganda and was underwriting so many front organizations that it no longer needed the Bund for this purpose. To be sure, some of the leaders of these groups had concurrent membership in the Bund.

[53] Germany's call for the immediate withdrawal of its nationals and related prohibitions did not mean that every existing connection was severed. In view of the number of Bundists who belonged to other pro-Nazi and/or German and German-American organizations, and since Nazi agencies continued to utilize non-Bund related organizations in its propaganda campaign (see Kipphan, *Deutsche Propaganda*, chs. iii, iv), a case could be made that Germany continued to give indirect support to the Bund after March 1938. The truth is that Germany (especially the DAI) retained limited contact with some members of the Bund in order to realize its aims in America. However, there has been a tendency to overemphasize the extent of these connections after March 1938 (see Rogge, *Official German Report*, p. 35, and Smith, *Deutschtum of Nazi Germany*, pp. 103–104). Unless the German records and the materials in the National Archives have not yielded all their treasures, the sources indicate that German support of the Bund ended with the March edict. See "Bericht über den Amerika-deutschen Volksbund," 1939, T-81/145/183278–300. As Kipphan has shown, by the summer of 1938, the German propaganda campaign in America was in full swing and was aimed at the entire American population. Regarding these efforts, see Foreign Ministry (Ribbentrop) to Dieckhoff, March 29, 1938, *DGFP*, D, I, 698; "Ernst Hepp Interrogation" (DNB correspondent, New York, 1935–1940; press attaché, Washington, 1940–1941), "U. von Gienanth Interrogation" (exchange student in United States, 1930–1932; attaché, German Embassy, Washington, 1935–1941), "W. E. Tannenberg Interrogation" (Mixed Claims Commission, Washington, 1923–1933; first vice-consul, Chicago, 1933–1937; first secretary, Washington, 1937–1941), "Heribert von Strempel Interrogation" (first secretary, Washington, 1938–1941), RG 59; and Rolf Hoffmann's correspondence, T-81/25–29. For activities of Manfred Zapp (Transocean News Service), the German Library of Information, the German Railroads Information Office, Welt Dienst, the German student-exchange program, the American Fellowship Forum (Friedrich Auhagen), VDA (Günther Orgell), and the Fichte Bund (Oscar Pfaus), see *Hearings*, Part VII; Rogge, *Official German Report*, ch. ii; Frye, *Nazi Germany and the American Hemisphere*, chs. vi, ix, x; and Kipphan, *Deutsche Propaganda*, ch. iv.

Otto Albert Willumeit, for example, a Bund official in Chicago, was one of the guiding lights of the German-American National Alliance (Einheitsfront), which was founded in October 1938 and was made up of German-Americans. As far as Berlin was concerned, this group had taken the place of the Bund in the Midwest and was deemed to be strictly American.[54] Kuhn's organization, in brief, had long outlived its usefulness.

It must be kept in mind that Berlin found it extremely difficult to sever its connections with the Bund overnight. Germany's relationship with the group had had a long and complicated history. At any given time between 1934 and 1937, more than one Nazi agency was in some way involved with the Bundists. At the very moment when the Nazi officials were meeting on February 3, the Bund was receiving propaganda from the Auslandsorganisation, the German Foreign Institute, and Rolf Hoffmann's Overseas Press Office of the NSDAP, and some German nationals were in contact with the Volksdeutsche Mittelstelle.[55] Although some German agencies disobeyed the edict at first, by the end of the year it was being observed.

No one was more concerned by Kuhn's tactics and the fact that some Nazi agencies were still in contact with the Bund than Ambassador Dieckhoff. In the months preceding the *Kristallnacht* pogrom and his recall shortly afterward, he sent to the Foreign Ministry several requests asking officials to investigate violations of the edict. In June, he claimed that "certain connections still exist here and there which give rise to the belief among the leaders of the German-American Bund that the separation contemplated in the order of February was not really meant to be taken seriously." [56] He had good reason to believe this. Hans Borchers, the consul general in New York, wrote in a report to Dieckhoff that the "situation seems to be aggravated by boastful remarks in public by inexperienced Bund leaders concerning allegedly good and secret re-

[54] The German-American National Alliance held its first meeting in October 1938. According to the Dies report, it had a membership of eighteen thousand. On consulate aid to the group, see *Hearings*, Part VII; and Frye, p. 155.

[55] Hoffmann's correspondence with the Bund's newspaper divisional headquarters, July 10, 1939, Sept. 4, 1939, T-81/26/22516ff.

[56] Dieckhoff to Foreign Ministry, June 2, 1938, *DGFP*, D, I, 708.

lations with government and Party authorities in Germany."
Borchers also contended that he had reason to suspect that the
Volksdeutsche Mittelstelle was still maintaining a limited correspondence with some Bundists; he cautioned, however, that any
further decrees concerning the Bund would be interpreted by
Washington as an admission of guilt.[57] Consul Baer in Chicago
also suggested that Germany take a laissez-faire stance, because he
believed that the Bundists were "attempting to sabotage the execu-
tion of the German order . . . by make-believe changes" and because the Bund would shortly collapse.[58] But the Bund, though
weakened by the withdrawal of many German nationals, did not
collapse.

Dieckhoff knew that officials in Washington placed little stock in
the March edict. In May, the House of Representatives passed the
Dies resolution and requested the Speaker to form—or revive—a
committee to probe into all supposed un-American activities. Martin Dies took his assignment as head of the committee very seriously, too seriously as far as the administration was concerned.
Never content with the amount of money allotted and forever ex-
panding the scope of the investigation, Dies replaced Dickstein in
the German press as the number-one "German hater." He was also
no darling of the Roosevelt Administration. Harold Ickes commented that Dies was a "hair shirt" for the administration and that
his "chief objective in life [was] to smear" the party in power. At
first, Dies received little cooperation from government agencies,
but as the published testimony of witnesses underscored the congressman's allegations of rampant foreign subversion throughout
the country, he received continued funding for his probe. The fact
that Ickes and the President had little use for his demagoguery no
longer mattered.[59]

[57] Statement of Consul General Borchers (New York), May 31, 1938, *DGFP*,
D, I, 709.
[58] Statement of Consul General Baer (Chicago), May 30, 1938, *DGFP*, D, I,
710. Cf. statement of vice-consul, San Francisco, May 29, 1938, D, I,
712–713.
[59] The committee's allegations and copies of letters concerning Dies's
charges that the Justice Department and the administration would not cooperate are in *UA*, pp. 1–10. Ickes' undisguised disdain for Dies has been well

To be sure, few people questioned the evidence concerning German activities in America. What many found disturbing was the expansion of the elastic concept of un-Americanism to include its application to the American Civil Liberties Union, the CIO, New Deal agencies, and activities as well as attitudes. With Dies's probe into the so-called Nazintern in mind, Cordell Hull told Dieckhoff in July 1938 that the "activities of Germans in the United States, with or without the approval of their government, [were] contrary to the Constitution and our laws" and were further endangering the relations between the two powers.[60] This, of course, was what Dieckhoff had feared all along. The Germans could not rid themselves of their creation.

---

documented; his diary indicates the depth of his dislike (*Secret Diary of Harold I. Ickes,* II, 455, 506–507, 528–529, 546, 574). During the war, Dies advertised that he planned to submit to the President a list of seventeen thousand suspected Nazi sympathizers (many of whom were former Bundists). Dies wanted the FBI to keep these people under constant surveillance. Roosevelt had little use for this proposal. James Rowe, Jr., assistant attorney general, wrote to Marvin McIntyre: "It takes three FBI agents to watch one person on a twenty-four hour basis. There are 3,000 FBI agents. Assuming they are busy on something else, we will need 51,000 more agents. I assume the President will go along with the appropriation" (Aug. 19, 1942). See also Dies to Roosevelt, Aug. 15, Oct. 19, 1942; J. Edgar Hoover to attorney general, Aug. 17, 1942; McIntyre to Dies, Oct. 26, 1942; correspondence between Justice Department and Dies, 1942, Official File, 320, FDRL.

[60] Cordell Hull, *Memoirs* (New York, 1948), I, 584.

CHAPTER **12**

Toward the Final Collapse

During the early formative years of the German dictatorship, American commentators were concerned by the re-emergence of German militarism. Others, many of whom were Jews, representatives of the amorphous liberal community, or old-fashioned idealists who had welcomed Germany's transition to a Republic as the partial fulfillment of America's assumed mission, were dismayed by Germany's racial practices and the rebirth of the *Obrigkeitsstaat* (authoritarian state). A genuine coalescence of anti-Nazi feeling came in the weeks following the *Kristallnacht:* for many Americans racial politics and expansionist imperialism spelled aggression. Few people bothered to examine the roots; Germany's re-emergence as a great and militaristic power seemed almost inevitable. Some Americans, moreover, were disturbed by the rapidity with which the Nazis had consolidated their rule. Had the Germans gone mad? they asked. After all, wasn't the Führer thought to be a madman? The popular belief was that Hitler had created a slave state, using the flexible materials he found at hand, that was no better, no worse than Stalin's Russia.[1]

This idea was reinforced by refugee intellectuals and scholars.

---

[1] In general, American newspapers were concerned more with the course of German foreign policy than with the Jewish question. Except for the outcry following the *Kristallnacht* pogrom, American editors did not demonstrate great concern for the fate of German Jewry. Questions about the rise of irrationalism in Germany and about Hitler's sanity were raised by several American newspaper and radio correspondents early in the history of Nazism. Later in the decade, writers concerned themselves with the spread, not with the roots, of Nazism; many writers and correspondents (with good reason) accepted the Third Reich as a permanent factor in world politics.

Each had a tale to tell. The theme was always the same: the Nazis were sinister men, and their leader would someday unleash a world war. Those fortunate enough to get out of the Reich were thought to be the most intelligent, and many were. These people viewed themselves as political and religious exiles. These modern counterparts of the Huguenots found refuge in universities, art centers, and cities. They were not greeted with open arms by job-hungry Americans, and the government did little to ease their plight. They were still Germans; many were also Jews and intellectuals. Transplanted intellect and talent did not count for much in a nation beset by seemingly insoluble economic and social problems.[2]

Americans were frightened by the disturbing news from Europe and Asia. Japan's merciless bombing of Chinese cities and the fall of Nanking and Canton were harbingers of the immediate future of that part of the world. In March 1939, when the rump Czech state had been destroyed, the accords reached at Munich were being viewed as a mistake. After the final dismemberment of the Czech state, it could no longer be argued that Hitler's designs were confined to ethnic German areas. German expansionism and the rapid spread of fascist or fascoid regimes were viewed as potential threats to the United States. To be sure, few Americans argued that the United States should become directly involved in curbing the expansion of foreign powers. But many Americans did agree that something should be done to curb the foreign "isms" brought to America. This meant a cleaning-out of foreign elements at home. Nothing seemed more foreign than Fritz Kuhn's Amerikadeutscher Volksbund.

When the New York grand jury looked into the celebrated Spanknöbel Affair in 1933, the McCormack-Dickstein Committee issued a public report in the winter of 1935, and Martin Dies charged treason in 1938, the culprits were the same people—the

---

[2] America's relation to the persecution of the Jews and the Holocaust has been the subject of much debate. Most writers agree that the American government did little to ease the plight of German and, later, European Jewry. See Arthur D. Morse, *While Six Million Died: A Chronicle of American Apathy* (New York, 1968); Wyman, *Paper Walls: America and the Refugee Crisis;* and Feingold, *The Politics of Rescue.*

Bundists and their supposed supporters in Germany. By their own admission, they were Nazis, and their opponents felt there was no room for them in American life. Unlike other right-wing or pro-German groups, the Bundists did not phrase their appeal in the name of Americanism; they did not hide the fact that their call was racially exclusive and that Hitler, not the President of the United States, was their leader. They were seen as foreigners and aliens mouthing subversive ideology. At the time of the Dies probe, a news-hungry public believed more than ever that the Volksbund was a foreign force in American life. The German edict of February 1938 did little to dispel the belief that Berlin was still behind the Bundists.

Fritz Kuhn and his followers realized that anti-Nazi sentiment was rising at a feverish pace. In spite of their public statements, they knew that not only the Jews now wanted them quieted, if not deported. In the mid-1930's, the charge leveled against the Bundists was that they were distributors of Nazi propaganda; it was argued that they fostered hate and were Hitler's henchmen. The Bundists did not deny these allegations, and the McCormack-Dickstein investigation found truth in them. In spite of the probes and the thousands of pages of testimony they produced, it became obvious to concerned Americans that there was little that could be done to dismantle the Bund movement. The Bund was labeled a conspiracy, a hate group, and a subversive organization; but except when it violated ciyil-rights statutes on the local level (as in the Riverhead case), it was difficult to obtain an indictment against the Bund.

In the middle of 1938, however, the people whom Kuhn called his enemies (and there is no denying that they were) changed their tactics. To be sure, there was never an organized plot to persecute the Bundists, but there were several concerted efforts to harass the Bund, to make life uncomfortable, and, if possible, to obtain indictments under existing statutes. Frequently, Bund locals and camps had their tax records examined; their liquor licenses were suspended and in some cases revoked. Bundists were bothered by police surveillance of their meetings. Up to this juncture in the group's history, the pressure had been subtle and had been applied at infrequent intervals. After the Bund's so-called time of troubles began, subtle pressure became outright coercion. In the New York metropolitan area this was especially true. Kuhn often said, "They are out to get me." Unquestionably, this was the case.[3]

Furthermore, the allegations leveled at the Bund carried a different force and content. Whereas John McCormack and Samuel Dickstein had charged that the Bund was the key outlet for Nazi propaganda and therefore constituted a subversive organization, Martin Dies cried treason: "The United States was no exception to this diabolical scheme, for Hitler has already planted in our midst many of his trusted agents who were carrying on their treasonable work unmolested." [4] Dies had no intention of leaving the Bund unmolested. He enlarged the definition of "un-Americanism" to include a wide spectrum of charges. In a section of the Dies report

[3] In 1938, the Justice Department made a study to determine whether Kuhn could be denaturalized under existing statutes; the broader issue was whether the Bund was in violation of any Federal laws. The government concluded that it would be difficult to revoke Kuhn's citizenship (obtained in 1934), since its representatives would have to prove that Kuhn was not well disposed toward the good order and happiness of the United States at the time of his naturalization. On efforts to denaturalize Kuhn, see Fritz Kuhn to Matthias Correa, Sept. 1, 1942, files 18–415, FRC. The first major Bundist to have his citizenship revoked was West Coast leader Hermann Schwinn, in 1939 (*Schwinn* v. *U.S.* [C.C.A. 9th] 112F [2d] 74, affirmed 311 U.S. 616). On the trial of the six directors of the German-American Settlement League, operators of Camp Siegfried (the Riverhead case), see transcript of proceedings (charges included violation of the 1923 New York State Civil Rights Act), container 194, RG 131. On the McNaboe probe (New York City, June 1938), see Kuhn to State Senator John McNaboe (about Kuhn's willingness to appear), container 153, RG 131. The "Revised Statutes of the State of New Jersey," 1937, suggests that existing legislation was revised in an effort to obtain an indictment against leading Bundists in that state and against the directors of Camp Nordland. By 1938, it was illegal in New Jersey to wear the uniform of a foreign nation and to print or distribute materials that could incite to violence (Title 2: 173–10, -11; 157B, B-2, -3, -4, -5, -6, -7). In the same document, an unnamed specialist in New Jersey's legal division cited a Pennsylvania decision in the case of *Commonwealth* v. *Benjamin*, 10 Pa. & D. Co. 775 (1928), which held that the police could interfere in a meeting held in a private hall. This decision ("the constitutional right to freedom of assembly is necessarily subject to restraints") became the basis for New Jersey's assertion that it could enter Camp Nordland and other known Bund haunts. Documents pertaining to the dismantling of the Bund in New Jersey are available in the collection of the ADL.

[4] *Hearings* Part VII, p. 1. In 1940, Dies published *The Trojan Horse in America*.

VII. Fritz Julius Kuhn addressing a Bund rally in 1937. (National Archives.)

entitled "What Are Un-American Activities?" Dies indicated his concept of Americanism and un-Americanism:

> It is as un-American to hate one's neighbor [if] he has more of this world's material goods as it is to hate him because he was born into another race or worships God according to a different faith.
>
> The American Government was established to guarantee the enjoyment of these fundamental rights. . . .
>
> The characteristic which distinguishes our Republic from the dictatorships of the world is not majority rule but the treatment of minorities. . . .
>
> Americanism is a philosophy of government based upon the belief in God as the Supreme Ruler of the Universe; nazi-ism, fascism, and communism are pagan philosophies of government which either deny, as in the case of the communist, or ignore as in the case of the fascist and nazi, the existence and divine authority of God. Since nazi-ism, fascism, and communism are materialistic and pagan, hatred is encouraged. Since Americanism is religious, tolerance is the very essence of its being.[5]

[5] "What Are Un-American Activities?" Section A, "Americanism Defined," *UA*, pp. 10–11.

The assertions, of course, were not in accord with the realities of American life in the 1930's. There was much disagreement about Dies's ideas. But as far as the Bundists were concerned, the charge of un-Americanism was synonymous with treason. In the fall of 1938, Dies broadened the scope of his probe to include an investigation of espionage and requested the FBI to look into the activities of Bundists working in the navy yards and airplane factories.[6]

VIII. Amerikadeutscher Volksbund meeting at Camp Nordland, New Jersey, 1939. (National Archives.)

The pressure on these people was heavy and constant. The German nationals in the movement—persons who had not completed the naturalization process—felt especially vulnerable. Tired of what they considered harassment, fearful of being caught in a na-

[6] Dies's allegation that "large numbers of Bundists were spying for Germany was unfounded (see note 53, below). The Volksbund became indirectly involved in the spy scare when Bundist Günther Rumrich was arrested and charged with espionage in 1938. On German spy activities in America, see Farago, *The Game of the Foxes*; on the Justice Department's concern about Dies's exaggerations, see Frank Murphy to Roosevelt, Jan. 5, 1939, President's Secretary's File, 10B, FDRL.

tional house cleaning and charged with treason, and increasingly
aware that the Bund was essentially what it always had been, a
movement of German nationals and not a German-American organization, many of the emigrants of the 1920's packed their belongings and returned to Germany. The exodus began shortly after Berlin issued the February edict and continued for nearly two years.
These *Rückwanderer* (returnees) hoped Germany would provide
what they had looked for in the United States. For the most part,
they returned to their native towns and cities and found employment; but by 1940, most found themselves in the military.

During the first years of the war, Kameradschaft-USA kept them
informed of each other's whereabouts. Their wartime correspondence had a pathetic quality. Albert Lieb wrote from the Russian
front in February 1942 that "life was primitive" and wished that
the war was over; other letters reported the death of former friends
from America.[7] In general, their letters reflect the realization that
they had wasted the best years of their lives. They were also disturbed by the fact that the Bund had made no impact on American
policy—at least the type of impact their leaders had predicted.
The one-time local leader of the Bund in San Diego, John Lutz, expressed this feeling in a brief but trenchant statement: "The U.S.A.
is already a forgotten part of the struggle." [8]

The exit of these people seriously weakened the Bund movement. Many had been members since 1933; others had belonged to
the Teutonia Association and Gau-USA. They were the "old fighters,"
stalwarts committed to National Socialism. They had supported
Fritz Gissibl after the Spanknöbel Affair, had transferred their allegiance to Kuhn in the middle of the decade, and more important,
had served Germany in a hostile environment. The returnees were
the nucleus around which the Bund had been built. Because they
believed in and adhered to the *Führerprinzip*, the organization

[7] Albert Lieb to Kameradschaft-USA, Feb. 14, 1942, T81/551/5325656.
Early in the war, Kameradschaft-USA produced a mimeographed newsletter,
"Mitteilungsblatt der Kameradschaft-U.S.A." The newsletter recorded the deaths
of former comrades and the whereabouts of others. Several examples can be
found in T-81/144/183178–92.

[8] Letter by John Lutz, former local leader, San Diego and San Francisco,
Dec. 18, 1941, T-81/140/177993.

had survived chronic intraparty quarrels and the impact of external pressures. They were the Bund's bureaucracy and had made it
possible for the Nazi movement in America to evolve from the
Teutonia Association to the Volksbund. They were the people
Kuhn depended on to enforce the leadership principle at the local
level. Although Kuhn had done much to protect the Bund from the
law, he had done little to ensure the continuation of the movement in the event of his own demise or the removal of trusted
functionaries at the lower levels.[9] Moreover, it was increasingly
difficult to get American citizens to fill the positions vacated by ex-
iting German nationals after 1938. Many Americans of German extraction preferred to hide behind pseudonyms and join the Bund as
"sympathizers," not members, and therefore could not hold important (and public) positions. The departure or withdrawal of the
German nationals was an unanticipated disaster. Gradually the
chain of command started to break down, and although replace-
ments for high-level posts were found, they lacked the dedication
of the "old fighters." [10] (See Appendix V.)

Some of the returnees were replaced by native-born or naturalized Americans. The German-born element, including individuals
on their way toward American citizenship, still constituted the
largest part of the membership. Kuhn, however, was careful to
avoid further criticism and selected only American citizens to fill
vacated positions. By the fall of 1938, the names Rudolf Markmann, George Froboese, James Wheeler-Hill, Gerhard Wilhelm
Kunze, August Klapprott, Hermann Schwarzmann, and Henry von
Holt started to appear as frequently as Kuhn's in the Bund's newspapers.[11] Their growing importance became obvious at the Bund's
national convention in September 1938.

[9] Lists of former Bundists and Bund leaders who returned to Germany,
T-81/140/177820ff; 141/179443. Cf. Dies committee list of Bund leaders in
the United States, *Hearings*, Part VII, pp. 67–69. By 1939, more than half of
the people on Dies's list had returned to Germany.
[10] It will be recalled that the first Bundists to return were the organizers of
the Teutonia Association, Fritz Gissibl (1936), Sepp Schuster (1936), and Walter Kappe (1937).
[11] Prominent Bund officials in the period 1937–1938 included Rudolf Markmann (East Coast leader); George Froboese (Midwest leader, 1937–1940; last

This meeting was another turning point in the Bund's history. Six hundred and thirty-two delegates gathered for a three-day convention at the Turnhalle in New York's Yorkville section at a time when the organization was under attack from the Dies committee. The convention was also held at a time when the gathering of groups of Bundists engendered violence. In New York, special units of the police department were assigned to guard Bund haunts and rallies. Most important, the Turnhalle meeting was held when there was growing suspicion among the members that their leader had been less than honest with them—that his statements of friendship with Hitler and Göring were lies, that the often repeated claim of German support was false. Gone were the jubilant days of the period of the Olympic trip, as everyone, including Kuhn, was aware. Whereas the February edict marked the end of German involvement with the Bund, the national convention later that year marked the beginning of the end of the Volksbund's efforts to unify Americans of German extraction. September 1938 witnessed the start of the Bund's last effort to "Americanize," a poorly timed and ill-conceived effort to reach "all white patriotic Americans." [12]

The convention began on September 3. The Bundists were fed and housed at the Bund's expense. They heard their leader deny that Germany had disavowed either him or the movement. He claimed that his trip to Germany in March had been a complete success, but he refused to say whom he had met. In effect, the leader said he could never be questioned: "Either a confidence exists which gives me free action or no such confidence exists, in which event you have the opportunity today to deprive me of this

Bund leader, 1941); James Wheeler-Hill (national secretary-business manager; arrested in 1939 and later convicted of perjury—had testified under oath at the time of Kuhn's trial for larceny that he was an American citizen); Gerhard Wilhelm Kunze (public-relations director and press manager, 1937–Sept. 1939); August Klapprott (restaurant operator, Camp Nordland, 1937–1938); Hermann Schwarzmann (district leader, Ordnungs-Dienst, Queens, New York); and Henry von Holt (Bronx County unit leader). A list of new appointments for 1937 is in Bund Command XIII, Sept. 14, 1937, ADL.

[12] Plans for the convention can be found in Bund Commands XIX (July 12, 1938) and XX (Aug. 16, 1938); excerpts from the minutes of the 1938 Bund convention appear in "Evidence," pp. 68ff. CF. Bell, *In Hitler's Shadow*, pp. 74–79.

trust." [13] They did not, and Kuhn was re-elected by the delegates.

In the ensuing months Kuhn became suspicious and began to equate all dissent within the ranks with treason. "The most dangerous opponents of a fighting movement," he wrote in October, "are those who work secretly to undermine the leadership." [14]

The evidence, though circumstantial, suggests that the dissatisfaction with Kuhn stemmed, not only from his tendency to fabricate, but also from a growing suspicion that he was embezzling funds from the treasury. The Bundists involved in his conviction for embezzlement were known in Bund circles as the three K's: Gerhard Kunze, who was in charge of public relations and publicity at the time of the convention and replaced Theodor Dinkelacker as national youth leader in October; August Klapprott, a one-time friend of Kuhn's and the operator of a restaurant near Camp Nordland in New Jersey; and Wilbur Keegan, a part-time attorney for the Bund who drew a weekly salary from the organization. According to one report, the three K's had discovered that Kuhn was stealing from the Bund. At the time of the convention, they were powerless to do anything about it. The following spring Kuhn was charged and later convicted of forgery and larceny. The New York district attorney, Thomas Dewey, who was instrumental in obtaining evidence against Kuhn, had gained access to the Bund's records with the help of the three K's.

In December 1939, with Kuhn on his way to Sing Sing to serve a two-and-a-half- to five-year sentence, Kunze took over the leadership of the Bund and had Kuhn officially expelled from the movement. This gave greater currency to the rumor that Kunze, Klapprott, and Keegan "had Kuhn railroaded" in order to get their hands on the Bund's treasury and the fifty-thousand-dollar defense fund collected on Kuhn's behalf. According to Henry von Holt, a

[13] "Evidence," p. 79. Regarding his trip to Germany and meeting with Captain Wiedemann, Kuhn said: "I gave you my word of honor that a denial of our organization in Germany would have caused me to stand before you today and state 'I can no longer undertake the responsibility of continuing the leadership of the Bund and I herewith withdraw.' Then you could have perceived that the continuance of the Bund would be useless" (*ibid.*).

[14] "Report to Bundists on the Results of the Convention," Bund Command XXI, Oct. 8, 1938.

staunch supporter of Kuhn and leader of the Bronx division, the three *K*'s knew as early as August 1938 that the end of the movement was in sight and wanted to pocket the treasury funds. Wilbur Keegan the attorney managed to quiet the rumors by threatening Holt and others with libel.[15]

One thing is certain: at the time of the national convention Kuhn sensed that some of his immediate subordinates were not fully in agreement with him. He told the delegates that they had come to New York to "decide whether my policy was the correct one and in which direction the Bund shall be led in the future."[16] Kuhn and the delegates agreed that there was a future for the Bund; they also agreed that the direction in which the Bund had been moving since 1933 might not have been the best one. Although it was reported that the Bund had recruited 4,852 new members in 1937, the delegates knew that their group was what it had always been —a German, not a German-American Bund. Recruitment statistics and the February edict had made this clear. Kuhn and the leadership did not, however, see themselves at fault. The Bund leader admitted privately that he believed the German government was to blame and had been to blame since 1933. Had Germany given unqualified financial and ideological support, the movement would not have faltered. In public, he used the age-old and time-tested technique of reflecting blame on others—in this case, the Jews— and since the major thrust of the Bund had been against American and world Jewry, he did this with a minimum of effort.[17]

Since the appearance of the 1938 German edict, Bund propagan-

[15] It must be emphasized that the story of the three *K*'s derives from circumstantial evidence (based on information available in the collection of the ADL). The story received greater currency after Kuhn's arrest in May 1939. Keegan's papers, in RG 131, are exempt from public disclosure; on Henry von Holt's analysis of the intra-Bund controversy and his expulsion from the organization on April 26, 1940, see his sworn statement, Denaturalization Proceedings, Henry von Holt file, 18–394, FRC.

[16] "Evidence," pp. 62ff.

[17] Only two policy changes were implemented after the Kuhn-Wiedemann meeting: Kuhn announced that the Bund would not attempt to become a political party—"This can be considered when the Bund is an organization of millions" (Bund Command XXI, Oct. 8, 1938); and the Bund abandoned the "*Heil*, Hitler" greeting and the use of Nazi symbols.

dists had been denying that Germany had disavowed the movement; they boldly asserted that the "Jewish circle" in the State
Department had fabricated the story. In the spring of 1938, Kuhn's
anti-Semitism had taken on a new virulence, adopting all the pseudoscientific theories of Germany's foremost Jew baiter, Julius
Streicher. Bund handouts became distinctly pornographic, depicting the Jews as a race of filthy sexual perverts bent on destroying
the purity of American womanhood. The Jews were thoroughly dehumanized and accused of treasonous activities. "Jewish-Marxist
Internationalism," read one handout, "will only lead to war against
all nations combating Jewish Domination and Bolshevism." [18]

The Volksbund's stepped-up hate campaign prompted some
Bundists to conclude that their leader might countenance the use
of violence to eliminate the so-called Jewish pest. Gradually an extremist element emerged, led by Hermann Schwarzmann, the
leader of the Queens, New York, Ordnungs-Dienst. He maintained
that the only solution to the Bund's and the nation's manifold
problems was the elimination of the Jews. As early as June 1937,
he had declared that the time would come "to wipe out the Jew
pigs." [19] At the convention in the Turnhalle, the call for blood was
in evidence. Rudolf Markmann told the delegates: "You all know
that the government in Washington is 100% Jewish and is committed against Germany. Here is the last harbor of the Jews. We can
expect a hot conflict concerning it here." [20] In an effort to exploit
native anti-Semitism in America, the Bundists decided to direct
their appeal to "Free America," to what Kuhn called "Gentile
America." In effect, this meant that Kuhn had dismissed most
Americans of German ancestry as thoroughly Americanized. His

[18] "Which Way America?" handout, ADL. See also Bund Propaganda and
Related Materials, Fragmentary Evidence, Records Relating to German House
and Related Organizations, containers 150–170, 332A–321, RG 131.

[19] Statement of Hermann Schwarzmann to Ordnungs-Dienst (Queens, New
York), June 17, 1937, "Evidence," p. 68.

[20] Statement of Rudolf Markmann, 1938 Bund convention, *ibid.*; West Coast
leader Schwinn argued that the Bundists "must bring the attack on the Jews
further into association with politics, economics, and culture. I can assure you
that you have a thankful subject in this conflict. The frame of mind of America is against the Jews" ("Evidence," p. 67).

appeal to their children had also failed. Now he hoped to fill the
ranks with other native-born Whites.[21]

In a strange but understandable way, Kuhn owed much to Martin Dies. By September, Dies seemed to be more concerned with
the Communist threat to America than with the Nazi menace.
Kuhn hoped to widen the Bund's base by rapidly converting it into
a militant anti-Communist and isolationist group. By doing so, he
believed that he could pick up support from the emerging isolationists, native anti-Semites and scores of right-wing organizations.
At the Turnhalle meeting the Bund adopted a syncretic eight-point
program. It called for a "White, Gentile America," which meant
the control of labor unions by Gentiles, the elimination of Moscow's alleged influence, the breaking of diplomatic ties with the
Soviet Union, the banning of the Communist Party in America and
treason trials for its leaders, the denial of entry permits for all refugees, a cleaning-out of the Communist elements controlling Hollywood, and a return to the policy of General—later, President—
George Washington: no foreign entanglements. In subsequent
weeks, the Bund also added *The Free American* to the title of its
newspaper *Deutscher Weckruf und Beobachter* and adopted what
Kuhn thought were "more American looking uniforms." [22]

These changes were, for the most part, merely window dressing.
The men and women wearing the new uniforms had not changed,
the base of the Bund was not enlarged, and the Bundists still
swore allegiance to Hitler and the Reich. To achieve what it considered Americanization, the Bund had to change its propaganda.
It appealed "For a Gentile Controlled America": "WHEREAS, this
Nation was conquered, pioneered and built by White Men, whose

[21] "*Amerikadeutscher Volksbund,* Nation-wide Militant Organization of FREE
AMERICANS of German Stock, Purposes and Aims," 1938, handout, ADL.

[22] Leuchtenburg, *Franklin D. Roosevelt and the New Deal,* p. 280; Ogden,
The Dies Committee, pp. 32–34, 41–45. On the implementation of the program adopted at the convention, see Bund Command XXI, Oct. 8, 1938. The
first issue of the *Deutscher Weckruf und Beobachter and The Free American*
appeared September 29, 1938. Changes in Bund uniforms had been accomplished by January 1937 (see Bund Command VI). By September 1939, the
wearing of Bund uniforms had been outlawed in several states (Bund Command XXIII, Sept. 8, 1939).

Culture, Form of Government and Ideals of Americanism are being undermined and destroyed by an alien minority with an unassimilable code, therefore be it RESOLVED, that we demand a socially just, White-Gentile ruled United States."[23] It also called for the furtherance of anti-Communism (the elimination of "the madness of class warfare!"), support of the Bill of Rights (to put an end to the "invasion and plundering of offices and homes WITHOUT SEARCH WARRANTS!"), and the end of the New Deal, degenerate art, hate-breeding commentators on the "Jewish radio" ("Winchells, Peglers, Brouns, Lores, Thompsons-Levys and Clappers"), and antipatriotic pacificism "in subverted Pulpits, demoralization of Old and Young through de-Christianization of Institutions and Observances!" Furthermore, it appealed for Washingtonian isolationism with one corollary: keep America out of all future conflicts, but pray for the destruction of "Jewish England" and Bolshevik Russia. In practical political terms, all this meant that America should give unqualified support to German foreign policy. The Bund was eclectic and borrowed from the isolationists, the native fascists, and the arguments of the traditional right. But unlike many organizations on the right, the Bund's adhered to two basic principles: racial anti-Semitism and unaltered support of German internal and external policies.[24]

The Bund was increasingly willing to cooperate with individuals and organizations on the right. It had done so before 1938 under the direction and influence of Bundists who had joined other organizations. On the West Coast, Bund locals had worked closely with Pelley's Silver Shirts earlier in the decade. In the Midwest and the East, it had not been uncommon for the Bund to invite members and speakers from the more than a score of fascist and pseudo-Nazi groups that had sprung up in opposition to the New Deal or

[23] "Which Way America?" and "For a Gentile Controlled America," handouts, ADL.

[24] At the close of the convention, Kuhn told the delegates that they could best serve Germany by supporting delegates pledged to keep America out of a future conflict ("Evidence," p. 93). After the outbreak of the European war in 1939, Kuhn outlined a five-point program: (1) call for absolute neutrality, (2) protest against all "lying reports" (e.g., Germany, not Poland, started the war), (3) declare war against "Jewish profiteering war-mongers," (4) make the slogan "Keep America Out" a reality, (5) refer to the nonpayment of war debts by America's allies in World War I (Bund Command XXIII, Sept. 8, 1939).

because of sympathy for Italy, Germany, or the cause of Russian nationalism. At Camp Nordland in New Jersey, representatives of the Ku Klux Klan and Salvatore Caridi, president of the North Hudson Chapter of the Italian Ex-Combattenti, had been frequent speakers.[25]

In exchanging speakers and participating in joint functions, each group retained complete autonomy; cooperation leading to a merger would require a partial relinquishment. In late 1938 and throughout the following year, it was rumored that the Bund was attempting to form a national right-wing coalition. It seems that for a brief period Kuhn was in favor of a merger with the Italian Black Shirts, Anastase André Vonsiatsky's Russian Nationalist Revolutionary Party, Donald Shea's National Gentile League, and the groups led by Louis McFadden, George Deatherage, Gerald L. K. Smith, General George van Horn Moseley, and Joseph McWilliams. But the leaders of these extremist groups—except McWilliams, head of the Christian Mobilzers—wanted to retain their autonomy and were reluctant to join forces with a group that was the object of a stepped-up Federal investigation.

Despite their understandable reluctance, they permitted their members to attend Bund-sponsored functions. In fact, Bund meetings in the New York area—at Innisfail Hall, Ebling's Casino, Schwabenhalle, and the Triborough Palace—became increasingly non-German in composition. In February 1939, the anti-Semitic rabble rouser Russell Dunn addressed a Bund rally in Brooklyn. Of an estimated two hundred persons in the audience, 25 per cent

[25] The Bund held joint meetings with Caridi's group (e.g., at Camp Nordland in September 1937); with Josef Santi, New York commander of the Liktor Assozion (on July 4, 1937); with John Finzio, leader of the Circolo Mario Morgantini (on August 29, 1937); with Donald Shea's National Gentile League, Joseph McWilliams' Christian Mobilizers, and Anastase A. Vonsiatsky's Russian Nationalist Revolutionary Party. Reports of cooperation among these groups can be found in *Hearings*, pp. 1462–1466, and *UA*, pp. 110–112. Information about activities in Innisfail Hall, Schwabenhalle, Ebling's Casino, and the Yorkville Casino is available in the collection of the ADL. Vonsiatsky was a German agent. He was born in Russia; following the Revolution, he fought with the Whites and later fled to Paris. In the 1920's, he married Marion Ream, daughter of the Chicago financier Norman Ream. In 1934, he founded the International Russian Fascist Party and was elected its first leader (*Vojd*) (Farago, *The Game of the Foxes*, pp. 443ff).

were Germans, 25 per cent Irish, 20 per cent Italian, and the remainder belonged to the Christian Mobilizers.[26] The figures suggest what was happening to the Bund in late 1938. Although the Bund's actual membership was contracting and was composed primarily of ethnic Germans, those attending its public functions were mainly non-German. More and more, observers noticed that meetings were attended by anti-British working-class Irish, Russian émigrés, Italian ex-servicemen, Coughlinites, and lower-middle-class and working-class native Americans. Kuhn encouraged these people to join the Bund as sympathizers and in June 1939 created still another subdivision, the Friends of the German-American Bund. There is little evidence to suggest that they took advantage of the Bundesleiter's offer; most preferred to remain anonymous in the crowd.[27]

Another change was taking place. Schwarzmann and Kunze, who was elevated from national recruiting leader to deputy Führer in September 1939, were opposed to a merger and the admission of non-Germans on the ground that Nazism was for the Germans and no one else. The Italians, the Russians, and the Irish might be kindred spirits, but they were not Aryans. On December 15, 1939, exactly ten days after Kuhn was convicted and sentenced to prison, Deputy Führer Kunze announced that the Bund was not contemplating a merger with any other group and that the movement did not "exist to father untried groups. . . . The Bund remains free!" He then dismissed the whole idea of a merger as absurd and, perhaps with the fallen Bund leader in mind, wrote, "It is unfortunately a German weakness, often observable in Bund members, to throw oneself into the arms of some non-German who is friendly." [28]

Several weeks after Kuhn announced the new Americanization program, he realized that he had to retain the Volksbund's Germanness in order to preserve its ideological consistency and to pla-

[26] Report dated Feb. 8, 1939, ADL.

[27] In Bund Command XXII (June 1, 1939), Kuhn explained this change: "Every Aryan friend of our movement, regardless of his nationality, can now help in the construction of our bitterly [sic] needed movement, until it reaches out into every locality in the country and touches all of the German American element."

[28] Bund Command XXVI, Dec. 15, 1939.

cate dissenters within the ranks. Abrupt ideological reversals did not rest well with people who had been propagandized into believing that their group was exclusively Aryan; also, the watering-down of the Bund's appeal to German-America came at a time when Hitler had catapulted a racially conscious Germany to the center of the western stage. In an effort to quiet his opposition and further heighten racial awareness, the Bund continued to have functions that were, by definition, separatist—that is, closed to all non-Germans. This obvious departure from the Bund's American orientation came less than one month after Kuhn announced the group's future course at the national convention.

In October the Bund was not invited to participate in New York's annual German Day program. The reluctance of other organizations to be seen in public with the Bundists was understandable in light of the Volksbund's involvement with the law and the fact that the German consulate had urged non-Bund-related German groups to keep away from the Bund. As far as Manfred Zapp, director of the New York office of Transocean, the consulate staff, and the personnel at the German Library of Information were concerned, Kuhn was *persona non grata*.

In early October, Kuhn decided to sponsor his own version of German Day and scheduled it for October 30—*Der Tag des Amerikadeutschtums von Brooklyn*. He instructed Nicolay to invite only pro-Nazi German singing societies, sport organizations, and workingmen's groups. But most of the groups that took part in activities were merely Bund-created front organizations, refuges for the still active element of German nationals in the Bund. At this and other distinctly separatist functions, Bund leaders stressed that National Socialism was for the Germans and for the Germans alone, that there was one leader, Adolf Hitler, and that the German spirit would cure America.[29]

By the start of the new year it was clear that Kuhn's syncretic movement was trying to be many things to many people. Some extremists admired the spirit that still pervaded Bund meetings, the uniforms, the night-time rallies—in short, the *élan* of National So-

[29] "Deutscher Tag 1938: Der Tag des Amerikadeutschtums von Brooklyn, 30. Oktober 1938," T-81/29/25652–3.

cialism. Many anti-Semites believed that the American Nazis had
an answer to the "Jewish question," which they associated with the
New Deal, the media, and the Left. For the most part, however,
the McWilliamses and Edmondsons found the Bund convenient for
furthering their own fantasies, grievances, and what may loosely be
called ideologies. Surely this was the case with the Knights of the
White Camellia, the Christian Mobilizers, and the northern units
of the KKK. For them, the Bund's racial-political theories were
only modifications of existing white-supremacy doctrines. There
were, of course, many fellow travelers—isolationists, people who
had been dislocated by the Depression and had a personal griev-
ance against Jewish shopkeepers in their neighborhoods, and people who hated the British or the Blacks or the Pope. Many later
managed to group together under the elastic rubric known to
Americans as isolationism. Admittedly, most isolationists did not
hate the Jews or, for that matter, anyone; but in the ranks of the
isolationists there were many haters and pro-Nazis. The isolationists stayed clear of the Bundists, and after the invasion of Poland,
the Bundists were seen as a threat to their cause. The Bundists,
who had long been viewed as interlopers, were now viewed as un-
touchables.[30]

The deterioration and final collapse of the Bund movement were
rapid and irrevocable. Although the end had been in sight for
some time, the group's disintegration was much faster than some
people had anticipated. After December 1939, no one, including
the Bundists, considered the Amerikadeutscher Volksbund effective. Its formal, that is, officially declared, death came five days before the surprise Japanese attack on Pearl Harbor. The eventual
destruction of the Bund was predictable; the causes of its destruction were not very complex and, by now, were quite obvious. Cast
off by the Germans, under constant pressure from Federal and
local authorities, financially desperate, depleted in numbers, and
with its members openly expressing doubt about a duplication of
the Hitler feat in America, the Bund could no longer sustain itself
in its adopted environment.

[30] Wayne S. Cole, *America First: The Battle against Intervention,
1940–1941* (Madison, Wis., 1953), pp. 119, 122.

After the start of the next year, 1939, even the once buoyant
Kuhn acknowledged that the Bund could not continue unless its recruitment, financial, and political situations changed dramatically.
All signs pointed in the opposite direction. Despite the fanfare afforded the organization in the nation's press, its fortunes approached a new low in mid-1939; the pressure brought to bear on
the Bund by local authorities in New York and by Dies's elastic
definition of un-Americanism forced hundreds of Kuhn's supporters
to leave the movement. When the Dies committee received an additional hundred thousand dollars to continue its work and the indefatigable congressman announced that the Right as well as the
Left would come under his close scrutiny, the Bundists knew he
was not bluffing. The restaurant owner in Yorkville, the toy distrib-
utor in Richmond Hill, Queens, and the small shopkeeper on St.
Anne's Avenue in The Bronx no longer wanted their names or the
names of their businesses on Bund literature or on its mailing lists
and withdrew from the group.[31]

The preliminary findings of the Dies committee pointed to un-
American activities carried on by Reds in the government, the
unions, and the movie industry; these activities were deemed especially dangerous—part of a Red plot to take over the nation. The
Nazis were regarded as a threat of a different kind. Hitler's agents
in the "Nazintern" were seen everywhere—in the shipyards, in the
aircraft factories, in America's Yorkvilles. Following the path
blazed by the McCormack-Dickstein Committee, Dies outlined the
history of the Bund since 1924 and concluded that the Bundists
constituted a subversive, conspiratorial, and un-American threat to
the United States. Besides giving a blanket condemnation of the
Bund's activities, he showed the extent of German propaganda efforts and uncovered a number of Nazi front organizations. Admittedly, the original conclusions were somewhat exaggerated and the
role assigned to the Bund was grossly magnified. Despite the in-
consistencies, the preliminary findings pointed to Hitler and his

---

[31] On the cancellation of advertising in the Bund's publications, see "Lists
of Cancellations," container 137; "Cash Ledgers," 1939, container 205; collection of letters from merchants canceling advertising and complaints concerning
the nonpayment of bills, 1937–1938, container 142, RG 131.

supporters in America as archetypal enemies, unequivocal threats
to American civilization. They gave the word "Nazintern" new
meaning, and soon "Fifth Column" and "Trojan horse" became
household words. The jelling of anti-Nazi sentiment was swift, and
the House responded by extending the life of the committee.[32]

It was fourteen years after the founding of the Teutonia Association in October 1924. The Bund had come a long way since several
young Germans opened the association's headquarters. The National Socialist movement in America had survived purges, investigations, and Germany's efforts to destroy it. Its several
corporations owned camps, hundreds of acres of land, stores, a re-
tirement home in New Jersey, a casino in Yorkville, and claimed to
have a membership of a hundred thousand in its fifty-eight nationwide branches. In all probability, the Bund had less than one-fifth
that number. Numbers did not seem to matter; Dies admitted that
his head counts were estimates of the number of persons "willing
to be seen" at Bund functions. What really counted was that the
Bund enjoyed a national reputation. The only people who seem to
have been aware that the Bund was receiving more publicity than
it warranted were the group's leadership and German officialdom.

After Munich, few Americans thought Hitler was a joke. He was
no longer a funny little man with a Chaplin mustache; he was the
great dictator, an enemy who would have to be deterred or defeated. But millions of Americans felt that was a job for the Russians or Western Europeans. A catastrophe was in the works, but
Americans did not want to get involved in preventing it or even in
effecting a *détente.* Instead, they thought it would be best to do
some thorough house cleaning at home. No event in the history of
the Bund movement made more obvious to a nationally conscious
America the Nazi threat at home than did the widely publicized
Pro-American Rally in Madison Square Garden on February 20,
1939. The Nazi menace was no longer viewed as an abstraction—a
concoction of the Jews, the refugees, the Left, or the German haters; it was no longer merely a European concern. Today, more

[32] The life of the Dies committee was prolonged by a vote of 344 to 35. For
the administration's view of the committee (Ickes referred to it as "a hair
shirt"), see entry for Dec. 18, 1938, Ickes, *Diary,* II, 528–529.

than thirty years later, the name Fritz Kuhn can still conjure up memories of a man standing before a thirty-foot picture of George Washington, singing praises to the German Führer. For these Americans and the millions who have forgotten all about it, the Bund's perverted display of Americanism was what un-Americanism was all about.

The planning of the gala George Washington's Birthday celebration began in November, when Kuhn and his immediate subordinates learned that the appellate division of the New York State judicial system had overturned an unfavorable decision against the German-American Settlement League.[33] The news that the Bund intended to rent Madison Square Garden spread rapidly among right-wing political groups in New York, and many of these wanted to be included. At first, Kuhn was cool to their overtures. In fact, he became increasingly reluctant to hold the rally at all. Because the Bund was low in funds, he believed that his organization would derive greater publicity if the New York Police Department called the rally off.[34] But the planning had gone too far, and the event had received much publicity. Responding to the cry that the Bund should be barred from holding this function, La Guardia and the American Civil Liberties Committee answered that it was the Bund's prerogative to exercise its civil rights. Obviously, the anti-Nazi La Guardia saw certain advantages in a pro-Nazi rally in mid-Manhattan.[35]

The Bund's plans were carried out according to schedule. Thousands of tickets were sold to the general public. After bickering with the representatives of the Central Committee of Affiliated Groups—a loose coalition of native right-wing groups in New York—Kuhn decided that the Garden rally would be a Bund affair. Kuhn, who was not known to have a keen sense of humor, even

[33] *Deutscher Weckruf,* Nov. 10, 1938. On plans for the meeting, see Kuhn to George Froboese, Jan. 13, 1939; Kuhn to Hermann Schwinn, Jan. 13, 1939, container 140, RG 131.

[34] Based on information available in the collection of the ADL which indicates that one of the reasons why the Bund was low in funds was because it had recently purchased the Yorkville Casino, a beer hall in Yorkville.

[35] Council for the American Civil Liberties Committee to Fritz Kuhn, Feb. 14, 1939, container 140, RG 131.

sent invitations to Martin Dies and New York State Senator Mc-
Naboe, who had completed an unsuccessful investigation of the
Bund's affairs the previous summer.[36]

The rally was held in the evening. Guarded by two thousand
New York City policemen, three thousand of Kuhn's OD men
marched into a filled-to-capacity Madison Square Garden.
Twenty-two thousand people sat through several hours of what
Kuhn called "pro-Americanism." Froboese, Kunze, Markmann, and
Kuhn compared Hitler to Washington, called for a united fascist
front, denounced Roosevelt, predicted that the Bund would have a
million members by 1940, asserted that the "Jew can never create
values" and that the Jews were social parasites, war profiteers who
had become rich in every American war, and suggested that Jewish teachers be removed from "Gentile schools." Some Americans
considered the speeches a misuse of Kuhn's and his comrades' citizenship. The speakers also helped discredit the isolationist cause
by attempting to fuse isolationism with anti-Semitism.[37] There were
several fist fights between hecklers in the audience and Kuhn's OD
people. One man, Isadore Greenbaum, broke through the line of
OD men guarding Kuhn and tried to attack the Bundesleiter. The
guard fell upon Greenbaum and dragged him off the stage. Kuhn
later cited the attempted assault as a violation of his civil rights and
as evidence of a Jewish conspiracy.[38]

---

[36] General admission to the rally was forty cents, seventy-five cents, or one
dollar. An itemized statement of the proceeds showed that the Bund collected
$13,048.17: from box office sale of tickets, $2200; national sale of tickets,
$8661; sale of materials at the Garden (programs, etc.), $2116 (handwritten
statement, n.d.; Fritz Kuhn to Martin Dies, Jan. 13, 1939; Kuhn to State Senator McNaboe, Jan. 13, 1939, *ibid*.). Plans for the Madison Square Garden
rally called for the inclusion of Donald Shea's National Gentile League, the
American Nationalist Party, the Crusaders against Communism, and representatives of the Christian Social Justice Party. At an organizational meeting held
at the Bronx Wintergarden (a combination beer and dance hall on Washington and Tremont Avenues), the Bund leaders decided to exclude these groups
(based on information available in the collection of the ADL).

[37] The addresses of leaders Kuhn, Kunze, Schwinn, Froboese, Markmann,
and Wheeler-Hill were published in the spring: *Six Addresses on the Aims
and Purposes of the German-American Bund: Madison Square Garden, February 20, 1939* (New York, 1939), container 38, RG 131.

[38] "Report of the New York Bund Rally," Feb. 27, 1939, *DGFP*, D, IV,
675–676; *New York Times*, Feb. 21, 1939, p. 1.

IX. Bundesleiter Fritz Julius Kuhn addressing the Pro-American Rally, Madison Square Garden, New York, February 20, 1939. Note the Ordnungs-Dienst men and New York City police in front of the stage. (National Archives.)

Newspaper coverage of the Pro-American Rally was not confined to the American press. British and French dailies carried detailed accounts, and editorials pointed to Kuhn as America's Henlein. Germany's coverage of the rally indicated the dilemma that the Party had created for itself by 1939. As much as a year after Germany had broken all existing connections with the Amerikadeutscher Volksbund, the German public was still being told that Kuhn and the Bundists stood almost alone in the fight against the Jewish-Communist conspiracy in the United States. On February 22, the *Völkischer Beobachter* cited Greenbaum's attempted attack on Kuhn as one more example of Jewish control of the United States. Another German newspaper reported that Greenbaum had been arrested and was later given a ten-day suspended sentence. "For this horrible act of violence," commented the writer, "the Jew Grünbaum [sic] received ten days in jail. America, land of the free!" [39]

[39] "Jüdischer Attentatsversuch auf den Leiter des Amerika-Deutschen Volksbundes—Neuyorker Massenversammlung gegen die Verjudung der USA —'Ohne Steuben kein Washington,'" *Völkischer Beobachter*, Feb. 22, 1939. On Germany's reaction to the sentencing of Greenbaum, see "Land der Frei-

The attendance of twenty-two thousand people at a Bund-sponsored rally and the fact that a Jew had attempted to assault Kuhn
had obvious propaganda value for the Germans. The Ministry of
Propaganda and diplomatic personnel in the United States dis-
agreed about the value of the rally. From New York, Consul General Hans Borchers reported that the rally had tarnished Germany's image in the United States and had done great damage to
the isolationist cause.[40] The Consul General's evaluation of the impact of the rally was correct. If Kuhn's purpose had been to draw
attention to his organization, he was extremely successful. *Life*
magazine, *The Nation, Christian Century*, the *New York Times*,
and a host of other publications raised serious questions concerning the advisability of permitting the Volksbund to continue its
existence and contended that it was part of the German spy network. There seems to have been little disagreement: the Bund
must be dismantled.[41] For many, the dissolution of the Bund meant
the successful conviction of Kuhn, not of minor Bundists. But few
people knew how to go about dissolving the organization. Under
existing statutes, Kuhn and most of his followers were in a legal
twilight zone. The government knew this; more important, Kuhn
knew it.

Although the government had temporarily halted its pursuit of
Kuhn, authorities in New York City had not. The city's mayor, La

heit," *Rhein.- Westf.-Zeitung* (Essen), Feb. 22, 1939. Ten days after the Bund
rally, an anti-Nazi rally was held in New York's Carnegie Hall. The guest
speakers included New York's Governor Herbert Lehman, Dorothy Thompson,
Thomas Dewey, and Robert Wagner ("Program," March 3, 1939, container
140, RG 131).

[40] Borchers reported that the Bund's most recent "Americanization" program
did little to disguise its German character and that its continued existence was
a disruptive factor in German-American relations; he urged Germany to "win
back" its nationals in the United States and "hope that they could become
useful citizens in Germany" (Feb. 27, 1939, *DGFP*, D, IV, 675–678).

[41] The so-called spy scare in the late 1930's was in part related to the activ-
ities of the Bund. Examples of spy-scare literature are: Otto D. Tolischus,
"Hitler Enlists Germans Everywhere," *New York Times Magazine*, Nov. 21,
1937; David Cort, "Democracy Unlimited," *Life*, 9 (Aug. 19, 1940), 68–71;
Demaree Bess, "Hitler's Weapon against Us," *Saturday Evening Post*, 213
(Aug. 3, 1940), 32ff; and J. Edgar Hoover and C. R. Cooper, "Enemies within
Our Gates," *American Magazine*, 130 (Aug. 1940), 18ff.

Guardia, did little to disguise his disdain for the Bundists. His reputation as a staunch anti-Nazi did little to endear him to Kuhn and
the authorities in Berlin. The man whom Goebbels labeled the
"half-Jewish German hater" wanted Kuhn behind bars and, although some Germans dismissed his pursuit of Kuhn as a publicity
stunt aimed at diverting attention from several scandals in his administration, his opposition to Nazism was genuine.[42] La Guardia
likened features of the Bund to those of organized crime: the cult
of the untouchable leader, the extortion of protection money from
small businessmen, the use of thugs and front organizations, and
the fencing of goods—in the case of the Bund, the fencing of foreign propaganda. In sum, he considered the Bund a racket. After
the widely publicized rally in Madison Square Garden, the mayor
gave the go-ahead for an investigation of the Bund's financial activities. La Guardia, the young and aggressive District Attorny
Thomas Dewey, who had a reputation for racket busting, and William Herlands, a friend of the mayor and a well-known lawyer, reasoned that somewhere Kuhn had made a mistake and that the road
to an indictment might be found in the Bund's ledger books. Such
a tactic was not new. Law-enforcement agents had learned a great
deal from the investigation of Al Capone's and other racketeers' tax
delinquencies. The discovery of irregularities in the Bund's accounts would make unnecessary the difficult and perhaps unenforce-
able charge of un-Americanism or conspiracy. Where Dickstein,
McCormack, and now Dies had failed, the man of Italian-Jewish
descent—the "little Flower"—would succeed. The charge had to
be concrete; the conviction had to be final. The illusion that the
Bundists were beyond the reach of the law was about to end.

In April, La Guardia organized a "Special Tax Emergency Investigation" and placed Herlands at its head.[43] Ostensibly charged
with the task of ascertaining whether the Bund had paid the New
York City tax on the sale of Nazi paraphernalia, Herlands and his
aide, City Treasurer Almerindo Portfolio, enlarged the scope of
their probe to include the examination of the records of the group's

[42] Hans Thomsen to Foreign Ministry, May 26, 1939, *DGFP*, D, VI, 588.
[43] William B. Herlands to Mayor La Guardia, May 17, 1939, Herlands, "Report of Tax Investigation," ADL.

six separate corporations. A careful scrutiny of the Bund's tax records revealed that each corporation had violated many tax regulations (more than forty were cited by Herlands); under existing laws, however, these violations were not serious enough to result in a long-term sentence for Kuhn, since settlements out of court were possible. Later that month and before the Herlands report was made public, Dewey decided that more information would be necessary. Realizing that Dewey meant business, Kuhn hurriedly tried to put the Bund's house in order. He engaged an accountant, Bundist Horst Otto Wegener, and had the group's financial records audited; he ordered the New York branch's secretary, Max Rapp, to examine the tax records carefully and to pay debts (the payments led to the rapid depletion of the Bund's bank accounts at several branches of the Manufacturers Trust Company); he requested Bundists to keep detailed records of their expenses.[44]

In spite of these measures, Kuhn did not act fast enough. On May 2, 1939, Dewey and several of his agents entered the Bund's offices in Yorkville and seized the group's financial records. Later that year Kuhn sent an eleven-page affidavit to Attorney General Frank Murphy claiming that Dewey was "involved in a conspiracy against him" and that the district attorney had entered the Bund headquarters without a subpoena, violating Kuhn's constitutional rights.[45] Although there was no substance to these allegations, Kuhn tried to convince his followers that "the Jewish-controlled District Attorney, Thomas Dewey, seized upon gangster methods

[44] The Herlands investigation found that Max Buchte (manufacturer of uniforms for the Bund), Karl Kienzler (a partner in Kienzler and Schimpf, Inc., jewelry importers and distributors of Bund jewelry), Fred Hackl (president of Hackl Press, Inc., one of the Bund's publishers), and two Bund officials, Carl Nicolay and Fritz Schwiering, were liable for back taxes. (Nicolay and Schwiering sailed for Germany while the investigation was in progress.) On Kuhn's belated efforts to put the organization's finances in order, see "A. V. Publishing Co., Audit Report, 1939," and "Letters between Horst Wegener and Fritz Kuhn, 1939," container 205; "Tax Records of the GAB, New York City Sales Tax Payments," container 199; and "Financial Reports for 1939," container 134, RG 131. Wegener was later appointed "Bund schooling leader" (Bund Command XXXIIIA, June 21, 1940).

[45] Fritz Kuhn to Frank Murphy (attorney general, 1939), June 1939, container 142, RG 131. Kuhn's allegation was groundless. See transcript of *People v. Kuhn* (5 vols.), containers 48–49, RG 131.

and broke into my office and into the residences of two Bund administrators without warrants, and seized books and other things in the hope of finding something against us and especially against me." [46] As far as Kuhn was concerned, Dewey was an "unscrupulous, ambitious politician who believe[d] that by taking care of the Bund he [could] get the Jewish votes in his campaign for the presidency." [47] The district attorney found what he was looking for. In the ledger books, auditors discovered that Kuhn had apparently misappropriated part of the $14,548 of the proceeds from the February rally. Kuhn was indicted by a New York County grand jury and later released after posting five thousand dollars from the Bund's fifty-thousand-dollar bail fund. Of course he pleaded not guilty to the charge. In an effort to prevent Kuhn from fleeing the county, La Guardia requested the State Department to seize Kuhn's passport.[48]

Between the time of Kuhn's arrest and the opening of his trial on November 9, 1939, the disintegration of the Bund accelerated. Sensing that many of his followers shared Dewey's suspicion that he had embezzled funds, Kuhn assured them that he had not "embezzled one cent" and that he did not have to defend himself before the membership.[49] In late May he left New York for a nationwide inspection of Bund locals. En route to Chicago, he was arrested and charged with bail jumping, although he later claimed that Dewey had given him permission to leave New York City.[50]

[46] "Statement of National Leader Kuhn to the Membership," June 1939, container 142, RG 131. Cf. Bund Command XXII, June 1, 1939.

[47] Bund Command XXII.

[48] "Woes of a *Führer*," *Newsweek*, 13 (June 5, 1939), 12. Kuhn posted bail with no difficulty. The Bund had established a "fighting fund" in 1937. When the bail was raised to fifty-thousand dollars in September 1939, Kuhn was forced to borrow additional funds from unnamed moneylenders (Bund Command XXVI, Dec. 15, 1939, Part IV, "Liens for Bail").

[49] In Bund Command XXII, Kuhn proclaimed his innocence: "I don't believe that I have to defend myself to the members, and it is only in their opinions that I am concerned. I believe I have shown after years of service that I have led the Bund honorably and honestly. I declare through this command upon my word of honor, I have not embezzled one cent from the Bund. I can account for every expenditure which I was authorized to make by the National Convention."

[50] Bund Command XXII.

His arrest was a miscalculation, since it re-enforced the Bundists' belief that Dewey was part of a conspiracy directed against their leader. This interpretation of their leader's problem was apparent throughout the annual Volksbund convention in July. Meeting in Yorkville's Turnhalle, dissident factions within the Bund were temporarily quieted in the face of so many problems; in consequence, Kuhn was once again re-elected, given continued control over the organization's finances, and authorized to take all the necessary steps to fight the district attorney. Meanwhile, across the Hudson, state officials had other surprises, as the pace of the Bund's disintegration quickened. In New Jersey a law was passed which prohibited the wearing of uniforms resembling those of a foreign power or political party; in what only could be interpreted as a coercive tactic, Camp Nordland had its liquor license revoked. Both these actions signaled the beginning of New Jersey's dismantling of the Bund and its related affiliates.[51]

In August, Kuhn was subpoenaed to appear before the Dies Committee. After receiving permission from Dewey to leave New York, he arrived in Washington in the middle of the month. During five hours of testimony, he asserted that the Bund was not a Nazi organization; rather, it was an American organization working for peace. His testimony proved to be somewhat of a sensation. He repeatedly banged his hands on the table and alluded to a conspiracy led by Dewey that was aimed at railroading him to prison.

[51] The fact that many of Kuhn's alleged tormentors were Jewish or partly Jewish accorded with the organization's view of America. Kuhn was depicted as an innocent victim of "Jewish Hate Mongering." One Bund handout reads:

Help Fight the Mad Informers Hounding Fritz Kuhn by the Hate-Blinded, Desperate International Jew and His Politician Slaves!
What is the concern of Dewey about the Bund's money?
Fritz Kuhn is the Bund!
Grant Us Loans to Cover Bail Bonds!
Fritz Kuhn Personifies the Persecuted German Element!
He shall Win! [T-81/413/5158081]

Nicolay drove home the same theme after he returned to Germany. See his speech "Im Weltkrieg hatten die Amerikadeutschen viel zu leiden," 1941 T-81/144/182667. On the Bund's troubles in New Jersey, see materials concerning the Nordland case (Richard Schiele, Paul Schaarschmidt, Carl Schiphorst, and George Neuppert), ADL; and copies of legal briefs and transcripts of testimony, *State of New Jersey* v. *Klapprott and Others,* container 49, RG 131.

Frequently, Dies and other members of the committee cautioned him against making any statement which could be construed as contempt. Needless to say, Kuhn's testimony produced few new revelations. The same cannot be said of the testimony of Helen Vooros, a nineteen-year-old former member of the Bund's Youth Division. She told the committee that she had been sent to the Reich to be educated in National Socialism. Far more startling was her suggestion that homosexual practices were taking place in youth camps. The committee was shocked; her testimony underscored what Dies and others had long believed: un-American activities not only subverted the political structure but also undermined the moral fabric of the nation.[52]

The combined impact of these probes brought the movement within an arm's length of disaster. The year 1939 proved fatal to the Bund; it began with the publication of the preliminary findings of the Dies committee in January and the massive Pro-American Rally in February; ten months later Kuhn was in prison after having been found guilty of larceny and forgery on December 5. The following day Gerhard Wilhelm Kunze (who had been appointed deputy Führer on September 8) convened a secret meeting of the Bund's executive committee and had Kuhn expelled from the organization. During the preceding ten months the debacle had quickened. Aware that the end was in sight, the Volksbund's creditors wanted their money, Bundists who had purchased ten-dollar shares of preferred stock in the A. V. Publishing Company cashed in their shares, subscribers to the newspapers and other publications canceled their subscriptions and requested Kuhn to destroy the ad-

[52] The thrust of the committee's argument was that the German-American Bund was an un-American organization which was "diametrically opposed to the principles of Americanism, as set forth in the Constitution and the Declaration of Independence." The preliminary report (committed to the whole House on January 3, 1939) maintained that the Bund (and a host of other right- and alleged left-wing groups) were receiving foreign support and were bent on undermining the nation ("Summary of Findings," *UA*, Part VI, pp. 118ff). Throughout the proceedings, Kuhn stressed that the Bund was an American organization working for the improvement of German-American diplomatic relations; at one point in his testimony, he asserted that the Amerikadeutscher Volksbund was *not* a Nazi organization. Some of the materials pertaining to his testimony in October are in container 142, RG 131.

dressograph plates with their names on them: in sum, the rank and file defected en masse. In early September, two of the Bund's major advertisers, Hapag-Lloyd Lines and the Hamburg-Bremen Steamship Company, cut off all contact with the group, thus ending a financial connection which had begun in 1933. The prevalent feeling in Berlin and among the consular people in America was that Kuhn was getting what he deserved, but belatedly. In October, Kunze wrote to the German government, requesting some support —if only moral—for his leader, who he claimed was still listed as a German citizen in Berlin. On October 30, Kunze received an answer from Hans Thomsen, chargé d'affaires at the German Embassy in Washington, who wrote that Kuhn had unequivocally lost his German citizenship and was now an American citizen; Germany could do nothing and, moreover, would do nothing, since it had never had "any relations with the German-American Bund or its officials." Upon hearing the news of Kuhn's conviction in December, Consul General Borchers commented that the Bundesleiter and his loud-mouthed lawyers had alienated everyone; he was finished, and the movement was about to die.[53]

[53] On cancellations of subscriptions and newspaper advertising, see Hamburg-Bremen Steamship Company to German-American Bund, Sept. 6, 1939; Hapag-Lloyd Shipping Lines to Fritz Kuhn, Sept. 6, 1939; Cancellation List (23 pages), container 137, RG 131. On the expulsion of Kuhn from the Bund, see Hans Thomsen to G. W. Kunze, Oct. 30, 1939, *ibid.;* and Minutes of Executive Committee Meeting of the GAB, Dec. 6, 1939, container 16. On Germany's view of Kuhn's manifold problems, see Karl Goetz to Fritz Gissibl, July 1939 ("Kuhn's behavior is a disgrace"), T-81/144/183237–8; and Hans Borchers to Foreign Ministry, Dec. 8, 1939, T-81/502/5264838–41. Several Bundists were enlisted by Abwehr as spies and potential saboteurs. According to Farago, *The Game of the Foxes,* W. Othmer (Trenton unit, German-American Bund), Gustav Guellich (Brooklyn unit), Otto Willumeit (one-time Chicago unit leader, founder of the German-American National Alliance), and Kuhn's successor, Gerhard Wilhelm Kunze, were enlisted after 1940 (pp. 345, 442–447, 502–503). It should be emphasized that these men were recruited because they had a special skill (the construction of long-range radio equipment) or access to materials or plans needed by Germany (Guellich worked for U.S. Steel). There is absolutely no evidence to suggest that Germany recruited these men because they belonged to the Bund; nor were the Bundists used en masse as saboteurs. To be sure, Germany had little use for persons well known to the FBI and other government agencies. See Martin Dies to Roosevelt, Aug. 15, 1942; J. Edgar Hoover to the attorney general, Aug. 17, 1942, Dies file, 10B, FDRL.

Between the Pro-American Rally in February and his conviction in December, Kuhn attempted to keep his movement intact. While awaiting trail, he adjusted the Bund's viewpoint to accord with the ideological turnabout demanded by Germany's signing of the non-aggression pact with the Soviet Union in August. He said that the Molotov-Ribbentrop pact was the beginning of the end of Marxist-Communist domination of Russia and cited the fall of Litvinov as evidence. The Jews, he argued, had lost at their own game; "Germany's interests come first for the German People and . . . it is no more Germany's job than any other country's to carry a crusade into Russia with the object of changing that Country's political system." [54] After the outbreak of the war, Kuhn instructed the Bund to maintain complete neutrality, but also to "war against Jewish profiteering war-mongers" and to fight for a "Gentile, Christian American Nationalism and the uprooting of all atheistic, international Jewish Marxism and related phenomena!" [55]

Two weeks after the outbreak of the war in 1939, Dewey tried to silence Kuhn by raising his bail from five thousand to fifty thousand dollars. To the surprise of the district attorney, Kuhn managed to post bail and was released from jail in early October. After the money was delivered, a concerted effort was made by the FBI to trace the serial numbers on the bills, which were in large denominations. The result is not known. In the meantime, Kuhn engaged an attorney, Peter L. F. Sabbatino, and together the two men prepared the Bundesleiter's defense to answer twelve charges of embezzlement.[56]

The case of *People* v. *Fritz Kuhn* opened on November 9, 1939.

[54] "Statement of the German American Bund: The Russian-German Trade Agreement and the Non-Aggression Pact," Sept. 7, 1939, ADL.

[55] *Ibid.* Cf. Bund Command XXIII, Sept. 8, 1939. It is instructive that Kuhn, who feared the outcome of his trial and the long arm of the law, told his followers not to collect money for the German war effort "since it is contrary to the Neutrality Act" (*ibid.*, Part VI).

[56] The legal forms and receipts for the fifty thousand dollars (dated October 5, 1939) are in container 142, RG 131. The money was paid in large denominations; the serial numbers of these bills were recorded by the government (container 134). On Kuhn's engaging of Sabbatino, see *Peter Sabbatino v. G. W. Kunze*, transcript of testimony, March 10, 1941 (after the trial, the Bund did not pay Kuhn's lawyer, and Sabbatino sued Kunze), container 205.

For the next twenty days the chief prosecutor, Herman J. McCarthy, tried to prove that Kuhn had embezzled funds from the Bund's corporations, claiming that he had squandered them on women and entertainment. Much to the chagrin of Kuhn's wife, Elsa, McCarthy produced several "Dear Fritzi" letters and canceled checks that had been used to pay the moving expenses of a Mrs. Florence Camp, one of Kuhn's girl friends. Sabbatino, in turn, argued that Kuhn's private life had no bearing on the case and that his client could not be accused of larceny because, in keeping with the "leadership principle," he had ultimate control over the organization's finances. Sabbatino's defense was excellent, and for a while it looked as if Dewey would not win the case. Sabbatino's arguments ate away at the indictments. Eventually, the case rested on the allegation that Kuhn had not paid a legal fee of five hundred dollars to a lawyer who had defended six Bundists in the German-American Settlement League case the previous year. Armed with the Bund's ledger books as evidence, McCarthy attempted to convince the jury that although Kuhn claimed he had paid the fee, in reality he stole money and forged the sum in the ledger book. To the very end Kuhn maintained his innocence. The jury felt otherwise. After eight and a half hours, it found Kuhn guilty of larceny and forgery, and he was sentenced to serve a term of two and a half to five years in Sing Sing. It was December 5, 1939. The Fritz Kuhn era had ended.[57]

Following his conviction, the Bund's propagandists boldly asserted, "Kuhn is the Bund." Unquestionably, he was. In spite of his many shortcomings and the fact that he was a notorious liar, a crude anti-Semite, and in the end a convicted embezzeler, Kuhn managed to transform the nearly moribund Friends of the New Germany into a vigorous movement. And he accomplished this with little or, later, no German support. This man whom most Americans looked down upon as a notorious demogogue, a Nazi puppet, and a cheat, never commanded the nearly religious veneration evoked by an appearance of Hitler. But in the heyday of the Bund, from 1936 to 1938, he did command the allegiance of thousands of

[57] Transcript of testimony, *People* v. *Kuhn;* copies of legal briefs, containers 48–49, RG 131. Cf. Rogge, *Official German Report,* pp. 128–129.

followers. The one-time chemist from Munich had catapulted the Bund into the national limelight at the very moment when the German leader had moved Germany to the center of the world stage. Despite the excitement the Volksbund aroused, it was a failure by American and German political standards. Although Kuhn made inroads into the community of German nationals, he failed to gain support from German-Americans. Like his predecessors—Spanknöbel, Gissibl, Schnuch—they viewed Kuhn as a stranger, an interloper propagating a foreign ideology. Once it was clear that German-Americans were eschewing the Bund's overtures the myopic Bundists spent most of their time in haunts in Yorkville and elsewhere. In their self-imposed isolation, they perpetuated a so-called *völkisch* way of life in their camps, beer gardens, and meeting halls; for them, the German way of life meant racism, beer, marching, and *völkisch* solidarity. Blinded by their views, they dismissed anything and anybody that did not fit into their preconceived scheme of things. They clung to a mythical image of the old Germany, and since most of them had left their homeland before 1925 they remembered only what they wanted about Germany. Strangely, except for a handful, most never saw Hitler's Germany firsthand. They believed what they were told and accepted as true what they saw in German-supplied movies. They tried to experience National Socialism while living in the United States and exempted themselves from American life. Kuhn's successors were no exception. Kuhn left his followers a legacy of lies, myths, and debts. Somehow, his followers had to resolve the problems their imprisoned leader left behind or disband the movement.

CHAPTER **13**

The End of the Pursuit

The challenge fell to two men, August Klapprott, a thirty-three-year-old former bricklayer, and Gerhard Wilhelm Kunze a one-time chauffeur-mechanic from Camden, New Jersey.[1] Both had joined the Friends of the New Germany in late 1933, but neither had held an important post until 1937. Kunze was a hard worker and a dedicated Nazi. Between November 1937 and April 1939 he worked for the Bund on a voluntary basis, which seems to have impressed Kuhn. More important, he was one of a handful of native German-Americans who committed themselves completely to the Nazi cause. Consequently, he rose very rapidly in the Bund's administrative structure. After Kunze had served as national public-relations director and recruiting leader, Kuhn appointed him deputy Bund leader on September 8, 1939. On that day, Kuhn also appointed Klapprott leader of the Eastern Department, a position that was becoming increasingly more important in light of the Bund's dwindling membership in other regions. It is not clear why Kuhn entrusted the leadership of the Bund to these two men at such a crucial point in the group's history. It had been long rumored in Bund circles that Kuhn suspected both men of collaborating with Thomas Dewey. With Kuhn's trial scheduled to open in early November, perhaps Kuhn made these appointments as a conciliatory move and believed that once he had won his case, he could return to a unified Bund movement. At any rate, there is no

[1] For biographical data on Kunze, see Appendix III, below; on Klapprott, see *Hearings*, Part VII, pp. 64–66. Transcripts of Kunze's and Klapprott's testimony before the Dies committee (Oct. 1–2, 1940) are in *Hearings*, pp. 8251–8353, 8285–8307.

evidence to suggest that Kuhn unwillingly appointed them, and Kunze assumed the titular leadership of the Bund shortly after Kuhn's trial began.[2]

But if Kuhn suspected that Kunze wanted him out of the way, his worst suspicions were borne out. The day after he was sentenced, on December 6 Kunze called a special secret meeting of the Bund's national executive committee, whose members were Hermann Schwinn, August Klapprott, Willy Luedtke, Gustav Elmer, and James Wheeler-Hill—the organization's most trusted leaders. Now that Kuhn had been found guilty, Kunze imposed his will on the movement. Kuhn was deposed from his offices and expelled from the Bund. The committee also decided to give Elsa Kuhn an unstated sum for her maintenance and instructed the Bund's lawyer, Wilbur Keegan, to start an appeal for Kuhn.[3] As will be seen, they had absolutely no intention of pursuing the appeal and, in fact, wanted to keep Kuhn in prison.

Kunze organized several rallies on Kuhn's behalf. On December 30, for example, an estimated five hundred people gathered at Ebling's Casino (a third belonged to the Christian Mobilizers). Here and at other rallies a collection was taken for Kuhn's appeal; Kunze said that "qualified lawyers devour huge sums of money." The money was never used for this purpose, nor was it used to pay off the Bund's debts (the German-American Settlement League was seventeen thousand dollars in debt); instead, Kunze used it to defray operational expenses. When some Bundists raised questions about the appeal and the disposition of the money, Kunze referred their queries to the discipline committee, which was controlled by the Ordnungs-Dienst. For the moment the dissenters were quieted, but only for a moment. Kunze's misappropriation of the appeal money raised a storm of protest. In the words of one of Kuhn's sup-

[2] On Kuhn's appointments of Kunze and Klapprott, see Bund Command XXIII, Sept. 8, 1939, ADL. An assertion that Kuhn was railroaded is in a letter from Bundist F. W. Yockel to Klapprott, n.d., container 142, RG 131.

[3] Minutes of Executive Committee Meeting of the German American Bund, Dec. 6, 1939, container 16, RG 131. James Wheeler-Hill withdrew from the Bund on December 28, 1939. Willy Luedtke replaced him as business manager (Bund Command XXVII, Jan. 12, 1940). Gustav Elmer was elevated to Bund treasurer on March 10, 1940. (Bund Command XXIX).

porters, Fred W. Yockel, "These guys are lining their pockets while Kuhn rots in prison." Unconcerned by such comments, Kunze continued to solicit money from locals throughout the country.[4]

In January 1940, Kunze sent Keegan to inspect locals in all major cities. The purpose of the trip was to determine whether unit leaders wanted to organize a nationwide campaign for funds on Kuhn's behalf. According to the minutes of a second secret meeting of the executive committee, Keegan did little to encourage the appeal of Kuhn's conviction. On January 29, 1940, Keegan dismissed Kuhn's lawyer, Peter L. F. Sabbatino. At this point Sabbatino realized that the Bund's new leaders never intended to attempt to reverse Kuhn's conviction. Sabbatino seems to have been disturbed, not by the prospect of his client remaining in Sing Sing, but by Kunze's refusal to pay Kuhn's legal fees. (A year later, Sabbatino took Kunze to court and won the case.) Sabbatino rallied to his support several of Kuhn's staunchest supporters, including his wife, Elsa, who seemed to have recovered from the shock of the revelations, some months before, of her husband's night life. Unfortunately for the imprisoned Bund leader, none of these people held important positions on the organization's executive committee. In desperation, Mrs. Kuhn wrote to the leaders of several Bund locals and appealed for their help. In turn, Kunze issued a scathing blast aimed at ending what he dubbed rumor-mongering:

Recent rumors are to the effect that we in Bund Headquarters are responsible for his conviction and that we are trying to thwart the appeal because we want him out of the way, and I am seeking his office, etc., and that it is necessary to disregard Bund Headquarters and to support the appeal alone.

These are all monstrous insults of persons who are still seeking means to destroy the movement. Every comrade, especially if he is an OD Man, knows what the propagator of such murder stories deserves.[5]

[4] Materials on the repercussions of Kuhn's conviction and rallies on his behalf are in container 16, RG 131. On the discipline committee, see Bund Command XXVI, Dec. 15, 1939; on Kunze's denials that he was involved in Kuhn's arrest and conviction, XXVIII, Feb. 15, 1940; on the costs of the appeal, XXIX, March 10, 1940. On the allegation that Kunze was getting rich at Kuhn's expense, see Yockel to Klapprott, n.d., container 142, RG 131.
[5] Bund Command XXVIII, Feb. 15, 1940. On Keegan's tour of the locals throughout the United States and his problems with Sabbatino, see "Meeting

In March, Kunze stopped perpetrating the hoax that the new leadership was behind Kuhn. Claiming that the defense of the Bund leader had already cost ten thousand dollars (in addition to the five thousand borrowed from moneylenders for Kuhn's first bail bond), Kunze announced that a successful appeal was impossible. Why further weaken the movement, he asked? Certainly Kuhn would understand. He also informed the Bundists that Kuhn had formerly withdrawn from office on February 22, 1940. Although Elsa Kuhn, Henry von Holt, Fred Yockel, and several other Kuhn stalwarts complained, there was little they could do. In a letter to the membership, Yockel suggested that Bundists might comfort their former leader by sending gift packages to his new address: 354 Hunter Street, Ossining, New York—Sing Sing Prison.[6]

Kunze's contention that the Volksbund was in such serious financial trouble that it could not undertake a renewed defense was not as fraudulent as Kuhn's loyal followers asserted. The organization's financial records reveal that the Bund's income from advertising and contributions stopped after Kuhn was indicted. Throughout the spring of 1940, Bund officials depleted the Bund's savings in a frantic effort to ward off creditors who threatened to foreclose on the organization's properties. In the heyday of the Bund, owners of small restaurants, beer distributors, landlords, and printers had permitted the organization to run up large debts on credit. Now they wanted their money and threatened to engage legal counsel. At the Manhattan branch of the Manufacturers Trust Company, for example, the A. V. Publishing Company had a balance of three hundred dollars on October 31, 1939; on December 12, the balance dropped to ninety-one dollars, and by March, to less than five. The Bund's financial statements give evidence of a nationwide financial debacle. Throughout the spring and summer of 1940, the disaster

of Executive Committee, February 17, 1940," Container 16, RG 131. The details of Elsa Kuhn's fight with Kunze over her husband's appeal are available in the collection of the ADL.

[6] "Meeting of the Executive Committee, June 2, 1940," container 16, RG 131. In Bund Command XXIX (March 10, 1940), Kunze wrote, "Fritz Kuhn knows also that a useless weakening or restriction of the movement is not to be permitted regardless of how blameworthy the methods were which brought about his downfall." See also Yockel to Klapprott, n.d., container 142, RG 131.

continued. In July, Kunze announced that the Bund had severed all connections with the German-American Settlement League (which operated Camp Siegfried). He claimed that its directors had incurred a huge debt, and he disclaimed any responsibility. Despite the financial collapse, the Bund's new leaders—Kunze, Klapprott, Elmer, Rapp, and Luedtke—continued to draw salaries, enjoyed the privilege of petty-cash accounts, and drove new automobiles.[7]

Kunze's achievement of ascendancy over the Bund was a Pyrrhic victory; it had quickened the pace of the organization's disintegration. During the Volksbund's national convention that was held at the Fatherland House in Chicago in late August 1940, Kunze was elected to fill the post vacated by Kuhn. Although he had gone through the mechanics of leading, there was little left to lead. At best, the newly elected Bund Führer (Kunze preferred this designation to president or Bundesleiter) could count less than fifteen hundred followers (this estimate is based on newspaper subscriptions, not on membership lists). Between November 11, 1939, and October 10, 1941, he issued twenty-four Bund commands, drafted a new constitution, dismissed members out of hand, made more than a score of new appointments, devised elaborate auditing procedures, instituted "fighting funds," assumed direct control over most of the Bund's subsidiaries, supported the isolationist cause, and went on a national tour. All this availed him little. The end of the Bund was no longer in sight; it had finally arrived.[8]

[7] Income tax returns, bank statements, payroll books, containers 15, 171, 189, 209, RG 131. Kunze severed connections with Camp Siegfried in July 1940. See Klapprott to the membership, July 8, 1940, container 153.

[8] Bund Commands XXIV–XLIX, Nov. 11, 1939–Nov. 1941. On finances, see payroll books, 1941, containers 193, 194, 195, RG 131. Copies of the Bund constitution (1940), are in containers 17 and 37. On the convention of 1940 and the Bund's role in the isolationist controversy, see Transcript of Meeting, National Convention, Aug. 31–Sept. 1, 1940 (held in German House, Chicago), containers 16–17. See also correspondence between Froboese and unit leaders, 1940, container 15. Kunze urged his followers to join the America First Committee as a means of showing their support of Germany's war aims. Several weeks after he wrote the letter, John Flynn, chairman of the America First Committee in New York, announced that members of the Bund were not eligible for membership (Cole, *America First*, p. 119).

During this period the Bund resembled the Friends of the New Germany in the latter's early formative months. Day after day metropolitan newspapers carried reports of fights between Bundists; in general, they erupted over the disposition of the group's remaining resources. Fights also took place between the Bundists and McWilliams' Christian Mobilizers (Kunze referred to him as a "sheenie stooge"). The Bund was also collapsing in Los Angeles, Philadelphia, Chicago, and elsewhere. At the time of the Japanese attack on Pearl Harbor, most of Kunze's remaining followers had either dropped out of the movement or had joined native German-American singing societies and other cultural groups.[9]

Unlike Kuhn, Kunze was not a cautious leader. He did little to isolate the Bund from outside attack; in fact, he compounded the Bund's manifold problems. In August 1940, for example, he advised aliens in the Bund not to answer a question on the alien registration form. Three months later, he urged Bundists to register for the recently organized draft but to refuse induction. He argued that the Selective Service Act was unconstitutional and violated the "Germandom" of every Bundist. Few of his followers paid any attention to these Bund commands; those who did were later charged with subversion or draft evasion.[10]

The debacle was nearly complete. The organization's business manager was convicted of perjury in December 1939; West Coast leader Schwinn was denaturalized the following November. By the summer of 1941 the Bund had been outlawed in California and Florida, and Camp Nordland had been closed by New Jersey. Play-acting in a collapsing world, the Bundists assembled for their last national convention, in Chicago, on August 20, 1941. Kunze

[9] "Reports of Bund Activities in Yorkville (New York), November 6, 1941–December 11, 1941," German-American Bund folder, ADL.

[10] The Alien Registration (or Smith) Act was passed on June 28, 1940. Kunze's instructions concerning the Smith Act are outlined in Bund Command XXXV, Aug. 15, 1940. In September the Selective Service Act was approved. The first draft registration was on October 16, and the first draft numbers were selected on the twenty-ninth. Kunze's instructions to his followers concerning registration are in Bund Command XXXVII, Oct. 1, 1940. During the war, several Bund leaders were convicted of counseling resistance to the Selective Service Act; the unfavorable decisions against these men were reversed by the high court in 1945. See Polenberg, *War and Society*, p. 49.

announced that in light of the government's freezing of the group's remaining assets, it would be impossible for the Bund to pay its debts. More important, he later told the delegates that he intended to step down:

If each of you had earnestly approached the negligent Bund members and sympathizers and appealed to their honor we would have succeeded. Since this lack of success strikes back at the leadership I have decided that it would be right to give the matter to another Bund officer and let him try in his way to call forth the necessary willingness to sacrifice.[11]

Kunze's resignation was not accepted, however. In early November he disappeared. Bewildered by Kunze's actions, his deputy George Froboese called together the members of the Bund's executive committee on November 13. Froboese told the committee that Kunze's conduct was reprehensible and that his failure to appear at this crucial meeting suggested that he no longer wanted to be part of the organization. With a stroke of a pen in a world at war, Bund Führer Kunze was removed from his post. Froboese instructed Willy Luedtke, the Bund's secretary, to communicate the decision to Kunze. But he was nowhere to be found. Kunze, who was an agent at large for the German Abwehr and in close contact with the Ukrainian *vojd*, Anastase André Vonsiatsky (which may account for Kunze's insistence that the Bund would remain free from other right-wing groups), had gone into hiding in November. In early 1942, the German spy apparatus arranged for his escape to Mexico. Later that year Kunze was picked up by Mexican authorities and returned to the United States, where he was later convicted on several counts, including espionage, and sentenced to fifteen years in prison.[12]

On December 2, acting Bund leader George Froboese issued the last Bund command, Number L. Unlike previous commands, this one was in the form of a letter to the handful of stalwarts remain-

[11] Bund Command XLVII, Sept. 8, 1941. On the freezing of the Bund's assets (Executive Order 8389), see DKV to Manufacturers Trust Company, Aug. 11, 1941, container 204, RG 131.

[12] Minutes of the Executive Committee Meeting of the German-American Bund, Nov. 13, 1941, container 16, RG 131. On Kunze, see Farago, *The Game of the Foxes*, p. 446.

ing in the organization. In a somber appraisal of the group's manifold troubles, Froboese admitted defeat and urged his comrades to brace themselves for hard times ahead:

We all wanted the fight, we have therefore the obligation to persevere. Our old homeland also recently had men who believed it was necessary to undertake steps which would lead faster to victory in order to establish peace [the sinking of the U.S. destroyer *Reuben James* on October 30?]. They are today one illusion poorer; through this step which they undertook they were sentenced to useless work. . . . We must carry on, comrades! [13]

Five days later the Japanese attacked the United States at Pearl Harbor; on the eleventh, the Germans and the Italians declared war on America. The nightmare which had plagued the minds of most Bundists was at last realized: they were stranded in the homeland of the enemy.

In a technical sense, the leaders of the Bund never declared the group defunct. The courts pronounced its several subsidiaries bankrupt, and the A. V. Publishing Company went into receivership.[14] George Froboese, the man who had warned his comrades to prepare themselves for troubled times, committed suicide on June 16, 1942. He was en route to New York City to answer a Federal grand jury subpoena. After December 7, 1941, the government kept a close watch on many Bundists who had made up the rank and file in the organization, but did little else.[15] However, most of the

[13] Bund Command L, Dec. 2, 1941.

[14] On the disposition of the Bund's remaining assets, see financial statements and canceled checks, New York Tax Commission, 1946–1947, container 209, RG 131.

[15] In general, the rank and file were left unmolested by the government (in sharp contrast with the treatment of the Japanese-Americans—Nisei—and foreign-born Japanese—Issei). Many former Bundists served in the armed forces, while others joined local German *Vereine*, which were kept under close surveillance. See "Membership Cards of *Vereine* in Philadephia," container 213, RG 131; and "Reports on Bund Activities in the New York Metropolitan Area, November 13, 1941, to July 15, 1942," ADL. Of special interest are the wartime civil-liberties cases. See *Keegan* v. *U.S.* 325 U.S. 478 (1944); *Hans Max Haupt* v. *U.S.* 330 U.S. 631 (1947); and *Henry Baumgartner* v. *U.S.*, 322 U.S. 665 (1944).

men who had directed the movement found themselves in serious
trouble during the war years.

Thirteen months after the Japanese attack on Pearl Harbor, on
January 5, 1943, Fritz Kuhn was taken from his prison cell to the
Foley Square Court House in lower Manhattan. Kuhn and nineteen of his associates had been indicted for retaining allegiance to
a foreign power at the time of their naturalization, in violation of
the Nationality Act of 1940.[16] During the pretrial maneuvers in the
fall and early winter of 1942, Kuhn tried to convince the government not to continue its denaturalization case against him. In a letter to the court he claimed that he had "worked for understanding
between the two nations" and, more important, that he could not
be tried under the Nationality Act, since he was naturalized on

---

[16] The pretrial briefs, letters, and materials relating to the denaturalization
proceedings in *U.S.* v. *Fritz Julius Kuhn and Nineteen Other Cases* are filed
under Fritz Kuhn, Civ. 18–415, FRC. The motion to consolidate the twenty
cases was approved in the fall of 1942. The nineteen others were William
Kunz, Herbert Finders, Konrad Koehler, Henry von Holt, Leo Cyler, Her-
man Hoeflich, William Heller, Ernst Sotzek, Gotthilf Faigle, Richard Schmidt,
Werner Ulrich, Martin Heinrich, Urban Kugler, Franz Schneller, Paul August
Rausch, Carl Steger, Franz Wunschel, Ernst Schwenk, and Fred Hackl.
Throughout the 1930's, many individuals (e.g., Samuel Dickstein and Judge J.
Wallace Leyden, Hackensack, New Jersey) and groups (e.g., the Non-Sectarian
Anti-Nazi League) had called for the denaturalization and deportation of all
Bund officials. In the fall of 1937, Judge Leyden asserted that membership in
the Prospective Citizens' League was sufficient to deny a prospective citizen
naturalization. The Justice Department declared that such denial was not possible under existing statutes. After the passage of the Nationality Act, the government found it possible to obtain indictments against individuals who "retained an allegiance to their native lands" at the time of their naturalization.
See Justice D. J. Bright, "Opinion," *U.S.* v. *Fritz Julius Kuhn and Nineteen
Other Cases*, pp. 18 ff, Civ. 18–415. In 1944, the Supreme Court set aside the
denaturalization ruling against Henry Baumgartner, a member of the Bund,
who had been convicted of fraudulently taking the oath of allegiance to the
United States in 1932. In consequence, the unfavorable decisions against other
Bundists were overturned. The denaturalization cases should not be confused
with the sedition cases (against the propagandist George Sylvester Viereck,
William Pelley, Hans Diebel, etc.). See Rogge, *Official German Report*, ch.
vii; and Polenberg, *War and Society*, pp. 48–49. The much publicized Nordland case (1940–1941) found nine Bundists guilty of promoting race hatred in
New Jersey. See "Bund Leaders Indicted and Sentenced in New Jersey, January 21, 1941, Conclusion," Statutes Examination, German-American Bund
folder, ADL.

December 3, 1934.[17] The government's attorneys thought otherwise; they maintained that Kuhn and his associates had not been
"well disposed to the good order and happiness of the United
States" at the time of their naturalization and throughout the Bund
years.[18] Initially, the government wanted to try each of the twenty
men separately, but Kuhn, who had declared himself a poor person
on September 14, 1942, and therefore had a lawyer assigned to defend him, raised no objections when a motion was made to consolidate all the cases into one.

By this time he was a broken man. According to Matthias Correa, his lawyer, Kuhn was in poor health and spirits. After two
years in prison, his few remaining contacts with the outside world
had ended. His former lawyer was demanding payment of legal
fees. His wife, Elsa, their son Walter Max, and their daughter Waltraut had returned to Germany. Kuhn's world had collapsed, and
he was about to become an enemy alien in America.[19]

In U.S. v. Fritz Julius Kuhn and Nineteen Other Cases, the government's attorney argued that the defendants had deceived the
United States at the time of their naturalization and had joined
and/or helped an organization closely related to the National Socialist German Workers' Party. The government's attorney claimed
that since its founding in 1924, the Bund had been based on blood
and had fostered hatred and that its subsidiary the Prospective
Citizens' League had worked to circumvent the law by urging aliens to move toward citizenship, if only to remain in the Bund or
its affiliates. In turn, the defendants argued that what the prosecu-
tors said was untrue and that the Bund's activities and their own
were perfectly legal. One defendant, Henry von Holt, a former unit
leader from The Bronx, told the court that during the "entire time
[he] was such a member and Unit Leader [he] heard no one say

[17] Fritz Kuhn to U.S. District Court, Southern District, N.Y., Sept. 1, 1942,
Civ. 18–415, FRC. It will be recalled that Kuhn filed for naturalization on
June 28, 1934, and was issued a certificate on December 3, 1934.
[18] Stenographer's report, minutes, Dec. 30, 1942, ibid.
[19] Kuhn declared himself a poor person on September 14, 1942; he was
later assigned a government lawyer, Matthias Correa, to defend him. In April
1945, troops of the U.S. Army's 55th Division located Kuhn's wife and two
children in Germany (New York Times, April 19, 1945, p. 1).

anything anti-American or advocate an allegiance to Germany." [20] The government was prepared to counter such assertions point by point. Armed with letters and reproductions of statements made by the accused, it maintained that the Bund's often repeated dictum "A divided allegiance cannot suffice" was in itself enough to obtain a judgment against the defendants.

After weeks of arguments and counterarguments, Justice D. J. Bright submitted a seventy-four-page opinion on March 18, 1943. For those individuals who had long pointed the finger at the Bundists and cried "un-Americanism," Bright's opinion represented a high-water mark in the government's pursuit of supposed subversives. The justice asserted that some of Kuhn's statements at the 1938 national convention violated the oath he had taken at the time of his naturalization. Kuhn had said to the Bundists: "Need I remind you, for instance, that Henlein had no swastika flag and also gave no ['*Heil*, Hitler'] greetings; despite this, it was a Nazi organization. The means justify the end." [21] "No alien," argued Bright, "can take this oath with any mental reservation [and he cannot] retain allegiances or fidelity to his homeland." Eleven of the twenty defendants declared Bright, never had any intention of becoming "good Americans" and had always placed the well-being of Germany before that of the United States. Evidence for his allegations was their joining an oath-bound organization which was ultimately controlled by ideas originating in Berlin. Basing his decision on the materials gathered by the government, Bright recommended the denaturalization of eleven of the defendants. Later that year, on May 27, Kuhn and his ten former comrades were served with a copy of the judgment in the Foley Square Court House: as of June 1, their American citizenship was null and void. Later that month, Kuhn was paroled and transferred to an internment camp in New Mexico.[22]

The government's pursuit of the Bundists did not end with the prosecution of the denaturalization cases (several of the judgments

[20] Copy of indictment. Kuhn's response is in a letter he dictated to Correa, Sept. 1, 1942, Civ. 18–415. FRC. The statement of Henry von Holt during arguments for consolidation is in *ibid*.

[21] "Opinion," pp. 6ff.

[22] Court records, May 27, June 1, 1943, Civ. 18–415, FRC.

were later reversed). After the war, Kuhn was deported to his native land on the grounds that he was an enemy alien and "dangerous to the public peace and safety of the United States." Upon his arrival in Germany, the former Bundesleiter was questioned by American occupation authorities. In April 1946, Kuhn was released. For the next year, Kuhn was a free man. He returned to his native Munich and found employment in a small chemical factory, where he worked as an industrial chemist. A year later, in July 1947, Kuhn was arrested by Bavarian de-Nazification officials. The fifty-one-year-old Kuhn was charged with having close ties with the German Führer and with attempting to transplant Nazism to the United States. Once again, the notorious liar was caught in his own game; he had concocted a relationship with Hitler in order to prop up his standing. In January, he was interned in the Dachau camp after being questioned by American investigators of war crimes. To be sure, Kuhn was not a major war criminal; he was considered to be among the small fry. But once more (and for the last time) the name Fritz Julius Kuhn was in the limelight. With the help of a friend, thirty-two-year-old Hedwig Munz—a countergirl in an American air-force installation—Kuhn escaped from the camp. Kuhn did little to hide his identity; in fact, he even made application to live in the French zone.

In April 1948, Kuhn was tried and sentenced *in absentia* to ten years at hard habor. His lawyer, Otto Gritschneider, and the witnesses were also absent. The de-Nazification court reached its verdict after five hours of deliberations. Six months later he was captured in the French-zone town of Bernkastel. When asked how he had managed to escape from the camp, he told police officials that the "door was open and so [he] went through." While in prison Kuhn appealed the verdict and was set free in 1950. He died in Munich one year later, on December 14, 1951. Four years before, Munich Police President Franz Pitzer had said to Kuhn: "If you hadn't worked for a guy like Hitler you wouldn't be here today." Kuhn had answered: "Who would have known that it would end like this?" [23]

[23] "Fritz Kuhn Mysteriously Escapes from Dachau as He Awaits Trial," *New York Times*, Feb. 4, 1948. See also *ibid.*, Feb. 5, 1948; and "Bavaria Finds Kuhn a Major Nazi Offender," *New York Herald Tribune*, April 21,

Fate dealt a harder blow to Heinz Spanknöbel, the first Bund leader and the man to whom the Bund owned its organization and structure. It will be recalled that Spanknöbel returned to Germany in 1933 while under indictment as an unregistered agent of a foreign government. Upon his return to his native Magdeburg he found work in a leather-goods factory. He was later drafted into the Wehrmacht. In 1953, twenty years after the widely publicized Spanköbel Affair, the Justice Department instructed the FBI and occupation authorities to check into his whereabouts; the government wanted him returned to the United States to stand trial. It was discovered that he had died of starvation in a Soviet prison camp in 1947. Upon receiving the news, Assistant United States Attorney B. P. Atterbury recommended an entry of nolle prosequi, and the case was closed.

Former Bundesleiters Ignatz Griebl and Reinhold Walter were more fortunate and survived the war in Germany. The fate of Fritz Gissibl remains a mystery. In October 1944, he held the rank of SS *Obersturmbannführer* (equivalent to lieutenant colonel in the U.S. Army) and was serving on the eastern front. Of the men who served as leaders of the Bund between 1933 and 1939, only Dr. Hubert Schnuch returned to his former occupation; he served as principal of the Brooklyn Academy until his death in 1958.[24]

In the prewar years, Kuhn and his Bund cohorts often said, "They are out to get us." They could not have been closer to the truth if the "they" the Bundists referred to is enlarged to include not only anti-Nazis, but also an increasing number of Americans whose perception of the Bund was not influenced by class, ethnic background, or faith in isolationism or intervention. This amor-

---

1948. On Kuhn's exchange with Police President Pitzer, see *ibid.*, June 17, 1948. On Kuhn's recapture, see "Fritz Kuhn verhaftet," *Tagesspiegel* (Germany), June 18, 1948.

[24] Memorandum of B. P. Atterbury, July 8, 1953, *U.S. v. Spanknöbel*, file C95–936, FRC. Griebl fled to Germany in 1938 after he was named part of an Abwehr spy ring (Farago, *The Game of the Foxes*, p. 65; Rogge, *Official German Report*, p. 338). Reinhold Walter seems to have returned to Germany (T-81/31/28320ff). On Fritz Gissibl's later history, see Appendix III, below. On Schnuch, see *Yale University Doctors of Philosophy, 1861–1960* (New Haven, 1961).

phous and widely diverse group was convinced that the Bundists were outside the bounds of what was elastically defined as Americanism. Congressman Dies had made a reputation as America's chief interpreter of what constituted such activities. His definition and the use of the subpoena offended many—conservatives, liberals, and moderates alike. But these very people were also offended and distraught at the sight of Bundists parading in Nazi-style uniforms. In an America that was undergoing rapid social and cultural change and at a time when Nazism was viewed as a threat to the peace of the world, they felt there was little room for those who had brought Nazism to America.

The Bundists' interpretation of their fate accorded well with the Hitlerian image of the United States. By the end of the decade German propagandists were boldly asserting that the Jews were on the verge of a complete victory and that little could be done to extricate their racial comrades from the grip of Roosevelt-Jewish-capitalist forces. In late 1938 and into the war years America was depicted as a vast Jewish citadel. The use of this imagery helped the Ministry of Propaganda to explain to the German people German-America's failure to unify into a genuine pro-German force. It also permitted the Germans to explain the failure of the Bund. The picture of a movement hounded by local, state, and Federal authorities whose probes had culminated in the destruction of the Bund was adjusted to fit a broader view of the Americans. From the Nazi propagandists' point of view, what better material could the German image makers have at their disposal than Mayor La Guardia, Samuel Dickstein, and Martin Dies destroying the only genuine Nazi organization in the country? The Bund's failure, then, was not seen as Germany's failure; it was seen as one more victory for international Jewry.[25]

This distorted explanation received full expression just five weeks before the invasion of Poland. On Sunday, July 23, 1939, an exhibit, "The Struggle of German-America," opened in the DAI's House of Germanism in Stuttgart. It was meant to explain to the German public the failure of Nazism in America. The exhibit's sev-

[25] *Aussendeutscher Wochenspiegel* (Germany), 29 (Aug. 8, 1941); *Diktator Roosevelt*, VDA publication, T-81/149/152135.

eral displays had been provided by the Party's Central Archives in Munich and by the *Rückwanderer,* those Bundists who had returned to their homeland. When the exhibition closed in late August, more than fifteen thousand people had visited the House of Germanism, and the exhibit had toured ten cities in the Reich. These people saw and heard the official explanation of what had taken place in America.[26]

The program and format were prepared by former Bundesleiter Fritz Gissibl. Under his careful supervision, DAI staffers arranged the displays in order to provide "the general public with a view of the struggle for National Socialism in America." [27] Not only did visitors find a pictorial and documentary history of the Bund, but also what Gissibl called "living examples"—former Bundists and their families. The unsuspecting and highly propagandized visitors could not help concluding that the Bund was once a dynamic and politically viable organization which had attracted thousands of recruits and had made significant inroads into the German-American community. But the visitors were told that the Bund's path into American *Deutschtum* had been blocked by the Jews, who, like their racial brothers in pre-Hitler Germany, had managed to gain control of the government and the nation.[28]

The visitors, then, were led to believe that the ubiquitous Jew had managed to frustrate the German-backed Bund's efforts to unify *Deutschtum* in America and that the Star of David would soon rise over Washington—in short, that America was about to be Judaized and could be counted among the enemy nations. The Jews' successful campaign to destroy the Bund was the beginning of a wider and more violent attack against millions of Americans of Germany ancestry. The prosecution of Kuhn and the Bundists was

---

[26] "Amerikadeutschtum im Kampf," program, T-81/144/183204–5. On preparations, see T-81/144/180054ff.

[27] "Amerikadeutschtum im Kampf." Cf. "Das Amerika-Deutschtum im Kampf mit dem Weltjudentum," address by Carl Nicolay, May 21, 1939, T-81/142/180206.

[28] The exhibit was a three-part history of the Bund movement (1) "Nazism in America, 1924–1933"; (2) "World Jewry against the Germans, in Words and Pictures, 1933–1939"; (3) "National America against Jewry and Bolshevism, 1939——" (T-81/142/180047–8).

seen as only the start of a wider assault, and visitors to the House of Germanism in Stuttgart left with the impression that there was little that Germany could do to reverse the course of American history.

The Bund movement began with a lie; it also ended with a lie. Nazi propagandists argued that America's diverse roots would prove its nemesis. Since they believed racial weakness was tantamount to death, they claimed that the United States could never sustain itself in war despite its enormous material assets. This aspect of the Hitlerian world view eventually proved fatal to the Third Reich.

APPENDIXES
BIBLIOGRAPHICAL NOTE
INDEX

German Immigrants Entering the United States, 1880 - 1933[*]

Year	Number	Year	Number
1880	15,042	1907	37,807
1881	210,485	1908	32,309
1882	250,630	1909	25,540
1883	194,786	1910	31,283
1884	179,676	1911	32,061
1885	124,443	1912	27,788
1886	84,403	1913	34,329
1887	106,865	1914	35,734
1888	109,717	1915	7,799
1889	99,427	1916	2,877
1890	92,538	1917	1,857
1891	113,554	1918	447
1892	119,168	1919	52
1893	78,756	1920	1,001
1894	53,989	1921	6,803
1895	32,173	1922	17,931
1896	31,885	1923	48,227
1897	22,533	1924	75,091
1898	17,111	1925	46,068
1899	17,476	1926	50,421
1900	18,507	1927	48,513
1901	21,651	1928	45,778
1902	28,304	1929	46,751
1903	40,086	1930	26,569
1904	46,380	1931	10,401
1905	40,574	1932	2,670
1906	37,564	1933	1,919

* Not including Austrians.

Source: The Statistical History of the United States from Colonial Times to the Present (Stamford, Conn.: Fairfield, 1965), Series C 88-114, pp. 56–57.

Regional Organization of the Amerikadeutscher Volksbund

Region I (Eastern Department): Maine, New Hampshire, Vermont, Massachusetts, Rhode Island, Connecticut, New York, New Jersey, eastern Pennsylvania, Delaware, Maryland, District of Columbia, Virginia

Region II (Eastern Department): North Carolina, South Carolina, Georgia, Florida, Alabama, Mississippi, Tennessee

Region III (Midwestern Department): western Pennsylvania, West Virginia, Kentucky, Ohio, Michigan, Indiana, Illinois, Wisconsin

Region IV (Midwestern Department): Minnesota, North Dakota, South Dakota, Iowa, Missouri, Nebraska, Kansas

Region V (Midwestern Department): Arkansas, Louisiana, Oklahoma, New Mexico

Region VI (Western Department): Colorado, Utah, Arizona, Nevada, California

Region VII (Western Department): Montana, Wyoming, Idaho, Oregon, Washington

Source: Based on the organizational charts of the German-American Bund, *Hearings*, Part IV, Appendix, pp. 1503–1504.

Selected German Officials and Bund Personnel Cited

Bohle, Ernst-Wilhelm. Born Bradford, England, July 28, 1903; moved to Capetown, South Africa, 1906; Bachelor of Commerce degree, Berlin, 1923; NSDAP, 1931; AO chief, 1934–1945; State Secretary in the Foreign Ministry, 1937–1941.

Borchers, Hans. Born Germany, 1887; Doctor of Jurisprudence, Berlin, Heidelberg, 1908; German consulate, New York City, 1933–1941; NSDAP, 1936; retired from diplomatic service, 1944.

Csaki, Richard. Born Rumania, 1886; director, DAI, 1933–1941.

Dieckhoff, Hans Heinrich. Born Germany, 1887; counselor of embassy, Washington, 1922–1926; counselor of embassy, London, 1926–1930; Foreign Ministry, British and American affairs, 1930–1936; head of political section, April–August 1936; acting State Secretary, August 1936–April 1937; ambassador to United States, March 1937–December 1941; recalled to Germany, November 1938; head of American Committee, Foreign Ministry, 1940–1943; ambassador to Spain, 1943–1944; NSDAP, 1941.

Emerson, Edwin ("Colonel"). Born Germany, January 1869; alleged maternal grandson of Samuel Ingham, Secretary of the Treasury under President Andrew Jackson; graduated Harvard, 1891; personal secretary of Andrew White; covered Spanish-American War for *Harper's Weekly;* POW in Germany, 1917–1918; director, Friends of Germany, spring–summer, 1933; director, American section, Friends of the New Germany, 1933–1934.

Fürholzer, Edmund. Born Germany, 1886; Freikorps, 1920–1921; emigrated to United States, December 1926; founded *Deutsche Zeitung* (New York), 1927–1928; staff writer, *Brooklyn Daily Eagle,* 1930–1931; campaigned for Hoover, 1928, 1932; returned to Germany, February 1933; German representative of Transocean News Service, in Far East, 1934–1939.

Gissibl, Friedrich (Fritz). Born Germany, March 9, 1903; emigrated to United States, December 1923; NSDAP, 1926; cofounder, Teutonia Association, October 1924; Bundesleiter, FONG, 1933–1935; returned to Germany, March 1936; staffer, DAI, 1936–1939; founder, Zentrale der Kameradschaft-USA, 1938; SS *Obersturmbannführer*, Poland, 1941–1944.

Griebl, Ignatz. Born Germany, 1899; artillery officer, German army; emigrated to United States, 1925; M.D., Long Island Medical College, 1928; surgeon, Harlem Hospital, New York, 1928–1933; Bundesleiter, FONG, September–October 1933; Abwehr activities, 1930's; returned to Germany, 1938.

Kappe, Walter. Born Germany, January 1905; NSDAP, 1923; emigrated to United States, March 1925; propagandist, Bund movement, 1926–1937; returned to Germany, June 1937; staffer, DAI, 1938–1940; Abwehr, 1940–1942; trained saboteurs who landed in United States, 1942; eastern front, 1942–1944.

Kloss, Heinz. Born Germany, 1904; joined DAI, 1927; specialist in American affairs.

Kuhn, Fritz Julius. Born Germany, May 1896; Germany army, 1914–1918; Freikorps, 1921–1922; degree in chemical engineering, Munich, 1922; emigrated to Mexico, 1923; entered United States, 1927; Bundesleiter, Amerikadeutscher Volksbund, 1936–1939; naturalized, 1934; convicted of larceny, 1939; denaturalized, 1943; deported to Germany, 1945; convicted by de-Nazification court, 1948.

Kunze, Gerhard Wilhelm. Born Camden, New Jersey, January 1906; chauffeur-mechanic; acting Bundesleiter, December 1939–September 1940; Bundesleiter, September 1940–December 1941; fled to Mexico, 1941; returned and convicted on several counts, including espionage, 1943.

Manger, Paul. Born Germany, 1897; no profession; leader of Gau-USA, 1931–1932; returned to Germany, 1938.

Nicolay, Carl ("Papa"). Born Germany, 1879; propagandist and writer, Amerikadeutscher Volksbund, 1936–1939; returned to Germany, 1939.

Schnuch, Hubert. Born Germany, 1892; emigrated to United States, 1913; returned to Germany, 1914; German army, 1915–1918; Freikorps Wesel, 1920; employed by International Harvester Corporation, Germany, 1921–1922; returned to United States, 1923; taught at Berlitz School, New York; Ph.D., Germanic languages, Yale University, 1934; president, FONG, 1934–1935.

Schuster, Josef (Sepp). Born Germany, 1904; NSDAP, 1921; Fifth SA Company, 1923; emigrated to United States, 1927; organizer, OD; *Gauleiter,* Eastern Division, FONG; returned to Germany, 1936; Kameradschaft-USA, 1939–1942; SA *Standartenführer;* eastern front, 1941–1944.

Spanknöbel, Heinz. Born Germany, 1893; emigrated to United States, 1929; organizer and first leader, FONG, 1933; returned to Germany, 1933; employed in leather-goods factory, 1933–1941; German army, 1941–1944.

Strölin, Karl. Born Germany, 1890; son of Prussian general; captain, German army, 1915–1920; doctorate in economics, Berlin, 1923; NSDAP, 1931; appointed Lord Mayor of Stuttgart and honorary president, DAI, 1933; visited United States, 1936.

Thomsen, Hans. Born Norway, 1891; German citizen, 1913; NSDAP, 1938; chargé d'affaires, German Embassy, Washington, 1938–1941; minister to Sweden, 1943–1945.

Wertheimer, Fritz. Born Germany, 1884; director, DAI, 1919–1933; emigrated to Porto Alegre, Brazil, 1938.

Selected Newspapers Published by the American Bund Movement

Nationalsozialistische Vereinigung Teutonia
  Vorposten. Irregularly, 1924–1932. Chicago and Detroit.

Gau-USA
  Amerika's Deutsche Post. Irregularly, 1931–1933. New York.

Freunde von Deutschland
  Die Bruecke. Irregularly, 1933. New York.

Bund der Freunde des Neuen Deutschland
  Deutsche Zeitung. Bimonthly, August–December 1933; weekly, spring, 1934. New York.
  Das neue Deutschland. Weekly, August–December 1933. New York.
  Deutscher Beobachter. Daily, November 15, 1934–October 24, 1935; weekly, November 15–20, December 20, 1934; semiweekly, November 27–December 15, 1935. Official publication, November 15, 1934–January 3, 1935. During the Haegele-Schnuch affair, Haegele's splinter group used the same title, January 10, 1934–October 24, 1935; Haegele's group changed the name to *National American*, December 15, 1935. New York.
  Philadelphia Deutscher Weckruf und Beobachter. Monthly, December 1934–October 1935.

Amerikadeutscher Volksbund
  Deutscher Weckruf und Beobachter. November 1935–September 1938. New York.
  Deutscher Weckruf und Beobachter and the Free American. September 1938–December 1941. New York.

Selected Bund Leaders and Subordinates Who Returned to Germany, 1938-1940

Ach, Karl. Group Leader, New York City.
Biele, Norbert. OD leader, Philadelphia; director, Bund Camp Deutsch-
   horst.
Dinkelacker, Theodor. Youth leader.
Ex, Alfred. Cofounder of Teutonia Association.
Flick, Karl. OD leader, Brooklyn, New York.
Fuchs, Anton. Bund leader, Pittsburgh, Pennsylvania.
Goeppel, Allen. Assistant Bund leader, Pittsburgh, Pennsylvania.
Gries, Heinz. District leader, New Haven, Connecticut.
Haas, Hugo. Youth leader, Brooklyn, New York.
Hein, Gottlieb. District leader, Oakdale, California.
Hutten, Heinz, District leader, Staten Island, New York.
Kessler, Martin. District leader, Cleveland, Ohio.
Lage, Henry. Bund leader, San Francisco.
Lutz, John. Bund leader, San Diego, California.
Merker, Oskar. Bund leader, St. Louis, Missouri.
Meyer, Hans. OD leader, Manhattan, New York.
Nasse, Eberhard. Youth section leader, Manhattan, New York.
Nicolay, Carl. Propaganda leader, New York City.
Notle, Karl. OD leader, Franklin Square, New York.
Othmer, Waldemar. Bund leader, Trenton, New Jersey.
Purwien, Hermann. Local leader, South Bend, Indiana.
Röll, Engelbert. Treasurer, Friends of the New Germany.
Schlenz, Friedrich. Local leader, Chicago, Illinois.
Schrick, Michael. OD leader, New York City.
Schwarzmann, Hermann. OD leader, Queens, New York.
Seegers, Henry. Bund leader, Reading, Pennsylvania.
Wagner, Henry. Acting Bund leader (1938), Brooklyn, New York.
Wax, Max. Local leader, Cincinnati, Ohio.
Weiss, Helmut. Bund leader, Dayton, Ohio.
Wenisch, Willi. OD leader, Pittsburgh, Pennsylvania.
Zimmermann, Hans. Propaganda section chief, New York City.

Source: Zentrale der Kameradschaft-USA, membership applications, T-81/
140–142.

Bibliographical Note

Many of the sources for this study are housed in archives in the United States. After World War II extensive parts of the records and papers of the NSDAP, the Foreign Ministry, the Deutsches Ausland-Institute, and other German agencies were microfilmed and deposited in the National Archives in Washington. The volume of the archival collections makes several guides indispensable. Of special importance are the mimeographed guides prepared by the American Historical Association's Committee for the Study of War Documents and the National Archives and Records Service: "Guides to German Documents Microfilmed at Alexandria, Va." (1958——), available from the National Archives, Washington, D.C. Of great value are George O. Kent, editor, *A Catalog of the Files and Microfilms of the German Foreign Ministry Archives, 1920–1945* (3 vols.; Stanford, Calif.: Hoover Institution on War, Revolution and Peace, 1962–1966); and Gerhard Weinberg *et al., Guide to Captured German Documents* (Montgomery, Ala.: Air University, 1952) and the *Supplement* (Washington: National Archives, 1959). The Hoover Institution houses materials from the NSDAP *Hauptarchiv*. They are listed in *NSDAP Hauptarchiv: Guide to the Hoover Institution Microfilm Collection,* compiled by Grete Heinz and Agnes F. Peterson (Stanford: Hoover Institution, 1964).

This bibliographical note is not exhaustive. Books, articles, memoirs, periodicals, published documentary collections, and literature distributed by the Bund and related organizations are cited in full in the footnotes. I note here only unusually valuable archival collections.

Materials are in widely scattered locations. The Bund's reports, handouts, and leaflets, the "Outline of Evidence against the German-American Bund," prepared by the Justice Department in 1942, and the "Bund Commands Issued by the Bundesleiter, October 1936 to December 1941" are available to qualified scholars in the collection of the Anti-Defamation League of B'nai B'rith, New York. Most of the materials in this collection are in English. The Archives, YIVO Institute for Jewish Research, New York, houses the Noah Greenberg Collection of Anti-Semitic Materials Distributed in the New York Metropolitan Area, 1933–1945. The late Noah Greenberg, a Brooklyn lawyer, collected newspaper articles, leaflets, handouts, and pamphlets distributed in New York City. Throughout the Hitler years, he carefully pasted these materials into twenty-five notebooks. Also at the YIVO Institute are a small collection of records from the Reich Ministry of Interior, 1927–1934 (file NFI 18), and the financial reports of the German Foreign Institute (DAI), February 1937 (file 18A).

Unquestionably, the richest and by far most comprehensive collection of records relating to the history of the Friends of the New Germany, the Amerikadeutscher Volksbund and related organizations, Deutsches Haus in California, and the German Railroads Information Office are in the Office of Alien Property, APA World War II Seized Enemy Records, Record Group 131, Washington National Records Center, Suitland, Maryland. This collection also includes the Bund's five-hundred-volume library. In accordance with Section 552 of the Administrative Procedure Act (5 U.S.C.A. 552), portions of this collection are not available to researchers, since their release for public inspection would constitute an unwarranted invasion of the personal privacy of people mentioned in the records. In spite of the "limited access" qualification, the numerous documents (in English and German) provide scholars with a rare insight into the inner operations of an extremist organization. Although the list of documents in this collection indicates an orderly arrangement of materials in more than two hundred containers, a cursory inspection of the contents of the containers indicates otherwise. The only sources that are arranged in an approach to an alphabetical or chronological order are the records of the German Railroads Information Office and materials dealing with American tourists in Germany.

The Federal Records Center, New York, recently made available to researchers the records of the United States District Court for the years 1930 to 1945. Documents pertaining to the denaturalization of Fritz Kuhn and nineteen others (1942–1943) are filed under Civ. 18-415. Individual case record numbers are listed in the Kuhn file and can be obtained from the Washington Street depository of the Federal Records Center. Materials relating to the Spanknöbel Affair and Heinz Spanknobel's fate after 1945 are filed under C 95-936.

The Franklin D. Roosevelt Library at Hyde Park, New York, yielded little information on the history of the Bund movement. Interesting, but by no means extensive, documentation relating to Roosevelt's feud with Martin Dies is contained in the Dies folder, Official File 320. The Hugh Wilson folder, in the President's Secretary's File, Germany, Official File, 1933–1944, and the President's Personal File, Germany, 1934–1938, 198A, provided insight into Roosevelt's and his immediate associates' reaction to the *Kristallnacht* in November 1938.

The files of newspapers consulted are as scattered as the other collections. Newspapers published by the Bund in the New York metropolitan area (1933–1941) are in the Newspaper Division of the New York Public Library. Reports of Bund activities which appeared in German and British newspapers are in the German-American Bund Folder at the Wiener Library, Institute of Contemporary History, London.

Many documents are available on microfilm. Especially important are four microfilm collections.

1. *Records of the German Foreign Ministry Received by the Department of State,* Microcopy T-120, National Archives, Washington. Of special interest to scholars engaged in the study of German-American diplomatic relations in the 1930's are the materials in the files of Ernst-Wilhelm Bohle (AO), the files of Sections III and IX of the Foreign Ministry, the files containing the correspondence with the Carl Schurz Memorial Foundation, and "*Deutschtum* and the Race Question in the United States, 1920–1935" (roll 5189).

2. *Captured German Documents Microfilmed at Alexandria, Virginia,* Microcopy T-81, National Archives, Washington, includes *Records of the National Socialist German Labor Party* and *Records of the Deutsches Ausland-Institut, Stuttgart,* Part II: "The General Records." Documents in this collection reveal the inner workings of the NSDAP and the Deutsches Ausland-Institut, and Germany's relationship with overseas Nazi groups. The published guides do not do justice to the rich variety of materials. Although I have cited more than ninety rolls of microfilm, I have read twice that number. Here again, a word of caution is in order. The materials relating to Germany's relationship with the Bund and the history of the Bund movement are scattered throughout this collection. The documents recorded on the many rolls of microfilm will yield their treasures only as a result of a painstaking reading of each frame. Unquestionably, this collection was my most important single source.

3. Department of State, *Special Interrogation Mission: Reports on Interrogation of German Prisoners-of-War, Made by Members of the*

Department of State Special Interrogation Mission (September, 1945 to September, 1946), Headed by DeWitt C. Poole, General Records of the State Department, Record Group 59, Microcopy 679 (3 rolls).

4. The *NSDAP Hauptarchiv* Collection at the Hoover Institution consists of 134 rolls of microfilm. Of special value are rolls 27 (folder 531, Documents Relating to the Work and Activities of Wilhelm Schneider); 35 (folders 680–710, "Deutschtum im Ausland"); and 57 (folder 1386, "Deutsches Ausland-Institut, 1939/40"). The few valuable documents revealing the early history of the Bund (1924–1932) are in this collection.

Index

Volksbund für das Deutschtum im Ausland, *see* League of Germans Abroad
Volksdeutsche Mittelstelle, *see* Ethnic German Office
Volksdeutscher Rat, *see* Ethnic German Council
Vollbehr, Otto, 193
VoMi (Volksdeutsche Mittelstelle), *see* Ethnic German Office
Vooros, Helen, 208, 333
Vonsiatsky, Anastase André, 319 & n, 344
Vorposten, 95, 115, 117, 362
VR (Volksdeutscher Rat), *see* Ethnic German Council

Walter, Reinhold, 164, 173, 174, 179, 186, 273
Weber, Eugen, 156
Wegener, Horst Otto, 330
Weimar Republic, 25, 26, 44, 57, 64, 85, 150, 223
Weizsäcker, Ernst von, 284, 287-288
Welles, Sumner, 283
Wertheimer, Fritz, 43-48, 51, 51 n. 20, 52, 53, 361; *see also* German Foreign Institute, World War I and
Wheeler-Hill, James, 239, 312, 329

White, Andrew, 87
Whyte, A. P. Luscombe, 207
Wiedemann, Fritz, 202, 284-285, 297-298, 299
Wilhelmstrasse, *see* Foreign Ministry
Willumeit, Otto Albert, 302
Wilson, Hugh, 35-37, 278
Wilson, Woodrow, 89, 102
Winrod, Gerald, 194, 204
Winterhalder, Hans, 135 n. 14, 136, 142, 144
Winterscheidt, Severin, 216, 217
Wittke, Carl, 70
World Economic Conference, 105
Wortmann, Dietrich, 88
Wunschel, Franz, 346n

Yale University, 165
Yockel, Fred, 341

Zapp, Manfred, 301 n. 53, 321
Zentrale der Kameradschaft-USA (after 1941, Amerikadeutsche Kameradschaft), 275 & n. 2, 311, 352
    former Bundists and, 92 n. 12, 147-148
    German-American Bund and, 351-352
    relationship with DAI, 92 n. 12
Zimmermann, Hans, 216

THE NAZI MOVEMENT
IN THE UNITED STATES
1924–1941

Designed by R. E. Rosenbaum.
Composed by Vail-Ballou Press, Inc.,
in 10 point linofilm Caledonia, 3 points leaded,
with display lines in Helvetica Medium.
Printed offset by Vail-Ballou Press.
Bound by Vail-Ballou Press
in Columbia book cloth
and stamped in All Purpose foil.